INVOLVING DIALOGUING SHARING

Elementary Teacher Education

from a Global Perspective

新时代小学教育专业建设与小学教师教育研究丛书
丛书主编：刘慧

走近 对话 共享

小学教师教育研究的全球视野

刘慧 唐斌 主编
魏戈 杨天 鲁华夏 副主编

天津出版传媒集团
天津人民出版社

图书在版编目（CIP）数据

走近 对话 共享：小学教师教育研究的全球视野 / 刘慧，唐斌主编；魏戈，杨天，鲁华夏副主编. — 天津：天津人民出版社，2022.3

（新时代小学教育专业建设与小学教师教育研究丛书/刘慧主编）

ISBN 978-7-201-17743-4

Ⅰ．①走… Ⅱ．①刘… ②唐… ③魏… ④杨… ⑤鲁… Ⅲ．①小学教师—师资培养—研究 Ⅳ．①G625.1

中国版本图书馆 CIP 数据核字(2021) 第 204046 号

走近 对话 共享：小学教师教育研究的全球视野
ZOUJIN DUIHUA GONGXIANG：XIAOXUE JIAOSHIJIAOYU YANJIU DE QUANQIU SHIYE

出　　版	天津人民出版社	
出 版 人	刘　庆	
地　　址	天津市和平区西康路 35 号康岳大厦	
邮政编码	300051	
邮购电话	（022）23332469	
电子信箱	reader@tjrmcbs.com	
策划编辑	武建臣	
责任编辑	林　雨	
特约编辑	武建臣	
装帧设计	汤　磊	
印　　刷	天津新华印务有限公司	
经　　销	新华书店	
开　　本	710 毫米×1000 毫米　1/16	
印　　张	28.25	
插　　页	2	
字　　数	370 千字	
版次印次	2022 年 3 月第 1 版　2022 年 3 月第 1 次印刷	
定　　价	96.00 元	

"新时代小学教育专业建设与小学教师教育研究"丛书
序

　　新时代中国小学教育专业如何建设？面向未来的小学教师如何培养？这是当代小学教师教育者必须要回应的时代之问。本套丛书是我们——首都师范大学初等教育学院迎接新挑战、抓住新机遇、乘势而上的实践探索与理论研究答卷。

　　我国小学教师中师培养的历史已有百年，而本科层次培养的历史却很短。首都师范大学初等教育学院，作为我国小学教师本科培养的首批单位之一，其建设发展的历程，也是当代中国小学教育专业建设与小学教师本科层次培养历程的"缩影"。在"十四五"开局之年，面向未来的教师教育改革与创新，我们认为，有必要将我们在小学教师教育理论研究与实践探索过程中的一些重要事件、主要成果整理出版，通过回顾历史来把握当下、创造未来；也为推动具有中国特色的小学教师教育体系、世界先进水平的小学专业建设贡献我们的微薄之力。

　　首都师范大学初等教育学院，1999 年由两所中师——具有百年历史的通州师范学校和颇具影响力的北京第三师范学校合并升格成立，至今走过了 22 年的发展历程。在此期间，经历了学院文化的大学化、小学教育专业性质的定位、小学教育专业人才培养模式的形成与发展、初等教育学学科建设的确立与起步等至关重要的发展阶段与事件；并在国家一系列教师教育政策的指引下得以迅速发展,取得了显著成绩,被誉为全国小学教育专业的"领头雁""带头羊"。在此过程中的关键事件,可以分为三类。

一、关于小学教育专业建设的政策、项目与成效

在 20 年时间里,对小学教育专业建设产生重要而深远影响的国家政策与项目主要有以下几个:

2007 年,教育部评选国家级特色专业,我校和上海师范大学小学教育专业首批入选。这是建立不足 10 年的高师小学教育专业得到国家认可与重视的"信号",是对全国小学教育界(简称小教界)的莫大鼓舞。一些省市也相继开展特色专业评选活动,小教界有多家单位入选。由此开启了我国小学教育专业特色建设的探索之旅,小教界围绕着小学教育专业特色"特"在何处、小学教育专业的核心品质到底是什么等问题进行深入探索。这是推动我国小学教育专业关注自身性质、特色建设,注重内涵发展的重要力量。

2011 年,根据《教育部 财政部关于"十二五"期间实施"高等学校本科教学质量与教学改革工程"的意见》和《关于启动实施"本科教学工程""专业综合改革试点"项目工作的通知》,我校于 2012 年组织申报"高等学校专业综合改革试点"项目,我院小学教育专业的申报得到了学校的支持并获得立项。经过 3 年的建设,完成了"以人才培养质量为核心,进一步改革人才培养模式,凝练人才培养特色,为小学输送优秀教育工作者,在全国小学教师教育院系中起到引领和示范作用"的建设目标,实现了人才培养模式、教学团队建设、新课程体系建设等具体目标,开启了我院小学教育专业综合改革之路。

2017 年,我校接受北京市教委对高校本科专业审核评估。我们通过撰写"本科教学工作审核评估汇报报告",从学院发展概况、办学特色、人才培养目标的实现、质量保障体系建设、存在的问题与努力方向、建设规划等六个方面认真梳理了建院以来的教学工作,为日后申报一流专业建设点和撰

写师范专业认证自评报告打下了坚实基础。

同年,北京市属高校一流专业建设工作启动,我院小学教育专业入选首批一流专业建设单位。2018年5月,我们组织骨干教师团队,研究并依据一流专业建设的具体要求,对我院小学教育专业建设现状、专业建设存在的问题、专业建设目标、专业建设的主要举措等方面做了进一步的梳理与研究。在此过程中,参与撰写的教师思想观念、思维方式不断发生转变,对一流专业建设的理解不断加强。

2018年9月4日,我院接到通知,被指定为全国小学教育专业认证"打样"单位。依据教育部颁布的《普通高等学校师范类专业认证实施办法(暂行)》,经过两个月的高效工作,我院小学教育、美术学(小学教育)、音乐学(小学教育)接受了教育部师范类专业"联合认证",开启了中国小学教育专业认证的历史,也正如教育部教师工作司任友群司长在认证反馈会上所指出的:"为我国的师范教育发展史留下了浓墨重彩的一笔。"这一过程,不仅仅是完成了专业认证这项工作本身,更是梳理与反思了我院小学教育专业的建设历程,研究与憧憬了小学教育专业的未来发展。

2019年,教育部颁布了《关于实施一流本科专业建设"双万计划"的通知》,我院小学教育专业经过层层选拔,入选了首批"国家级一流本科专业"建设点,这一成绩的取得,得益于前期大量的基础性工作,不仅是扎实的实践探索,更是针对小学教育专业与小学教师教育的学术研究。可以说,我院小学教育专业能入选首批"国家级一流本科专业"建设点,一路走来,每一步都很坚实,每一步都展现了学院追求卓越、敢为人先的探索与创新精神。2020年,根据学校要求,对照《一流本科专业建设点推荐工作指导标准》科学编制一流本科专业3年建设规划方案,提出了深化专业综合改革的六大主要举措,3年后的成效将使我院小学教育专业建设再上新台阶。

二、关于小学教师教育的政策、项目与成效

2010 年,教育部启动教师专业标准研制工作,我院有幸在顾明远先生的指导下开展"小学教师专业标准"研制工作。在一年多的研制过程中,我们认真梳理了各国教师专业标准及其相关标准的有关内容,反思了我院小学教育专业建设经验,整理了我们对小学教育和小学教师教育的研究成果,尤其是对小学教师与中学教师的异同的探析,逐步厘清了小学教师专业标准的理念、维度、领域、基本要求等框架与内容,并完成了《小学教师专业标准解读》的撰写。由此不但进一步推动了小学教师教育研究,而且整体提升了我院教师团队的小学教师教育专业水平,尤其是带动了大学学科教师向小学教育专业教师的转型,为我院的发展提供了强有力的专业教师团队。

2014 年,教育部出台《关于实施卓越教师培养计划意见》(称为 1.0 版),全国小教界共有 20 家入选,我院小学教育专业是其中一员。如何理解"卓越""卓越教师"的内涵,成为影响卓越教师培养计划实施的关键。对此,我们突破"学科教学"本位的思想与思维"禁锢",提出卓越小学教师的核心是以"儿童教育"为本,并积极探索培养模式,"一体两翼一基"培养机制,解答了"卓越小学教师应如何培养"的问题。

2019 年,正值我院成立 20 周年,我们积极筹备承办了以"走近·对话·共享——多元取向小学教师教育伦理与实践"为主题的首届"小学教师教育国际会议",来自中国、芬兰、法国、匈牙利、冰岛、日本、韩国、瑞士、澳大利亚、美国等 10 个国家 102 个不同单位(其中包括 78 所大学)300 余位专家学者参加,分享了各国小学教师教育的理念、模式以及质量保障机制等,为推进国际多元取向小学教师教育模式的彼此交流,共享过去、现在与未来,做出时代贡献,开启了国际小学教师教育模式跨文化、跨领域、跨时空对话的新篇章。

三、关于课程建设的政策、项目与成效

小学教育专业课程建设，既是小学教育专业建设的重心，也是小学教师培养的主渠道，因此如何构建小学教育专业课程体系成为小学教育专业建设与小学教师教育的关键问题。

2012年，教育部教师工作司开展"教师教育国家级精品资源共享课"建设项目，我们申报的《小学生品德发展与道德教育》课程入选，经过3年的建设，在"爱课网"上线，并于2015年出版同名教材，之后又在"中国大学慕课"上线。此课程及教材自上线与出版以来，持续受到小教界同人的关注与使用，尤其是在师范类专业认证以来，落实立德树人的根本任务，小学德育课成为小学教育专业的必修课，2020年，《小学生品德发展与道德教育》课程荣获线上线下混合教学"国家级一流本科课程"。

2013年，在教育部"专业综合改革试点"项目下，开展小学教育专业课程地图研制工作。依据所提出的小学教师核心素养及其指标体系，创制了小学教育专业课程地图。这是基于小学教师理念、理论的对小学教育专业课程体系的设置，突破了之前课程设置的经验性与随意性过重的现象，首创"333"式课程结构，使专业课程内在逻辑清晰、层次清楚，体现科学性、规范性、系统性；确立了"儿童&教育"专业核心课程体系，解决了长期以来该专业核心课程不明的理论难题，实现了课程设置"精致化"，在小教界兼具开创性和示范性。

2016年，教育部颁布《关于组织实施中小学幼儿园教师培训课程标准研制工作通知》，我院承担了"教师培训标准——小学品德与生活（社会）学科教学"研制项目，借此全面深入地研究了小学德育理论与实践及小学德育课程与教学，这一标准研制工作的完成，不仅有利于我院2019年在小学教育专业中增设小学德育方向，也为组织开展小学德育学科骨干教师培训打下坚实基础。

　　总之，高校小学教育专业建设，在我国还是"新事物"，本科层次小学教师培养历史仅有 22 年。在这段历程中，上述所列政策、事件起到了关键作用，在此我们选取了小学教师教育国际会议、小学教育专业认证、小学教师培养模式、道德与法治课程建设等整理出版。未来，我们还将陆续选择影响我国小学教育专业建设与小学教师教育发展的关键事件，进行整理出版。这既是我国小学教育专业建设与小学教师教育研究的现实历程，也是未来的史料；既是鲜活的个案，也是典型的代表；既是实践的呈现，也是理论的贡献。我们愿为此付出与努力。

刘慧

2021 年 9 月 25 日于西钓鱼台嘉园

序　言

　　当代中国小学教师教育研究走向世界,是时代的必然诉求,也是应有的姿态。在新时代教师教育振兴行动兴起之际,首都师范大学初等教育学院,被誉为全国小学教育专业发展的"带头羊""领头雁",正值建院 20 周年之时,积极筹备承办了以"走近·对话·共享——多元取向小学教师教育伦理与实践"为主题的首届"小学教师教育国际会议",为各国小学教师教育研究者、一线小学教师搭建跨文化、跨领域、跨时空对话平台,分享各国小学教师教育的理念、模式以及质量保障机制等,为推进国际多元取向小学教师教育模式的彼此交流,共享过去、现在与未来,做出时代贡献。会议的召开是对新时代的响应,也是我院 20 华诞之际向全国小学教师教育界的献礼!

　　首届"小学教师教育国际会议"于 2019 年 10 月 24 日至 25 日在首都师范大学召开,由首都师范大学、中国教育国际交流协会教师教育国际交流分会主办,首都师范大学初等教育学院承办,教育部小学教师培养教学指导委员会为会议提供学术支持。来自中国、澳大利亚、芬兰、法国、匈牙利、冰岛、日本、韩国、瑞士、美国等 10 个国家 102 个不同单位(其中包括 78 所大学)300 余位专家学者参加,其中,教育部小学教师培养教学指导委员会委员,全国首批本科层次小学教育专业单位,如东北师范大学、南京师范大学、上海师范大学、杭州师范大学等同人共聚会场。出席会议的出版社有:人民教育出版社,教育科学出版社,高等教育出版社,北京师范大学出版社,华东师范大学出版社等,报纸杂志社有:《人民日报》《光明日报》《中国教育报》《人民教育》《教育科学研究》《中国德育》等。这样的盛况在中国小学教师教育发展史上有着里程碑意义。

会议得到了教育部教师工作司高度重视。司长任友群教授莅临会议并致辞。任友群司长在致辞中指出,教育是民族振兴、社会进步的重要基石;教师教育是教育事业的源头活水、工作母机。新中国成立 70 年来,我国教师教育得到了巨大的发展,小学教师教育是其中重要的组成部分。6 到 12 岁是小学教育所覆盖的年龄段,是孩子从儿童成长为少年,从不成熟到逐渐成熟,身心发展、习惯养成、品德形成的关键时期,这是人生非常重要的阶段。中国人讲的是养正于蒙,小学老师正确的价值取向、科学的教育教学方法,对于下一代的成长意义不言而喻,肩负着小学教师培养任务的小学教师教育更是责任重大。近年来,我国积极推进小学教师教育模式改革,提升培养质量,主要采取了以下措施:一是开展综合培养,二是推进"U—G—S"协同育人,三是重视信息技术的应用,四是实施师范类专业认证。目前,中国的基础教育和教师教育领域仍然有许多值得研究探讨的话题。比如,如何更好地适应基础教育教学改革需求进行小学教师培养? 如何提升小学教师培养的水平? 如何吸引更多的优质生源报考师范院校? 5G 时代智能环境下怎样实现信息技术与教师教育深度融合创新发展? 我相信,各国的实践和专家们的思考交流会给我们很多启发。

首都师范大学校长孟繁华教授指出,任友群司长的报告对中国教师教育有关问题有些精辟的论述,总结为三个"最"。第一,小学教育专业是最大的一个专业。首都师范大学小学教育专业就是最大的,一年招生 400 多名;第二,小学教育专业是最重要的专业,小学即是面向未来,孩子是祖国的未来,民族的未来;第三,小学教育专业是最有前途的一个专业,是阳光的专业,特别是在现在的社会背景下,未来的发展空间非常大、非常具有潜力。所以说时代赋予我们的责任重大,使命光荣,我们会不忘初心、牢记使命。

首都师范大学领导高度重视本次会议,孟繁华校长到会致辞并做主题发言。他在致辞中说,我们很高兴与各位领导、来宾、朋友相聚在首都师范大学,共同研讨小学教师教育既有经验与未来发展,这是见证中国乃至国际小学教师教育发展的一场盛会!我校初等教育学院小学教育专业是国家特色专业,也是中国最早一批本科层次小学教师培养的专业。作为北京市培养小学教师的基地,初等教育学院每年向北京市乃至全国小学一线输送各层次的毕业生,多年来已经形成了小学教师培养、小学教育研究、小学教育服务三位一体的发展特色。"面向未来,培养什么样的人,怎样培养人"是当今教育的一个重要议题,在小学阶段,无论是童蒙养正,还是培养创新人格,都离不开教师的人格及专业影响。在中国,习近平总书记曾这样比喻,今天的学生就是实现中华民族伟大复兴中国梦的主力军,广大教师就是打造这支中华民族梦之队的"助梦人"。在全球化背景下,小学教师教育的未来走向是很多国家教育发展共同关注的话题,拓展国际视野,有助于了解不同国家对小学教育的共同关切,更自觉地认识和把握小学教育的发展规律,以及对小学教师的要求、挑战,同时更好地理解文化多样性。世界各国在如何培养小学教师方面,有着各自的经验和探索。期待多方的经验能够互相激荡,共同启发,皈依之道,与时同行。真诚地希望能在对话、分享交流的过程中,共同探索小学教师的未来之路。

会议开幕式由首都师范大学副校长李晓娟教授主持。她指出,2019 小学教师教育国际会议是我校国际化进程当中的一件大事,更是国内小学教育专业建设中的一次空前的盛举。教师是立教之本,兴教之源,而教师教育研究是挖掘和释放教师潜力,保障和提升教师质量,转变和完善教师培养的重要基础。21 世纪以来,世界各国的小学教师教育均面临诸多前所未有的挑战和机遇,既有共性又有特性,变革的呼吁此起彼伏。在我校初等教育学院承办此次国际会议之际,广邀海内外专家学者共聚一堂,分享理论,交流经验,探讨困惑,展望未来,可谓恰逢其时,我相信此次会议不仅能使各位与会代表收获颇丰,更能为大家打开一扇窗户,构建一个平台,在国际化视野下更好地推动全球小学教师教育的研究与实践进展。

杨志成副校长在会议闭幕式上致辞。他说,我一直参与这个会议的筹备过程。1 年前，我跟刘慧院长交流这个会怎么准备？我问她以前开没开过？她说他们考察了本科层次小学教育专业发展 20 年来的国际交流情况，仅有四个院校召开相对规模有限的会议，而我们要召开的是在更多国家、更大规模上关于小学教师教育的国际会议，具有开创性的会议。小学教育很重要，小学教师教育很重要，这个会很重要，具有开创性意义！今天召开这个会议，还面临一个新的时代。无论是从联合国教科文组织发布《教育 2030 行动框架》，还是中国政府出台的《中国教育现代化 2035》，都标志着人类教师教育进入一个新的时代。这个新的时代，用一句话概括就是人类世界教育进入百年未有之大变局中。人类 400 年来的"把一切知识交给一切的人"的教育，在今天随着互联网、大数据、云计算，变得可能了，因此面临这样的挑战，世界意义的小学教师教育研究具有重大的时代价值，需要和全世界的同行共同研究。教师教育具有世界价值、开创价值、时代价值，应建立一个"世界小学教师教育研究与发展共同体"。

会议由三个主论坛和三个分论坛组成。三个主论坛分别为"国际视野""中国经验""多元共享"，国内外 18 位专家分享了迎接未来的教育、多元化世界背景下小学教师教育、小学教师教育的未来发展趋势、各国小学教师教育发展历史及其状态等。在三个分论坛上，24 位国内外专家学者围绕小学教师培养理念与模式、未来小学教师教育发展路向、小学教师教育质量保障为主题开展报告研讨，探索了多元取向的小学教师教育新理念、新思路和新策略。其中，变革是各国共同面对的问题，在应对中，各国各有其经验。

"国际视野"主论坛，由北京师范大学顾明远教授所做的题为"迎接未来的教育"主题报告拉开了序幕；美国密歇根州立大学彭恩霖教授站在批判性想象视角，剖析了多元化世界背景下的小学教师教育；韩国首尔国立大学白淳根教授探讨了小学教师教育的未来发展趋势；日本东京学艺大学岩田康之教授聚焦质量保障分享日本小学教师教育发展的动态；芬兰赫尔辛基大学文德教授以芬兰的跨文化教师教育为例，探讨了面向小学教育多样性的师范生培养问题；北京师范大学教育学部部长朱旭东教授论述了一流小学教师教育体系的重构。本论坛由首都师范大学刘慧教授和蔡春教授主持。

在"中国经验"主论坛上,多位专家分别立足各校本土实践,分享了小学教师教育的中国经验。首都师范大学校长孟繁华教授报告了构建 U—D—S 教师教育共同体,培养高质量专业化教师;东北师范大学教育学部初等教育学院院长刘学智教授介绍了他们"本硕一体·全科·融通"卓越小学教师培养模式的实践探索,天津师范大学教育学部杨宝忠教授报告了"厚实学养 聚焦能力——天津师范大学小学教育专业 20 年发展",湖南第一师范学院党委副书记刘志敏教授分享了湖南第一师范学院乡村公费师范教育的改革与实践,南京晓庄学院教师教育学院党支部书记曹慧英教授介绍了他们"1 + X 主辅学科、全程知行合一"的小学教育专业培养模式,临沂大学社会科学处处长李中国教授报告了"精准扶贫"提升乡村学校薄弱学科教师素养的创新探索。本论坛由首都师范大学王智秋教授和上海师范大学惠中教授主持。

在"多元共享"主论坛上,首都师范大学初等教育学院院长刘慧教授报告了中国小学教师培养模式的变迁、探析与未来展望;匈牙利罗兰大学初等教育与学前教育学院副院长乔堡·西科斯先生立足变革,分享匈牙利小学师资培养的经验;澳大利亚悉尼大学教育与社会工作学院教育系主任默瑞·普林特教授探讨了面向全球公民教育的小学教师教育;日本创价大学副校长铃木将史教授呈现了基于创价教育哲学的创价大学人本主义取向的教师教育样态;冰岛大学教育学院扬·卡亚兰教授就冰岛教师教育中的认知暴力问题进行了分享;澳门城市大学教务长李树英博士高度关注新时代新技术环境下教师专业发展中的教育智慧。会议由人民教育出版社刘立德研究员和首都师范大学教师教育学院院长田国秀教授主持。

闭幕式上,在分论坛报告分享环节,六位学者分别代表三个分论坛六个半场进行总结性分享。

首都师范大学初等教育学院魏戈副教授对分论坛(一)上半场的总结:日本创价大学教育学部董芳胜副教授从同课异构入手,探讨了小学教师如何提升自己的反思性实践和教学的主体性。法国波尔多大学教育研究院副院长雷吉斯·马莱教授聚焦全球公民素养教育,从多元文化的视角来探讨 21 世纪全球公民对小学教师教育培养提出的挑战与机遇。瑞士图高教育大学艾斯特·布伦纳教授分享了瑞士全科型小学教师培养理念与模式,介绍了瑞士小学教师如何同时承担七个不同科目的教学。魏戈本人介绍了采用"1 + 1 + 1"的嵌套模式开展培养师范生实践性知识的行动研究,证明师范生的实践性知识可以"前移",即在教师入职前提高教育教学熟悉度,以减缓实习所面对的实践冲击。

天津师范大学司成勇教授对分论坛下半场做了总结:大连大学师范学院院长庞国彬教授从本科层次的小学教师职前、职后衔接沟通的视角,从职前培养、入职适应和职后发展三个层次分析如何进行卓越教师的培养。陇南师范高等专科学校初等教育学院院长张永明教授探讨了专科层次农村卓越教师的培养模式,从师德养成、课程建构、实践体验和综合考核四个方面进行陈述。首都师范大学初等教育学院副院长孙建龙副教授分享了他们的办学理念、办学模式、课程建构的思考,分析了卓越小学教师的品质培养和课程建构。浙江师范大学教师教育学院教育系主任王丽华副教授探讨了小学教师培养中儿童研究的缺失问题及原因,强调应重建学习观、知识观和课程结构。

洛阳师范学院教育科学学院赵丹妮副教授对分论坛(二)上半场进行了总结分享:台北市立大学视觉艺术学系高震峰教授提出应基于儿童的立场,通过儿童美术设计、师生家长共创绘画的多元形式,运用后现代的技术,让绘画与儿童建立联结。高等教育出版社小教教育分社社长肖冬民强调抓住卓越教师培养建设的核心,实现师德课程、师德案例的再现,为每个学生建立师德档案。浙江师范大学教师教育学院蔡连玉副教授提出了教师的教育惩戒伦理的 1 阶和 2 阶规范。首都师范大学初等教育学院李敏教授报告了小学教师德育专业化的愿景与进展,指出在当前立德树人的教育政策背景下,亟须培养小学教师的德育专业化能力。

江苏连云港师范高等专科学校初等教育学院朱萍院长分享了分论坛

（二）下半场的发言：台湾师范大学艺术学院院长赵惠玲教授、首都师范大学初等教育学院朱永海副教授、澳门化地玛女子学校刘丽姝校长和美国俄克拉荷马州立大学教育学院王秋颖教授。他们分别从美感素养、智能教育、自主学习和数字素养等不同视角展开了有高度、有深度，更有温度的对话交流，分享彼此对小学教师教育的理论与实践的思考。四位学者涵盖了小学、中学、大学，分布广、层次多，既瞻前又顾后，使职前培养与职后培训珠联璧合。

首都师范大学初等教育学院副院长张志坤副教授对分论坛（三）上半场报告进行总结：日本创价大学教师教育研究生院铃木词雄副教授介绍了该院注重实践和培养高度专业的实践性人才，提出对于一年制研究生的质量保障问题的困惑；研究生岩田秀满展示了去年在中国小学实习时的照片；研究生山本美纪介绍了日本小学实习的情况及其大学所学课程；研究生滨佳子介绍了在职教师和研究生的学习过程，指出日本小学更加注重集体活动。首都师范大学初等教育学院唐斌副教授以首都师范大学小学教育专业在完成专业认证后的持续改进研究项目为例，阐述了以内部质量保障体系中生成的问卷调查结果为依据，改进师范专业毕业生的培养质量的思路和策略。延边大学师范学院小学教育系主任崔梅花副教授简要介绍了他们的培养模式、课程体系、教学改革和以专业化建设促进学生自主发展的情况。美国明尼苏达大学教育学院克里斯汀·麦克马斯特教授认为可以通过数据采集、整理和分析形成教学方案，促进个性教学，介绍了 DBI 项目的具体步骤。

最后，沈阳师范大学学前与初等教育学院小学教育系主任樊涛博士做总结分享：南京师范大学小学教育系主任易晓明教授围绕研究型全科教师的内涵、培养目标、培养机制、课程设置和课堂教学等方面进行介绍。杭州师范大学教育学院肖正德教授探讨了农村小学全科教师的内涵与特质、乡村属性的教学能力与培养路径。青海师范大学教师发展中心主任武启云教授介绍了他们"两基础一专业一特长"的模块化综合课程结构，提出了小学全科教师培养的非选择全员培养模式。重庆师范大学初等教育学院院长林长春教授介绍了高素质农村小学教师卓越人才培养目标,以及"文科 + 艺体""理科 + 艺体"的模块和"1 + 1 + N"课程层级模式。

在闭幕式上,教育部高等学校小学教师培养教学指导委员会秘书长王智秋教授做了总结发言。她用八个字概括了这次国际会议,即"广度""长度""深度"和"温度"。广度即对"小学教师教育"这个主题的研讨非常广泛,体现在跨城乡、跨层次、跨学科、跨文化和跨界。长度主要指时间的跨度长,历史回顾与未来展望都体现在本次国际会议中。深度是指许多学者提出了很有理论深度、发人深省的问题,但实践中的发展道路仍任重道远。所谓温度是指参会代表都对小学教师教育投入了满满的热情,对未来人类社会儿童的健康成长充满了热切的期望。闭幕式由首都师范大学国际合作交流处处长、国际文化学院常务副院长韩梅副教授主持。

本次会议的成功举办,体现了学校层面、学院层面探索全球视野下小学教师教育未来发展的决心和力度;见证了初等教育学院在大规模国际会议从筹备到举办的实力与成长,展现了我院教师团队的学术风采。

全球小学教师教育对话的序幕已经拉开,持续不断地"走近、对话与共享"是我们的未来之路,我们即将相见于 2021 第二届小学教师教育国际会议上,愿更多的同人参与,让我们在教师教育的国际舞台上讲好中国小学教师教育的故事!

2021 年 8 月 16 日于西钓鱼台嘉园

目　录

Contents

第一编　教师教育未来变革

PART Ⅰ：Future reform of Teacher Education

迎接未来的教育

顾明远

北京师范大学资深教授

摘要:"人工智能＋教育"正在改变着教育的生态、教育的环境、教育的方式,教育管理的模式。充分认识"人工智能＋教育"的育人功能,是当前教育工作者遇到的重要挑战。要适应这些变化,教育教学方式就要发生变革。教师要利用人工智能、大数据等技术的优势,重点为学生的学习营造适合的环境;指导学生正确获取信息、处理信息的策略和方法;帮助学生的个性化学习设计科学的、合适的学习方案;以及帮助学生解决自学难以解决的疑难问题。但技术的变革不会改变教育传承文化、创造知识、培养人才的使命,不会改变立德树人的根本目的,更不会改变教育的本质。教育必须同时具备学生和教师两个基本要素。学生精神世界需要教师的言传身教。简言之,人只能由人来培养,不能完全交给机器来培养。

关键词:人工智能＋教育;人工智能;教育;教师

教育是未来的事业,习近平总书记说过"教育决定着人类的今天,也决定人类的明天"。当今社会已经进入一个瞬息万变的时代,国际政治风云变幻、科学技术日新月异,互联网、人工智能正在改变着世界。变化的迅速,难以预测。我们不仅要了解今天的社会,还要了解明天的社会,了解社会发展的趋势,为未来做准备。教育要有先导性、前瞻性。今天人类已经进入了人工智能的时代,有的学者认为,过去的蒸汽机、电动机和计算机的出现,社会还有几年的时间来适应技术带来的变化。今天变化已经随时随地了,迅速之间就以数字化的形式遍布了全球。教育是未来的事业,教育是为未来社会培养公民,因此教育必须适应科学技术的变革而引起的社会经济的变革。

同时,我们今天的青少年生活在这个变革的时代,他们的生活方式和思维方式已经大大不同于我们这一代,他们是互联网、人工智能时代的原住民。因此,对他们的培养方式,我们也必须改变。人工智能＋教育,改变着教育和学习的一切。

今年3月,联合国教科文组织曾经发布一个报告《教育中的人工职能:可持续发展的挑战与机遇》。这个报告指出,人工智能技术能够支持包容和无处不在的学习访问,有助于确保提供公平和包容式的教育机会,促进个性化学习并提升学习成果。

5月,首届国际人工智能和教育大会在北京召开,发布了《人工智能与教育北京共识》这样一个宣言式的文件,提出了各国要制订相应的政策,探索利用人工智能促进教育创新的有效战略和实践。

前不久中共中央、国务院公布了《关于深化教育改革全面提高义务教育质量的意见》(以下简称《意见》),《意见》指出,促进信息技术与教育教学的融合应用以提高教育质量。那么信息技术的发展,将引起教育的哪些变革呢?互联网、人工智能改变着教育概念、教育的生态环境,改变着教育的形态、教育的方式、师生关系、家庭关系,等等。这种变革是非常深刻的,颠覆了整个传统教育的观念,教育工作者需要认识这种变革,迎接新的挑战。前不久,我到江阴去开会。我的母校小学,已经开始将数据中心、教师办公室、云课堂运用到学校。教育的概念变化了,学习的渠道拓宽了。以往的学习主要在学校里进行,现在可以在多种场合,利用多种媒体学习,特别是在网上学习,在虚拟世界学习。学习已经不限于学校,也没有年龄的限制,正规教育与非正规教育、正式教育和非正式教育结合起来,使得人人可学、处处可学、时时可学。

教育的目标也转变了。以往的教育只是传授知识，而且只重记忆不重能力，只重结果不重过程。现在是创新时代，科学技术日新月异，今天需要培养创新人才，才能适应未来社会的变化。因此教育的目标要改变，需要培养学生批判性、创造性思维能力和实践能力。所以我有的时候讲，课堂教学的本质就是改变人的思维，思维可以改变世界。我们说乔布斯改变世界，那就是因为他发明了个人电脑。我们说马云改变了商业模式，现在电商很发达。都是思维的变化的结果。

经济合作与发展组织 2012 年提出，21 世纪的学生必须掌握四方面技能。

第一，思维方式，要培养创造性、批判性思维，问题解决、决策和学习能力。

第二，工作方式，沟通和合作能力。

第三，工作工具，会运用信息技术和信息处理能力。

第四，生活技能，作为一个公民，他的生活、职业及个人与社会的关系。

互联网正在改变着人们学习的方式，如果说工业革命使机器代替了人的部分体力，信息革命使电脑代替了人的部分脑力，而互联网则把人的脑力联系起来，扩大了人类的大脑，变成了人类共有的大脑，知识成为人类共同的财富。人们可以在互联网上获取各种知识，讨论各种问题，人类的智慧可以共享。知识已经是全人类的财富了，不是一个人的财富。

教学方式的变化，教师要充分发挥学生的主体性，未来教育最重要的变化是教师的教转变为学生的学。学生通过自我学习，发现问题，提出问题，自己去探索，或者与同伴合作，互相探讨。教学要改变单向传授知识的方式，合理地使用互联网，启发学生探索，师生之间、学生之间互相沟通。正如《意见》中指出的，要融合运用传统和现代技术手段，合理地使用互联网，探索基于学科课程综合化教学，开展研究性、项目化合作学习。这里提到的是融合运用传统和现代技术手段，也就是说运用先进技术手段，也不排除传统的教学手段，两者要结合起来。

互联网为个性化学习、个别化学习提供了条件。以往的教育以集体学习为主,班级授课制只能照顾大多数学生的学习水平,不能照顾到学生的个别需要。信息技术在教学中的应用,可以使教师更好地根据学生的兴趣和爱好,为每个学生设计个性化的学习计划。不仅促进了课程的多样化、学习方式的多样化,而且扩大了学生选择的机会、选择的权利。学生可以自主选择、自主学习。

互联网改变了师生关系,老师已经不再是知识的唯一载体,知识的权威。学生已经不是只依靠课堂上教师的知识传授,而是可以通过各种媒体获得信息和知识。教师主要是为学生的学习营造一个舒适的环境,指导学生正确获取知识、处理信息的策略和方法;为学生设计个性化的学习计划,帮助学生解决一些疑难问题,教师可以定位为设计者、指导者、帮助者。

人工智能、大数据可以作为教师的有力助手,大数据可以帮助老师随时了解学生的学习情况,帮助他们解决困难,还可以帮助老师批改作业,用不着老师批改。可以替代老师做一些机械式的劳动,减轻教师的负担,使教师有更多的时间和学生接触沟通。老师负担减轻了,不是休息,而是用更多的时间跟学生沟通。正如《意见》中所说,"双教师模式"就是包括教师和虚拟教学助理,助理可以接管教师的日常任务,使他们有更多的时间专注于对学生的指导和一对一的交流。

"人工智能 + 教育",可以远程地、免费地为农村和边远贫困地区提供优质教育资源,不仅使那里的学生能够在线上学习到优质的课堂教学,而且可以提高那里教师的专业水平,从而更快缩小城乡教育差距。最近很多学校采用了远程教学,四川成都七中就用慕课、远程教育,在云南培养一批教师。他们把优质的课堂传到那去了,学生就参加线上学习了。最近我到石家庄外国语学校,他们也是用远程教学培养山区的一些教师。人工智能还可以利用大数据对教育进行有效的管理,运用大数据了解学生的学习情况。

信息技术的发展,引起教育的变革是毫无疑问的。但是我们必须明确地认识到,一是利用信息技术的目的是提高教育质量,是培养学生的创新能力,不是技术主义,为技术而技术。二是充分认识"人工智能 + 教育"的优势在哪里? 有没有风险? 如何趋利避害,规避风险? 现在我们一谈到未来的教育,往往就是从技术的角度,刚才我讲的那一套都是从技术的角度,"人工智能 + 教育"改变教育的形态,教育的方式,等等。但是我们考虑未来教育是不是光从技术的角度呢? 我觉得还是要从整个的未来社会的发展来考虑我们到底要培养什么样的人。另外,我们对"人工智能 + 教育"的优势在哪里? 信息技术教育的优势在什么地方? 它的特点是什么? 可能我们现在还不是太清楚,比如说人工智能、大数据具有虚拟性、互动性、个性性、开放性等特点,还有没有其他一些优势可以用到我们的教学上? 另外用到教学上有没有风险? 大数据可以了解学生学习的情况,随时了解学生的学习和生活。但是大数据用了以后有没有风险? 如果把数据发到家长微信群里,家长之间会不会出现一些矛盾? 出现一些问题? 学生隐私能不能得到保护? 对这些问题我觉得还是应该搞清楚。前一阵大家讲了很多"人工智能 + 教育"改变教学,但是对于"人工智能 + 教育"优势在哪里? 风险在哪里? 我觉得我们的认识还不够清晰,还要很好地研究。

另外,教育的本质不会变。互联网使教育发生了重大的,可以说是革命性的变革,但是教育的本质不会变。教育的传承文化、创造知识、培养人才的本质不会变,立德树人的根本任务不会变,正如联合国教科文组织在《反思教育》报告中讲的,"教育应该以人文主义为基础,以尊重生命和人类尊严、权利平等、社会正义、文化多样性、国际团结和为可持续的未来共同承担责任"。

2015 年联合国教科文组织的这个报告非常重要,讲到了当今的形势。联合国教科文组织成立 70 年来有三个重要的报告。

第一个报告,《学会生存:世界教育的今天和明天》,讲科学技术的发展引起社会的变革,人类进入了知识化社会,提出了终身教育的概念。

第二个报告,1996 年《教育:财富蕴藏其中》,那个时候正是资本主义经济最繁荣的时期,再加上苏联解体,认为冷战结束了,和平来了,人们抱着乐观主义态度。认为到了 21 世纪就能够解决很多的疑难问题。但是 2001 年就出现了恐怖主义，现在的恐怖主义越来越厉害，同时环境污染越来越厉害。该报告提出了学习的"四个支柱"：学习认知、学习做事、学习与人相处和学习发展，对教育发展还是有影响的。

第三个报告，《反思教育》的提出，要以人文主义为基础，要培养尊重生命、尊重人类，促进和平，促进社会的可持续发展。这个报告是针对当今时代的特点提出来的。《反思教育》报告提出：当今教育要超越狭隘的功利主义和经济主义，回归教育的本原，教育是人的权利，是社会发展的基础，是全社会的公益事业。习近平总书记在全国教育大会上讲："培养什么样的人，怎么培养人，为谁培养人，是教育的根本任务。"教育永远要把培养学生的思想信念、道德情操放在首位，培养德才兼备的未来的公民。

教育的本质是什么？可以概括为，教育的本质是提高人的生命质量和生命价值，提高人的生命质量是通过教育提高人的生存能力，能够过上有尊严而幸福的生活；提高人的生命价值，通过教育使他有知识、有能力，有高尚的思想品德，能够为社会、为人类做出应有的贡献。教育的本质是把提高生命质量和生命价值结合起来。

学校和教师会不会消亡？有的学者提出来学校要消亡，教师要消失。联合国教科文组织的报告提出，回答是否定的。《反思教育》报告中说，学校是人走出家庭，走向社会的第一个公共场所，是人的社会化的第一步。人都要走进社会，教育本身就是社会化的过程，那么把孩子关在家里可不行，孩子走出家以后，学校是他进入社会的第一个公共场所，是人的社会化的第一步。儿童进入学校不仅学知识，更重要的是学做人，学会与人沟通和交流，培养良好的社会情绪。学会尊重人、热爱人，这要在学校形成。有的人开玩笑说是一个人死了突然醒过来，一看世界都变了，唯独学校和教堂没有变。我觉得这也不稀奇，因为教堂和学习都是塑造人的心灵的地方，是培养信仰的地方，它不会变。我觉得这有一定的道理，教堂和学校不会变，其他的都可以变。人工智能可以改变实体工厂、实体的生产甚至于商业模式，但是对教育的本身不会颠覆,因为教育是要培养人的。

　　学习是人类集体的行为,个性化学习不是个人学习。《反思教育》中指出,学习既是个人行为,也是集体的努力。学习是由环境决定多方面的现实存在,教育不只是个人发展的条件,而是人类集体发展的事业。个人的发展不是孤立的,而是在人类社会共同发展的进程中发展的,学校是学生集体学习、共享学习成果的最好的场所。所以个性化学习、个别学习,不是一个人孤立的学习,而是要在集体中的个人学习。报告讲,学习是集体的活动和行为,可以因材施教,但是因材施教不等于说把孩子孤立起来,自己一个人学习那是不行的,因为他生活在现实存在里。教师也不会消失,信息化、互联网改变了教育环境和教学的方法。但是技术永远只是手段,不是目的。教师的教育观念、教育方式方法需要改变,但教师培养人才的职责没有改变。儿童的成长要有思想信念、有道德情操,有扎实学识,有仁爱之心的教师的指导、帮助。人只能由人来培养,不能由机器来培养。教师的自身魅力和人格魅力时时刻刻影响着学生,今年10月5日是世界教师日,联合国教科文组织为世界教师日定的主题是:"年轻教师:职业的未来",旨在突出当今教师面临的特殊困难。报告指出,教师面临的诸多问题,包括学生家长不再全力支持教师对课堂和学生的权威。联合国教科文组织认为,教育领域的另一个问题是,有人认为技术、人工智能和自动化将导致一些人认为人工服务多此一举,这是批评的话。联合国教科文组织与国际劳工组织、联合国儿童基金会,联合国开发计划署及教育国际的领导,在一份联合致辞中写道:"如果没有新一代积极热忱的教师,无数学子将错过学习机会,或是继续错失素质教育的权利,由于教师的工资低,不受到重视,吸引和留住人才成了问题。"这个报告中讲到很多教师遇到的困难,遇到的问题。在我国也存在,我国尊重教师的风尚还没有完成,尊重教师、信任教师、依靠教师的风尚还没有很好地建立起来。

　　现在家校关系很紧张,家长对教师的要求有的时候是无理的,提出很多问题。联合国教科文组织等在致辞中指出:我们赞美世界各地全心奉献的教师,他们每一天都在不懈努力,从而确保世界每一个角落都能实现"人人接受公平素质教育"并促进"人人都有终生学习的机会"(世界教师日对教师的致辞),可见对教师的重视。

当前"人工智能 + 教育"还存在什么问题?

一是认识问题,广大教师还没有认识到"人工智能 + 教育"的特点和它的优势,还比较迷茫。

二是软件跟不上,缺乏应有的适应教育教学的软硬件。如适合学生自学的软件、利用大数据进行教学管理的软件、个性化学习课表设置的软件,等等,软硬件跟不上,所以现在"人工智能 + 教育"还停留在概念、口号上,理想上。

三是广大教师还不太会运用信息技术来改进教育教学,需要进一步提高技术能力。

Education for the Future

Mingyuan GU

Distinguished Professor, Beijing Normal University

Abstract:"AI Empowered Education" is changing the ecology, environment and modes of education as well as the models of educational management. Fully understanding the educational functions of "AI + Education" therefore presents a great challenge to educational practitioners. To adapt ourselves to such changes, we must innovate our education and teaching. So, teachers should avail the AI and big data technologies to mainly create proper learning environment for students and to guide students through the strategies and methods of acquiring and handling information appropriately. They are also expected to aid students in designing scientific and suitable personalized learning plans, and help students solve the problems that are too difficult for them to handle independently.

However, the technological reforms will not transform the missions of education, such as inheriting culture, creating knowledge and cultivating talents. Neither will they change the moralizing and nurturing aims of education, nor the nature of education. Two essential elements are contained in education simultaneously, namely students and teachers. And a student's spiritual world is influenced by the teacher's personal example as well as verbal instruction. In sum, human beings can only be cultivated by their own kind, not totally trained by the machines.

Key words: AI Empowered Education; AI; Education; Teachers

多元互通加强交流，共育人类启蒙良师

——在首都师范大学 2019 小学教师教育国际会议上的致辞

任友群

教育部教师工作司司长

摘要：教师队伍体量最大的是小学教师，小学老师正确的价值取向、科学的教育教学方法，肩负着小学生的培养任务，责任非常重大。培养高层次的小学教师，成为师范教育改革发展的一个重要课题。教育在每个国家都是民族振兴、社会进步的重要基石，所有国家都非常重视自己的教育，只是有时限于财力和历史条件，各国的教育手段和方式可能在不同阶段会有不同。2018 年，我们国家政府出台了《关于全面深化新时代教师队伍建设改革》文件，即 4 号文件，提出了义务教育学校侧重培养素质全面、业务见长的本科层次的老师。整个国家的差异表现在不同的区域不能完全一根线划下去。我们主要实施了以下措施。①开展综合培养。②推进 U—G—S 的协同培养教师的机制。③重视信息技术的应用。④实施师范类专业认证。此外，中国的基础教育和教师教育领域仍然还存在很多需要研究的问题和克服的困难。我们需要注重思想的交流共享，国际之间交流可以取长补短，相互促进。上海两次比萨测试和对教师的问卷，虽然上海教师有一些不足，但显示出中国在基础教育方面取得的长足进步，并使其走向世界舞台。各国的基础教育和教师培养都要服务于本国的经济社会文化的发展。

教育是民族振兴、社会进步的重要基石；教师教育是教育事业的源头活水、工作母机。新中国成立 70 年来，我国教师教育有了巨大的发展，小学教师教育是其中重要的组成部分。

6～12 岁左右是儿童向少年过渡，从不成熟到逐步成熟，身心发展、习惯养成、品德开始形成的关键时期，这一时期的教育在人的一生发展中起着重要的启蒙作用。在中国，面向 6～12 岁孩子的小学教育是义务教育的起始阶段，受到国家高度重视。目前，我国共有小学约 17 万所，在校生超过 1 亿人。回想新中国成立之初学龄儿童入学率只有 20%，今年我国小学净入学率为 99.95%，我认为以后还需要努力到 100%，不能让一个孩子在小学阶段没有学上。现在全国小学教师约 610 万，占义务教育教师人数比例超过 62%。中国人讲"养正于蒙"，小学教师正确的价值取向、科学的教育教学方法，对人类下一代的成长意义重大，肩负小学教师培养任务的小学教师教育更是责任重大。

在中国，小学教师教育主要由师范院校承担。1951 年，教育部召开第一次全国初等教育和师范教育工作会议，初步确立了我国师范院校培养各级教育师资的基本方略，小学教师培养由中等师范学校承担。改革开放后，随着经济社会快速发展，培养高层次的小学教师成为师范教育改革发展的重要课题。1984 年，江苏南通师范学校率先招收培养专科层次的小学教师；1985 年，全国第一所专门培养小学教师的高等师范院校——上海师范高等专科学校建立；1995 年，教育部研制《大学专科程度小学教师培养课程方案》并颁发全国试行。20 世纪 90 年代中期以后，开展本科学历小学教师培养的呼声不断加强。1997 年，上海师范高等专科学校并入上海师范大学，全国第一个初等教育学院成立；1999 年，上海师范大学、南京师范大学、东北师范大学和杭州师范学院本科层次小学教育专业开始招生。目前，我国开设本科层次小学教育专业的院校 225 所，开设专科层次的 193 所。2018 年，中国政府出台关于全面深化新时代教师队伍建设改革文件，提出为义务教育学校侧重培养素质全面、业务见长的本科层次教师，为当前和今后一段时期小学教师教育指明了重点和方向。当然,一些发达地区率先在小学教师中增加硕士层面毕业生的比例,这也完全符合时代要求。

近年来,我国积极推进小学教师教育模式改革,提升培养质量,主要采取了以下措施:

一是开展综合培养。2014 年,教育部启动实施卓越教师培养计划,2018 年,升级实施卓越计划 2.0,探索借鉴国际小学全科教师培养经验、继承中国养成教育传统的培养模式,培养素养全面、专长发展的卓越小学教师。东北师范大学、首都师范大学等 20 所高校作为卓越小学教师培养计划实施单位做了大量探索,积累了不少经验。2018 年,教育部等五部门印发《教师教育振兴行动计划(2018—2022 年)》,提出"通过公费定向培养、到岗退费等多种方式,为乡村小学培养补充全科教师"。重庆、湖南、江西、河南等省(市)积极推进农村小学全科教师定向培养。我曾经去过湖南第一师范,湖南一师以小学教师为重点面向乡村开展地方公费师范生定向培养,办得很好,是代表中国中西部地区的一个案例。加强辖区内相对欠发达县域的优质师资补充,既是国际培养的趋势,也是中国传统文化的重新回归。在中国传统文化中,有鼓励出身寒门的优秀人才从教的优良传统。

二是推进 U—G—S 协同。U—G—S 协同,即高校(University)、地方政府(Government)、中小学校(Schools)协同培养教师机制。由地方政府统筹规划本地区中小学教师队伍建设,预测教师需求,做好招生培养与教师需求之间的有效对接;高校将社会需求信息及时反馈到教师培养环节,优化整合内部教师教育资源,促进教师培养、培训、研究和服务一体化;中小学全程参与教师培养,促进教师专业发展。首都师范大学与北京市各区县的 60 余所小学建立合作共建伙伴关系,以合作小学作为教育实践基地,同时通过合作共建,充分发挥了首都师范大学服务首都基础教育的作用。

三是重视信息技术应用。信息技术既是教育教学改革的手段,也是需要教给孩子们的教育教学内容。在 2013 年建设的 200 门教师教育国家级精品资源共享课中,小学教师教育课程 50 门,占总数的四分之一,2017 年遴选公布的国家级精品在线开放课程（MOOC）中也有不少。近年来，机器人、人工智能在小学教育教学中的探索十分蓬勃。许多小学将机器人作为科学探究的工具和平台，开展了丰富多样的科学探究活动，促进学生科学探究能力的提升，对小学教师的信息素养及跨学科教学能力提出了新要求。我们曾经做过在边远乡镇中小学中开展编程教育的试点研究，想了解边远地区的孩子对新技术的认知与城里的孩子是否有本质的区别，结论是没有本质区别。也就是说，只要给这些孩子足够的条件，他们都能学会我们现在希望他学会的东西。从这个角度来说，对于全中国的农村基础教育改革和发展，我是充满信心的，但是在师资和教育教学方法等方面还有很多工作要做。人工智能在中小学智能教学系统、智能网络阅卷系统、智能决策支持系统、智能仿真系统等方面得到了应用，在促进教学相长、提高阅卷工作效率、减少教学资金投入、促进中小学整体教育质量提升等方面发挥了优势和作用。不少高校积极应对，在师范人才培养中整合新技术、开设新课程，推动师范生信息素养的提升。

　　四是实施师范类专业认证。2017 年，教育部印发《普通高等学校师范类专业认证实施办法（暂行）》，坚持"学生中心、产出导向、持续改进"的认证理念，开展纵向三级，横向囊括小学教育、中学教育、学前教育、职业技术师范教育和特殊教育专业五类的师范类专业认证。专业认证对照师范毕业生核心能力素质要求评价师范类专业人才培养质量，并将评价结果应用于教学改进，推动师范人才培养质量持续提升。2018 年，首都师范大学小学教育、美术学（小学教育）、音乐学（小学教育）3 个专业率先进行师范类专业认证的第二级认证"打样"，全国目前已有首都师范大学、南京晓庄学院、杭州师范大学等 9 所院校 11 个专业通过了小学教育第二级师范类专业认证。

　　我曾经去南通拜访李吉林老师。李吉林老师一辈子就是一名普通的小学语文老师，但作为情景教育创始人，她获得了全国首届"基础教育国家级教学成果"特等奖。70 年辛勤耕耘，70 年积极探索，中国的小学教师教育事业为国家的基础教育改革发展培养了大批优质师资，做出了卓越贡献。然而中国的基础教育和教师教育领域仍然有许多值得研究探讨的话题和需要克服的困难。比如,如何更好地适应基础教育教学改革需求进行小学教师培养?如何吸引更多优质生源报考师范专业?当然也包括小学教育。我最近去过好多综合性大学,就是希望推进综合性大学在中国的师资培养上做出一定的贡献。还有5G时代智能环境下怎样实现信息技术与教师教育深度融合创新发展?我相信,各国的实践和专家们的思考交流会给我们很多启发。

刚才芬兰教授的演讲引发了我的共鸣。实际上,芬兰的基础教育一直是中国学习的榜样。上海的两次PISA测试和对教师的问卷都显示出上海在基础教育方面取得的长足进步。也正是因为2009年首次PISA的测试,使得全世界基础教育的研究开始关注中国。在上海的两次教师测试中,上海教师所表现出的综合素质是非常高的,很多指标排在全世界第一,但也有几个指标,如鼓励学生用信息技术解决问题等比较薄弱。

因此,通过国际交流能够更清晰地看到自己的长处和短板,有利于相互取长补短。正如萧伯纳说:"你有一个苹果,我有一个苹果,彼此交换一下,我们仍然是各有一个苹果;但你有一种思想,我有一种思想,彼此交换,我们就都有了两种思想,甚至更多。"各国基础教育及其教师培养皆服务于本国经济、社会、文化发展,因其多元不同而各有特色、精彩纷呈。今天的会议为多元取向的小学教师教育提供了走近、对话、交流、共享的机会,希望此次会议能给每位嘉宾带来新的启迪,期待本次会议的成果能对推动各国小学教师教育发展有所裨益!

Diverse Communications Should Be Strengthened for Cultivating Excellent Primary Teachers

Youqun Ren

Abstract: The largest number of teachers is primary school teachers. Primary school teachers need to have correct value orientation and scientific teaching methods. Primary school teachers shoulder the task of training primary school students, which is very important. Training high – level primary school teachers has become an important issue in the reform and development of normal education.

Education is an important cornerstone of national rejuvenation and social progress in every country. All countries will attach great importance to their own education, but sometimes limited to financial and historical conditions. Different countries may have different means at different stages. In 2018, our national government issued the document "on comprehensively deepening the reform of teachers′ team construction in the new era", namely document 4, which proposed that compulsory education schools should focus on the cultivation of undergraduate level with comprehensive quality and professional expertise, and cultivate undergraduate level teachers for compulsory education schools. The differences of the whole country are reflected in different regions, and cannot be drawn down in one line. We have mainly carried out the following measures. 1. Carry out comprehensive training. 2. Promote the mechanism of U – G – S to train teachers in coordination. 3. Pay attention to the application of information technology. 4. Carry out the professional certification of normal school. In addition, there are still many problems to be studied and difficulties to be overcome in the fields of basic education and teacher education in China. We need to pay attention to the exchange and sharing of ideas. International exchanges can complement each other's strengths and promote each other. Although there are some deficiencies in Shanghai Teachers, the two pizzas tests and the questionnaire for teachers show that China has made great progress in basic education and made it to the world stage. Basic education and teacher training in various countries should serve the development of their own economy, society and culture.

构建 U－D－S 教师教育共同体，培养高质量专业化教师

孟繁华

首都师范大学校长，教授

摘要:在"反哺、激活与超越"理念的指导下,首都师范大学形成了以"理论与实践双向激活,职前职后一体化"为基本特征的实践取向的教师教育模式。以大学—区域—中小学(U—D—S)组成的教师教育共同体,有助于构建"五位一体"的教师教育实践体系,推进整体区域教育变革,并促进教师教育学科群建设。经历 20 年探索,首都师范大学教师教育取得了显著成效,并形成了独具特色的"首师大模式"。

关键词:U—D—S;教师教育共同体;专业化教师

一、指导思想:反哺、超越与激活

首都师范大学是国家"双一流"建设高校、北京市与教育部"省部共建"高校,是北京市基础教育教师队伍的摇篮。作为首都教师培养的重要基地,首都师范大学自 2001 年以来,率先在国内创设"教师发展学校",逐渐摸索出"高校—区域—学校"(U—D—S)教师教育共同体模式。经过十余年的不断进阶,我们的师资培养观念与实践不断发生变化。终于在 2009 年前后,形

成了"反哺、超越与激活"的教师教育核心理念。在此理念的指导下,形成了理论和实践双向激活、职前职后一体化为特征的教师教育的"首师大模式"。

(一)反哺:凸显中小学实践的丰富性

所谓的反哺,即凸显中小学实践的丰富性,用中小学的实践问题、经验和智慧反哺高校教师教育。北京市有中小学生 1 亿人,600 多万教师,每一个课堂都是丰富的教育教学"实验室"。我们在凸显中小学教育教学实践丰富性的过程中,鼓励大学教师到中小学现场汲取鲜活的实践智慧。这么多的学校,这么多的老师,他们在个人实践中不断地有这样或那样的智慧涌现出来,值得大学教师学习。而丰富的实践经验又能激发大学教师教育的活力,改进大学教师教育。倘若大学教师教育的教学内容,都能够来自鲜活的中小学实践,那么职前教师教育就能够做到既扎根理论学习,又面向生动的实践。总之,中小学要反哺大学,因为她们具有丰富的实践性。

(二)超越:摆脱经验路径依赖

所谓"超越",就是摆脱既往的路径依赖。我们习惯于这样讲课、这样教学,几十年如一日。有些教师非常驾轻就熟,掌控能力也非常强,但是有可能陷入了路径依赖的怪圈。这里所谈的"超越"包括两点含义:一是大学教师教育既要基于基础教育的实践,又要突破经验的局限。中小学教育实践虽然丰富,但是有时候这些日常的经验,不可复制、并非完美,也存在这样或那样的问题。因此,不是所有的一线经验都适合纳入高校教学的体系中来。二是要超越既往的传统,避免堆砌中小学经验,要开拓理论自觉的实践空间。比如,某位中学教师经过他/她个人专业的成长,最后成长为特级教师,深受学生欢迎,和他/她的努力程度有关。但是其他教师也都很敬业,有的却成不了特级教师。背后的原因恐怕与经验的路径依赖有直接关系。因此,我们应该摆脱教师教育的路径依赖,构建适切的、适用的教师教育专业理论,这是教师教育改革的基本职责。

（三）激活：推进理论和实践创新

理论来自实践，通过教育实践，我们生成了一种新的教育理论，这就实现了理论创新。在这个基础上，又有一些新的实践问题出现，倒逼我们必须挖掘深层的教育理论。要实现深层次的理论创新，就要实现"激活"——理论和实践的双向激活。在教育实践过程中，有的问题是浅显的问题，很难成为理论的问题。但是借助理论的视角进行解读，就能挖掘出实践背后深层次的理论难题。因此，通过理论创新对实践有激活的作用，而实践又激活新的理论，这种理论和实践的双向激活，是首都师范大学多年来探索的指导思想。在教育理论与实践开放的状态、融合的互动关系中，激活新一轮更丰富、更深刻的理论建构与实践探索。

二、教师教育改革的实践举措

（一）完善教师教育学科群建设

新时代教师教育的使命是培养"有理想信念、有道德情操、有扎实学识、有仁爱之心"的高素质专业化教师。我们首先需要整合教育学科内部各个学科，完善教师教育的"首师大模式"，同时协同教育学科和各个教学学科建立教育专业生态的体系，实现理论与实践开放、合作的双通道的"U—D—S共同体"。在这个基础上，构建教师教育的课程和教学体系，实现教师专业素养提升，共同推进理论和实践的双提高。

（二）构建"五位一体"的教师教育工作体系

教师教育学科建设和教师培养工作有时会发生偏差，比如，学科评估主要是考察知识的创新，发表了多少有影响力的论文，以及重大的成果；而教师教育旨在培养更多的好老师，这两者的目的之间存在偏差。在教师教育导向之中,培养好教师的目标推进了我们的工作,而不是学科建设。但是我们办学的终极目的是培养好老师。如何化解这两者的矛盾呢?我们认为,应该按照实践要求推进理论建设,在教师教育工作过程中,教育实践需要什么样的好老师,教师教育研究就朝哪个方向发展理论。进而按照理论要求推进标准建设,按照标准要求推进课程建设,按照课程要求推进实验室建设,最终按照实践要求推进基地建设。这样一来,"U—D—S"才真正成为一个共同体,实现了"实践、理论、标准、课程、实验室、专业基地"五位一体的工作状态。

(三)夯实 U—D—S 教育共同体,推进区域教育整体变革

首先,北京市的各个区域构成了一种良好的合作伙伴关系,实质性地推动了区域教育的实践。学校和区教委,它们是我们的"客户端";客户端也要参与到我们教师培养的过程中来。

其次,构建学校教育、家庭教育、社会教育共同的生态体系。学校教育不是整个教育的全部,我们现在提倡"三全"育人,家庭、社会、学校协同育人是我们首都师范大学努力的方向。学校最近成立了家庭教育研究中心,是教育部关工委、北京市关工委和首都师范大学构成的一个生态体系,是我们协同育人的目标。我认为,如果教育能够激发、启迪人的生命力,唤醒人的精神状态,构建人的生存方式,那就是"正教育",不符合这些标准的就是"负教育",或者是"零教育"。"零教育"就是对人的发展没有起到什么作用,"负教育"就是背道而驰。说实话,我们很多教育工作者在做负教育的事,打着教育的旗号干着负教育的工作。所以教育工作首先要明白教育的本质是什么,教育的目的和追求是什么,这是最根本的方面。所以构建家庭教育、学校教育、社会教育协同育人的良好生态显得尤为重要。

最后,变学科导向为需求导向。学科导向是高等学校现在追求的核心竞争力,需求导向就是更加准确、定位教育实践的需求。从学科导向转向需求导向,告诉我们应该形成充满活力的教师教育模式,这是一种职前、职后

一体化的全新模式。

三、教师教育改革的总体成果

首都师范大学是北京基础教育师资培养的重要基地,北京市现任的 5 万名中学教师中,首都师范大学的毕业生占到 55%;北京市幼儿教师中,我校的毕业生占到 94%;在北京市特级教师中,我校毕业生占到一半以上,部分学科达到 90%。目前,首都师范大学已经形成了鲜明的教师教育办学特色,具有教师教育"学前、小学、中学"一体化的培养体系。近年来,在北京市教委的支持下,我校不断优化师范生的招生计划,扩大师范生的招生名额,并尝试探索本硕博贯通一体化的教师培养模式。

近年来,我校师范生培养质量显著提高,与基础教育的实践契合度明显提高,不断有中小学校长向我们反馈这样积极的消息。借用习近平总书记的话:"首都师范大学是一所很好的学校,是一所很有分量的学校,特别是在基础教育方面功不可没,培养了大量人才,整个学校状态很好,技术很好,前景很好。"我们用习近平总书记给我们的鼓励,来不断激励自己提升我们的教师教育质量,为北京市乃至全国培养更多高质量专业化的教师。

Building a U – D – S Teacher Education Community to Cultivate High – Quality Professional Teachers

Fanhua Meng

Professor, President of Capital Normal University

Abstract: Under the guidance of the concept of " feedback, activation and transcendence", Capital Normal University has formed a practice – oriented teacher education mode with the basic characteristics of "mutual activation in theory and practice, integration of pre – service and in – service". The teacher education community consisting of University – District – School (U – D – S) helps to build a teacher education system with the model of "five – in – one", to accelerate the education reform of the whole region, and to promote the construction of the teacher education course group. After 20 years of exploration, the teacher education program of Capital Normal University has achieved remarkable results and formed a unique "CNU mode".

　　Keyword: U—D—S; Teacher education community; Professional teachers

论一流小学教师教育体系重构

朱旭东

北京师范大学教育学部部长，教授

摘要: 鼓励一流综合大学参与小学教师培养，一流小学教师培养的师范院校资源整合，提升应用型本科院校小学教师培养的一流学科建设，构建独立专门的小学教师培养院校体系，构建"互联网＋"小学教师培养体系和小学教师教育学科体系。

关键词: 一流小学教师培养；教师培养体系；互联网＋

我在北京师范大学珠海校区上完课以后，一个本科生给我写了这么一段话："小学教师的门槛几乎是教师门槛里最低，这意味着发育最关键的时候，在认知发展、情感发展和社会性发展的起步时比其他时期更容易受到低质量的教育。"他觉得这存在风险性。把这个大学生的话拿到第一个来讲的原因是，国家现在确实很重视这个问题。中共中央、国务院发布了一个报告，里边也提到了小学教师学历要提升至师范专业专科和非师范专业本科。

在有关小学教师培养的目标和模式、课程和机构的变迁等方面，学者们都做了一些探索。例如首都师范大学的王智秋老师，她做了新中国成立后小学教师教育的变迁，历史怎么发展过来的有关研究。总体上来讲，前面这些研究都是给我们提供了很好的启示、启发和基础，但是我觉得还是要加强对小学教师教育体系的研究。

我先从问题入手，一流大学的小学教师教育参与度太低。截至 2019 年 6 月 15 日这一天，全国本科城市高等学校共计 1265 所，其中开设小学教育专业、本科专业共计 211 所，和刚才任友群司长的数据相差无几。其中 985 大学有 0 所，211 有 4 所，双一流大学有 7 所，但还不是教师教育，也不是教育学科，跟教育学科没有关系。三无大学指的是非 985，非 211，非双一流大学总共 201 所。请问我们的小学教师教育怎么能够在高水平上培养呢？这一数据当然是由历史原因造成的，137 所里边就两所师范大学，华东师范大学还没有小学教师教育。好在北京师范大学在我对小学教师培养的不断坚持和努力之下，设置了一个硕士层次的小学教师教育专业。

师范大学怎么不进行小学教师的培养？我们不断向学校有关领导提出一定要建立小学教师教育的专业。首都师范大学已经在培养本科生了，就不抢人家的饭碗了。但是无论如何要有这样的责任和担当做这样的工作。所以两年前，应该已经有两届学生毕业了，我们的小教专科人数很少，只有 20 人，但是也算是小学教师的培养。小学教师教育金字塔型的体系基本没有变，20 年了，30 年了，还是这个样子。

为什么这么说呢？小学教师教育办学层次低，生源质量缺乏保障，关键是小学教师教育机构太大了！

因此，实施教师教育供给侧结构性改革十分迫切，底端的教师教育机构任务十分艰巨。我们可以看一下，3 年前我国小学教师教育专业在校人数的数据。可以看到，大量的小学教师的培养，其中师范大学总共 13643 人。那么其他的都是哪些大学在培养？给大家提供另外一个数据，2011—2017 年小学新入职教师学历区域差异。东部地区整体提升了，其中研究生学历从 2.7% 上升到 4.77%，本科学历从 59.34% 到 72.21%。可是我们看到中部地区或者西部地区，本科毕业生从 2011 年的 46.07% 到 2017 年 67.13%。我只是说新入职的教师的量显然跟已经在职的教师的量不可同日而语。所以总体上，从教师学历的角度来讲，我们离世界一流的小学教育，在我看来还是比较远的。拿上海来说，说明不了中国教育、小学教师整体水平高。底端的小学教师教育体系又不完善,我指的是区县教师教育体系,基本没有,要有也可能是一个学科的一到两个教研员,在管理区县的某一个学科的整个教研,而且教研体系呈现重事不重人的状况。

所以我们说要健全地方教师教育体系建设。在我们的意见当中也提出了——机构和专业培训者队伍。小学教师教育机构的压力太大了,办学资源严重匮乏。我们跟诸多的办小学教育的这些院校在访谈、调查过程中,发现确实面临着严峻的问题。本科、硕士、博士点制度资源必须要去争取,同时创新力不足。互联网+教师教育体系,小学教师教育急需构建。我们的教师教育的课程教学等诸多环节停留在传统的状态,包括信息技术、学习科学、认知科学、科技与教育的深度融合等,都还处在一个初始状态。

教师教育者的专业师资队伍数量严重不足,质量也不高。从教师教育的角度来讲,博士学历数量严重缺乏。有一个问题我必须要提出来,小学教育学和小学教师教育学的学科边界其实是没有建立起来的。我以为小学教育学研究的是在小学里边如何开展小学教育,但是小学教师教育是要关注在大学里面、在小学教师培养机构里面,怎样培养教师有关的学科体系。通过小教的同人们的努力,小学教育学、小学教育这个体系应该说在过去20多年来,取得了非常大的成就。但是小学教师教育应该说是严重的滞后于我们的小学教育学的。我认为这两个是有联系,但是完全不同的概念。

大学教师做小学教师培养工作,首先要把我们自己大学里面,小学教师如何培养和学科体系如何建设开展研究,这才是真正在大学工作的一个本分。但是这个领域我们探索的不多。

为此,我说要重建新时代一流的小学教师教育体系,在我们国家其实解决小学教师教育体系有两个"欠账"的问题。一方面是要整体提升小学教师教育体系。就是前面我提到的,一流大学参与小学教师教育几乎为零,为什么会形成这样一种局面?这方面有诸多因素,但是从国际经验比较的角度来讲,美国的一流大学里边是有培养小教的。那么为什么中国不可以有?北京大学为什么不可以有?南京大学成立陶行知教师教育学院,但是它将来只培养中学教师，而不会培养小学教师吗？我认为还需要关注小学教师教育。另一方面是解决均衡优质的教师教育体系很不充分的问题。首都师范大学也是培养小教，但是跟西部某一所大学开展的小学教师教育，两者之间的差距其实还是很大。中国小学教师教育的问题，在我看来还是有这么两个"欠账"，国家需要解决。

为此我说要重构新时代中国一流大学的小学教师教育体系。中国一流的师范大学、一流的中国大学要去培养小学教师。过去十几年来，我在不同的会议上就呼吁，慢慢开始若干一流大学已经关注基础教育，他们也慢慢开始进入中小学里边去，开始关注培养教师相关的一些工作。我以为只有中国的一流大学进入教师教育当中的时候，才能提升中国的教师教育的整体水平。

其次，重构新时代中国专门、独立的教师教育体系。我们并不认为小学教师都应该由综合大学来培养，应该存在专门培养小学教师的院校。所以提出来借鉴国际经验，建立培养小学教师教育的大学。我们要有大学层面的小学教师的培养，从而能够争取到更多的学位点资源，比如硕士点和博士点。现在我们严重受制约的很多院校，因为不是一级博士学位点，导致这些博士点根本就建不起来。那么我们的小教怎么办？教师培养怎么办？也要呼吁有关机构真的要让我们的小教，成为一所大学，大学当然是有这个条件、资格去申请博士点，哪怕是教育博士。

再次是重构新时代中国区县教师教育体系。我有一个基本观点，就是只有中国的区县教师教育体系构建并完善，才能真正振兴教师教育。我们现在区县教师教育的概念基本是没有的。为此我们要不断呼吁，区县的人大报告、政府报告，不管什么报告，总得把教师教育这个概念写入报告中，让我们的政府官员和我们的老百姓都知道，教师教育不是可有可无，它是一项事业。事业当然要进入政府的工作报告中。

我们要构建区县小学教师教育新体系，这也是我自己过去几年来一直在凉山州，三区三州在做的一项工作，就是帮助这些地区建立区县教师教育体系，当然也包括小学教师教育体系。我们提出区县教师发展中心、教师专业发展学校、校本教师专业发展中心、名师工作室构成的区县教师教育体系,试图打破过去我们只有一个进修学校,而现在要整合成为一个教师专业发展中心这样一个局面,让区县教师教育能够多元化、多个机构来培养教师,这是我目前正在现场开展的一个推进区县教师教育的一项工作。

最后是重构新时代中国互联网 + 小学教师教育体系。现在的孩子从娘胎开始就与手机结缘了,我们不能无视他们的原生性环境,未来的孩子从一开始就与信息技术与互联网共同生存是一种发展趋势。所以北京师范大学教育学部成立慕课发展中心。成立慕课发展中心的目的就是希望教育学部的师生要进入线上线下的学习格局当中去。孩子已经是在互联网生存状态里边了,我们大学培养教师的课堂,还不是线上线下,情何以堪啊?虽然国家也有很多慕课中心,但是我认为线上线下混合学习,和只打开一个电脑看,是两个不同的概念。

小学教师教育要积极地融入教育发展前沿趋势当中。脑科学与小学教育怎么跨学科运用?学习科学至少成为小学教师教育的重要课程。人工智能(AI)环境下的小学教师教育体系要重构,实现人机共存。互联网 + 环境下的小学教育过程建构,以及科技推动小学教育改革等,无论从方法论、价值论还是实践论上,都需要有教师教育和科技的融合。

前不久教育部基础教育司、教师工作司召集北京师范大学与 10 所师范大学的副校长开了一个务虚会,说师范院校要引领基础教育改革,要服务于基础教育,让我们北京师范大学提出一个针对"到底该怎么引领?该怎么服务?"的方案。也就是说,基础教育司也要来关注我们的师范院校的发展。当然,最先受到影响的就是教师培养。我们的教师培养如何去适应今天我们的小学教育当中的一系列的新的变化?同时更重要的是去引领它。

总之,小学教师教育面临的问题还是很多。比如说西方国家流行的阅读、数学、科学、道德与法制、艺术和运动,我们前面研究的角度——分科、全科、综合,等等。但是对于小学教育来讲,要先构成小学教育自身的一个学习结构,再来看教师该怎么培养。之前我参加北京师范大学和中国科学院合作的科学教育研讨会,我也发现这些问题几乎无人问。所以,我们是任重而道远,改革开放40多年确实取得了巨大的成就,但是我们依然面临着太多的问题。

最后,呼吁大家建立小学教师教育学科,这是在大学里边有你的地位的基本门道。这是中国的特色,我觉得这需要今天小教界的各位专家、老师们共同一起来努力,我也愿意为小学教师教育做出努力!

On the Reconstruction of First – Class Elementary Teachers Education System

Xudong Zhu

Professor, Dean of Faculty of Education, Beijing Normal University

Abstract: The following strategies are recommended concerning the reconstruction of first – class elementary school teacher education system: (1) First – class comprehensive universities are encouraged to participate in elementary school teacher education; (2) Normal institutions setting out to cultivate first – class elementary teachers are advised to integrate their resources; (3) Application – oriented institutes are expected to boost their construction of first – class elementary teacher education programs; (4) A specific and independent system of elementary teacher education institutions can be constructed; (5) "Internet plus" elementary teacher training system and elementary teacher educational discipline system are advised to be constructed.

Key words: First – class elementary school teacher education ; Teacher education system ; Internet plus

德育教师专业化：溯源与展望①

李 敏 刘 慧

首都师范大学初等教育学院，教授

摘要：小学德育工作走向专业化，急需开启职前培养小学德育师资的人才培育通道。为此，需要回顾历史、展望未来，厘清德育理论发展与德育实践推进的阶段成果与形势，综合考虑师资、课程、人才需求等重要办学条件，科学稳妥地推进小学德育师资培育的职前师范教育，引领德育教师专业化发展。

关键词：德育教师专业化；教师德育专业化；小学德育

一、发展溯源：从"教师德育专业化"到"德育教师专业化"

近年来，"专业化""专业素养"等概念被教育各界广泛讨论。教育部于2012年颁布了《中小学幼儿园教师专业标准（试行）》，又于2014年展开中小学幼儿园教师培训课程标准研制工作。2019年3月18日，习近平总书记在北京主持召开学校思想政治理论课教师座谈会并发表重要讲话："思想政

---

① 本文系2019年教育部人文社科规划基金项目"小学教师德育素养的结构要素与培育机制研究"（项目编号：19YJA880023）阶段性成果。

治理论课是落实立德树人根本任务的关键课程。青少年阶段是人生的'拔节孕穗期',最需要精心引导和栽培。思政课作用不可替代,思政课教师队伍责任重大。"①

这一系列指向教育发展和教师队伍建设的重要政策文件和工作,加强了全社会对"教师德育专业化""德育课程建设"等工作的关注和投入。它昭示着一个重要的发展趋势——我国的教育理论、政策与实践均在逐步明晰德育专业化与教学专业化之间的相对边界。

相对于教学专业化专注于学科与教学,德育专业化旨在关心每一名教师的育德意识和育德能力。早在 2007 年,檀传宝教授就提出了"教师德育专业化"的命题。② 他认为,教师作为德育工作者的历史可以划分为三个阶段:第一阶段是德育工作者的未分化时期,其对应的是经验型教育阶段,特征是教育几乎等于德育,"教师即人师",所有教师都是德育工作者;第二阶段是教师逐步分化为"专门的德育工作者"和"非专门的德育工作者"阶段,与之对应的是近现代专业化教育阶段。这一阶段的一般科任教师(非专门的德育工作者)常常会误解工作分工,将德育责任完全推诿给所谓的"德育教师";第三阶段是指向教育专业意义上的教师"德育专业化"阶段,这一阶段的特征是包括德育教师在内的全体教师都应走向德育专业化。③

在对教师德育专业化的阶段描述中,第二阶段实际上指出了德育教师急需专业化的"现实需求",第三阶段实际上提出了全员教师需要走向德育专业化的"理想形态"。

从师资队伍建设来看,中学阶段已经通过思想政治专业的人才培养,一定程度上满足了中学德育教师实现专业化的"现实需求"。然而在小学阶段,我们一直以来缺失相应专业的职前人才培养环节,以至于我国小学阶段的德育教师队伍始终处在"杂牌军"和"不专业"的境况之中。由此可以得

---

① 《习近平主持召开学校思想政治理论课教师座谈会》,新华社,2019 年 3 月 18 日。

② 檀传宝:《德育教师的专业化与教师的德育专业化》,《教育研究》,2007 年第 4 期。

③ 檀传宝:《主动回应时代的呼唤:努力推进"教师德育专业化"》,《人民教育》,2012 年第 18 期。

知,推进小学德育教师的职前培养是当前教师德育专业化建设的一个重要阶段和组成部分,而这种职前培养也将为在职的一线德育教师实现专业化成长提供方向引领和具体指导。

二、现实诉求:在德育实践与理论交互砥砺中前行

毋庸置疑,小学德育教师队伍的培养需要兼顾先进的德育理论发展和现实的德育实践需求,从中探索适合当下我国小学德育师资培养的职前与职后教育教学体系。

(一)于德育实践中明晰小学德育工作指向

在此,我们可以从内容和形式两个方面,归纳当前小学德育实践开展情况。

首先,从小学德育工作的内容分析。学校教育中,常规的德育工作是围绕小学生的品德发展和社会性发展来聚合德育内容的。其中,品德发展所涉及的德育内容包括:道德教育、国情教育、行为习惯养成教育等;社会性发展所涉及的德育内容包括:公民素养教育、心理健康教育、媒介素养教育、法律教育等。这些德育内容既是指导学生健康成长与生活所必需的给养,又是鼓舞学生参与社会、贡献社会的重要引领。

其次,从学校德育工作的形式分析。随着德育研究和实践的不断深化,教育决策者和实践工作者也超越了一直以来,在认识与选择德育形式时,偏于偶发性、主题化、活动化的倾向,而趋于从稳定性、区块化、育人性等方面,考虑和规划德育形式。从实际的小学德育实践来看,[1]直接德育课程、各类活动、教师风貌、班级管理、学科教学、校外实践、校园环境、管理文化、课堂文化,甚至校园中的群己关系,都已被视为重要的德育形式。

---

① 刘慧:《小学德育实践》,高等教育出版社,2012 年,第 17～20 页。

由此，我们可以看到，学校德育工作实际上是一个全面、系统的工程。正如 2017 年教育部印发《中小学德育工作指南》所提出的"三全育人"体系，要"努力形成全员育人、全程育人、全方位育人的德育工作格局"。

无论从内容还是形式来看，当下的小学德育工作都需要走向专业化的方向，逐渐明晰各项德育工作背后所需要的知识基础和能力基础。

（二）与时俱进的德育理论为培养专业化德育教师夯实专业基础

不可否认，德育发展至今，已成为一个独立的学科领域。其研究成果日趋丰硕，形成了自己的研究范式和众多理论流派，已有一些高校设有德育方向的硕士点和博士点。

从实际情况看，德育领域已形成相对成熟的科目群，包括德育原理、德育社会学、德育心理学、德育与家庭教育、德育与班级管理，等等。借助科研机构与高校力量的研究动力，目前已极大地推进了德育理论的繁荣与发展，生活德育、情感德育、欣赏型德育、生命德育、生态体验德育等，已经逐渐走进德育实践领域，并日益发挥着理论引领作用。

而如何将这些理论成果切实转化到德育实践中去，并在实践中加以完善与创新，一方面要依靠一线教师的职后学习与培训；另一方面，急需创设和发展职前相关专业，以更好地传播、吸收这些新理论，为未来的德育工作提供优良的教师队伍，也为当前的在职教师培训提供专业理论指引与培训课程的参照。

三、照见未来：以职前培养推进小学德育教师专业化

1996 年，国家教委印发《关于师范教育改革和发展的若干意见》的通知，要求逐步增加本科学历的中小学教师培养，提出"高等师范本科教育学制为四年，高等师范专科教育学制由二、三年并存逐步过渡为三年，中等师范教育学制由三、四年并存逐步过渡为四年"。截至当前，经历 20 多年的师范教

育改革,我国小学教师教育取得了长足进步,以夯实基础、综合培养为一致方向;同时,越发注重专业素养的培育,并借助多样化的教师职后培训积累了丰富的教育教学经验。

优良的师范教育发展为小学教育专业进一步实现培养"素养全面、专长发展"的专门化师资人才,创造了很好的基础。依托师范教育实现小学德育教师的专门化培养,已提上了议事日程。在师范院校落实培养小学德育教师的行动需要考虑三方面的条件。

（一）师资条件

承担培养小学德育教师的高校师资应该在专业上是多元的,自身具备较好的理论研究素养与实践应用能力,以实现"素养全面、专长发展"的人才培养目标。在学历上也应有较高的要求,应建设具有博士学位的高校师资队伍。基于对德育理论与德育实践的双向考虑,高校师资的专业背景需要涉及伦理学、政治学、社会学、德育学等相关专业或方向,以胜任德育理论研究与传播及小学德育实践的工作需要。

（二）课程建设

专业化的小学德育师资培养主要依靠合理的课程架构。基于已有师范教育以及近年来教师职后培训经验的积累,我们认为,小学德育专业方向课程应涉及几大类:

一是专业方向基础类课程。这部分课程会提供专业德育师资所需要的多个学科支撑,为小学德育工作者打下坚实的理论基础。课程将涉及伦理学基础、政治学概论、法学概论、德育原理等小学德育的基础理论科目。

二是专业方向核心类课程。这部分课程需要细致考虑如何实现德育理论与德育实践的对接,在德育理论的"实践化"和德育实践的"课堂化"方面下足功夫。课程将聚焦小学德育专业的核心课程,包括道德与法治课程标准与教材分析、教学设计、儿童组织与思想意识教育理论与实践、研学旅行课程等。

　　三是实践教学类课程。这部分课程主要指向师范生教育教学实践能力的锻炼和提升,包括经过达到一定量的道德与法治课堂教学实践、少先队活动(课)实践、教育教学实习、科研指导课程等。此外,有条件的师范院校还应为小学德育方向的师范生开设读书课程,以及形式多样的素养类课程,包括舞蹈、钢琴、书法、科学、家庭教育等课程。

　　这些课程设置基于小学德育教师队伍的现状,考虑学校德育工作的具体内容,希望也能借此为一线德育教师实现自身的专业化发展提供引领和借鉴。

(三)人才需求预测

　　推进小学德育专业师资的职前培养,还需要进行有效的人才需求调研。小学德育方向的毕业生,未来将主要求职于小学"道德与法治"课程任课教师,以及少先队大队辅导员岗位。为此,一方面需要对区域范围内小学德育岗位的人才需求进行调研,另一方面,需要积极联合当地教育部门,在体制上捋顺小学德育教师的现实供需关系,为该方向毕业生就业创造良好的条件。随着德育工作在学校教育中地位的不断加强,以及对其实效性的不断强调,可以预见,中小学校对于道德与法治及少先队专业教师的需求会越来越大。因此,毕业生的就业形势与前景会更加广阔。这也为解决当前我国普遍存在的德育教师"兼职"状况,确立德育教师的专业地位,规划了美好的前景。

　　推进实现小学德育教师的职前培养是落实国家"立德树人"根本任务的有力行动。如何尊重小学教育的规律性和特殊性,关照小学儿童的需要和特质,开展规范有效的德育工作,急需依托具有专业能力的教师来进行。为此,高校小学教育开设德育方向,无论对于德育理论还是德育实践,都具有重大的历史意义与现实价值。这既是一种高校办学的实践探索,更是一种以"产学研"的方式建设德育理论的研究进程,它将为国家培养出一批又一批专业扎实、综合能力强的小学德育工作者。

Professionalization of Moral Education Teachers: Traceability and Prospect

Min Li   Hui Liu

Abstract: The moral education in primary schools is becoming more and more professional, so it is urgent to open the channel of cultivating moral education teachers. Therefore, we need to review the history and look forward to the future, clarify the stage achievements and situation of the development of moral education theory and the promotion of moral education practice, comprehensive consideration of important school conditions such as teachers, courses, and talent needs, scientifically and steadily promote the pre - service teacher education for the cultivation of primary school moral education teachers, leading the professional development of moral education teachers.

Key words: professionalization of moral education teachers; professionalization of teachers´ moral education; primary school moral education

智能教育时代下人机协同智能层级结构及教师职业形态新图景①

朱永海　刘　慧　李云文　王　丽

首都师范大学初等教育学院

摘要:人工智能逐渐成为国际竞争的新焦点和国家重大战略。通过文献分析和国家规划文件研究,指出智能教育既是指用人工智能技术辅助教育,也是指培养学生个体智能发展的教育。人工智能时代下的智能最终将进化成为由人的生命主导的"'机器智能+'人"的人机协同智能层级结构(HISHMC),即人机协同基础:计算思维;协同支撑:计算智能、感知智能、认知智能;协同接口:智能环境(智能系统、智能平台、智能媒体);协同主体:认知智能、情感智能、志趣智能和创新智能。智能教育时代,教师的职业形态将变成人机协同工作,教师将聚焦于凸显生命特质的职业能力;提供高端服务品质;促进人机协同的智慧教育;探寻生命整体意义;师生共同感悟生命实践形成新的职业形态。

关键词:智能教育;个体智能;人机协同智能层级结构;智慧教育;生命教育

---

①　基金项目:教育部学校规划建设发展中心第二批未来学校(中小学、幼儿园)实验研究重点课题"开放融合的'互联网+'学习生态研究"(CSDP18FS1102)。

人工智能成为国际竞争的新焦点,世界主要发达国家把发展人工智能作为提升国家竞争力、维护国家安全的重大战略。我国依托"互联网＋"这一国家战略,奠定了"人工智能＋"发展的良好基础,使人工智能技术得到了飞速发展,"未来已来"的世界图景已经展现在我们眼前。随着 2017 年国务院《新一代人工智能发展规划》发布,提出培育智能经济、建设智能社会、建设智能教育;2018 年《教育信息化 2.0 行动计划》提出要大力推进智能教育,探索泛在、灵活、智能的教育教学新环境建设与应用模式。智能教育是顺应智能环境下的教育发展,因应信息技术特别是智能技术的发展,成为"互联网＋"教育变革的又一个实践热点。2017 年《地平线报告》都认同从移动学习进阶到了人工智能,以及从提升素养、整合学习形式到重塑教师角色的难度升级。① 作为人类,我们如果不快速提升自己、改变自己,就很可能会被外界强制性改变,②教师职业便是首当其冲,本文抛砖引玉以期引起大家讨论。

一、未来已来:人工智能技术及其在教育中的应用

当前人工智能快速发展,呈现出深度学习、跨界融合、人机协同、群智开放及自主操控等新特征,推动经济社会各领域从数字化、网络化向智能化加速跃升。③ 人工智能的关键技术主要有:知识表示方法、机器学习与深度学习、自然语言处理、智能代理和情感计算等。④ 智能校园、立体化综合教学场、基于大数据智能的在线学习平台、智能教育助理等是人工智能增强型教

① 高媛、黄荣怀:《〈2017 新媒体联盟中国高等教育技术展望:地平线项目区域报告〉解读与启示》,《电化教育研究》,2017 年第 4 期。
② 互联网思想:《月付薪水的数字员工机器人已到岗,这是你离失业最近的一次》,搜狐,http://www.sohu.com/a/244656315_464025。
③ 杜占元:《人工智能与未来教育变革》,《首届"教育智库与教育治理 50 人圆桌论坛"》,2017 年。
④ 闫志明:《教育人工智能(EAI)的内涵、关键技术与应用趋势》,《现代远程教育研究》,2018 年第 2 期。

育的四种微观层次的应用形态。① 伍尔夫等人（Beverly Park Woolf et al., 2013）总结了人工智能教育的五项关键研究挑战，包括个性化学习导师的研制、21 世纪核心能力培养的支持、基于学习交互数据的分析、服务的普及性、为终身学习服务。② 近年来，基于海量结点的神经网络的机器翻译，实现自然语言处理，达到了人类专业水平；对话式人工智能系统，为用户带来包括情感语音讲解、声纹识别等能力在内的自然语言交互技术；移动 AR 技术与 AI 需要相互加持，二者信息相互补充、叠加，为人类感知信息提供了新的方式；通过生物特征识别技术，可以较为有效地识别即将要实施的人的行为，从而做出行为预测；像素级声源定位系统能识别出视频中发声的物体，并将声音分离出来；智能流程自动化（Intelligent Process Automation）增加基于深度学习和认知技术的推理、判断、决策能力；人性化和个性化的智能代理技术从经验中不断自我学习，根据环境调整自身的行为，可以在用户没有给出十分明确的需求时推测出用户的意图、兴趣或爱好，并按最佳方式代其完成任务；入耳式人工智能，作为一种常见的智能穿戴设备，可以无限延续使用时间和场景，可收集行走步数、心率和体温，等等，还可以通过内置陀螺仪捕捉用户头部移动和位置状况。③ 从阿尔法围棋（AlphaGo Zero）的设计来看，它不需要连入网络，不需要大量的数据支撑，而是"小数据"，完全从零开始自主学习和迁移学习，这种学习能力远远超出了过去对简单人工智能的想象。④ 人工智能在教育中有十二种主要作用，⑤国外有关研究证明：将人工智能结合到在线测试系统设计中，能有效解决来自教师、单一教学模式及当下其他大学英语教学存在的问题，诊断学习者的问题，并给予学习者行之有效的人工智能训练之体验，从而有效增强学习者的自主学习意识，强化学习者

---

① 苏令银：《论人工智能时代的师生关系》，《开放教育研究》，2018 年第 2 期。

②③ 成都准星云学：《不新鲜！人工智能早已从 3 方面渗入美国教育》，百度，https://baijiahao. baidu. com/s？id = 1586462472005122726&wfr = spider&for = pc。

④ 杜占元：《人工智能与未来教育变革》，《首届"教育智库与教育治理 50 人圆桌论坛"》，2017 年。

⑤ 余胜泉：《人工智能教师的未来角色》，《开放教育研究》，2018 年第 1 期。

的自主学习能力,提高教学质量。① 在当下在线教育基础上探讨与人工智能结合应用成为一大重要研究热点。② 未来已来,我们必须要对人工智能和人类智能发展有一个清晰的梳理,把握人工智能教育应用及教师的地位和作用。

二、本质回归:智能教育时代对人的本质再认识

(一)机器智能和人机协同智能层级结构

1.机器智能

从技术的角度来看人工智能的发展经历了三阶段:计算智能、感知智能和认知智能。计算智能能存会算;感知智能能听会说;认知能力能理解会思考,即具有抽象思维、形象思维和灵感思维等思维能力。③ 目前,人工智能整体上还处于"感知智能"阶段,"认知智能"只是初期阶段。这三种智能主要是倾向于对"智力"的模拟,是一种狭义的智能,未涉及生物机体的情感和生命层面。

2.人的本质

人工智能无法取代人类,就在于人类与机器之间有几大差异:机器鲜见发现问题的能力,机器不具备社会属性和心理属性。④ 人类的属性可分为生物属性和社会属性。⑤ 人与机器、生物、人之间的差异来界定人的本质属性,具体包括:①人类和机器相比而呈现出的生物属性(包括情感属性);②人类和动物相比而呈现出的(高级)思维属性;③人与人相比而呈现出的社会属

①　Fu R.,Design and Application of the Artificial Intelligence in Online Test of English Computer,*Agro Food Industry Hi – tech*,No. 3,2017,pp. 2390 – 2393.

②　Zheng X.,Application of Distance Education Combined With Artificial Intelligence,*Agro Food Industry Hi – tech*,No. 1,2017,pp. 555 – 559.

③　于继栋:《人工智能为数字营销带来的新变革》,移动营销峰会,2016 年。

④　赵勇:《未来,我们如何做教师》,《中国德育》,2017 年第 11 期。

⑤　刘国城、晁连成、张忠伦、叶平:《生物圈与人类社会》,人民出版社,1992 年,第 40 页。

性(包括文化属性)。所以人应该具备基本的生物属性、思维属性和社会属性。

　　人类的生物属性是人之所以为人的生理基础,尤其是生物机体和情感特点是机器难以突破的。作为生物本能的人类应该保障自己的生物机体和情感特点不被替代,并得以继续强化。而人类的思维理性和文化倾向又在不断地引领或调节着人类适应社会发展。人类既要守卫着作为生物本能的有机体,又要不断调整自身以适应社会科技及环境发展,"生物本能"与"文化倾向"之间必然会形成张力而相互制衡,并借助"思维理性"在二者之间进行调节,影响着人类在人工智能时代何去何从的人类及社会发展方向。

　　3. 人机协同智能层级结构

　　在讨论人工智能时,我们必须对"人类智能"进行全面的界定,以便探讨人工智能对人类智能模拟及智能教育培养对人类智能培养的广度和深度。智能,在《汉语大辞典》①的解释是:①智谋与才能;②指智力;百度百科的解释是:智能是智力和能力的总称。② 从概念来看,智能不仅包括认知智能,还包括智谋、才能和能力。关于人类智能比较公认的理论有左脑智能和右脑智能,以及霍华德加德纳提出的"多元智能理论"。

　　人工智能也不仅仅是在模拟人类的认知智能,还包括模拟人类的情感、社会交往等综合品性。Huang 提出了"人工智能工作替换(AI job replacement)"理论,指出服务性工作要求的四种智能,从低级到高级智能依次为:机械智能(mechanical)、分析智能(analytical)、直觉智能(intuitive)和移情智能(empathetic)。③ 祝智庭指出:智能主要涵盖认知智能、情感智能和志趣智能,这些智能与品性的融合形成了智慧。④ 这恰好符合我们前文所述的人的

----

① 《汉语大辞典》,汉辞网,http://www.hydcd.com/cd/htm19/ci369724s.htm。

② 《百度百科》,百度,https://baike.baidu.com/item/智能/66637? fr = aladdin。

③ Huang M,Rust R T.,Artificial Intelligence in Service,*Journal of Service Research*,No. 2,2018,pp. 155 - 172.

④ 《30 年后,你家孩子凭什么拼过人工智能? 就凭这 4 点》,搜狐 ,http://www.sohu.com/a/242369106_389102。

思维属性、生物属性和社会属性;以上三种智能表现出来的是一种综合体,即人类智能和机器智能之间的重要差异——创新智能。智能时代教育的基本理论应该是强调"知行创合一"①。整体上形成了广义的"智能",或称为"智慧"。我们将人类智能和机器智能结合起来,构建了一个"人机协同智能层次结构模型"(HISHMC, Hierarchical Intelligent Structures in Human - machine Collaboration),如图 1 所示,分四个部分:人机协同基础:计算思维;协同支撑:计算智能、感知智能、认知智能;协同接口:智能环境(智能系统、智能平台、智能媒体);协同主体:认知智能、情感智能、志趣智能和创新智能。每个部分又根据功能和层次的不同,分成若干个层级,简单地理解为低阶智能和高阶智能两个层级(具体高低层级,限于篇幅问题不再赘述)。

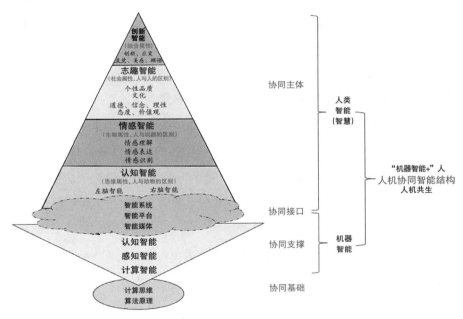

图 1 人机协同智能层级结构模型

基础层:主要包括计算思维和算法原理,是人和机器共有的能力;既是

---

① 陈琳:《匹配 AI 时代的教育要素变革》,中国智能教育大会,2018 年 8 月 8 日。

人工智能的基础,也是人机协同智能的基础。① 当前学界对此已经有了足够的认识,应用计算机科学的思想与方法来解决问题,以便人们更好地理解和分析复杂问题,形成具有形式化、模块化、自动化、系统化等计算特征的问题解决方案。②

支撑层:生物与机器联姻的时代,无论是生物还是机器,其实都是进化体。世界上所有对象的本质组成都是一样的,"生命"和"机器",都只不过是人类规定概念而已。③ 人工智能在计算智能方面进化速度已经远远超出了人类;在感知智能方面正在赶超人类,诸如人脸识别等,尤其是近些年来随着深度卷积神经网络(Deep Convolutional Neural Network,DCNN)的引入,人脸识别的准确率得到跨越式提升,已经应用在课堂教学中学生的脸部表情分析,将传统课堂教学进一步数据化,为大数据分析和智能教育奠定坚实的基础。人工智能技术已经强大到了一定的程度,可以极大地提高工作效率,帮助人类有效地解决问题,以至于不得不构建"人机协同智能层级结构",走向人机统一,成为"人机协同智能层次结构"的重要支撑。

接口层:也可以称之为内部的智能环境,主要是各种智能媒体、智能平台和智能系统的集成体。人类和机器应该是相通的,"边界最精彩"④。在接口处人类的认知智能和机器的认知智能最终将会走向无缝融合,借助最为直接的嵌入式或者穿戴式智能设备,实现合二为一。"接口"在教育领域主要表现为以下几个方面:

一是智能媒体,未来人和机器智能结合,不仅仅借助"场"和"空间"等虚拟方式,还有更多地借助"泛在智能设备",通过微型化、生物化、智能化的可穿戴设备(如谷歌眼镜、VR 头盔),尤其是可嵌入人体内的智能设备,发挥人机接口的作用,来实现人机智慧结合,智能芯片辅助人类特定器官的功能。

---

① 祝智庭、彭红超、雷云鹤:《智能教育:智慧教育的实践路径》,《开放教育研究》,2018 第 4 期。
② 任友群、隋丰蔚、李锋:《数字土著何以可能?——也谈计算思维进入中小学信息技术教育的必要性和可能性》,《中国电化教育》,2016 年第 1 期。
③④ [美]凯文·凯利:《失控》,东西文库译,电子工业出版社,2016 年,第 103~107 页。

二是智能平台,作为人机协同智能层级结构的最为核心的一个部分,用于直接处理人机协同工作,如国际商业机器公司(IBM)的沃森(Watson),通过自然语言处理和机器学习,从非结构化数据中揭示意义,目前已经成为一个基于云的认知系统,能够进行基于自然语言的理解、假设生成进行推理、以证据为基础的学习,自然方式交互等。

三是智能系统,让智能平台在特定情境下应用而开发,具有特定功能,如数字员工、智能助医和智能导师等。目前,芝麻街正与IBM Watson合作开发各种"个性化学习工具"以适应不同孩子的学习方式。它可以明白每个儿童独特的互动方式,并能够分析每位儿童输入和互动的内容,再针对他们的学习风格对每次接触进行个性化处理。同时,随着每一次互动的进行,Watson能够不断进行自身优化,以匹配每个学生的学习模式。[①]

主体层:主要是人类智能部分,包括认知智能、情感智能、志趣智能和创新智能。人工智能技术的进步就是要实现对"人类智能"的完美模拟,必然朝着类人的方向发展。随着人工智能技术一个个的攻破,计算智能已经超过了人类,"感知智能""认知智能"也可能会在将来逐步超越人类智能。这样便可能有三种结果:一是人在进化人工智能的同时也在不断地改造自己,人将变成"人工智能+"人,人机和谐相处,机器作为人类忠实的助手辅助人类。二是人类和机器和谐相处,二者互不隶属,自然界中又多了一个"智能物种",都成为自然界中平等的主体,各司其职。三是机器智能全方位超过人类智能,机器智能将重新定义"人",或者是说人工智能机器就是新种类的人——机器人类,人就会从属于机器而成为机器的一个"附属物",届时"生物人类"的价值和定位将会由未来"机器人类"去讨论和决定。如果出现了第三种情况,人的"主体性"地位已经丧失,人的主体价值已经不存在了,已经脱离了我们本文讨论的价值和意义;第二种情况不是本文探讨的范围;本

文关注的是第一种情况,人类智能在"人机协同智能层级结构"中是"主体智能",智能教育就是要夯实人机协同的基础——计算思维,并充分利用人工智能中的计算智能、感知智能和认知智能等机器智能,不断增强作为主体价值的人类智能中的情感智能、认知智能、志趣智能和创新智能。机器智能的发展目标是协同或辅助作用,不断地强化人类智能。

4.机器智能的"天花板"是人的本质特征

对教师职业形态的研究,需要对人工智能能够达到的人类智能的水平有一个定位:机器智能的"天花板"是人的本质特征——生命,机器智能难以拥有情感智能、志趣智能和创新智能中的高阶智能成分。譬如美国有个研究团队在探究人工智能是否可以替代课堂上的教师,迄今为止,尝试是不成功的。[①] "最蹩脚的建筑师也比最巧妙的蜜蜂优越",即便是像今日头条的人工智能实验室获得"吴文俊人工智能科学技术奖"的自动撰写新闻稿的人工智能技术及其发明,也是对"互联网信息摘要",而不是创作。[②] 人工智能技术或媒体终端可以嵌入人体,可以强化生命,但不能突破生命,不能改变生命的主要特征,本文的探讨是在人的主体地位得以确保的前提下展开的。幸运的是,人类除了"认知智能"之外,还有更加重要、更加高级、更加全面的生物特征和社会特征,这些都是非结构化的,极具个性化的智能特征,机器智能在可预见的未来内是无法超越的。

(二)智能教育界定及其本质回归

1.智能教育定义

周建设指出:智能教育是利用人工智能技术,依据教育大数据,精准计算学生的知识基础、学科倾向、思维类型、情感偏好、能力潜质,结合习得规律和教育规律,合理配置教育教学内容,科学实施因材施教,促进学生个性

---

① 苏令银:《论人工智能时代的师生关系》,《开放教育研究》,2018 年第 2 期。
② 周小白:《机器人写稿时代来了? 今日头条写新闻机器人拿下人工智能大奖》,百度,http://baijiahao. baidu. com/s? id =1587724569605066302&wfr = spider&for = pc。

化全面发展和核心素养全面提升。① 苏令银指出对人工智能存在的两种理解:狭义上,把人工智能看作是一种计算机程序,以智能的方式处理知识的特定方面,帮助人类执行特定的任务;广义上,是把人工智能理解成成功模仿人类认知的计算机程序。② 张进宝指出:狭义的智能教育定位于"以人工智能为内容的教育",培养掌握机器智能技术的专业化人才;广义的智能教育则定位于最终实现个体智能的提升,不仅掌握人工智能等技术,还能初步具备未来工作中实现人机合作的能力。③《教育信息化2.0行动计划》指出要充分利用智能技术加快推动人才培养模式、教学方法改革。基于此,智能教育的内涵包括对人工智能在教育中的三种理解:一是作为内容,以人工智能为内容的教育;二是作为手段,利用人工智能辅助教育;三是作为目的,促进学生智能发展的教育,在教育中培养学生的四种主要智能与智慧。本文主要探讨的是后两个维度之和,即智能教育是利用人工智能技术辅助教育,及其用于促进学习者智能发展的教育。有四个层面的意思:一是用人工智能技术辅助教育,但这是一种不完全的智能教育;二是促进学习者智能发展且用了人工智能技术,而不是泛泛地利用其他非智能技术,否则就会使智能教育的范畴无限扩大,毕竟传统教育也是促进了学习者智能发展。三是利用人工智能技术创设环境等促进学习者生命特质的智能发展,包括认知智能的中高阶智能,如分析、综合、评价等批判性思维;情感智能中的高阶智能,如情感理解;志趣智能中的高阶智能,如文化品质与个性品质;创新智能的创新和应变等。四是智能教育的目的是促进人类智能主导的"'机器智能+'人"的人机协同的智能结构,是 AI + BI 的教育:人工智能(AI)已经成为现实,但我们更加强调生物智能(BI)④。未来教育的重要特征是要基于

---

① 周建设:《人工智能与教育的深度融合》,中国智能教育大会,2018 年 8 月 8 日。
② 苏令银:《论人工智能时代的师生关系》,《开放教育研究》,2018 年第 2 期。
③ 张进宝、姬凌岩:《是"智能化教育"还是"促进智能发展的教育"》,《现代远程教育研究》,2018 年第 2 期。
④ Pekka Peura:《翻转课堂,让学生成为自己的老师》,第四届中国未来学校大会,2017 年。

脑、适于脑、促进脑。①

2. 智能教育是对人的本质回归——生命教育

真正智能教育的目的,应该是人类智能和机器智能的完美协调,让机器智能辅助人类智能发展,构建人机协同智能层级结构体,从而实现达成"完人"和"智慧"的教育,是完人教育、智慧教育、人性教育、生命教育,是一种有"温度"的教育。智能教育是教师在人工智能时代的重要任务。任何技术背景下,教师的核心任务都是聚焦在"人"的培养上。培养"完整人"这个根本的教育目的,不受互联网+、大数据技术,或人工智能技术所干扰和束缚。随着人的寿命不断增长,当下出生的一代婴儿,他可能到2100年还是个活跃的公民,而仅在30年后,人工智能算法可能比人类自己还了解自己,操纵人类最深层的情绪和欲望。② 尤瓦尔·赫拉利(2018)指出若想拼过人工智能,人类必须具备③:一是理解和辨别信息的能力。二是不断学习、适应变化和学会改变的能力。三是独立思考的能力,让自由天性自然绽放出来。四是一定要跑得比算法更快。这些不可替代的价值,就是人的生命内在的自由与活力,越是在机器智能飞速发展的时代,愈加彰显人类生命和智能的特殊性,引领社会的能力。项贤明认为:智能教育时代,德行和情感等人性特有的东西应当受到极大的重视,从现在起就建立一种"人性为王"的教育。④ 凯文·凯利指出:未来我们需要让自己做更感性,人情味更浓的事情,要活得更像人。⑤ 刘慧指出:如果我们想要回归人的本质,生命的学习就是返璞归真的途径,教育必须要回到生命本身和生命特性本身来认识与理解教育——生命教育。⑥

---

① 董奇:《未来教育的重要特征是要基于脑、适于脑、促进脑》,搜狐,https://www.sohu.com/a/258768746_484992。

②③ 《30年后,你家孩子凭什么拼过人工智能?就凭这4点》,搜狐,http://www.sohu.com/a/242369106_389102。

④ 项贤明:《人工智能与未来教育的任务》,《华东师范大学学报(教育科学版)》,2017年第5期。

⑤ [美]凯文·凯利:《失控》,东西文库译,电子工业出版社,2016年,第103~107页。

⑥ 刘慧:《生命教育内涵解析》,《课程·教材·教法》,2013年第9期。

三、生命教育：智能教育时代教师实践新形态

人工智能时代教育的技术手段和目标重点都发生了一定的变化，智能教育背景下的教师职业图景的探讨，也是对新时代下的人才培养的全面思考，具体表现在以下几个方面：

（一）教师工作技能：更加聚焦于具有生命特征的职业分工，体现生命回归

首先，教师的职业分工越来越细化。随着各国人工智能战略规划的逐步落实，人工智能逐步替代人类体力劳动和技能型工作。社会对从事低技能工作的劳动者需求将会大幅降低，人们需要的是更高素质的劳动者。[①] 智能教育会愈发呈现混合学习、在线学习、泛在学习、情景学习和非正式学习等"互联网＋"学习形态，学校将呈现开放办学状态，教师的职业分工将会更加精细化和个性化，而且这种分工在当下在线教育时代已经拉开了序幕。教师个体或人工智能都只从事其中某一个或几个环节，呈现特定局部功能化角色的特点。智能教育时代下，这种精细化的分工得以强化，借助大数据"喂养"或迁移学习，人工智能将会替代教师实现录像、自动推荐和传播学习资源，甚至是有情感的讲解、智能助教答疑、自动命题与批阅、学习障碍自动诊断与及时反馈、心理素质测评、综合素质报告等，帮助学生发现自己潜在的兴趣特长，成为教师的有力工具和伙伴，并基于数据驱动决策等[②]。

其次，教师承担的职业分工越来越凸显生命回归。有研究表明，不太可能被机器人取代的工作，其特征有[③]：社交能力、协商能力及人情练达的艺术；同情心、扶助和关切；创意和审美。而教师职业恰好需要具备这些特征，

[①]　Yildiz M，Yildirim B F，The Effects of Artificial Intelligence and Robotic Systems on Librarianship，*Turkish Librarianship*，No.1，2018，pp.26－32.

[②③]　余胜泉：《人工智能教师的未来角色》，《开放教育研究》，2018 年第 1 期。

教师的本质特征在于以人育人。实验表明：当使用者在实验中不是与人工智能交流时，使用者有更加开放、更加认同、更喜社交、更加认真及自我揭示的倾向。[①] 毕竟"人"具备之所以为"人"的关键特征，教师承担诸如能力培养、价值引领、情感感化、信念确立、德性养成等教育角色的现象将会日益凸显。[②③] 人工智能时代，教师要回归人性，[④]承担的角色分工，将更加侧重于能够凸显认知、情感、志趣和创造智能等高阶能力定位。有些教师则可能在多个方面同时肩负责任，如教学、测评、身心健康和职业发展规划等。

（二）教师工作特点：更加聚焦于体现高端品质的职业特征，凸显生命价值

相关数据显示，教师职业的被取代率只有0.4%，虽然教师"职业"被取代的可能性非常小，但大量的教师"岗位"和"角色"都会逐渐被人工智能所淘汰与更新，人工智能向教育提出了新的诉求——个体智能的提升和对个体生命的关照，要求教师对传统教学部分角色进行替换、改造与螺旋提升。

首先，机器可以替代的、无须生命参与的、机械重复性的教师工作将会被淘汰。"人工智能工作替换"指出：人工智能工作代替基本上发生在任务（task）层面，而不是职务（job）层面，并且从较低级的智能工作开始取代人类的工作，分析智能也将变得不那么重要，会被人工智能逐渐所替代。[⑤] 当下在线教育中的教学团队中主讲教师、助教、辅导老师、资料整理员等都普遍存在，都将由人工智能替代，而教师则需要利用学习诊断与分析工具，及学习者个别特征，分析其中有价值的信息，再开展有针对性地教学，这对教师

---

① Mou Y, Xu K., The media inequality: Comparing the initial human – human and human – AI social interactions, *Computers in Human Behavior*, No. 72, 2017, pp. 432 – 440.

② 苏令银：《论人工智能时代的师生关系》，《开放教育研究》，2018年第2期。

③ 余胜泉：《人工智能教师的未来角色》，《开放教育研究》，2018年第1期。

④ 赵勇：《未来，我们如何做教师》，《中国德育》，2017年第11期。

⑤ Huang M, Rust R T., Artificial Intelligence in Service, *Journal of Service Research*, No. 2, 2018, pp. 155 – 172.

提出了更高的职业技能要求。

其次,呈现典型生命特质的教师多元化角色,有助于提升教师的高端品质。教师角色分化精细,并转向特定功能的生命教育实践的感悟者,需要教师具有较高的职业素养,首先要具备教学研究素养。随着机器智能的发展,教育研究者需要不断地以"生命"和"机器"为对象开展研究,保证人之所以为人的核心品质。教学设计者与资源开发者的角色,必然是承接教学研究者的工作,将研究成果转化为教学方案和资源;并依托教学者角色,以生命教育实践的形式参与到生命教育的活动之中。

再次,专业实践领域的教师跨界供给来源多样化,有助于提升教师整体质量。由于人工智能介入,教师存在的唯一理由必然是转向复杂性和综合性等高阶能力的发挥,或者由掌握专长及特殊实践领域的专业人群来承担,如某个领域的科学家、工程师、科技馆与博物馆馆员、为中小学提供 AP(Advanced Placement)课程的高校教师、校外辅导机构名师,以及"身怀绝技"的独立教师个体户等,为在校学习者提供个性化、情境化、综合化的课程,或引入其相关在线课程等开展教学。在人工智能时代下的跨界融合及开放办学理念下,这部分兼职专家会为传统课程注入教学活力,教师职业及教学团队构成都将发生明显变化。

最后,"互联网思维"和"后喻文化"会深刻影响学习者对高品质教学的需求。智能教育时代,学习者从"数字土著居民"进化成为特征更加明显的"App 一代",教育将会进入全虚拟时空,民主、平等、共享、去中心化等"互联网思维"和"后喻文化"会渗透进 App 一代的骨髓,决定了他们对优质教育的需求。

教师将变成一种具有生命价值的高端职业,不仅仅表现为要掌握复杂的信息技术等职业技能、使用各种学习分析工具诊断学习等,而且还要能够培养高阶思维、丰富情感和综合结构化认知等生命特点的"个体智能",并能理解生命教育特征。未来的教师资格证取得,学科知识与传统教学技能不再是重要的门槛;衡量教师的主要标准是教师对网络文化的理解能力、自身生命特质的彰显能力、自身生命状态的活跃程度、对学生生命机能的挖掘能力、生命教育感悟与实践能力,这些才是人工智能时代教师之所以为"人师",凸显生命价值的核心能力。

(三)教师工作目的:更加聚焦于追求人机协同的智慧教育,达成生命智慧

伴随智能助教的逐渐应用,人机结合的教师职业将是我们迎接智能时代最普遍的形式。[①]《教育信息化2.0行动计划》中提出:以智能技术为手段、以融合创新为目标、以智慧教育为先导理念。"智慧"的背后,除了需要先进的教育教学理念,更是离不开人工智能技术的支撑,[②]教师团队是人工智能和人类智能协同完成的智慧性工作,体现在以下几个方面:

第一,在智慧教学环境方面的协同。人类智能和机器智能之间协同,离不开二者之间有效的接口,可通过多种方式开发和丰富人机协作的"智慧接口",《新一代人工智能发展规划》提出,包括:一是,开发基于大数据的在线教育平台。二是,开发智能助教,建立智能、快速、全面的教育分析系统。三是,建立以学习者为中心的智慧教育环境。随着人工智能研究的发展,网络虚拟空间的人机交互朝着人性化和个性化的方向迈进,极大地改善了学习者的学习环境。[③] 但目前已经建设的智慧校园,主要还是停留在统计和自动化层面上,智慧性和智能性都不足,尤其是在促进智慧的生成上,智能教育助理也亟待开发。

第二,在智慧教学手段方面的协同。除了被用于佐治亚理工学院Watson智能机器人助教外,还有多种"数字员工",如奔驰公司销售代表Sarah,

---

① 杜占元:《人工智能与未来教育变革》,首届"教育智库与教育治理50人圆桌论坛",2017年。
② 马玉慧、柏茂林、周政:《智慧教育时代我国人工智能教育应用的发展路径探究——美国〈规划未来,迎接人工智能时代〉报告解读及启示》,《电化教育研究》,2017年第3期。
③ Song Y,Qiao Q,Ge R,Construction of the Classroom Teaching Capability System of English Teachers Based on an Artificial Intelligence Environment,*Agro Food Industry Hi – tech*,No. 1,2017,pp. 511 – 515.

Autodesk 软件公司客服 Ava,苏格兰皇家银行的数字银行家 Cora,她们已不再是简单的聊天机器,而是有着灵敏的"情感反应"的虚拟"数字员工",能与人类交流,也可辅助人类决策,和人类员工将无缝对接。① 未来教师规模会适当地减少,智慧教学手段成为主要方式。"人机双师"的协同将成为未来教师工作的新形态。② 人工智能可以实现学习路径优化、自适应考试、自动任务建模等,并在测评领域实现过程的全自动化。③ 著名的"乔布斯之问"有望得到解决:未来教师工作模式就如同当前的医生和护理师,教师借助各种人工智能和大数据技术等先进的仪器设备进行"体检"或"诊断病情";确定"病症";分析"病因";开出个性化学习的"治疗方案";并进行"护理"。研究结果表明,人工智能能够帮助英语教师提升教学能力,④并越来越多地通过执行各种任务重塑服务,构成创新的一个主要来源,同时也正威胁着人类的工作。⑤

第三,在智慧教学生成方面的协同。人机协同的教育不仅仅、也不应该停留在"诊断病情"层面上,而更应该放在"激发生命活力"层面上。对于教育来说,就是放在引导和启发学生形成创新观点和教学个性化层面上。"教育"的英文单词来源于拉丁文,其意义不是"赋予",而是"激活""点燃"。在智能教育时代,教学应该是智慧的生成,对学习者进行精准"画像",深入进行学习者特征分析,把握学习者的知识基础、认知特点、多元智能倾向、学习风格和学习态度等问题,推测出学习者的意图、兴趣或爱好,并将会按最佳方式提供学习方案,为人类教师主导方案设计和个性化项目学习提供参考和选择。尤其是线下课堂教学,生成性教学要求从生命的高度、用动态生成

---

① 互联网思想:《月付薪水的数字员工机器人已到岗,这是你离失业最近的一次》,微信,https://mp.weixin.qq.com/s/k0KqZMfP4anMMaTybLa7XA。

② 祝智庭、彭红超、雷云鹤:《智能教育:智慧教育的实践路径》,《开放教育研究》,2018 第 4 期。

③ 余胜泉:《人工智能教师的未来角色》,《开放教育研究》,2018 年第 1 期。

④ Tang W,Liang X,Research on the Construction of Classroom Teaching Ability System OF English Teacher based on Artificial Intelligence,*Agro Food Industry Hi – tech*,No. 1,2017,pp. 1064 – 1067.

⑤ Huang M,Rust R T.,Artificial Intelligence in Service,*Journal of Service Research*,No. 2,2018,pp. 155 – 172.

的观点看待教与学,为学习者提供基于学习能力水平的个性化学习时空、学习需要、学习方式、学习资源和学习指导,找到学生的"痛点"和"启发"的时机,"不愤不启、不悱不发",从而为学生的思维发展提供固着点和"导火索"。机器短期内还很难替代人类提出深层次的,尤其是由好奇心和兴趣驱动的问题。① 作为教师应该充分发挥人类智能的作用,唤起学习者的感情参与,引导他们联想、想象和符号思维,合理有效地引导学生思维上的跨越,诱导学习行为和知识经验的生成,实现教学参与者之间的思想观念与情感体验的充分接触与碰撞,形成各种异质要素之间的互动、对话和交融,开启创新思维,产生创新火花,形成生成性资源,促进智慧教学生成。

第四,在智慧教学内容方面的协同。以人机协同智能层级结构体构建的智能教育,一方面,应该注重培养学习者和机器合作解决问题的方法与责任。一是培养一定的"计算思维",教会学习者理解人工智能的逻辑过程,掌握机器学习的原理和机制;二是注入适度的"数字血液":让学习者了解不同应用情境(或专业领域)中的深度学习等人工智能算法,② 包括自适应机器人技术、机器学习系统、自然语言处理技术、情绪识别、预测性分析和增强智能等,③ 理解解决生产生活中各种问题的方法原理。另一方面,主要是培养以创新为特征的多元智能,注重培养学习者左右脑学习适当地互补,但不是强调齐头并进。人工智能与多元智能的空间结构之间有着一定的对应关系,④ 已被广泛应用到各种右脑型教学之中,包括机器人能够动作捕捉、素描速写、钢琴弹奏评价,为运动员提供最佳教学方案。⑤

第五,在智慧教学目的方面的协同。人机协同教育是"1 + 1 > 2",甚至

① 杜占元:《人工智能与未来教育变革》,首届"教育智库与教育治理50人圆桌论坛",2017年。
② 苏令银:《论人工智能时代的师生关系》,《开放教育研究》,2018年第2期。
③ 互联网思想:《月付薪水的数字员工机器人已到岗,这是你离失业最近的一次》,微信,https://mp.weixin.qq.com/s/k0KqZMfP4anMMaTybLa7XA。
④ Hao Z, Cao C., Research on the Time Sequence Arrangement of Table Tennis Balls Based on Artificial Intelligence, *Agro Food Industry Hi – tech*, 28 (3), 2017, pp. 139 – 142.
⑤ 陈维维:《多元智能视域中的人工智能技术发展及教育应用》,《电化教育研究》,2018年第7期。

是"人类智能机器智能"或"人类智能机器智能",促进以"计算思维"为基础的"'人工智能＋'人"的协同智能层级结构培养,真正实现人机结合、跨学科整合、左右脑多元智能结合,既实现了人工智能支持教学,又实现了个体个性化智能培养,促进了人类智慧和创新不断发展,推动人机共生的智慧社会建设。

(四)教师工作内容:更加聚焦于探寻对人的生命整体意义,实现生命关照

"如果说人工智能让我们的机器越来越像人的话,在我看来,我们今天的教育却正在把人变得越来越像机器"①。智能教育时代,应该挖掘教育生命意义,不要被技术遮蔽生命的兴趣、价值和意义。②

首先,生命整体性包括个体智能中"逻辑思维"的生命特征。人类和人工智能在培养左右脑学习者方面也有一定的分工和擅长之处。以"语言"与"数理逻辑"为主要智能形态的左脑型学习,是可量化、可数字化的,人工智能可以对其进行无缝记录,提供强有力的分析与诊断,并基于此判断学习者的认知特点和兴趣特长。

其次,生命整体性包括个体智能中"丰富情感"的生命特征。教育的目的是促进思维能力和综合素养培养。生命的整体性是个人情感、价值观、人格等的综合表现,教育中情感培养主要包括:情感识别、情感表达和情感理解。情感形成的本质是"非逻辑推理可感形式"③。由于人工智能机器没有生物机体的生命特征,也难以短时间内模拟出连人类自己到目前为止都尚不清楚的人的大脑的个体符号及其加工系统;对于这种以无意识的"非推理逻辑形式"为主要特征的情感表达和理解,显然人工智能参与性比较低。而

---

① 项贤明:《人工智能与未来教育的任务》,《华东师范大学学报(教育科学版)》,2017 年第5 期。

② 刘慧:《生命教育内涵解析》,《课程·教材·教法》,2013 年第 9 期。

③ 朱永海:《基于知识分类的视觉表征研究》,南京师范大学博士研究生学位论文,2013 年。

情感的另外一个特征就是"可感形式",可以借助人工智能较为有效地识别,包括人脸识别、声纹识别和眼球识别,为教学搜集较有价值的信息,也可以较为有效地识别人的情感特点,直接调整反馈到教学之中,辅助教师进行情感交流,优化情感价值观教育。在人机协同智能机构中,人类可以主要负责情感理解,识别与表达交给机器来做,①为培养"完整的人"的教育提供所必要的基础。

再次,生命整体性包括个体智能中"创新思维"的生命特征。创新思维很大程度上体现在方法论的创新上,而机器学习的方法、规则目前都是人为规定好的,很难超越自我、实现自我创新。② 右脑型学习者,教学内容不易被机器和人工智能所量化处理,需要教师更多地进行个别化指导与评价,体现在多元智能中的空间、身体运动、音乐、人际、内省、自然探索等方面,这些方面恰好都是个体智能中的核心智能——创新能力所关注的思维特质,可以依据生物特征识别技术,为学习者呈现整体样貌,帮助学习者实现联想、直觉、灵感、顿悟等,从而为学习者创新思维的培养奠定基础。

最后,生命整体性包括人机协同智能层级结构构建,人要保持独立性和完整性。《纽约客》有一个画报:一群机器人匆忙地行走在大街上,只有一个人坐在地上进行乞讨。寓意当下教育培养的、生活在未来的学习者一定不能和机器"抢饭碗",当下人类在体力和认知智能都已经或者很快被淹没在人工智能的洪流中,沦落为向机器人行乞的"乞丐"和"机器附属物"。人要恰当地利用人工智能的人性化和个性化接口,保持适当的独立性。人机协同去中心化的时代,连接才是王道。在教学中,培养孩子了解自我、认清自我的能力,找准符合自己生命特点的兴趣和特长,明确自己的发展方向,希望在人生中实现目标。根据社会发展及人的生命内在的自由与活力,不断地调整自身的行为,提高处理问题的能力,努力成为专业人才,成为一个不

---

① 祝智庭、彭红超、雷云鹤:《智能教育:智慧教育的实践路径》,《开放教育研究》,2018 年第 4 期。

② 杜占元:《人工智能与未来教育变革》,首届"教育智库与教育治理 50 人圆桌论坛",2017 年。

容易被控制和支配的人。

（五）教师工作方式：更加聚焦于师生共同感悟的生命实践，践行生命教育

个体生命是目的性与工具性的并存，[1]智能教育同样既把人工智能作为一种工具，也要将提升个体智能作为一种目的。

首先，智能教育把"生命"作为"教育目的"和"教育内容"。库克曾提出：人们真正担心的，不是人工智能发展会使机器像人一样思考和做事，而是随着人工智能的发展，人会变得像机器一样思考和做事[2]。智能教育必然是一种生命教育，可以从两个方面来看：一是智能教育的重要使命之一必然是追问生命的意义与价值。如果你知道自己想要什么，人工智能技术能帮助你达成目标；但如果教育培养出来的"人"，都不知道自己想要什么，人工智能就很容易为人类塑造目标、控制人类的生活。[3] 智能教育中最为宝贵的就是生命，给学习者以生命的力量、情感的体验、生活的感悟和精神的慰藉，体现生命活力，把"人"培养成"人"。否则，人无生命，谈何以智能，又何以"人工智能"。二是，智能教育要坚持情感教育、生存教育、挫折教育、感恩教育、责任教育、死亡教育及终身教育等内容和取向。[4] 如未来智能教育在"死亡教育"中，必须要让学习者能够正视死亡，引导人类思考"要不要活那么久"的人类责任问题。

其次，智能教育把生命教育看作是一种"教育方法"和"教育形式"。教育作为一种人类的生存方式，是属于"生活世界"的，[5]智能教育时代下的生命教育，要充分适当地利用人工智能技术为体验和感悟生命提供生命环境

---

① 刘慧：《生命教育内涵解析》，《课程·教材·教法》，2013 年第 9 期。
② 苏令银：《论人工智能时代的师生关系》，《开放教育研究》，2018 年第 2 期。
③ 中国教育报：《30 年后，你家孩子凭什么拼过人工智能？就凭这 4 点》，搜狐，http://www.sohu.com/a/242369106_389102。
④ 陈盛：《关注生命教育提升生命价值》，《现代教育科学》，2008 年第 6 期。
⑤ 杨桂青：《教育的功能不仅在于文化复制》，《中国教育报》，2010 的 9 月 26 日。

支撑和"智慧教育环境",教育要以人的生命为基点,回到群体的生命环境之中,转变方式,以人的主体性为基本前提,以生命感悟为主线,充分地认识学习者独一无二的特点,解放学生个性;关注个体生命的经历、经验、感受、体验与感悟,开发生命潜能,以生命教育生命。① 借助智能技术拓宽学习者在校学习期间的生存空间,跳出"特殊认知论"的框架,回归到更加丰富、活泼、开放的生活化的形式之中,在师生之间感悟生活、体悟情感和实践生命。通过这些开放性的生命活动,重在培养学习者整体结构化思维,形成非结构化思维与能力。智能教育时代下的未来教师,必然是在人工智能支持下的最为关注生命教育的一代教师,欣赏生命、激扬生命、展示生命、丰富生命、完善生命、美化生命、享受生命等是未来师生的主要教与学实践形式。②

四、小结

我们正在迎来生物与机器联姻的时代,最终将进化成为由人的生命主导的"'机器智能+'人"的人机协同的智能结构。智能教育就是要夯实人机协同的基础——计算思维的培养;充分利用人工智能中的计算智能、感知智能和认知智能等机器智能,不断增强作为主体价值的人类智能中的情感智能、认知智能、志趣智能和创新智能,机器智能的强化也是人机协同智能层级结构的必要组成部分,也应该不断获得增强(计算机科学工作者等重点考虑的事情),人类在某种程度上也要与机器之间互相满足。③ 在智能教育时代,从我国所处的时代特征来看,我们亟待转变教师角色,重塑人才培养目标,培养具有高阶思维能力、丰富情感、个性鲜明、创新能力强的未来一代人才,否则,当西方国家装备大量的机器人作为制造业"工人"时,制造业将重回西方本土,我国不仅在全球产业链的末端地位不保,甚至会被从全球产业

---

① ②　刘慧:《生命教育内涵解析》,《课程·教材·教法》,2013 年第 9 期。
③　Degani A,Goldman C V,Deutsch O ,et al,On human - machine relations,*Cognition Technology & Work*,No. 2 - 3,2017,pp. 211 -231.

链中清除出去,无法参与全球化制造。在智能教育时代,教育的使命从培养适应社会需要的人才,变成引领社会发展的人才;教师的使命要引领机器认知唤醒,引领人机协同智能进化,而且引领的速度一定要跑过机器智能发展的速度,最重要的是教师也得一次又一次地重塑自己;否则,我们都会被淹没在人工智能的洪流中,沦落为向机器人行乞的"乞丐"或"机器附属物",人类智能将失去作为主体的价值,一切归零。

Hierarchical Intellectual Structures in Human – machine Collaboration and New Perspectives of Teachers' Occupations in the age of Intelligence Education

Yonghai Zhu   Hui Liu   Yunwen Li   Li Wang

Department of Primary Educational, Capital Normal University

Abstract:Recent years have witnessed the phenomenon that Artificial Intelligence has becoming the new focus of international competition and major national strategy. Through literature analysis and study on national planning documents, we concluded that intelligence education has two meanings:one can be interpreted as utilizing AI technology to aid education,and the other refers to a kind of education that cultivating learners' individual intelligence. The intelligence in the age of artificial intelligence (AI) can finally evolve into Hierarchical Intelligent Structures in Human – machine Collaboration (HISHMC) with" ' Machine Intelligence + 'Human"led by human,which refers to the foundation of human – machine collaboration:computational thinking;the support of collaboration:computational intelligence, cognitive intelligence and sensing intelligence; the interface of collaboration: intelligent environment (intelligent systems, intelligent platforms, and intelligent media); the subjects of collaboration: emotional intelligence, cognitive intelligence, aspirational intelligence, creative intelligence. In the age of intelligence education, teachers' working skills will focus on the occupational ability of highlighting life quality; the working characteristics of the teacher will be expressed to provide the value of life in high service quality; their work content will emphasize on exploring the whole meaning of life, in order to achieve whole view of human life; the way of working will be that both teachers and students perceive life practice and carry it out.

Keyword: Intelligence Education; Individual Intelligence; Hierarchical Intelligent Structures in Human – machine collaboration; Smart Education; Life Education

The Future Development Directions for Elementary Teacher Education

Sun Geun Baek

Chair & Professor, Department of Education,

Seoul National University

Abstract: Education is one of the most important human activities to prepare for the future. Education is also very important for the development of the individual as well as local and global communities. In this context, UNESCO (2015) has emphasized ensuring inclusive and equitable quality education and promote life – long learning opportunities for all for the development of individuals and communities. However, the quality of education cannot exceed the quality of the teacher. On these premises, this article discussed specifically the direction of future development for elementary teacher education.

To do this, the characteristics of the future society so – called the Fourth Industrial Revolution Society were shortly reviewed, and the vision of elementary teacher education for the future was suggested as 'Fostering World – class Elementary Education and Research Professionals'. The four missions of elementary teacher education for the future were also suggested as 1) Cultivating a good person who strives to manage himself and develop himself continuously; 2) Fostering a competent instructor who can understand students well and provide them appropriate teaching – learning activities; 3) Training an expert who creatively researching and developing for education; and 4) Upbringing an active volunteer who contributes to the community with global citizenship.

In addition, the images of a desirable teacher were suggested as 1) a Moral and Educated Person, 2) a Competent Instructor and Learning Facilitator, 3) a Creative Research and Development Specialist, and 4) a Voluntary Contributor. Future qualified elementary teachers should have eight core competencies (Self – Management Competency (SM), Aesthetic Emotion Competency (AE), Theoretical Teaching Competency (TT), Practical Teaching Competency (PT), Creative Thinking Competency (CT), Research and Development Competency (RD), Local Community Competency (LC), Global Community Competency (GC)) and their sub – domains were also suggested.

Finally, there were some policy suggestions for implementing these developmental ideas for the future elementary teacher education.

Keywords: development direction, education, elementary teacher education, core competency

1. INTRODUCTION

Education is one of the most important human activities to prepare for the future. Education is also very important for the development of the individual as well as local and global communities. In this context, UNESCO (2015) has emphasized ensuring inclusive and equitable quality education and promote life – long learning opportunities for all for the development of individuals and communities.

However, it is very difficult to maintain and develop high – quality education for all students. One of the reasons is that the quality of education cannot exceed the quality of the teacher. That is why it is very important to cultivate good teachers to ensure a good education for all students and to continually develop.

On these premises, this article discussed specifically the direction of future development for elementary teacher education. To do this, the characteristics of the future society so – called the Fourth Industrial Revolution Society were shortly reviewed, and the vision and missions of elementary teacher education for the future were discussed. Besides, the images of a desirable teacher for the future were suggested. Finally, there were some policy suggestions for implementing these developmental ideas for the future elementary teacher education.

2. THE FOURTH INDUSTRIAL REVOLUTION SOCIETY

The new era that is often called the Fourth Industrial Revolution Society. The characteristics of the Fourth Industrial Revolution Society were discussed by so many professionals. For example, Schwab (2016) described that the fourth industrial revolution is fundamentally changing the way we live, work, and relate to one another. He wrote about industrial revolutions as follows:

The first industrial revolution spanned from about 1760 to around 1840. Triggered by the construction of railroads and the invention of the steam engine, it ushered in mechanical production. The second industrial revolution, which started in the late 19th century and into the early 20th century, made mass production possible, fostered by the advent of electricity and the assembly line. The third industrial revolution began in the 1960s. It is usually called the computer or digital revolution because it was catalysed by the development of semiconductors, mainframe computing (1960s), personal computing (1970s and 80s) and the internet (1990s). Mindful of the various definitions and ac-

ademic arguments used to describe the first three industrial revolutions, I believe that today we are at the beginning of a fourth industrial revolution. It began at the turn of this century and builds on the digital revolution. It is characterized by a much more ubiquitous and mobile internet, by smaller and more powerful sensors that have become cheaper, and by artificial intelligence and machine learning. Digital technologies that have computer hardware, software and networks at their core are not new, but in a break with the third industrial revolution, they are becoming more sophisticated and integrated and are, as a result, transforming societies and the global economy (Schwab, 2016, pp. 11 - 12).

Besides, Genovese (2017) mentioned a key goal of digital transformation in the Fourth Industrial Revolution Society is to provide a ROADS experience — Real - time, On - demand, All - online, DIY, and Social — for customers, partners, and employees. He also mentioned the Fourth Industrial Revolution is characterized by a confluence, convergence, and fusion of technologies that is blurring the lines between the physical, digital, and biological spheres (See Figure 1).

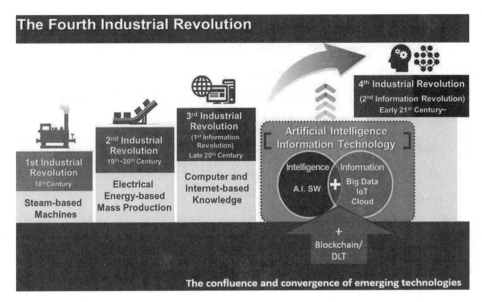

（Figure 1）The Fourth Industrial Revolution（Source：Genovese，2017）

In the era of the Fourth Industrial Revolution, we must prepare for various things. In particular, educators who must prepare for the future society must reform the goals, contents, methods, and evaluation of education. For example, Schwab（2016）suggested nurturing and applying four different types of intelligence in the new era：

> *The fourth industrial revolution may be driving disruption, but the challenges it presents are of our own making. It is thus in our power to address them and enact the changes and policies needed to adapt（and flourish）in our emerging new environment. We can only meaningfully address these challenges if we mobilize the collective wisdom of our minds, hearts and souls. To do so, I believe we must adapt, shape and harness the potential of disruption by nurturing and applying four different types of intelligence：*
>
> *—contextual（the mind）：how we understand and apply our knowledge*

　　—emotional (the heart): how we process and integrate our thoughts and feelings and relate to ourselves and to one another

　　—inspired (the soul): how we use a sense of individual and shared purpose, trust, and other virtues to effect change and act towards the common good

　　—physical (the body): how we cultivate and maintain our personal health and well - being and that of those around us to be in a position to apply the energy required for both individual and systems transformation (Schwab, 2016, p. 99)

　　Besides, OECD (2018, 2019) suggested three core foundations as particularly important to prepare students for rapid economic, environmental and social changes, for jobs that have not yet been created, for technologies that have not yet been invented, and to solve social problems that have not yet been anticipated:

　　—cognitive foundations, which include literacy and numeracy, upon which digital literacy and data literacy can be built

　　—health foundations, including physical and mental health, and well - being

　　—social and emotional foundations, including moral and ethics

　　These core foundations are the building blocks upon which context - specific competencies for 2030, such as financial literacy, global competency or media literacy, can be developed. They also form the basis of transformative competencies, which can be transferred across a wide range of contexts.

　　In addition, the World Economic Forum (2016) mentioned some jobs will disappear by 2020, others will grow and jobs that don't even exist today will become commonplace. It also mentioned creativity will become one of the top three skills workers will need in 2020（See Figure 2）

Top 10 skills

in 2020

1.　Complex Problem Solving
2.　Critical Thinking
3.　Creativity
4.　People Management
5.　Coordinating with Others
6.　Emotional Intelligence
7.　Judgment and Decision Making
8.　Service Orientation
9.　Negotiation
10.　Cognitive Flexibility

in 2015

1.　Complex Problem Solving
2.　Coordinating with Others
3.　People Management
4.　Critical Thinking
5.　Negotiation
6.　Quality Control
7.　Service Orientation
8.　Judgment and Decision Making
9.　Active Listening
10.　Creativity

（Figure 2）Top 10 Skills（Source：World Economic Forum,2016）

Educational reform is essential to promote these new knowledge, skills, and competencies needed to make a successful life in the new era. For this, the reform of teacher education must be preceded, because the quality of education cannot exceed the quality of the teachers.

3. NEW DIRECTIONS FOR ELEMENTARY TEACHER EDUCATION

The higher educational institutes provide many services and opportunities to students, staffs, and communities. The three major functions of the college and university are often referred to as education, research, and community services.

For example, in connection with those three major functions, Seoul National University（2019）pursues three core values：Learning, Creating, and Sharing. Firstly, SNU honors the ideals of liberal education, aiming to prepare students to be lifelong learners and contributors to global intellectual life. Secondly, SNU strives to create a vibrant intellectual community where students and scholars promote path – breaking endeavors in all fields of knowledge. Thirdly, SNU is committed to sharing its values and knowledge to promote peaceful co – existence with others on the world stage.

College of Education, Seoul National University (2019) also pursues three similar missions: 1) To train students to become experts in the field of education for the 21st century; 2) To become a world leader in the research of education as a center of East – Asian countries, and 3) To aim towards implementing education that is able to direct both local and international communities. COE – SNU also emphasizes that a teacher have to serve as a role model by combining profound knowledge with noble conduct and strong moral integrity.

From now on, considering the major functions of higher education institutions and the changes of the times, I would like to talk about specifically the new directions of elementary school teacher education, which is the main topic of this keynote speech. A summary of the new direction of elementary teacher education to prepare for the Fourth Industrial Revolution Society mentioned above is presented in (Figure 3). It was constructed based on comprehensive reviews of previous studies such as Baek, et al. (2017, 2019), Ministry of Education (2015), etc.

New Directions for Elementary Teacher Education

Vision	Fostering World-class Elementary Education and Research Professionals.

Mission	Cultivating a good person who strives to manage himself and develop himself continuously.
	Fostering a competent instructor who can understand students well and provide them appropriate teaching-learning activities.
	Training an expert who creatively researching and developing for education.
	Upbringing an active volunteer who contributes to the community with global citizenship.

Exemplary Models	Moral and Educated Person
	Competent Instructor and Learning Facilitator
	Creative Research and Development Specialist
	Voluntary Contributor

Eight Core Competencies	Self-Management Competency (SM) Aesthetic Emotion Competency (AE) Theoretical Teaching Competency (TT) Practical Teaching Competency (PT) Creative Thinking Competency (CT) Research and Development Competency (RD) Local Community Competency (LC) Global Community Competency (GC))

（Figure 3）New Directions for Elementary Teacher Education（Summary）

I want to suggest that the vision of elementary teacher education for the future is 'Fostering World – class Elementary Education and Research Professionals'. In connection with the vision, I also suggest the four missions of elementary teacher education for the future which are 1）Cultivating a good person who strives to manage himself and develop himself continuously;2) Fostering a competent instructor who can understand students well and provide them appropriate teaching – learning activities;3) Training an expert who creatively researching and developing for education;and 4) Upbringing an active volunteer who contributes to the community with global citizenship.

Besides the elementary teacher education for the future has to pursue the images of a desirable teacher which are 1) a Moral and Educated Person,2) a Competent Instructor and Learning Facilitator,3) a Creative Research and Development Specialist,and 4) a Voluntary Contributor. In the past,an excellent teacher should have a good character with the ability to teach with high qualities. In the new era,however,they are also required to have not only the ability to research and develop in education but also to be an active volunteer who contributes to the development of the community.

Therefore future qualified elementary teachers should have eight core competencies:1) Self – Management Competency (SM),2) Aesthetic Emotion Competency (AE),3) Theoretical Teaching Competency (TT),4) Practical Teaching Competency (PT),5) Creative Thinking Competency (CT),6) Research and Development Competency (RD),7) Local Community Competency (LC),8) Global Community Competency (GC).

Within each core competency,it consists of various sub – elements (Baek,et al.,2017;Baek,et al.,2019;Baek & Kim,2016;Ministry of Education,2015,2017;OECD,2005) (see 〈Table 1〉). For example,the´Self – Management Competency´consists of´Self – Reflection´,´Self – Development´,and´Self – Control´.

〈Table 1〉Sub – elements of Eight Core Competencies

Core Competency	Sub – elements
Self – Management Competency（SM）	– Self – Reflection – Self – Development – Self – Control
Aesthetic Emotion Competency（AE）	– Appreciation and Experiences – Expression and Creativity – High – Quality Life and Well – Being
Theoretical Teaching Competency（TT）	– Learning Theory – Understanding of the Learner – Contents Knowledge
Practical Teaching Competency（PT）	– Teaching Methodology – Coaching and Facilitation – Monitoring and Feedback
Creative Thinking Competency（CT）	– Novelty – Relevance and Reasonability – Usefulness
Research and Development Competency（RD）	– Critical Thinking – Research Methodology – Resolution and Evaluation
Local Community Competency（LC）	– Mutual Respect – Open – Mindedness – Participation and Belonging
Global Community Competency（GC）	– Multicultural Sensitivity – Inclusiveness – Global Citizenship

4. POLICY SUGGESTIONS

We should all keep in mind that a bright and desirable future is not just a-bout coming, but about achieving with systematic preparation and sincere efforts. There are some policy suggestions for implementing these developmental ideas for the future elementary teacher education that I mentioned earlier.

Firstly, each university or college needs to elaborate on its vision and mission by reflecting its founding philosophy and the ideas it pursues. The conditions or circumstances given to each institute may differ, so it will need to plan accordingly and concretely.

Secondly, to successfully push ahead with future directions for new changes, the open dialogues, communications, and public relations for reaching a general consensus should be strengthened.

Thirdly, human and material resources support should be expanded so that all members of the institute can participate actively. New changes or innovations always require extra efforts and expenses.

Lastly, each university or college must develop educational programs that are appropriate for a new era and to develop measurement tools that can monitor such educational programs and evaluate their performances. To manage the quality of each university or college education, improve its quality, and ensure its quality, it is necessary to establish an IR (Institutional Research) center for each institute to collect systematically educational data and monitoring the overall education system. IR center will become increasingly important for each university or college to the formulation of strategies for its survival and development by on–campus data utilization in the new era (Botha & Muller, 2016; Otomo, et al., 2015).

References:

1. Baek, S., et al. The development and the validation of six core competencies measurement scale for high school students in Korea. *Journal of Educational Evaluation*, 30(3), 2017, pp. 363 – 395.

2. Baek, S., et al. A study on the improvement of teacher education curriculum for future generations, *Seoul: Seoul National University*, 2019.

3. Baek, S., & Kim, H. Internationalizing higher education in Korea: Government policies In Y. C. Oh, G. W. Shin, R. J. Moon (Eds.), Internationalizing higher education in Korea: Challenges and opportunities in comparative perspective (pp. 29 – 50). *APARC*, Stanford University, CA, USA, 2016.

4. Botha, J., & Muller, N. (Eds.), Institutional research in South African higher education: Intersecting contexts and practices, *Stellenbosch: Sun press*, 2016.

5. College of Education, Seoul National University, *About COE*, *accessed September 4, 2019*, http://edu. snu. ac. kr/en/vision.

6. Genovese, W. Accelerating success in the 4th industrial revolution," *Huawei*, Nov. 30, 2017, accessed August 9, 2019, https://www. huawei. com/en/about – huawei/publications/winwin – magazine/29/accelerating – success – in – the – 4th – industrial – revolution.

7. Ministry of Education, The announcement and the confirmation of the general guidelines for the 2015 Revised National Curriculum (press release), *Sejong: Ministry of Education*, 2015.

8. Ministry of Education, General guidelines for the 2015 Revised National Curriculum: High school, *Sejong: Ministry of Education*, 2017.

9. OECD, The definition and selection of key competencies, *Paris: OECD*, 2005.

10. OECD, The future of education and skills: Education 2030, *Paris: OECD*, 2018.

11. OECD, OECD future education and skills 2030 conceptual learning framework, *Paris: OECD*, 2019.

12. Otomo, A., Iwayama, Y, & Mohri, T, On – campus data utilization: Working on institutional research in universities, *Fujitsu Scientific & Technical Journal*, 51(1), 2015 pp. 42 – 49.

13. Schwab, K., The fourth industrial revolution. Geneva：World Economic Forum,2016.

14. Seoul National University, *SNU brochures*, accessed September 4,2019, http：//en. snu. ac. kr/brochures.

15. UNESCO, Outcomes of the world education forum 2015, *Paris：UNESCO*.

16. World Economic Forum, *The 10 skills you need to thrive in the Fourth Industrial Revolution*, accessed August 9,2019, https：//www. weforum. org/agenda/2016/01/the－10－skills－you－need－to－thrive－in－the－fourth－industrial－revolution/.

小学教师教育的未来发展趋势

白淳根

韩国首尔国立大学教育学院教学系主任,教授

　　摘要：教育是人类面向未来最重要的活动之一,它对个体的发展及地区和全球的发展都至关重要。在这一背景下,联合国教科文组织(2015)强调要保证全纳、公平的素质教育,为所有人提供终身学习的机会以促进个体和整体的发展。然而教育的水平受制于教师的水平。基于这些前提,本文拟讨论小学教师教育的未来发展趋势。首先,本文简要论述了未来社会(即所谓的第四次工业革命社会)的特点,将面向未来的小学教师教育图景呈现为"培育世界级的小学教育及研究专门人才"。面向未来的小学教师教育包含四个层面：①培养可以持续地自我管理及自我发展的优秀人才；②培养能够很好地理解学生并为学生提供恰当教学活动的高水平教师；③培养可以创

造性地研究教育、发展教育的专家;④培养具有全球意识、乐于奉献的公民。其次,本文认为理想型的教师应该是一位道德高尚、学识渊博的人,一位能力的塑造者和学习的引领者,一位积极的研发专家和一位乐于奉献的园丁。未来高水平的小学教师应该具有八种核心能力:自我管理能力、审美体验能力、理论教学能力、实践教学能力、批判思维能力、研究发展能力、着眼全局的能力以及兼收并蓄的能力。最后提出一些面向未来实践这些理念的具体建议。

关键词:发展趋势;教育;小学教师教育;核心能力

新中国成立70年小学教师教育发展：回顾与展望

肖菊梅

湖州师范学院教师教育学院，副教授

摘要：新中国成立后，我国小学教师教育发展经历了整顿巩固期、曲折动乱期、恢复重建期、快速发展期、改革创新期五个阶段。小学教师教育发展在实现开放化的小学教师教育体系、建设专业化的小学教师队伍、形成多元化的教育培养模式，以及进行规范化的小学教师教育管理等方面取得一定成就。展望未来，小学教师教育发展应以"兴国必先强师"为理念，建设新时代小学教师教育体系；以服务小学教育发展为目标，推动优质小学教师教育均衡发展；改革师范生招生制度，优化课程体系，推动小学教师考核评价机制改革；依托"互联网＋"技术，促进小学教师教育信息化。

关键词：新中国成立70年；小学教师教育；教育发展

新中国成立70年来，我国小学教师教育发展经历了一段曲折之路，取得了一定成就。展望未来，小学教师教育须加快各方面发展，为国家基础教育改革与发展提供创新型人才。

一、新中国成立70年小学教师教育发展的历程

新中国成立70年来，可以将我国小学教师教育的发展历程分为五个阶

段：整顿巩固期、曲折动乱期、恢复重建期、快速发展期和改革创新期。

（一）整顿巩固期（1949—1957 年）

第一，对师范学校进行调整与改革。新中国成立初期，随着人民生活的安定和改善，国家建设事业的开展，全国初等教育有大规模的迅速发展。1951 年，教育部召开师范教育会议，决定今后三五年内应重点以短期训练的形式培养师资，今后五年要培养百万教师就依靠这种办法。1952 年颁布《师范学校暂行规程（草案）》和《关于高等师范学校的规定（草案）》，确定当前师范教育的工作方针是正规师范教育结合大量短期训练，并以短期训练为重点作为今后三五年师范教育发展的主要目标，且对初级师范学校的调整和设置做出一系列规定，促进了初级师范学校的迅速发展。1953 年，全国高等师范教育会议决定对中等师范教育进行调整，大量裁并初级师范学校，使得小学师资又出现短缺现象。1956 年，教育部颁布《师范学校规程》《师范学校教学计划》等文件，要求大力发展初级师范，通过举办速成师范和短期训练班的方式培养小学师资。同时对师范学校的性质、学制、课程设置、招生、培养目标等予以规范，加快了中等师范教育的发展。截至 1957 年，全国中等师范学校共有 592 所，其中中级师范为 492 所，在校生 244 万人，初级师范 10 所，在校生 51 万人。① 该时期我国中等师范教育由培养初级师范为主变为中级师范为主。

第二，开展小学师资培训。1952 年，教育部颁布《关于大量短期培养初等及中等教育师资的决定》，对前期小学师资培训过程中出现的脱离实际和盲目冒进现象进行改正，自 1953 年，停止招收小学师资短训班新生（除少数民族外）；对小学师资短训班的学员通过升学、保留作小学教师、动员回家等方式进行安置处理；师范学校可附设修业年限为一年的短期师资训练班；经

---

① 《"国培计划"将 5 年内培训 550 万中西部农村中小学教师》，新华网，［EB/（）IJ（2011 － 08 － 10）［2014 － 02 － 05］，http：// news. xinhuanet. com/2011 － 08/10/c_12183 9532. htm。

省、市教育厅、局批准,可设函授部。这种急需下的急用措施,使得中等师范生数量大增。据统计,1951 年上半年,中师在校生共 188167 人,1952 年初,中师在校生即达 29.5 万余人①,1954 年,全国中学教育会议规定将现有初级师范学校逐步改办为师范学校或小学教师轮训班。今后小学师资主要来源师范学校及招收初中毕业生进行训练一年的师范速成班。这一时期我国中等教育执行文教总方针,在整顿巩固中等师范教育、建立正规化的中小学教师培养和进修制度等方面,均取得了可观的成就。

其三,开展小学教师进修。1952 年,"中小学教育行政会议"召开,提倡建立教师业余学习进修学校并与函授、教育刊物结合起来。1953 年,北京、河北、江苏、浙江、安徽、福建、湖南等省(市)均举办了函授师范学校或在师范学校内附设函授部,有很多教师参加函授学习。教育部将各省市小学教师进修学校重点设置数、开支标准、老区小学教师在职学习重点补助费列入预算,使新中国中小学教师进修体系逐步形成。1953 至 1957 年,《关于中等学校及小学教师在职业余学习的几件事项的通知》《关于函授师范学校(师范学校函授部)、业余师范学校若干问题的规定(草案)》《关于举办小学教师轮训班的指示》等文件颁布,规定小学教师开展各种形式的进修,实现了小学教师进修制度化。

(二)曲折动乱期(1958—1977 年)

第一,调整与改革中等师范教育。1958 年全国教育行政会议颁发《1958学年度中等师范学校的教学计划》规定,在新形势面前,各地对原有教学计划,可以因地制宜作适当变动。师范学校的教育实习……鼓励学校大胆创造。至此,我国各级师范院校在"大跃进"的影响下进行了一系列"教育革命",对原教学计划和教材进行了所谓"革命性的大变革"。这些做法使中等师范学校的教学处于无序状态,教学质量严重下降。1960 年 5 月,教育部颁

---

① 何东昌:《中华人民共和国重要教育文献》,海南出版社,1997 年。

布《关于师范教育教学改革的初步意见》《关于改革中等师范教育的初步意见（草案）》等文件指出，中等师范学校设置的课程有 22 门之多，其中教育课程竟达七八门，占教学总学时的 30% 以上；中等师范学校的课程内容根本没有反映现代科学技术的内容等。伴随这种"革命"潮流，不断加深认识师范教育的一些问题，从一个侧面推动师范教育的改革与发展，取得了一定的成绩。据统计，1959 年，我国中等师范学校发展到 1365 所，在校学生 540075 人，而"大跃进"运动之前的 1957 年，全国中等师范学校只有 592 所，在校学生 295784 人，在短短两年时间内，中等师范学校的数目增加了近两倍，学生人数几乎翻了一番。1960 年，中等师范学校增至 1964 所，在校学生 838480 人。[①] 由于不顾历史条件和生产力发展水平盲目地发展师范教育，导致了师范教育质量大幅度的下降。1961 年，全国师范教育工作会议提出中等师范教育的任务、招生、培养目标、课程等，提出师范学校办好附小，附小的教师，应该挑选优秀的师范毕业生担任。这样有利于师范学校做好实习指导工作，提高师范生的质量。[②] 1963 年，教育部颁布《全日制小学暂行工作条例（草案）》规定了小学教师的任务、教学等。经过 1961 年至 1964 年的调整，使得发展过快、规模过大的中等师范教育得以控制和压缩。据统计，至 1965 年，中等师范学校由 1960 年的 1964 所减到 394 所，学生由 838 万减到 155 万，甚至降到低于 1957 年的水平。[③]

1966 至 1976 年的十年"文革"给中等师范教育发展带来极大破坏，导致小学教育质量急剧下降。1976 年，国家制定相应的政策，采取恢复设施和应急手段等。暂时缓解了"小学毕业教小学，中学毕业教中学"的现象。至 1976 年，全国中等师范学校的数目达到了 982 所，相当于 1952 年全国中等

---

① 何东昌：《中华人民共和国重要教育文献》，海南出版社，1997 年，第 166 页。

② 教育部计划财务司编：《中国教育成就（1994—1983）》，人民教育出版社，1985 年，第 272～281 页。

③ 张乐天主编：《教育政策法规的理论与实践》，华东师范大学出版社，2002 年，第 190 页。

师范学校的数目,在校学生达到了 304356 人,与 1957 年数目相当。①

其二,采取多种形式开展小学师资培训。新中国成立后,教师的学历不合格,据 1960 年对几个省市的统计,未达中师毕业的小学教师占 80% 以上(上述情况系指教师的学历统计,实际水平可能更低)。在业务能力上能够较好地完成现任教学任务的仅占 20%,一般能胜任的占 60%,不能胜任的占 20%。1960 年,"师范教育改革座谈会"规定小学教师中具有小学、初师和中师水平的,除胜任自己所教学科外,8 年内还应在几门主要学科上分别达到将来的高中、大学专科、本科毕业的水平。因采取多形式、多规格、多渠道的师资培训工作,全国小学教师进修学校学生数从 1957 年的 55.8 万人,到 1965 年增加到 109.5 万人,增加到 2 倍。毕业生数从 1957 年的 3800 人,到 1965 年增加到 91000 人,增加近 24 倍。② 1977 年《关于加强中小学在职教师培训工作的意见》颁布,确定了中小学教师培训的目标、机构、队伍、形式、规划等。

(三)恢复重建期(1978—1985 年)

其一,积极恢复和加强教育学院的建设和管理。1977 年以来,担负中小学教师培训任务的教育学院、教师进修学校虽得到恢复,但不少院校还是人、财、物缺乏,办学条件很差。这种情况不适合承担培训中小学在职教师、开设相关培训课程及开展研究等。1978 年,教育部颁布《关于恢复或建立教育学院进修学院报批手续的通知》,极大地促进了全国各地教育学院恢复与发展中小学教师培训机构的热情。1982 年《关于加强教育学院建设若干问题的暂行规定》指出,教育学院承担中小学在职教师和教育行政干部培训,是具有示范性质的高等学校及社会主义师范教育体系的组成部分。上述政策促进了教育学院数量的增长,即由 1978 年的 17 所发展到 1985 年的

---

① 张乐天主编:《教育政策法规的理论与实践》,华东师范大学出版社,2002 年,第 191 页。
② 教育部计划财务司编:《中国教育成就(1949—1983)》,人民教育出版社,1985 年,第 984 页。

216 所。①

其二,加强和发展中等师范教育。粉碎"四人帮"后的三年,师范教育重新得到恢复和发展。中等师范学校的教育质量正逐步提高,在校生人数比1965 年增长了两倍多。但从整体来看,小学师资数量不足、质量堪忧。据统计,"小学在校学生人数,1977 年比 1965 年净增约 3000 万人,按 1965 年小学生与专师实际比例 30∶1 计算,应增教师 100 万人。小学教师中中师毕业及以上的,1965 年为 47.4% ,1973 年下降到 28% 。1979 年小学教师中具有中等师范或普通高中以上学历的只占 47% "②。这样就出现了小学生毕业后教小学,中等师范、中学毕业教中学的普遍现象,小学教师队伍未能形成梯队,出现"青黄不接"的状况。1980 年颁布的《中等师范学校规程》《关于普及小学教育若干问题的决定》等文件明确规定中等师范学校的办学方针、任务、教学计划,以及普及小学教育任务、提高小学师资业务水平等。该时期中等师范教育发展在充分吸收了"文化大革命"前中等师范教育办学经验基础上,根据新的形势需要加以发展,使全国 1000 多所中等师范学校在拨乱反正之后,终于有"规"可依了。

其三,加强小学师资队伍建设。1981 至 1985 年,教育部颁发《关于中等师范学校招生工作的通知》《关于中小学教师队伍调整、整顿和加强管理的意见》《中小学教师职业道德要求(试行草案)》等文件,提出严格考核中小学教师,合格后发给教师合格证;规定中等师范学校招收初中毕业生;中小学教师要具备以身作则、为人师表的职业道德素养等;落实毕业生到师范院校任教情况,任何机关和单位不能要求合格的中小学教师担任其他工作,这在一定程度上保证了新教师的数量。

其四,培训中小学在职教师。1980 年,《关于进一步加强中小学在职教师培训工作的意见》要求组织有教学困难的教师先过好"教材教法关",再进

---

① 中国教育年鉴编辑部:《中国教育年鉴(1985—1986)》,湖南教育出版社,1988 年,第 12 页。
② 何东昌:《中华人民共和国重要教育文献》,海南出版社,1997 年,第 1648 页。

行系统的进修专业知识学习。1982 年,《小学教师进修中等师范教学计划
(试行草案)》规定,小学教师学习的主要学科与中等师范毕业程度相当且能
够胜任小学教学工作,函授和业余面授的学习年限一般为四年,离职进修学
习年限为两年。1985 年,《中共中央关于教育体制改革的决定》要求认真培
训和考核现有教师,中小学教师培训可由高校教师组织。小学在职教师进
修教学计划的制定与实施,有效地保证了小学在职教师培训目标和教学质
量的提高。

(四)持续发展期(1986—1999 年)

其一,确立了小学教师培养目标和教学内容。1987 年,《中等师范学校
培养目标(初稿)》规定,小学教师的培训须具有理想、师德、创新精神、知识
和技能、健康体魄、艺术修养等条件。1989 年,教育部颁发《三年制中等师范
学校教学方案(试行)》成为中等师范学校教学大纲和教材编写、实行必修
课、选修课、课外互动和教育实践相结合的依据,给予学校和地方办学自主
权,突出师范生,有力地推动了中等师范教育教学改革。1995 年,《全国小学
教师基本功训练现场经验交流会》指出小学教育处于启蒙教育阶段,是基础
教育中最基础的教育,对小学教师素质要求高有其特殊性,并把小学教师的
基本功训练(三字一话一画)作为继续教育的重要内容。

其二,加强小学在职教师培训,提升培训质量。1986 年,《关于加强在职
中小学教师培训工作的意见》要求进一步加强培训小学在职教师。1993 年,
《中国教育改革和发展纲要》明确规定,师范教育是培养中小学师资的工作
母机,要求加大投入办好师范教育,进一步发展培训师资工作,鼓励更多优
秀的高中毕业生报考师范院校,扩大定向师范生招生比例,建立师范毕业生
定期到中小学任教。1993 年《教师法》颁布,明确规定参加进修或培训是教
师的权利。1996 年,教育部颁布《关于师范教育改革和发展的若干意见》指
出,要重点培训合格率低的地区教师,使教师达到合格学历,保证培训的质
量。1999 年,教育部相继颁布《关于深化教育改革,全面推进素质教育的决

定》《中小学教师继续教育规定》《关于师范院校布局结构调整的几点意见》等文件,要求在 2010 年前后小学教师达到专科学历;中小学教师继续教育的形式包括非学历和学历教育;办好经济教育欠发达地区的中等师范教育,部分中师可并入高师院校,少数条件好的中师通过合并、联合、改组成师专,其余中师可改为培训机构或其他中等学校;各省、市、县各自设中小学培训机构。培训的重心由学历补偿教育转向继续教育。与恢复与整顿时期相比,该时期的中小学在职教师培训更注重培训质量的保障;明确各级各类在职教师的学历层次;在职教师培训包括学历补偿教育和继续教育。

其三,规范教师进修院校,教师教育体系逐渐走向开放。1986 年,《关于加强在职中小学教师培训工作的意见》规定了教师进修院校旨在培训中小学在职教师和农村职业中专教师,其办学特点在于其师范生、在职性和成人教育。据统计,至 1989 年,达到中师学历水平的小学教师比率从 1977 年的47.1% 上升到 71.4%。[1] 1996 年,全国第四次师范教育工作会议提出,"九五"期间要建设中小学师资队伍,即适度发展本科,按照需要发展专科。加强中等师范教育,中师学制由三年并存到向四年过渡,规定"普九"教师的学历合格率达到经济发达地区的水平,扩大小学教师具有专科学历的试验规模。会后,全国各地开始有计划、有步骤地加快小学师资队伍建设的步伐,我国中等师范教育事业又迈上了一个崭新的台阶。1998 年,《面向 21 世纪教育振兴行动计划》正式要求小学教师的学历大专化。在此精神指导下,中等师范学校开始升格和转制。在第三次全国教育工作会议精神的强力推动下,我国小学教师培养向高等教育迅速迈进。如何用"教师教育"来统整和总揽,从而建立一个既具有小学教师专业性质又具有高等教育学术水准的小学教师高等教育体系,这应成为小学教师教育研究的一个重要课题。我们应当继承百年中师的优良办学传统,吸取其在服务小学、培养小学教师方面的成功经验,将其合理地带入专科、本科小学教师的培养体系中去,进一

---

[1]　何东昌:《中华人民共和国重要教育文献》,海南出版社,1997 年,第 3060 页。

步推动小学教师教育专业化。1999 年,《关于深化教育改革,全面推进素质教育的决定》要求调整师范学校的层次和布局,师范性和非师范性高等学校均参与培训培养中小学教师,探索有条件的综合性高校创办师范学院等。这说明教师教育体系由单一封闭走向共同开放。

其四,规范中小学教师考核,实行教师资格制度。1986 年,教育部颁布《义务教育法》《中小学教师考核合格证书试行办法》等文件,要求加快培训培养师资,逐步实现小学教师达到中等师范学校毕业以上水平;推行教师资格考核制度,对合格的教师颁发教师资格证书;对不具备国家规定学历的中小学教师试行考核合格证书制度。1995 年,《教师资格条例》规定教师资格的分类、条件、考试、认定等内容,这为我国教师的资格认定提供了依据,较之教材教法考试更加严谨、规范。

(五)改革创新期(2000 年至今)

其一,构建相互衔接、开放的教师教育体系。2001 年,"教师教育"一词首先出现在《国务院关于基础教育改革与发展的决定》文件中,该文件提出要完善开放的教师教育体系,即以师范院校为主体、其他高校参与、培训培养一体化,对师范教育结构进行调整,逐步由二级师范过渡到三级师范。2002 年,中等师范教育尚未在教育部颁布的《关于加强专科以上学历小学教师培养工作的几点意见》文件中进行明确定位。"中等师范"字样也只能在《中国教育年鉴》中的师范教育统计表上出现。"中等师范教育"字样也不再出现在《中国教育事业统计年鉴》中。中等师范教育发展历史终结,被"教师教育"取代。

2004 年,《2003—2007 年教育振兴行动计划》提出,为促进教师专业发展和终身学习,须构建现代化的教师教育体系,即以有教师教育学院的高水平大学和师范大学为先导,协调发展研究生、本科、专科三个层次,加强职前教育和职后教育沟通,实现学历与非学历并举。2007 年,《国家教育事业发展"十一五"规划纲要》提倡具备条件的综合性大学参与培养培训中小学教师,逐步形成开放灵活、规范有序的教师教育体系,提高教师教育的层次和水平;严控教师准入制度,公开招聘新任教师制度。完善教师职务聘任制。制定和完善吸引优秀人才从教的政策措施,建立吸引优秀人才到农村任教的机制。随着教师教育办学层次的不断提升,1999 年到 2007 年,我国高等师范本科院校由 87 所增加到 97 所;开展教育硕士培养的院校由 29 所增加到 57 所;师范专科学校由 140 所减少到 45 所;中等师范学校由 815 所减少到 196 所。①

2012 年,教育部颁布《关于完善和推进师范生免费教育意见的通知》《国务院关于加强教师队伍建设的意见》等文件,规定部分师范院校推行免费的师范生教育,培养农村中小学骨干教师;建设农村中小学教师队伍,激励更多优秀人才去农村从教等。2014 年,教育部颁布《关于实施卓越教师培养计划的意见》规定重点探索培养小学全科教师的卓越培养模式改革,培养一批卓越小学教师,即热爱小学教育、具有广泛知识、能力广泛、胜任小学多学科教学等。2018 年,随着《关于全面深化新时代教师队伍建设改革的意见》的颁布,新中国第一个面向教师队伍建设的纲领性文件形成,凸显教师队伍建设的"极端重要性"地位。

其二,积极推进教师教育信息化建设。2001 年,《国务院关于基础教育改革与发展的决定》提出在全国乡镇以上的中小学基本普及信息技术教育。2002 年,《关于推进教师教育信息化建设的意见》提出,信息化是实现教育现代化的基础条件,加快建设教师教育的信息资源和基础设施。2018 年,教育部颁布《关于实施卓越教师培养计划 2.0 的意见》规定推进中小学教育教学改革要通过深化信息技术改革,升级实施卓越小学教师的培养计划,推动建设一流师范院校和一流师范专业,以期加快形成高水平师范人才培养体系。

其三,重点加强农村中小学师资队伍建设。2004 年,教育部颁布《国务院关于进一步加强农村教育工作的决定》规定把农村教育作为重中之重来

---

① 何东昌:《中华人民共和国重要教育文献》,海南出版社,1997 年,第 3060 页。

加快深化农村教育发展与改革。2007 年,《教育部直属师范大学师范身免费实施办法(试行)》提出重点加强建设农村小学师资队伍。2008 年,《教育部办公厅印发 2008 年中小学教师国家级培训计划的通知》提出实施国家级培训计划所面向对象主要是中西部农村中小学在职教师。2011 年,《关于做好"中小学教师国家级培训计划"实施工作的通知》则要求中小学进一步完善"国培计划"。据统计,"国培计划"实施以来共培训中小学教师 115 万人,其中农村教师占 95.6%,并计划将 5 年内培训 550 万中西部农村中小学教师。①

其四,完善教师资格制度。2000 年,《〈教师资格条例〉实施办法》规定进行各级教师资格分类。2010 年,《关于开展国家教育体制改革试点的通知》提出改革教师资格制度,即自 2011 年开始在浙江、广西等 8 省市开展教师资格考试和定期资格注册改革试点,从 2012 年开始再推动 6 省份试点,预计用三年时间在全国推行此制度。2013 年至 2014 年,教育部颁布《中小学教师资格考试暂行办法》和《中小学教师资格定期注册暂行办法》规定,中小学教师资格考试具备从事教师职业所必需的教育教学基本素质和能力的考试,参加教师资格考试合格是教师职业准入的前提条件。申请小学教师资格的人员须参加相应类别的教师资格考试;每 5 年一次注册中小学教师资格,对于不合格或逾期不注册的教师,不得从事教育教学工作。②

二、新中国成立 70 年小学教师教育发展的主要成就

新中国成立 70 年,我国小学教师教育虽经历曲折式发展,但在教师队伍建设、教师教育体系、教师培养模式以及教师管理等方面取得一定成就。

---

① 《"国培计划"将 5 年内培训 550 万中西部农村中小学教师》,新华网,http://news. xinhua-net. com/2011 −08/10/c_12183 9532. htm。

② 中国法制出版社编:《中华人民共和国教育法法律法规全书》,中国法制出版社,2017 年,第 549 页。

（一）小学教师队伍建设专业化

新中国成立后,我国小学教师队伍建设成就明显。小学教师数量呈现一种波动式的发展。据统计,1951 年上半年,中师教育在校生共 188167 人,1952 年初,中师在校生即达 29.5 万余人。① 受 1958 年至 1960 年"大跃进"运动的影响,中等师范教育学校规模和数量得以盲目扩大,在校生数量急剧增长。1959 年,我国中等师范学校在校学生 540075 人,而"大跃进"运动之前的 1957 年,全国中等师范学校只有 592 所,在校学生 295784 人,在短短的两年时间内,中等师范学校的数目增加了近两倍,学生人数几乎翻了一番。1960 年,师范学校增至 1964 所,在校学生 838480 人。由于不顾历史条件和生产力发展水平盲目地发展师范教育,结果导致了师范教育质量大幅度的下降。经过调整,师范教育得到了控制并被压缩。据统计,至 1965 年,中等师范学校学生由 838 万减到 155 万,甚至降到低于 1957 年的水平,全国中等师范教育基本上恢复到"大跃进"运动之前的水平。② 1966 年至 1971 年,全国停止招收中等师范学校学生。到 1976 年,全国中等师范学校的数目达到了 982 所,相当于 1952 年全国中等师范学校的数目,在校学生达到了304356 人,相当于 1957 年在校生数目。③ 截至 1995 年,我国有中等师范学校在校生共 8527 万人,且分布基本合理,质量稳步提高。至 2012 年,全国小学教职工 553.85 万人,专任教师 558.55 万人,学历合格率为 99.81%,生师比为 17.36∶1。④

随着小学教师数量波动,教师质量也随之发生变化。据统计,"1965 年,在小学教师中,中师毕业及以上的为 47.4%,1973 年下降到 28%,现在有不

---

① 何东昌:《中华人民共和国重要教育文献》,海南出版社,1997 年,第 166 页。
② 张乐天主编:《教育政策法规的理论与实践》,华东师范大学出版社,2002 年,第 190 页。
③ 同上,第 191 页。
④ 同上,第 192 页。

少的教师是中学程度教中学,小学程度教小学"①。1978 年,我国普通小学专任教师数是 522.55 万人;1979 年,全国小学教师具有中等师范或普通高中以上学历的只占 47%。2015 年,普通小学专任教师数为 568.51 万人。专任教师学历合格率普通小学为 99.90%。专科及其以上学历的小学专任教师占自身总数的 91.89%。② 近 70 年来,尽管我国小学教师教育的培养质量随着数量及制度等的变化呈现出"钟摆"现象,但随着国家基础教育的发展,我国小学教师教育的培养质量处于提升的态势,小学教师队伍也随之发展壮大。

(二)小学教师教育体系开放化

新中国成立初期,我国中师主要培养小学教师,培训则由县教师进修学校负责。随着基础教育的发展,这种单一封闭的教师教育体系不再适应小学教师教育的发展。1999 年,《关于师范院校布局结构调整的几点意见》提出调整改革中等师范学校,原有中师概念终将被取消。我国小学师资的培养层次也逐渐由高师专科、中师二级学校培养模式向高师本科和高师专科两级学校来培养,中师这一级办学层次已完成历史使命,不复存在。这是我国小学教师教育发展进步的里程碑。有学者认为,近年来,我国教师教育形成了三轨四级体系,即师范院校、综合院校、职业院校三轨和中专、大专、本科、研究生四级体系。在该体系中,培养我国教师的主体仍然是师范大学(师范学院)、师范专科学校和师范中专。随着小学师资培养的开放化,小学教师培训也逐渐一体化。新中国成立至 20 世纪 80 年代之前,我国小学教师培训包括各级进修院校、县地市教师进修学院。

1980 年,《关于师范教育的几个问题的请求报告的通知》指出各级教师进修院校是培训中小学教师的基地,成为师范教育体系中的重要组成部分。

---

① 何东昌:《中华人民共和国重要教育文献》,海南出版社,1997 年,第 166 页。
② 《中国教育统计年鉴 2015》,中国统计出版社,2016 年,第 1~2 页。

要求省、地(市)、县应分别设置一所教育学院(教师进修学校)分工培训中小学教师。

1986 年,《关于加强在职中小学教师培训工作的意见》规划用 5 年或更长时间去培训没有合格学历和不胜任教学的教师;组织具备合格学历和胜任教学的教师学习新的知识、教育理论和教学方法等,重点培养一批学科带头人和教育教学专家。20 世纪 90 年代,国家进一步加强了中小学教师的培训工作。1999 年,《中小学教师继续教育》规定实施"中小学教师继续教育工程"(1999—2002 年)及"中小学教师全员培训计划"(2003—2007 年);2003 年,"全国教师教育联络联盟计划"启动;2006—2008 年,"中小学骨干教师国家级远程培训"和"西部农村教师远程培训计划"颁布;2011—2012年,《关于大力加强中小学教师培训工作的意见》颁发等,上述措施推动了我国中小学教师教育培训一体化进程:省级教育学院(教师进修学院)——地市级教育学院(教师进修学院)——县级教师进修学院。

(三)小学教师教育培养模式多元化

新中国成立初期,我国小学教师由初级师范培养,招收小学毕业生,学制三年,达到初级中学文化水平。20 世纪 50 年代,停办初级师范,改为招收学制 3 年的初中毕业生,达到高级中学文化程度。20 世纪 60 年代至 70 年代末,招收初中毕业生培养小学教师的办学模式停办。自 20 世纪 80 年代,我国在小学教育培养模式上不断探索改革,主要包括以下四种模式:

一是初中毕业起点的 5 年制专科模式。此模式招收初中毕业生,学制 5 年,颁发专科文凭。20 世纪 80 年代,我国一些经济发达地区,如江苏、上海、北京、南京、广东等省份实行小学教师由中等提高到高等专科教育水平的改革试验。同时,国家教委颁发《全国教育事业十年规划和"八五"计划要点(草案)》提出创办五年制中等师范的试验,逐步提高具有专科和本科学历的小学教师比例。1992 年,教育部颁布《关于批准部分省(直辖市)进行培养专科程度小学教师试验工作的通知》,批准上海、北京、黑龙江、天津、辽宁、吉林等 17 个省市共 29 所学校开展初中起点的 5 年制专科试验,招生指标列入国家高教招生计划。1993 年,《关于继续搞好培养专科程度小学教师试验工作的通知》进一步明确了小学教师培养专科化程度。1994 年,国家教委对"专科程度小学教师"的培养目标、规格要求、学制、办学条件、管理问题提出了具体要求。这种五年制模式的试验工作走上了更加规范化的道路。

二是"5 + 2""2 + 4"模式。此模式是指初中毕业起点的本科培养小学教师的模式。"5 + 2"模式是指招收初中毕业生学习 5 年后,在拿到专科文凭的基础上,再学习 2 年拿到学士学位,如江苏省就实行了此种模式。"2 + 4"模式主要是指招收初中毕业生学习 2 年,达到中专水平,在此基础上再学习 4 年拿到本科文凭,如湖南省即实行此种培养模式。这两种模式继承了五年制初中毕业起点专科培养模式的办学传统和经验,有效提升了小学教育的办学层次和水平,这是小学教师培养机制的创新,加快了小学教师本科化进程。

三是高中毕业起点的 3 年制专科、4 年制本科模式。这种培养模式主要招收高中毕业生学制 3 年或 4 年,拿到专科和本科文凭。1997 年,教育部提倡把小学教育纳入高等教育发展范畴,探索在培养专科学历小学教师的基础上试验培养本科学历小学教师培养模式。为此,教育部组织由北京、上海、江苏、吉林、浙江等省参与的"培养本科学历小学教师专业建设研究"课题组讨论。1998 年,南京晓庄师范学院率先开展本科学历小学教师的培养试验。1999 年,此试验得以在北京、无锡、杭州、上海、常州等地推广。

四是本科毕业起点的 2 年制硕士模式。此种培养模式主要是采取小学教师达到硕士学历的办学层次。2004 年,首都师范大学首次招收小学教育专业硕士研究生。近几年来,此种培养模式已在全国多所师范大学和师范学院实行,如南京师范大学、上海师范大学、东北师范大学、湖州师范学院等。

（四）小学教师教育管理规范化

新中国成立以来,我国小学教师教育逐步实现了规范化管理,主要体现在如下三方面:首先是颁布了教师教育课程标准。2011 年,教育部颁布《教师教育课程标准(试行)》(以下简称《标准》),着重体现了国家对教师教育课程设置的基本要求,是制定课程方案、教材与课程资源开发、教学评价开展,以及认定教师资格的重要依据。《标准》提出小学职前教师教育课程要引导未来教师理解小学生的成长特点与差异、生活经验与现场资源、价值及独特性等。同年,教育部颁布《关于大力推进教师教育课程改革的意见》提出要贯彻落实教育规划纲要,深化改革教师教育,提高培养教师质量,加强高素质教师专业化队伍建设,必须推进教师教育课程内容的改革以及教学方法和手段的创新。

其次是小学教师专业标准的颁布。2017 年,教育部颁布《小学教师专业标准(试行)》,规定了小学教师的职责、标准、资格等。同时探讨了小学教师教育的理念、主要内容与实施建议等。是国家对合格小学教师专业素质的基本要求,成为小学教师开展教学活动的规范以及专业发展的基本准则,是小学教师培养、准入、培训以及考核的重要依据。

最后是小学教师资格制度逐步规范。1986 年,《义务教育法》的颁布,为教师资格方面的政策、法规、条例等提供法律依据,初步确立了我国教师资格制度。1993 年,《教师法》规定各级各类学校和其他教育机构中从事教育教学工作的教师必须具备教师资格。2000 年,《〈教师资格条例〉实施办法》颁布,正式推行我国教师资格认证制度。2011 年,《国家教育事业第十二个五年计划》规定改革中小学教师资格考试,从纵向和横向维度出发,建立"国标、省考、县聘、校用"的职业准入制和五年一周期的定期注册制度;资格考试的难度加大、科目增加、内容更广、报考条件更严格以及认证程序更加严格,大大提高了准入门槛。

三、新中国成立 70 年小学教师教育发展的未来瞻望

小学教育是基础教育中的基础,事关义务教育发展。2018—2019 年,教育部相继颁布《关于全面深化新时代教师队伍建设改革的意见》(以下简称《意见》)《教师教育振兴行动计划(2018—2022 年)》(以下简称《行动计划》)《加快推进教育现代化实施方案(2018—2022 年)》(以下简称《实施方案》)《中国教育现代化 2035》《关于深化教育教学改革全面提高义务教育质量的意见》(以下简称《意见》)《关于实施全国中小学教师信息技术应用能力提升工程 2.0 的意见》(以下简称《意见》)等,为小学教师教育发展的未来指明方向。

(一)秉持"兴国必先强师"的教育理念,构建新时代小学教师教育体系

《意见》强调兴国必先强师,要认识到小学教师队伍建设的时代意义和总体要求。强化小学教师承担国家使命和服务公共教育的职责,赋予中小学教师作为国家公职人员的法律地位。《行动计划》提出,"着眼长远,立足当前,以提升教师教育质量为核心,以加强教师教育体系建设为支撑,以教师教育供给侧结构性改革为动力,推进教师教育创新、协调、绿色、开放、共享发展,从源头上加强教师队伍建设,着力培养造就党和人民满意的师德高尚、业务精湛、结构合理、充满活力的教师队伍"。"在我们这样一个人口大国,义务教育发展任重道远。我国师范教育体系的建设不能照搬发达国家的模式,需要考虑到我国师范教育发展的历史、现有的条件,建设有中国特色的师范教育体系"①。因此,小学师范教育体系的建设也要根据我国中等师范教育发展历史以及现有条件,构建以师范院校(地方师范院校)为主体,

---

① 朱旭东:《关于深化教师教育改革的意见》,《光明日报》,2018 年 9 月 27 日。

综合性大学与中等职业学校共同参与、开放灵活的教师教育体系,开展小学教师培养模式创新,加强小学教育实习环节,加强小学教师师德修养及其教学基本功的训练,提高小学教师培养质量。我们要加大本科层次小学教师培养力度。健全以师范院校和高水平非师范院校参与、以优质中小学为实践基地的开放、协同、联动,有中国特色的小学教师教育体系。

(二)依据小学教育发展实际,推动优质小学教师教育均衡发展

回顾我国小学教师教育改革发展历程,小学教育发展状况是引发小学教师教育改革的深层动力。

《意见》指出,至2035年,我国计划培养造就数以百万计的骨干教师、数以十万计的卓越教师、数以万计的教育家型教师的愿景,并对提高小学教师质量和建设高素质的小学教师队伍进行具体部署。为实现此目标,《实施方案》提出要加强小学师德师风建设,深化改革小学教师管理制度,加强编制管理创新,修订小学岗位设置管理指导意见等。《意见》提出,优化配置小学教师资源,核定小学编制并制定核定标准,加快入编符合条件的非在职教师,制定公开招聘符合小学教师职业特点的办法,严控小学教师资格准入制度,及时调整教师资格定期注册制度。加大县镇与农村小学教师的双向流动、实行定期轮岗,建立乡镇内小学教师走教制度,实施好农村小学教师的"特岗计划"和"银铃讲学计划"。完善认定小学教师岗位分级,适当提高小学教师中、高级岗位比例,促进小学教师的教学积极性。上述措施的实施加快调整了小学教师结构性的失调,加强建设小学教师队伍建设,提高了小学教育发展水平。

(三)改革小学教育招生就业制度,优化小学教育课程体系,深化小学教师考核评价制度

《意见》指出,为保证师范生生源质量,可采取多种形式吸引优秀青年包括小学教育专业,如到岗定位、定向培养、公费培养等,完善免费师范生政

策,履约农村小学教师任教期限为 6 年。改革小学教育招生制度,鼓励一些教学条件好的地方师范院校实行提前批次录取或二次选拔方式选拔小学教师人才;提高师范生的培养层次,推进教师供给侧结构性改革,为小学教育培养素质全面、文化业务见长的本科层次教师。

《意见》提出优化实践为导向的小学教师教育课程体系,强化小学教师的"三字一话"教学技能训练,提高小学教师的学术水平。同时要保证小学教育师范生教学实践不少于半年。加强小学科学、地理等薄弱学科及特殊学校小学教师的培养等。

《意见》提出改革小学教师职称和考核评价制度。进一步完善小学师资管理制度,逐步实现小学教师的职称与聘用相衔接,将小学教师任教乡村薄弱学校且任教一年的教学经历作为申报小学高级和特级教师的必要条件。完善小学教师的职称评价标准,构建适当的考核评价体系指标,坚持小学教师德才兼备的全面考核,奖励教育教学突出成就的小学教师。加强小学教师职后管理,完善小学教师退出机制,提升小学教师专业化发展。

(四)依托"互联网＋教育"技术,促进小学教师教育信息化

随着"互联网＋"技术的发展,信息化、人工智能等新技术给小学教师的教育教学带来影响,因此要提升小学教师教育体系的创新力。《意见》提出,建立服务小学教师教学的各年级各学科数字化教育资源体系。利用"互联网＋"技术,有机融合教师培训与信息技术,转变培训小学教师的方式,结合线上线下的研修方式,结合小学教学实际,改进培训内容,切实提高小学教师的教学水平,促进其终身学习及其专业发展。同时,可推行小学教师自主选学培训内容,实行小学师资培训学分管理,搭建学历教育与培训相衔接的"立交桥"。另外,根据贫困地区乡村学校实际需要,加强乡村小学教师信息化的精准扶贫工作,开展多层次、多方式的"双师教学"小学教师培训模式。通过互联网,组成名师网络课堂与远程协同、城乡教师与乡村教师相结合的教研共同体,开展小学教师集体备课和研课之间的交流,长期开展远程授课

教师对乡村教师进行的"陪伴式"培训,定向帮扶提高乡村小学教师专业化水平和信息技术应用能力等。

Retrospect and Prospect of the Development of Primary School Teacher Education in New China in 1970's

Jumei Xiao

Huzhou Teacher Education College

Abstract: After the founding of New China, the development of primary school teacher education in China has experienced five stages: consolidation period, tortuous and turbulent period, recovery and reconstruction period, rapid development period, reform and innovation period. The development of primary school teacher education has made some achievements in realizing an open primary school teacher education system, building a professional primary school teacher team, forming a diversified education and training model, and standardizing the management of primary school teacher education. Looking forward to the future, the development of primary school teachers' education should take the concept of "rejuvenating the country first, strengthening teachers" as the principle, build a new era of primary school teachers' education system; promote the balanced development of high-quality primary school teachers' education with the goal of serving the development of primary education; reform the enrollment system of normal school students, optimize the curriculum system, and promote the reform of the evaluation mechanism of primary school teachers. Relying on "Internet +"

technology to promote the informatization of primary school teachers´education.

Key words：New China70 years；Primary school teacher education；Educational development

Developing Pre – service Teachers' Practical Knowledge through an Integrative Training Model

Ge Wei

Capital Normal University

Abstract:This paper reports a qualitative case study of a teacher training model as an intervention which aims to develop pre – service teachers' practical knowledge. Audio – recorded teaching sessions and interviews including learning diaries were analysed using qualitative thematic analysis to identify the learning conditions and learning trajectories of pre – service teachers in this program. The analytical results reveal tensions in crossing the boundary between theoretical thinking and practical thinking. While, the integrative model of curriculum practicum and reflection (CPR) in the program is of validity to develop pre – service teacher practical knowledge on four dimensions. The study suggests that when creating an intervention, student teachers benefit from reflection apparently.

Key words:practical knowledge, pre – service teacher education, reflection

1. Introduction

Practical knowledge is critical for teachers to handle dilemmatic situations (Lyons, 1990)[1], to bridge theoretical learning and practical enactment (Cochran – Smith & Lytle, 1999)[2], and to foster adaptive expertise (Männikkö & Husu, 2019)[3]. Numerous previous research focus on experienced teachers' practical knowledge (e. g. Elbaz, 1987; Connelly & Clandinin, 1985)[4] but pay little attention on how to cultivate pre – service teachers' practical knowledge before they come into the practical field. In this article, based on the author's personal experience and experimentation in a Chinese university, proposes an integrative training model entitled "Curriculum – Practicum – Reflection (CPR)" as an intervention to facilitate student teachers' cyclic – learning trajectory between theory and practice in teacher education program.

2. Conceptual background

The emphasis on the practical nature of teachers' knowledge appeared in Elbaz' (1981, 1983)[5][6] case – study work. Teachers' practical knowledge is more

[1]　Lyons, N, Dilemmas of knowing: Ethical and epistemological dimensions of teacher's work and development, *Harvard Educational Review*, 60, 1990, pp. 159 – 181.

[2]　Cochran – Smith, M., & Lytle, S. Relationships of Knowledge and Practice. Teacher Learning in Communities. *Review of Research in Education*, 24, 1999, pp. 249 – 305.

[3]　Männikkö, I., & Husu, J., Examining teachers' adaptive expertise through personal practical theories. *Teaching and Teacher Education*, 77, 2019, pp. 126 – 173.

[4]　Connelly, F. M. & Clandinin, D. J. *Personal practical knowledge and the modes of knowing: relevance for teaching and learning*, University of Chicago Press, 1985, pp. 174 – 198.

[5]　Elbaz, F., The teacher's 'practical knowledge': Report of a case study. *Curriculum Inquiry*, 11 (1), 1981, pp. 43 – 71.

[6]　Elbaz, F., *Teacher thinking: A study of practical knowledge*. London: Croom Helm, 1983.

than just knowing: it also incorporates aspects of the human experience such as 'feeling, judging, willing, and action' (Duffee & Aikenhead 1992, p. 494)①. As such, it is integrated from a variety of sources, from life experiences and beliefs to formal education and the contemporary context of teaching, and is in a dynamic state of flux.

For the purposes of this article, we are interested in pre – service teachers' practical knowledge; how it is developed in situ in initial teacher training programs, as well as how it is influenced by their theoretical learning, self reflection, and the context in which they are found teaching within their practicum experiences.

I accept the characteristics of the salient features of teachers' practical knowledge expounded by van Driel et al (2001, p. 142)②. These characteristics include:

• *It is action – oriented, accumulated on the basis of experience and available for immediate use in practice.*

• *It is context – and person – bound, allowing teachers to achieve personally valuable goals. The context of the teaching experience is broadly inclusive, incorporating both physical and cultural components. The teacher's disciplinary background is significant in shaping their response to the context.*

• *It is largely tacit knowledge: Sockett (1993, p. 47)③ describes this tac-*

---

① Duffee, L., & Aikenhead, G. Curriculum change, student evaluation, and teacher practical knowledge, *Science Education*, 76(5), 1992, pp. 493 – 506.

② van Driel, J. H., Beigaard, D., & Verloop, N., Professional development and reform in science education: The role of teachers' practical knowledge, *Journal of Research in Science Teaching*, 38(2), 2001, pp. 137 – 158.

③ Sockett, H., *The moral basis of teacher professionalism*, New York: Teachers College Press, 1993, p. 47.

it form of knowledge as being demonstrated when 'someone knows how to do when—not merely spontaneously'. This characteristic also makes the sharing of such knowledge difficult.

● It is a form of integrated knowledge, combining aspects of biography and education through the context of the educational experience.

● Beliefs are important, acting as a filter on what new knowledge is integrated into the individual teacher's practical knowledge. These beliefs are heavily influenced by their biography.

An important consideration for pre – service teachers is the extent to which the elements of their practical knowledge are not integrated: 'the novice is someone who perceives the unfamiliar teaching situation in terms of discrete elements and, in making use of new skills and knowledge, relies on rules rather than an integrated vision of practice' (Timperley et al. 2007, p. 11)[①]. A potent source of this conflict is pre – service teachers' (often deeply held) beliefs around teaching colliding with the press for practices that support inquiry. Given this, it is simply not realistic to expect pre – service teachers to integrate the elements of practical knowledge during their practicum.

In this article, therefore, I am considering the process by which this nascent integration proceeds, and how it is enacted in the teacher training programs. For this, the following research question is used to guide my action – oriented enquiry:

In what ways do pre – service science teachers integrate theory, practice

---

① Timperley, H., Wilson, A., Barrar, H., & Fung, I., *Teacher professional learning and development*, Wellington: Ministry of Education, New Zealand, 2007, p. 11.

and personal experience and how do those interventions support pre – service teachers to develop their practical knowledge?

3. Context

This paper is case study and also an action research conducted by the author at the Capital Normal University. Capital Normal University is a modern university focusing on teacher training ranging from different grades and different subjects. This study was conducted at the college of elementary education in Capital Normal University from March 2019 to October 2019. Totally 70 student teachers involved in this study.

Figure 1 shows the integrative model of curriculum, practicum and reflection in the initial teacher training program. It is designed as a zigzag model by which pre – service teachers have chance to incorporate theory and practice by their reflection. This article, thus, is an exploratory study to discuss the validity of this training model for developing pre – service teachers' practical knowledge.

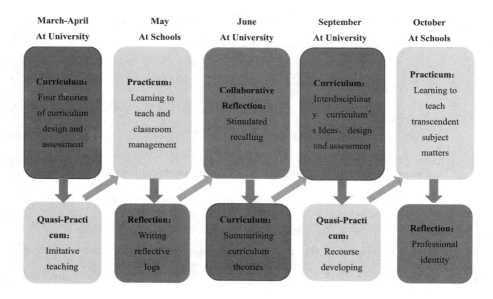

Figure 1　Design of the intervention

Considering the data collection and analysis, audio – recorded teaching sessions and interviews including reflective diaries were analysed using qualitative thematic analysis to identify the learning conditions and learning trajectories of pre – service teachers in this program.

4. Findings

4.1 Pre – service teachers' practical knowledge

While the different domains of teacher practical knowledge, craft and personal/interpersonal knowledge are closely interlinked, it may be helpful to identify key elements of each in relation to pre – service teachers. In terms of domain knowledge, this may highlight:

    • *depth and breadth of subject knowledge, though the level needed seems likely to vary according to the children's age, prior experience and level of attainment;*

    • *the ability to enable children to make links between different 'subjects' and domains of their experience, both in and out of school;*

    • *the need to balance a wide range of objectives, both across different aspects of children's development and in the short – and the long – term;*

    • *ways to develop attitudes, dispositions and values, as well as skills.*

Craft knowledge is harder to identify but would seem to encompass both deliberate and in – the – moment decisions, emphasizing aspects such as:

    • *sensitivity to prior experience and out of school interests of the class to aid planning;*

    • *planning which is both detailed and flexible, providing a broad and balanced range of experiences and activities appropriate to children's needs and stages of development;*

    • *adoption of a wide and varied range of versions of teaching to enable children to have access to different ways of representing and understanding experience, both individually and in groups of differing sizes;*

    • *scaffolding the differing needs of learners through ways of grouping selected according to aims and objectives, or what might be called differentiated differentiation;*

    • *monitoring of children's learning through a wide range of information feedback;*

    • *self – monitoring to enable adaptation and improvisation, depending on the cues and responses received from children, drawing from an extensive pedagogical repertoire.*

In terms of personal/interpersonal knowledge, the following seem especially important:

- *attunement to children's varied responses and how these affect both oneself and other children;*
- *the types, and continuities, of relationship established;*
- *judgement of the mood of a class, especially in situations where this is less adult – controlled or more volatile;*
- *attributes such as confidence to provide security to children, to enable changes of plans in the light of new information and to back one's own judgement;*
- *enactment of values in practice, given the importance for all, but especially young, children of learning by example and therefore of modelling.*

4.2 Reflective learning trajectory

Dewey (1933, p. 7) described "reflection" or "reflective thinking" as "active, persistent, and careful consideration of any belief or supposed form of knowledge in light of grounds that support it and future conclusions to which it tends" [1]. Killen (2009) identified teaching reflection as a deliberate attempt to understand or evaluate the success or otherwise of teaching and learning experiences in order

---

[1] Dewey, J., *How we think: A restatement of the relation of reflective thinking to the educative process.* Boston: Heath and Company, 1933, p. 7.

to shape future action or "reflection in action or on the run" (p. 103) ①. Based upon this, teachers employ "self – study" or "self – evaluative reflection" on the level of reflecting on individual lessons they teach (Smith et al. 2017) ②. Reflective practice can provide important insights into the ways in which personal beliefs and life experiences act as a lens or filter for framing and understanding past experiences.

In this study, I found that the reflective methods of pre – service teachers related to their theoretical underpinnings and practicum facilitate a deeper understanding of their own practices in different educational settings. As a student teacher said:

This training model provides a public forum for pre – service teachers' voices to be heard in order to bring to light the diverse, complex and challenging issues they are faced with during their practicum experiences.

Reflective practice is commonly used in teaching practicum programmes to bring to light routine interpretive activities that signify the beliefs and cultural assumptions of the knower. There is a growing recognition of the limitations of a narrow, results – oriented curriculum; and that since it is not sustainable in the medium – to long – term teacher education needs to focus more on a deeper and more flexible understanding of pedagogy. In the light of Pollard's notion that attainment and personal development should be mutually re – enforcing like intertwined strands of a rope, most of the session explores through discussion the implications

---

① Killen, R., *Effective teaching strategies: Lessons from research and practice* (5th ed.), South Melbourne: Cengage Learning, 2009, p. 103.

② Smith, P., Geng, G., & Black, P., Teachers as reflective practitioners. In G. Geng, P. Smith, & P. Black (Eds.), *The challenge of teaching: Through the eyes of pre – service teachers*, 2017, pp. 25 – 37.

of spiritual, moral, social and cultural development for learners and for teachers, to help explore what really matters for children. Three key outcomes, a sense of personal narrative, a need to belong and a sense of agency will be highlighted, and some of the pedagogical implications considered, notably those based on assumptions of children's capability. The session ends by considering briefly the extent to which this is achievable within the current climate.

Table 1　Four dimensions for teacher reflective learning

Spiritual who am I? where do I fit in? why am I here?	Moral how should I act? what sort of person do I want to become?
Social how should I interact with other people?	Cultural where do I belong? what is my identity?

Key points to be brought out in discussion, that these raise questions rather provide answers:

- *spiritual, not just about religion, but about meaning and addressing painful as well as enjoyable experience, with relationships central to this. who am I? where do I fit in? why am I here?*

- *moral, not just about right and wrong, and not predominantly conscious, but learnt more through example and habituation, as well as critical reflection via the conscious about what sort of person do I want to become? Jackson et al's book The Moral Life of Schools is a very powerful analysis of why explicit programmes are less important than what is implicit, what is unspoken is even more important than what is consciously taught;*

- *social, which means to connect yourself with the social context. It is a Vygotskian approach to identify human development as two planes, where the first plane stems from the external sociality*;

　　● *cultural, a particularly slippery word, but at root this is about questions such as where do I belong? what is my identity? Without these, children have little chance to become confident, creative learners. In Eagleton's (2000, p. 131)* [①] *words,* '*culture is not only what we live by. It is, also, in great measure, what we live for. Affection, relationship, memory, kinship, place, community, emotional fulfilment, intellectual enjoyment, a sense of ultimate meaning.* '

Vygotsky (1997) [②] suggested that the role of the teacher is to facilitate student learning through carefully structured social interactions and scaffolded teaching and learning activities. However, as both students and teachers must navigate a rapidly changing and increasingly complex environment, it is also crucial that teachers do not make assumptions about their students' background knowledge and experiences.

Vygotsky (1998) [③]described the dialectic of person and practice as a process of personal identity and practice. Pre – service teachers develop their own professional teacher identities over time as they draw on their own experiences as learners to navigate, understand and manage classroom situations. Consequently, teaching practices include engagement of pre – service teachers themselves in knowledge learning and this may require them to adjust their ways of thinking and behaving in the classroom.

Stetsenkom and Arievitch (2004) [④]explain that the learning journey of pre

---

①　Eagleton, T, *The Idea of Culture*, Oxford, Blackwell, 2000, p. 131.

②　Vygotsky, L. S., *Educational psychology*, Boca Raton, FL: St. Lucie Press, 1997.

③　Vygotsky, L. S., The collected works of L. S. Vygotsky, *Child psychology* (Vol. 5), New York: Plenum Press, 1998.

④　Stetsenkom, A. & Arievitch, I., The self in cultural – historical activity theory, *Theory and Psychology*, 14(4), 2004, pp. 475 – 503.

– service teachers is a period of self – transformation from a university student to a professional teacher. Edwards (2010)[1] and Roth (2006)[2] explain how histories, values and purposes lead to transformation. It is dissonance that leads one to question these histories, hence the importance of critical incidents and reflective practice.

During the reflective journal writings, student teachers focus on the self – transformation through reflective practice. By reflective practice, pre – service teachers' identities can be changed, especially when they are entering new classrooms and experience incidents that cause them to question their assumptions about teaching priorities and approaches. In 1999, Beach argued that "transitions are consequential when they are consciously reflected on, often struggled with, and the eventual outcomes changes one's sense of self and social positioning" (p. 114)[3]. In each of the following chapters, the authors have identified moments of uncertainty, of struggle, and a search for a resolution.

5. Concluding remarks

In this paper, I explored an integrative training model for initial teacher education. However, the deeper discussion need to be expanded to the new understandings of elementary teachers under the perspective of practical knowledge. U-

---

① Edwards, A., *Being an expert professional practitioner: The relational turn in expertise*, Dordrecht: Springer, 2010.

② Roth, M., Agency and passivity: Prolegomenon to scientific literacy as ethico – moral praxis, In A. Rodriguez (Ed.), *The multiple faces of agency: Innovative strategies for effecting change in urban school contexts*, Rotterdam: Sense Publishers, 2006, pp. 135 – 155.

③ Beach, K. Consequential transitions: A sociocultural expedition beyond transfer in education, *Review of Research in Education*, 24, 1999, pp. 101 – 139.

sing Hargreaves´ (2003) [1]analysis of key aspects needed in a knowledge economy, I highlight (Eaude, 2011, p 175) [2]that teachers should:

As catalysts,

- *promote deep cognitive learning;*
- *learn to teach in ways they were not taught;*
- *treat parents as partners in learning;*
- *build a capacity for change and risk;*
- *foster trust in processes.*

As counterpoints,

- *promote social and emotional learning, commitment and character;*
- *develop cosmopolitan identity;*
- *work and learn in collaborative groups;*
- *forge relationships with parents and communities;*
- *preserve continuity and security.*

As casualties, avoid the temptation to:

- *coach children to memorize standardized learning;*
- *learn to teach as they are told;*
- *work harder and learn alone;*
- *treat parents as consumers and complainers;*
- *respond to imposed change with fearful compliance.*

In order to achieve this goal, reflection plays a role as mediation for pre – service teacher development. Reflective teachers are those who are aware of the reasons behind the decisions they make and the consequences of those decisions.

---

[1] Hargreaves, *Teaching in the Knowledge society – education in the age of insecurity*, Maidenhead, Open University Press, 2003.

[2] Eaude, T., Thinking Through Pedagogy – Primary and Early Years, *Exeter: Learning Matters*, 2011, p. 175.

There are many issues within classrooms and schools and the wider educational context that teachers need to continually reflect on and sometimes as a result of reflection change their thinking and practice or question practices and innovations … Learning the skills of critical reflection can help them make sense of the situations they face and helping them learn these skills during their course of study can set them on a path to become reflective teachers in their future careers. This is a long process, the benefits of which will help them become more effective teachers, develop positive relationships and deliver better learning outcomes for the students they will teach (Smith et al. 2017, p. 25)[①]. It is suggested that uses reflective practice to connect the pre – service teachers' personal background with their placement experience around a self – selected topic. It also includes teacher educators' personal reflections on the pre – service teachers' reports on these issues of concern.

基于整合模式培养职前教师的实践性知识

魏　戈

首都师范大学初等教育学院博士

　　摘要:本文采用质性案例法,研究了一种致力于培养职前教师实践性知识的教师培训模式。将培训期间的录像、深度访谈材料及职前教师的学习日志作为资料,进行了主题式分析,从而得到职前教师在该项目中的学习结

---

　　① Smith, P., Geng, G., & Black, P., Teachers as reflective practitioners. In G. Geng, P. Smith, & P. Black (Eds.), *The challenge of teaching: Through the eyes of pre – service teachers*, 2017, pp. 25 – 37.

果与学习路径。研究结果揭示了职前教师教育项目在跨越理论性思维与实践性思维之间遭遇的张力。研究数据证明,这种整合了课程、实践与反思的 CPR 培训模式能够有效提高职前教师的实践性知识,并在精神性、文化性、道德性与社会性等维度上均有较好表现。该研究还发现,当教师教育者开发某种介入性培训项目时,职前教师的反思是贯穿理论与实践的桥梁。

关键词:实践性知识;职前教师培养;反思

第二编　小学教师培养模式探索

PART Ⅱ :Exploration of Elementary Teacher
Training Modes

中国小学教师培养模式:探析与展望

刘　慧

首都师范大学初等教育学院,教授

摘要:中国小学教师培养经历了长达百年的中师模式,于 20 世纪 80 年代开启专科模式,还未全面普及,于 1999 年步入本科模式,且发展迅速,到 2014 年实施卓越小学教师培养模式探索。本科层次小学教师培养历程中的主要研究议题有四大类,人才培养模式、专业建设、小学教师和初等教育学科建设;具有技能取向、知识取向、能力取向、实践取向、研究取向及人本取向等多种;小学教师培养的深层问题关涉师范性和学术性之辨、专业性和学科性之定位、全科性和分科性的理解、教育性和教学性的处理、儿童性和知识性的站位、现实性和理想性的矛盾等;对这些专业建设问题的科学回答有赖于学科建设,展望未来中国小学教师培养,必须迎接新时代的挑战,加强初等教育学、儿童学、小学教师教育学科建设,着力培养模式探索,如首都师范大学"儿童取向的卓越小学教师培养模式"探索。

关键词:小学教师培养模式;模式取向;学科建设;儿童取向

教师队伍建设是当代世界教育事业发展共同关注的关键因素。中国教师教育在改革开放的进程中取得了卓越成就,培养了支撑世界上最大规模的基础教育的教师队伍,积累了中国经验。尤其是中国小学教师培养,经过百年中师,于 20 世纪八十年代开始专科培养实验,九十年代末拉开了高师本科培养探索的帷幕。而今,小学教师本科培养之路虽刚刚走过二十年,却形成了多种培养模式,尤其是卓越教师培养计划实施以来。今天处在百年未有之大变局之际、"过去未去,未来已来"的新时代,教师教育面临新的挑战和新的历史使命,继往开来,与时俱进,推动教师教育创新,是当代中国教育的重大课题。本文围绕中国小学教师培养模式,从其历史变迁、高校小学教师培养模式探析以及未来展望三方面展开论述。

一、中国小学教师培养模式的变迁

(一)中国小学教师教育发展阶段

中国小学教师培养从 1897 年开始,盛宣怀在上海创办南洋公学,内设师范院培养各级教师,拉开了中国小学教师"中师"培养的帷幕。1902 年,张謇创办通州民立师范学校,这是第一个专门培养小学教师的学校。1935 年,国民政府教育部《师范教育令》等文件,基本形成了中等师范培养体系。新中国成立后,1952 年,教育部颁布了《中等师范学校暂行规程》等,逐步建立了三级教师培养体系,直到 1983 年。随着社会进步与基础教育的发展,对教师的需求由量转为质,小学教师的学历标准也在逐渐提升。1984 年,江苏省南通师范学校率先开启了培养专科层次小学教师的五年制师范试验,拉开了小学教师高学历进程的序幕。1985 年,上海师范高等专科学校、北京第三师范学校、北京通州师范学校、南京晓庄师范学校等举办小学教育大专班,开启培养专科层次小学教师的试验工作。1992 年起,国家教委决定在沿海和经济发达地区扩大试验。经过十年的实践探索,国家教委于 1995 年 2 月下发了试行《大学专科程度小学教师培养课程方案》(教师司〔1995〕4 号),有力地推动了试验工作的发展。至今仍有百余所专科学校承担培养小学教师的工作。

我国小学教师本科培养的帷幕于 1997 年拉开。当年,教育部提出将小学教育专业纳入普通高等教育,并成立了"培养本专科学历小学教师专业建设研究"课题立项组。1998 年,教育部师范司正式启动"面向 21 世纪培养专、本科学历小学教师专业建设"项目,在全国率先招收小学教育本科专业学生的高校有四所,从"1998 年度经教育部备案或批准设置的高等学校本科专业名单(教高函[1999]1 号)"中获悉,首批增设小学教育专业的高校有东北师范大学、上海师范大学、南京师范大学、杭州师范大学。在 1999 年度经教育部备案或批准设置的高等学校本科专业名单((教高函[2000]2 号)中,第二批增设小学教育专业的高校又有四所:首都师范大学、华中师范大学、四平师范学院、雁北师范学院(2003 年成为山西大同大学一部分),并于同年招生。后将两批并称为教育部首批招收小学教育本科生单位。

2002 年 9 月,教育部颁发《关于加强专科以上学历小学教师培养工作的几点意见》中指出:专科以上学历小学教师的培养要纳入高等教育体系;加强小学教育专业建设,努力办出特色,培养适应基础教育需要的小学教师。此后,高校本科层次小学教育专业发展迅速。到 2004 年已发展为 40 多家。据中国科学评价研究中心数据显示,2019 年,全国开设小学教育专业的高等院校总计有 225 所,专科 193 所。

综上,在中国小学教师培养走过百年中师历程,专科培养还没有大面积推广之前,就开启了本科层次培养之门,随之而来的是大批中等师范学校的"消失",高等师范专科学校和高师小学教育专业迅速发展,且成为我国小学教师培养的"主力"。

(二)"中·专·本"三层次小学教师培养的特点

我国百年中师形成了一套完善而卓有成效的小学教师培养体系,为中国培养了大量合格的小学教师,这些教师成为小学教育界的骨干和精英,到目前仍然活跃在小学教育战线上。中师模式的特点主要有以下几方面,一是选拔优秀的初中毕业生,学制 3 年或 4 年;二是定向于小学教师,以提高学生综合素质为基础,注重培养从事小学教育的信念与责任心,注重行为规范的养成、教学技能的训练、体音美全方位培养；三是主要侧重高中阶段的文化知识补偿教育，各学科知识齐头并进，毕业后能在小学同时教授几门课程。中师模式为当代中国培养全科教师积累了丰富的经验，这是一笔宝贵的财富，值得我们好好反思与借鉴。

专科层次小学教师培养的特点主要有：一是招生对象变为初中和高中生并存，其中，初中起点的学制 5 年，高中起点的学制 3 年；二是在培养模式上有单科、大文大理，也提倡综合培养，强调不分专业和不分学科，还有多科教学等。从中师走向专科，一个重要的标志就是出现了"学科"。在中师培养阶段，可以说是"无学科"的概念，但也不是综合，而是不强调"学科"。而专科的"学科"主要针对的是小学教学科目，而不是某一领域的知识体系，明晰这一点非常必要。即小学教育有什么样的教学科目，专科层次的小学教师培养就要"对接"培养。

在中国小学教师本科层次培养模式的构建过程中，各高师院校充分利用自身优势，形成了多种培养模式。从研究的角度对小学教师的本科培养模式进行分类，有两类划分方式，一是三分法，即分科型、中间型和综合型；另一是四分法，即"综合培养＋"分科选修、分方向培养、特色人才培养、大文大理。

值得一提的是对"分科型"的理解。"分科"之"科"是指知识体系之"学科"，还是小学教学科目？谁是此模式的代表？目前全国小教界似乎认为首都师范大学小学教师培养是"分科型"的代表，但我们在小学教师培养的办学理念、培养目标、培养模式等都坚持小学教育的综合性和小学教育专业培养小学教师的综合性，强调"综合培养，发展专长"，而不是分学科培养。那么为何会被"误解"？可能是因为我院小学教育专业分为小学语文、小学数学、小学英语、小学科学、小学信息、小学德育等六个方向。但这是在小学教育专业下"分方向"而不是"分学科"，两者非是同一含义。明晰这一点非常重要，这是小学教育专业建设中一个关键问题，是许多问题产生的根源所在。

（三）卓越小学教师培养模式的探索

在小学教育专业建设中,国家卓越教师培养计划具有重要作用。为推动教师教育综合改革,全面提升教师培养质量,2014 年教育部出台《关于实施卓越教师培养计划意见》(称为 1.0 版),全国小学教育专业共有 20 家入选(本科 19 家,专科一家)。各校根据对"卓越"内涵的理解、区域特点、学校类型以及各自优势等,形成了以教学科目多少与层度为标准的不同的培养模式,如"两专多能""一专两辅""两精通三主教"等,还有的从学历角度,将卓越教师培养定位在硕士层次。从总体上看,这些提法主要是着重于所培养的小学教师能在小学从事几门小学学科教学,所追求的培养方案是如何能涵盖或符合多科或全科的要求。之所以如此,主要原因是 1.0 版中卓越教师培养与全科教师关联,这导致对卓越的理解,主要围绕的核心词是全科。2018 年教育部又发布了《关于实施卓越教师培养计划的意见》(2.0 版),提出了培养"素养全面、专长发展"的卓越小学教师。这将进一步引导卓越小学教师培养模式的探索。

综上,我国本科层次小学教师的培养,经过二十年的探索,取得的一个重要成绩就是"打破"了"中小学"不分的局面,逐渐清晰了对小学教师的特性、小学教师与中学教师培养差异等的认识,明确了中学教师培养的"学科+教育""双专业"模式,并不适合小学教师培养,形成了具有自身特色的培养模式,并随着卓越小学教师培养计划项目的推进,开始迭代升级。如,首都师范大学由"综合培养、发展专长、注重研究、全程实践"的小学教师培养模式 1.0,迭代为"儿童取向"卓越小学教师培养模式 2.0,其核心是卓越小学教师之"卓越",并非在能教几门课上,而是儿童教育,卓越小学教师培养的重心是要突破"学科本位",回归"以人为本",体现以儿童为本,实施儿童教育。

二、本科层次小学教师培养模式探析

（一）本科层次小学教师培养历程中的主要研究议题

2014 年,中国高等教育学会教师教育分会小学教师教育委员编辑出版了《传承与创新——中国高等教育学会教师教育分会小学教师教育委员会十年纪实与探索》(2004—2013)一书,收录了自 2004 年建立到 2013 年发展历程中所开展的学术活动纪要和重要的研究论文。我通过对该书中十届年会主题和主要论文内容分析发现,小学教师本科层次培养历程中关注的主要议题与推动力量主要有四大类:一是有关小学教育专业人才培养模式问题,二是有关小学教育专业建设问题,三是有关小学教师的问题,四是有关初等教育学科建设的问题。

1. 关于小学教育专业人才培养模式的议题

这一议题,最早被人们关注的,主要包括人才培养逻辑起点问题、人才培养模式的变革问题、人才培养模式的实践取向问题、高校与小学联合培养小学教师的问题、农村小学教师培养模式问题、全科小学教师培养的模式问题,以及近年来的卓越教师培养问题模式研究。同时也提出了关于初等教育学科建设问题,此议题在接下来的学术年会中也有不断地深入,主要是如何进行学科建设以支撑专业建设的问题,包括学科与专业的关系、学科建设自身问题、学科专业一体化建设等问题。

2. 关于小学教育专业建设的议题

这一议题的研讨内容最为丰富,主要有:一是小学教育专业如何根植于大学文化。当时许多高师院校承办小学教育专业的学院是基于中师合并升格而来,带来的一个大问题是如何在高校文化环境中生存下去。也就是说,小学教育专业如何能根植于大学文化中来建设的问题。有关此问题,在小学教育专业发展过程中被持续关注多年,现在基本上不谈了。今日的小学教育专业建设,不再是怎么大学化的问题,而是在大学文化之中怎样建设的问题。

二是小学教育作为特色专业和专业特色的问题。2007 年教育部评选国家级特色专业,首都师范大学和上海师范大学的小学教育专业入选首批。之后一些省市开展地方特色专业建设。小学教育专业委员会年会围绕着什么是特色专业,小学教育专业特色何在、小学教育专业品质问题、专业标准问题等开展研讨。

三是围绕小学教师专业标准的讨论。2010 年,在顾明远先生指导下,我院承担并完成了小学教育专业标准研制工作,2012 年 2 月教育部发布了小学教师专业标准,这对小学教育专业建设有重要的意义。随之小学教育专业委员会年会更多是围绕与小学教育专业标准相关的议题展开研讨。

四是专业课程等问题。研讨的议题主要有专业课程、专业教材建设,实验课程体系建设,专业核心课程建设、教育部教师教育国家精品资源共享课建设等。值得一提的是,2013 年我院在教育部"专业综合改革试点项目——小学教育"中,进行了小学教育专业课程地图研制工作,这使我们对小学教育专业建设和发展的思考与研究,不再是基于经验的、现实的具体问题和自身所具有的优势,而是有了顶层设计、自上而下地整体的、系统的思考与构建,形成了一个从培养目标、指标体系到课程设置之完整的"课程地图"。这一探索成果在全国小学教育界引发强烈反响,有力推动了小学教育专业建设向着科学化、规范化、体系化迈进。

五是小学教育专业教师队伍建设。这是小学教育专业建设的关键,但由于小学教育专业主要是因社会需要而建,并非基于大学的学科专业建立逻辑,且采取合并升格、转型等多种途径与方式,故各校普遍缺乏独立的、高学历的、专业的、足够的教师队伍,这成为制约小学教育专业建设的重要因素。又因为小学教育专业作为高校的一个新专业,缺乏相应的初等教育学学科基础,也难有此学科毕业的博士生,故新入职的各学科教师,如何走进小学教育专业,成为此专业的教师,成为各高校小学教育专业建设中的一个新问题。所以小学教育专业教师队伍建设,成为 20 年来全国小学教育界关注的重要议题。至今,全国小学教育专业教师队伍建设现状已有很大变化,如,我院目前拥有一只百余人的专职教师团队,无论是博士学位教师所占的比例,还是教师专业发展程度上,都在不断提高。

六是小学教育专业与基础教育的关系问题,两者到底是什么关系? 其中有两个词,一个是引领,一个是合作。可以说,今天大学与小学的合作是比较普遍存在的,但是否能引领,却是一个问题。一定程度上讲,今天的基础教育改革正在"倒逼"师范教育的改革、转型,师范专业认证就是一个重要举措,接下来的几年,小学教育专业的工作重心是迎接师范专业认证。

3. 关于小学教师的议题

在小学教育专业建立之初,就在追问小学教师发展问题,当然这与小学教育专业建设是一体的,只有清晰前者,后者才能有的放矢。后来随着教师专业化的提出,小教界开始探索小学教师专业发展问题、小学教师专业能力培养问题、小学教师资格证考试问题、教师课程标准、小学教师专业标准、小学教师专业素养、小学教师核心素养等一系列问题。如,早在 2013 年,我院在小学教育专业课程地图研制时就提出了小学教师核心素养包括认识小学儿童、理解小学教育、教师自身发展三个方面,并依此构建了小学教师培养的三级指标体系,在此基础上设置了小学教育专业的课程体系。这与师范类专业认证所提出的课程体系应支撑毕业要求及培养目标,具有内在的一致性。

4. 关于初等教育学科建设

早在 2003 年就研究者发表论文提出要在教育学一级学科下设置初等教育学为独立的二级学科,2004 年全国小学教师教育专业委员会成立大会上,学科建设也是其中议题之一。但这些年来初等教育学科建设并不尽如人意,有一些具体的问题,如支撑小学教育专业建设的是初等教育学学科建设,还是初等教育学科建设,还是初等教育学院学科建设,还存在多种提法,并未澄清。对此理解的不同,所强调的侧重点也不一样。在我看来,初等教育学学科建设是以小学教育为研究对象的学科体系构建,是支撑小学教育专业建设的基础学科;初等教育学科建设还应涵盖初等教育的其他方面,初等教育学院的学科建设的概念更大,可以说涵盖初等教育学院关涉的所有学科建设。那么小学教育专业建设到底缺什么? 到底需要什么学科支撑? 什么才是支撑小学教育专业建设的基础学科? 还需要我们认真思考、研究。再有,所探讨的问题有学科建设怎么支持专业建设,学科建设与专业建设一体化的问题。

此外,2003 年开启了培养硕士层次小学教师的帷幕,如,首都师范大学初等教育学院借助本校教育学学科平台,在课程与教学论二级学科下招收小学语文和小学数学方向的硕士研究生,之后一些高校小学教育专业也陆续开始招收硕士生,所以小学教育专业委员会多次会议都涉及硕士层次小学教师培养问题的探讨,而今这个议题更为重要。不仅是因为在学科建设中,研究生培养、学位点建设是重要内容;而且在中国广袤的大地上,尽管不同区域对小学教师的学历需要不同,但北京、上海等一些发达地区的小学都需要硕士毕业生,这也是未来小学发展的需要。

(二)小学教师培养模式的"取向"分析

小学教师的培养模式,从中师到专科再到本科,各层次的着力点有何不同? 如果说中师模式的培养着力点在于教师基本功,专科培养模式重视学科教学技能,那么本科模式的着力点何在? 这是进入本科层次培养以来一直在讨论的话题。顾明远先生曾在 2008 年初等教育学学科独立论证会上指出,以往中师培养重视教师的技能,相对忽视教师的文化素养的培养。小学教师的培养应该强调文化底蕴、通识教育、养成教育,使之具有较高的文化水准,这样他们就会明白什么叫教育,什么叫孩子。这为本科层次小学教师培养着力点何在指明了方向。

在小学教育专业发展历程中,各高校不断探索本科层次小学教师的内涵、特质,并依据各自理解,形成了多种模式,其着力点,有的放在了学科知识上,有的是在学科教学,还有的是研究能力,近年来关注儿童成为新的着力点。其中,小学教师的研究能力,是今天本科层次小学教师必备的能力,更是研究生层次培养的重要方面,目前许多学校都很重视;而着力于小学儿童,则是伴随人本教育理念的推进、小学儿童作为初等教育学的逻辑起点的确立、促进儿童生命健康成长作为小学教师工作落脚点的明确等,才逐渐被个别培养单位意识到。

小学教师培养模式之不同着力点背后所反映的是不同价值取向。所谓取向,其实是一个方向性问题,是培养定位问题。由于对小学教育、小学教师认识与理解的不同,必然带来对小学教育专业建设定位的差异,进而反映在其人才培养目标、课程设置、培养方式等方面的侧重点的不同。概言之,上述不同着力点的培养模式,分别对应的是技能取向、知识取向、能力取向、实践取向、研究取向和人本取向。

(三)小学教师培养的深层问题

进一步思考小学教师培养的深层问题是什么?我将其归为这样几对矛盾:

一是师范性和学术性之辨。这不仅仅是我们小学教师培养、小学教育专业建设要回答的问题,而是教师教育面临的问题。那么师范性与学术性的关系到底是怎样的?对这一问题的回答会关涉诸如教师本体性知识是什么等一系列问题。

二是专业性和学科性之定位。我们是立足于小学教育专业,还是立足中文、数学等学科来培养小学教师,是有着不同表现的,如在人才培养方案的设计上,包括一直争议的学分分配上、课程设置上,都因站位不同而有所不同。

三是全科性和分科性的理解。全科的指向何在?是要培养小学所有科目都能教的小学教师,还是什么?是指向小学教师知识能力的综合性,还是指向小学教师的儿童性?再有,在小学教师培养中,全科要怎么分配学分?

分科要怎样分配学分？当然全科是否等于综合，也是一个需要厘清的问题。

四是教育性和教学性的处理。教育与教学虽为一体，没有无教育性的教学，但还是各有侧重。在一些情况下我们可能注重了学科教学，而忽视了学生教育，对小学教师而言，"立德树人"是根本任务，要培养学生成为有德之人，所以我们需要加强德育性。

五是儿童性和知识性的站位。在小学教育专业课程设置中，有关学科和学科教学的知识很多，而有关儿童的知识很少；在小学教师培养中，主要也是立足于学科知识和教学技能的获得，而理解儿童的课程很少。这种现象与我们对小学教育专业与小学教师的儿童性与知识性及其关系的认识与理解密切相关。

三、中国小学教师培养的未来展望

（一）迎接时代的新挑战

我们要迎接时代的挑战，首先，我们要深度理解时代的变化与未来发展的趋势。其中重点关注两个变化，一个是新时代人们对美好生活的需求，我们的教育能不能满足、帮助、引导人们过美好生活，是一个新的挑战，它不是在生存的层面上，而是在活得好的层面上。以往我们的教育主要服务于人的生存，未来教育必须服务于人过美好生活的需要。另一个是人工智能时代人们对生命意义与价值的追问与实现，人工智能改变了我们的生存方式，挑战了我们的智力、体力，也使我们从劳作中解放出来，有了更多的闲暇和自由。那么人的大量闲暇时间要做什么？人怎么过闲暇时光？这关涉的核心问题是人的心灵如何安顿、生命意义和价值问题，在2018年中国民众最关注的十大哲学问题的调查中"人生的意义与价值"已高居榜首，未来这个问题将更加凸显。

再有，我们必须清楚未来需要什么样的人？未来的人需要什么？在20

世纪末,社会所需要的人才应具有学习能力、实践能力、协作能力、创新能力,到了 21 世纪,社会所需要人才应具有批判性思维、沟通、合作和创意,到了 22 世纪,社会需要的是具有生命、情感、思维、创意之人。可见,伴随着社会的发展,所需要的人才越来越回归生命、回归人的整体,而非某些方面的能力或素养。有句话可谓一语中的:即"要想跟上 2050 年的世界,人类不只需要发明新的想法和产品,最重要的是得一次又一次的重塑自己"。这就是未来人最重要的落脚点:不断地"重塑自己"。所以我们的教育应明晰时代对人的要求,能为未来培养人,能培养适应未来、创造未来的人。

其次,我们必须要适应当代小学教育改革发展的趋势,我对这种趋势从两个视角来看,一个是小学的视角,我们看到今天许多优质小学在强调儿童中心、学科整合、体验学习;另一个是儿童的视角,在强调儿童中心时,注重儿童精神成长、儿童核心素养培育、儿童良好品行养成等。这既彰显了当代小学教育改革的方向、立场、原则与重心,同时也是回归小学教育本质的显现。

最后,未来的教育必须要"突破"适应于工业社会的传统教育范式,走向与后工业社会、人工智能时代相适应的教育范式,即突破批量化、标准化、流程化、程式化和同质化的教育范式,构建生命性、差异性、个性化、合作性和创新性的新教育范式。这一变革的实质是跳出"知识本位"的学科教育范式,回归"生命本位"的生命教育范式,只有生命才强调差异、个性、合作、创新等。

(二)加大学科建设力度

小学教师培养关涉四个核心概念,小学教育专业、小学教师、小学教育、小学儿童。我们要明晰这四个核心概念之间的关系,即小学教育专业与小学教师培养、小学教师与小学教育、小学教育与小学儿童、小学教育专业与小学儿童。对此,我们的理解是,小学教育专业是培养小学教师的,小学教师是为小学教育服务的,小学教育是满足小学儿童生命健康成长需要的,小学教育专业的人才培养、课程设置、教育实践,必须体现小学儿童立场,只有这样才可能培养出适应未来的小学教师。这也是我们在开展小学教育专业建设与初等教育学学科建设过程逐渐明晰的,所以小学教师培养是相当复杂的,不仅是学科基础与学科教学的问题,更是人学、儿童学的问题,这对小学教师教育者的要求也是相当高的,因为所有的人几乎都没有受过有关初等教育学和儿童学的训练。

这实质关涉三个学科建设问题,一是以小学教育为研究对象的初等教育学学科建设,二是以小学教师为研究对象的小学教师教育学学科建设,三是以儿童为研究对象的儿童学学科建设。这是支撑小学教育专业建设的三大主干学科,但目前均处在刚刚起步或将要起步阶段。正因为学科建设的匮乏,才导致小学教育专业建设还难以摆脱"经验"的束缚,因此未来我们必须要加大学科建设力度。在此,我就小学教师教育学科建设,着重谈一下有关小学教师、小学教育专业、小学教师培养的三个基本观点。

一是明晰小学教师身份。长期以来,对小学教师身份的认识,主要是小学学科教学者,如小学语文教师、小学数学教师等,这样的称谓实质是"学科教学"本位的教师观,对小学教师的身份定位在知识传授上。但小学教师不是小学学科教学者,而是儿童教育工作者,这是小学教师的职业身份所在。对此,2012年《国务院关于加强教师队伍建设的意见》做出了明确要求,"促进学生健康成长是教师的出发点和落脚点"。所以我们必须回到"儿童教育工作者"的立场来思考小学教师培养问题。

那么以儿童教育为本的小学教师是什么样的?概言之,就是能以儿童生命为基点,从儿童的立场出发,遵循儿童生命成长规律、阶段特性、儿童生命需要、生命样态等,思考、设计、实施小学教育教学;能为每个个体儿童生命的健康成长提供个性化的、适合的帮助。小学教师不仅是职业人,更是独特的生命个体,今天小学教师的发展,不仅是专业发展,更是作为一个完整之人的发展,这是教师发展的根本,也是小学教师教育学学科建设的原点。

二是认清小学教育专业特性。这是我们在2018年接受师范专业认证时备受困扰的一个问题。尽管小学教育专业发展已有 20 年,但对小学教育专业的特殊性还缺乏清晰的认识,对小学教育专业认证标准的解读缺乏理论支撑,因此撰写小学教育专业认证报告的定位成为一个难题。在我院小学教育专业被指定为全国小学教育专业认证"打样"单位,接受师范类专业"联合认证"专家进校的汇报中,我提出了对小学教育专业特性的认识,必须要"跳出"三种定式与思维:一是学科性 + 教育性,这是中学教育专业的特性,中学教师培养是"双专业",即学科专业 + 教育专业;二是教育学性质,这是注重"教育学"的教育学专业的性质;三是通识性 + 技能性,这是中师的性质。回归小学教育专业本身,寻找属于它自身的特性。

基于前期研究,我提出小学教育专业的特性主要体现为儿童性、综合性和养成性。小学教育专业建设是基于对儿童的认识与理解、促进儿童生命健康成长,并体现在人才培养的目标规格与课程设置与培养活动之中,故概括为儿童性;小学教育专业建设注重通识性、多学科性、多能力性,以体现小学教育、小学教师培养的综合性;养成性是指小学教育专业人才培养强调实践性、过程性与持续性。简言之,小学教育专业的实质是小学儿童教育专业。

三是理解小学教师教育性质。在我看来,小学教师教育是"同行 - 共在"的人的教育。所谓"同行"指的是大学教师、师范生和小学生之"三人"在小学教师培养过程中的"同行"。人的教育一定是有心的教育,是心中有人的教育,即大学教师在培养小学教师时,心中要有师范生,不仅如此,还要有小学儿童;师范生在学习成为小学教师时,心中要有小学儿童,只有从小学儿童出发来培养小学教师,才能培养出心中有儿童的小学教师。所谓"共在"指的是在小学教师培养中,过去、现在和未来的"共在",人、教育与环境的"共在"。

其实,相比于中学教师的培养,小学教师的培养更为复杂。在小学教育专业课程设置中,不仅包括小学各教学科目的学科基础与学科教学、教育学与心理学等方面内容,而且还包括儿童学、初等教育学等方面内容,后者对高校小学教师教育者而言也是挑战,几乎所有的人都没有受过有关初等教育学和儿童学的训练。未来必须要加大初等教育学、小学教师教育学、儿童学学科建设力度,不仅为了学科建设本身,而且也是促进小学教育专业教师队伍成长的最佳路径。

(三)深入探索卓越小学教师培养模式

无论是《教师教育课程标准》《教师专业标准》,还是《师范专业认证标准》,其基本理念都是强调以学生为本、学生中心,故小学教育专业人才培养模式必然要凸显学生为本;未来不能被人工智能替代的是生命、情感、感受和体验,而这正是未来小学教师安身立命之所在,故未来卓越小学教师培养的关键是在思想观念、思维方式与行动路径上突破学科教育本位,回归儿童教育本位。

在此,以首都师范大学小学教育专业为例来阐释小学教育专业人才培养模式的升级探索。首都师范大学小学教育专业,自建院以来,经过短暂的"大文大理"(1999—2001)培养阶段,进入了"综合培养、发展专长、注重研究、全程实践"培养模式(2002—2018),称为 1.0 版;经过师范专业认证,明确提出"儿童取向的卓越小学教师培养模式",称为 2.0 版。这一模式的探索开启于 2012 年"教育部专业综合改革试点项目",在探索小学教育专业综合改革过程中,围绕小学教师核心素养及其指标体系构建了小学教育专业课程地图、人才培养方案;2014 年明确了探索卓越小学教师培养模式,特别是 2018 年师范专业认证,深度反思了人才培养模式,进一步凝练特色、明确未来发展方向,提出了儿童取向的卓越小学教师培养模式,强调"具有未来教育家潜质卓越小学教师"培养目标、"儿童为本、师德优秀、主兼多能、人机协同、国际视野"的培养规格。

所谓儿童取向,强调的是小学教师的培养应基于小学儿童生命、以促进儿童生命健康成长为目的,能实施遵循儿童生命规律的小学教育。儿童取向既是教育的目的体现、人本教育理念的落实,也是实现教育之目的的必然要求。儿童是小学教育主体,小学儿童的生命成长、认识世界的方式、生活状态等是综合的、整合的,小学教育必然要遵循小学儿童生命成长特性,为其生命健康成长提供有效能量,小学教师必须具有以儿童为本的教育教学能力,这就要求小学教育专业建设应凸显生命性、儿童性、综合性,并落实在小学教育专业课程体系中。如我院将与"通识课程""实践课程"并列的"专业课程"设计成了三大模块:儿童类课程、教师教育类课程、专业方向类(主教 + 兼教)课程。

关于德育方面。"立德树人"是教育的根本任务,小学教师的培养必须落实这一个根本任务。目前我院的主要措施有,一是构建师范生师德养成体系,这是2019年北京高等教育"本科教学改革创新项目——师范生师德养成体系建设研究",从师德养成指标体系、师德养成课程体系、学生师德践行体系、教师师德示范体系、师德养成评价体系这五大体系展开研究,将师范生的师德教育落实;二是进一步推进教育部"三全育人"综合改革试点单位建设工作,挖掘学院办学思想、育人理念、学子精神的思想文化内涵,凝心聚力,形成全院师生认同并遵循的价值理念;三是德育课程与教材建设,包括小学教育专业德育课程与小学教育专业德育方向课程建设,并向国家级精品课程与教材建设方向努力。目前《小学德育实践》教材荣获北京市高等教育精品教材、入选"十二五"普通高等教育本科国家级规划教材,《小学生品德发展与道德教育》课程入选首批"国家级一流本科课程"(线上线下混合)。

关于儿童课程方面。这是我院近十年来重点研究领域,自2010年人才培养方案中增设《儿童研究专题》课程以来,尤其是2014年小学教师核心素养的提出,将"认识儿童"作为小学教师三大素养之一,并将此素养培养指标体系化,从儿童需要与表达、身体与健康、社会性与道德、认知与学习、安全与权利五个维度展开,将儿童研究与儿童课程开发与实施相结合,完成了《儿童需要与表达》《儿童权利与保障》《儿童性健康教育》《特殊儿童教育》等多门专业基础课、《儿童发展》《小学生心理辅导》等专业核心课、《儿童文学概论》《儿童文学作品赏析与教学》《儿童戏剧与创作》等专业方向课建设。目前,我院有关儿童课程开发已覆盖小学教育专业课程结构的全方位,未来还将进一步开展教育现场的儿童研究及儿童课程。

关于"大－小结合"课程。这是小学教育专业最具特色的课程,也是我院对小学教育专业开创性的贡献。小学教育专业具有自身特性,它不同于中学教育专业、教育学专业和中师教育,它的课程体系不能简单照搬、照抄高师的或中师的课程,必须要有专属于这个专业的"专有"的课程。而这个专属的课程就是"大－小结合"课程,即大学学科知识与小学教学内容相结合的课程,以前者为基础并向后者转化,直接"对接"小学教育教学的课程,这是培养小学教师的重要支撑,也是初等教育学学科建设的重要方面,目前我院已先后开发了《文本解读与文学鉴赏》《写作基础与儿童文学创作》《汉字学与识字教学》《语用学与语文教学》等一系列课程。

关于生命教育课程。生命教育是每个人的人生必修课,尤其是在学生时代,特别是师范大学生。这不仅源自他们自身正处在遭遇与思考生命问题的重要阶段,而且还源自他们未来所要从事的教师职业之需要。自 2007 年我院开始设置《生命教育》选修课,并在教育实习、毕业论文选题、科研课题中开展生命教育研究与实践探索,又于 2016 年设置"生命教育与班主任工作"兼教方向,设置了四门必修课,包括《多视角的生命解读》和《小学生命教育教师的素养与能力》两门基础课,《班级管理中的生命教育》和《生命教育课程与教学》两门核心课。

面对未来的小学教师培养,我们还要加大关于人机协同课程和国际视野课程建设,前者包括人工智能、多元读写、数据分析等课程;后者包括国际理解教育、比较小学教育等课程,并能在国际舞台上讲好中国小学教师教育的故事。

Analysis and Prospect of Elementary Teacher Training Modes in China

Hui Liu

Abstract: The origins of the cultivation of primary teachers in China could be traced back to the late 1890s, since when it had been a century – long task for the secondary normal schools. The junior college model was launched in the 1980s, but it was not fully popularized. In 1999, the undergraduate model has been adopted and developed rapidly. In such a background, the exploration of the excellent primary teachers' cultivation model has been initiated since 2014. Generally speaking, there are four key research issues on the journey of primary school teachers' cultivation at the undergraduate level, including the personnel? cultivation model, the major setup, the professional development of school teachers and the discipline construction of elementary education. Besides, the undergraduate program includes various kinds of orientation – skill orientation, knowledge orientation, ability orientation, practice orientation, research orientation, humanistic orientation and so on. Furthermore, the underlying problems of primary teachers' cultivation involve the dialectic relationship between practice and research, the positioning of professionalism and disciplinarity, the understanding of children – oriented education and subject – oriented teaching, the difference between cultivating children's integrated personality and delivering specialized knowledge, the contradiction between reality and ideality and so on. In a word, it depends on

the discipline construction to provide satisfactory answers to the problems listed a-
bove. Looking into the future of the cultivation of primary teachers in China, challenges of the new era? should be tackled? to strengthen the programs of elementary education, childhood education and primary teacher education. Efforts need to
be made to explore new cultivation models, such as the "children – oriented" excellent primary teachers' cultivation model of Capital Normal University.

Keywords: children – oriented excellent primary teachers' cultivation model, discipline construction, model orientation, primary teachers' cultivation model

当前小学全科教师培养模式的桎梏与突破

王智秋　许红敏

首都师范大学初等教育学院，南京晓庄学院

摘要:根据当前国家对小学全科教师培养的定位,培养院校必须明晰小学教育的价值及小学教师的专业身份定位、明晰小学学科学习与儿童发展的关系等关键立场,澄清全科教师内涵和专业属性,认识到当前培养目标的局限性、素质标准的模糊性、培养内容的低融合度和培养动力不足等桎梏存在。大学教师教育应当发挥对小学教育发展的价值引领作用,通过改变培养观念带动行动突破,逐渐凸显小学全科教师的普适性而非农村专属的专业身份,素质结构扬弃学科知识能力的排列组合,走向儿童发展立场的跨学科教育能力的形成,参与全科教师培养的小学和地方政府作为利益相关者,应突破任务导向的线性被动合作,达至协同互惠的良性互动模式。

关键词:小学全科教师;培养模式;普适性

引　言

随着国家对以师资队伍为核心的教育资源配置公平化的重视,近些年陆续通过多份文件下达关于卓越教师培养和农村教师队伍建设的相关指导意见与工作部署。其中关于"小学全科教师"培养的问题多次被提及。2012

年《关于大力推进农村义务教育教师队伍建设的意见》中提出"采取定向委托培养等特殊招生方式,扩大小学全科教师培养规模";2015 年《乡村教师支持计划 2015—2020 年》中提出"采取多种方式定向培养'一专多能'的乡村教师"。2014 年《教育部关于实施卓越教师培养计划的意见》中提出"针对小学教育的实际需求,重点探索小学全科教师培养模式,培养一批热爱小学教育事业、知识广博、能力全面,能够胜任小学多学科教育教学需要的卓越小学教师";2018 年《关于实施卓越教师培养计划 2.0 的意见》提出"面向培养素养全面、专长发展的卓越小学教师,重点探索借鉴国际小学全科教师培养经验、继承我国养成教育传统的培养模式"。2018 年 1 月《关于全面深化新时代教师队伍建设改革的意见》提出"鼓励地方政府和相关院校因地制宜采取定向招生、定向培养、定期服务等方式,为乡村学校及教学点培养'一专多能'的教师,优先满足老少边穷地区教师补充需要"。2018 年 3 月《教师教育振兴行动计划(2018—2022 年)》提出"通过公费定向培养、到岗退费等多种方式,为乡村小学培养补充全科教师"。六份文件中的"小学教师"内涵大致可分为两类,一类是在农村小学师资匮乏及整体素质偏低情形下所需要的"全科教师",其中"一专多能"的乡村教师提法也属于此,另一类是针对小学教育的实际需求,借鉴国际经验所需培养的卓越"全科教师"。

关于当前多所院校进行的小学全科教师培养行动也同上分为两类,但据实地调研及文献查阅,满足社会需求的培养定位院校远远多于后者,关于"小学全科教师"培养所开展的实证研究、思辨研究也是后者甚少。再加之当前非偏远农村地区小学教师"非全科化"尤为普遍,所以似乎也带来了一种普遍理解:优质教育环境下是不需要"小学全科教师"的,或者"小学全科教师"只能成为一种追求卓越的理想和少数"卓越学校"的需求,与当下的众多普通小学并无关系。真的是这样吗?

一、当前小学全科教师培养模式的普遍框架与桎梏

模式是对实践活动的简约化表述,培养模式简约地反映了教育实践活动中培养目标、培养规格、培养过程及评价等基本要素之间的规律性联系。[①] 就当前"小学全科教师"培养模式的全国普遍框架来看,存在一些窄化和异化小学全科教师内涵的现象,也正是这些束缚了小学全科教师培养的现状与前景。

(一)农村需求导向带来的培养目标局限

当前我国多数农村学校教师队伍匮乏,尤其是大量的小规模学校中限于教师编制数和小学生生源数量比例的原因,出现迫不得已的教师包班、复式教学、教师"一顶多"等现象,此时能够一师承担多门学科的教学成为一种无奈的"优化"配置手段。所以"全科"教师成为农村小学最大的供给,由此产生的"农村定向"的师范生源出入机制使全科教师培养目标在社会使命上表现出"扶贫济弱"的色彩,"扎根农村"的专业情意教育成为定向培养的必修课,也因此使全科教师的培养目标在服务去向上表现出区域局限性意味,同时"一顶多"的岗位定性使全科教师培养在历史使命上也表现出解决"当前区域发展失衡"的阶段性特征。

(二)多学科兼教导向带来的素质标准定位模糊

多学科兼教的需求使小学全科教师之"全"始终在"学科知识与能力"的数量上追求之多、之广,是"一专多能"还是"多专多能"抑或是"诸项全能",成为衡量小学全科教师之"全"的主要标准。"渊博"的学科知识和配套技能成为全科教师的重要素质标准,既然是标准就应有定性和定量的衡定,所掌

[①] 阴天榜、张建华、杨炳学:《论培养模式》,《中国高教研究》,1998 年第 4 期。

握学科的门类、门数、掌握深度如何来衡定,根据学科在小学中的地位、岗位实际需要还是遵从"多多益善"成为一种矛盾,也因此使全科教师的素质标准变得模糊不定、规则不一。

(三)大学学科壁垒带来的培养内容融合度低

自从取消中师,小学教师的培养开始进入大学模式中,不管是综合性大学还是师范专科学校,都不再以中师的"年级制"管理学生,换而为系部学院管理。系部学院多以学科归属而分,教师教育者也是以学科身份出现,这就带来培养者的"单一学科特性"和培养对象"全科特性"之间的供需矛盾。由此出现师范生学科课程的"拼盘化",针对将来的任教学科需要积累下各个学科的相关知识结构与课程教学理论、技能,学习内容"大容量"、负担重,同时学科逻辑融合度低。如果院校有师资队伍在学科方面较齐全的初等教育学院那是比较理想的现象,但随着大学学科建设的需要,更多教师教育者出于自身专业发展的需要而更倾向加入学科专属学院,所以全科教师培养内容难以避免课程"拼盘化"、知识分散、逻辑隔阂、融合度低。

(四)小学评价方式带来的培养动力不足

从当前小学教师接受的主流评价方式来看,"全科教师"在教师资格认定和职后专业技术评审中都在需要确定"任教学科"这一问题上遇到比较现实的矛盾。从2017年开始国家在教师资格认定时新设"全科教师"类别,但由于社会总体认可度低、局限性强,加之各地教师入职考试对任教学科的惯例要求等,使除"定向培养"之外的学生不敢涉入"全科教师"行列,也是有意去避免日后专业技术晋级时必须参加某一学科序列考核选聘时的困境。现象背后是当前社会对全科教师之"全"只是"学科之全"的浅表性理解,致使全科教师的专业身份内涵窄化,职场准入和选拔机制也因此带来了大学对"全科教师"培养的谨慎。

二、小学全科教师培养中关键立场的讨论

要想回答引言中最后提出的问题,我们需要首先讨论几个关乎小学全科教师培养中的关键立场。立场明晰,才能知道当前所出现的桎梏症结在哪里,也才可以更进一步去谈行动突破问题。

(一)小学教育与小学教师的价值定位问题

小学教育是人一生接受教育的基础学段,无论是"双基"教学还是"核心素养"教育,都十分重视小学教育这一基础作用,既是知识能力积累形成的基础,更是社会参与、人格养成、身心健康发展的基础。同时小学也是人生得以启蒙的阶段,"幼儿养性、童蒙养正""蒙以养正,圣功也",这些古训能传承至今说明其具有经典意义。不断灌输的知识教条与强化训练,增加的无非是儿童对知识教条的盲从与迷信,损耗的却是儿童自由自主的精神。显然,忽视"儿童之为儿童"的教育不仅忽视了儿童存在的意义,曲解了儿童教育的启蒙意义,而且不利于儿童的和谐发展。①

小学教师是儿童的启蒙者,是学生学习的启动者,而不是操控者,不能只顾把学生引向自己的教学计划、阐释和教学进程,而是必须尊重学生的自由,让他们找到自己的道路和自主权。② 小学全科教师有其自身的价值诉求,即推动小学回归知识、兴趣与人性的启蒙。③ 因此谢维和教授提及小学教育的价值时发表了自己的"顶灯理论",④并以顶灯照亮全程和中学实施分科教学的"探照灯理论"做了形象的对比,由此说明小学儿童成长需要的课

---

① 姚伟、索长青:《儿童启蒙教育意义的现代探寻》,《东北师大学报(哲学社会科学版)》,2013年第5期。

② [瑞士]安德烈·焦尔当:《学习的本质》,杭零译,华东师范大学出版社,2015年。

③ 江净帆:《小学全科教师的价值诉求与能力特征》,《中国教育学刊》,2016年。

④ 谢维和:《小学的价值》,《人民教育》,2015年第3期。

程应当是没有分明的界限和规约的,也继而说明了小学教育的奠基性作用。

(二)小学学科学习与儿童发展的关系讨论

核心素养理念下的小学学科学习主要是指在学科活动中进行学科知识的学习,但我们的知识并不总是以各门学科的方式严谨地、分门别类地发生在我们的生活需要里,也并不是一门学科的思维方式和观念就对应"认识和解决"生活中的某现象或问题。尤其是在儿童的生活里,世界以复杂性、偶然性、现象性朝向他们。6~12 岁的小学儿童不同于中学生具有抽象思维发展模式,他们的思维尚未细致分化,课程当强调综合化,学科知识的传递应以儿童的生活经验为基础,要求教师具有广泛的通识知识,不仅有能力关怀儿童认知方面的发展,而且要有兴趣和能力关怀儿童的情感精神生活。[①] 但我们的教育体系不是用起矫正作用的东西来抵制学科分开,而是服从于它。从小学它就教我们孤立对象(于其环境)、划分学科(而不是发现它们的联系)、分别问题(而不是把它们加以连接和整合)。[②] 所以在小学中,教师教学活动的设计与实施理应以综合化、情境脉络化、活动化的形式来呈现学习任务才适合该年龄段儿童的认知与情感发展方式。如现行的项目化学习(PBL),就是从某一个学科切入,聚焦关键的学科知识和能力,用驱动性问题指向这些知识和能力,在解决问题的过程中进行学科与学科、学科与生活、学科与人际的联系与拓展,用项目成果呈现出对知识的创造性运用和深度理解。[③]

(三)全科教师之"全"的内涵理解与专业属性

小学全科教师是相对于"授教单一学科内容的分科教师"而言,"全科"不应只是在增量上思考或只是在承担小学学科教学科目的数量上做"加

---

① 　朱小蔓:《认识小学儿童,认识小学教育》,《中国教育学刊》,2003 年第 8 期。
② 　[法]埃德加·莫兰:《复杂性理论与教育问题》,陈一壮译,北京大学出版社,2004 年。
③ 　夏雪梅:《在学科中进行项目化学习:学生视角》,《全球教育展望》,2019 年第 2 期。

法",而应把"全科"理解为一种综合能力。"全科"的关键在于能否以"全科"的背景、视野和能力展开多学科、跨学科的综合化教学,实现小学课程教学的科学整合。

所以,教师教育走到繁荣发展的今天,我们不应当再仅仅将全科教师培养视为一种教学劳动力的节约,而应当是一种科学的育人理念。全科教师也不应是以满副武装的学科门类知识为标志,而应当以具有学科融合的理念、具有整体认知儿童的能力为基准,[①]实现从教"多书"到育"全人"本位的转变。职前教师教育无须一味地想方设法创造更多的课时去传授自认完备的各科知识体系,而应当使师范生获取更多"关于儿童建构与习得知识的方法""儿童与知识之间微妙互动"的原理与实操。

(四)时代变革与全球视野中的小学全科教师性质

我国百年中师一直在培养小学全科教师,但那时并没有"全科"之说,默认为可以根据小学发展需要任意承担一门或多门学科的教学。这样的"全科"是在我们师资短缺、教育整体质量偏低、国家发展、知识更新都较为缓慢的情形下适用的教师,这种"全科"完成的依然是"分科"模式下的教学,即所谓"一顶多"和"任意切换",与我们上文所探讨的全科教师之"全"的深层内涵和专业性表现是不一样的。与美国、英国、芬兰、日本等国家的小学教师专业性内涵也是不一样的,在其他国家小学教师做着"全科"之事却并无须"全科"之冠名,那是因为无"分科"之对照,是一种默认的小学教师之应然与实然。芬兰的"现象教学(Phenomenon Based Teaching)"、日本的"班主任(Home Room Teacher)",小学教师为全科教师是一种存在常态,是"非分科"的小学教育教学的必然要求。美国小学全科教师具有较为漫长的历史积淀。这些国家的教师之"全科"、之"常态"都属于对小学教师专业身份的普

---

① 许红敏、曹慧英:《小学全科教师的内涵辨析与培养策略——基于江苏省的需求》,《教育理论与实践》,2016 年第 11 期。

遍认识,全科之"全"都是以儿童发展为逻辑起点,能够融汇各学科的知识来综合设计和开展教育活动的教师专业属性。因此,当前提出我国小学教师队伍的"全科"化是一件顺"势"而为的事,也是需要突破单一的"农村导向、阶段需求"等桎梏来重新审视实际教育发展需求的事。

三、小学全科教师培养观念的改变与行动突破

基于上述关键立场的讨论,对小学教师之专业身份定位和小学全科教师之"全"的深刻、全面认识,并结合当前培养现状中所表现出的观念偏颇、行动受限等,建议可做以下突破,以期为小学全科教师"正名"并"做实"。

(一)培养目标突破"农村学科专家"执念,凸显小学全科教师的普适性专业身份

为农村定向培养小学全科教师是我国当前缓解教师队伍困境之策,也是努力实现教育公平的国家支持战略。一名全科教师可以承担多学科教学任务,是在农村分科教学背景下最好的资源配置了,属于现阶段农村教育发展的实际需求。但"承担学科教学"只是全科教师的部分功能或者说阶段性功能,如果我们能够突破对全科教师的窄化认识,则可以转变其功能,实现从"学科教学专家"到"儿童发展启蒙者"的身份转变,这种转变不仅可以实现农村教学需要,而且具有城乡普适性。我们不能因为现阶段的局部需求而对"全科教师"的认识窄化,需要什么规格的小学教师由小学教育的基础性、小学儿童的成长需要及小学教师的专业属性决定。小学教师需要在人格上具有情感性和人文性,在知识结构上突出综合性,强调教育教学的技能性和艺术性,养成思维模式的半童性并具有教育现场的研究反思能力。[①] 全科之"全"非"学科之全",非一时农村之需,而是一种追求卓越的小学教师专

---

① 　王智秋:《小学教育专业人才培养模式的研究与探索》,《教育研究》,2007 年第 5 期。

业特质,此为普通小学的共有需求。

(二)素质结构突破"学科知识能力的排列组合",走向儿童发展立场的跨学科教育能力

全科之"全"并不排斥学科知识和能力,只是并不认同教师所具备的学科知识和能力,只是各学科之间的简单拼盘,失去了一个有机体应当具备的内在整合性。这种相互独立的学科领域会导致小学教师在实际教学中只能让自己的知识"轮番登场"。"在现今学校中已经可见的结果是:小学语文教师不一定会教小学历史课或数学课,数学教师也不见得能教语文课。低年级语文教师不会教高年级语文课……如不冲破这种人为设置的凝固分工的樊篱,势必成为"跛足的教师"。① 学科知识是儿童经验生长的重要组成部分,儿童的世界具有它自己生活的统一性和完整性。儿童一到学校,多种多样的学科便把他的世界加以割裂和肢解。② 所谓儿童立场,则是强调教育活动的逻辑起点与终点都应当是儿童发展。通过儿童自身参与,真正将外在知识与儿童现有经验相融从而促进儿童发展,儿童为体,知识为用,知识又是跨学科融合的、与生活经验能够相联系的知识。

跨学科教育也称整合教育(Intergrative Studies),是以普遍性、全面性的课程改革为中心,通过专业设置、课程结构、教材教法等方面的跨学科革新,使教学出现崭新面貌。例如,法国小学在 20 世纪 70 年代末的跨学科改革中,曾合并了所有的教学活动,并把这些活动分为法语、数学、文化娱乐、体育运动四组。③ 小学教师跨学科教育的能力就是在学科整合过程中培养儿童的素养与能力,教学活动不再围绕单一的学科进行,而是将着力点放在某个特定的关乎儿童世界的问题解决过程中,强调利用多学科的知识、跨越学

---

① 陈桂生:《"教师专业化"面面观》,《全球教育展望》,2017 年第 1 期。
② [美]杜威:《儿童与课程》,顾岳中译,赵祥麟校;吕达,刘立德,邹海燕:《杜威教育文集》(第1 卷),人民教育出版社,2005 年。
③ 刘仲林:《天地交而万物通》,广西师范大学出版社,2004 年。

科边界综合解决问题。在具体课程实施中，多学科式的做法始于内容和技巧，知识被固定于事前决定的顺序，而统整的做法则确认外在知识，然后依周遭的问题而安排其顺序。[①]

(三)培养主体双方突破任务导向的线性合作,达至协同互惠的利益相关者良性互动模式

经济伦理学家弗里曼（Freeman）提出："组织中的利益相关者是指任何能够影响公司目标的实现,或者受公司目标实现影响的团体和个人。"[②]在小学全科教师培养过程中,大学教师教育机构、地方政府、实习基地学校、定向就业学校以及师范生、教师教育者、小学生、教育行政管理机构等都属于这个组织目标的利益相关者,他们之间的协同互动形成一种利益相关者模型。

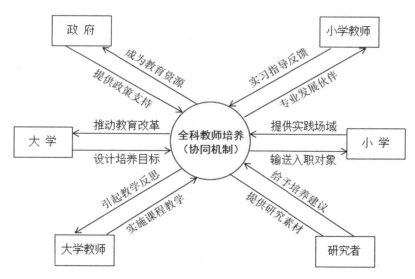

小学全科教师协同培养利益相关者模型

①　[美]James A. Beane:《课程统整》,单文经等译,华东师范大学出版社,2003 年。

②　[美]弗里曼:《战略管理——利益相关者方法》,王彦华、梁豪译,上海译文出版社,2006 年,第 55 页。

其中大学与小学为两个培养主体,常见的协同合作方式一般是大学学习与小学见实习、理论课程与实践课程分别承担、各司其职的模式,政府在双方之间发挥指导协调的中介作用,这种铁路警察、任务导向式的合作模式难以实现真正意义上的"协同发展"。实习基地小学不仅是提供实践场域、负责实习指导的贡献者、服务方,也是大学教师教育机构培养建议的供给者、反馈方,同时他们也是大学培养成果的消费者、享用方,先前的贡献也是在为得到一个更好的"产品"而投入的前期努力。大学既是小学全科教师的生产者、供应方,也是与小学开展教育理论与实践研究的合作方,研究促进培养质量、促进小学科学发展。政府和地方管理机构是区域教育质量的"责任人",为促进双方良性互动,应当主动推动合作,利用正确的价值导向在小学教育的发展、教师入职选聘、职后教育、教师教育等方面把握科学的方向、出台合理的评价方式,促进地方教师队伍的整体提升和地方教育供给侧需求的平稳合作。在这中间,还有一个隐形的旁观者但也可以称之为合作者的角色:全科教师培养的学界研究者,他采集互动过程中的各类资料,借用科学的解释框架为整体互动方提供冷静理智的行动指南,并建立这一领域的相关理论。以上多方在业已形成的"利益相关者"模型中实现协同互惠。

(四)作为培养主体和教育研究机构,大学要对小学教育发展起价值引领作用

关于小学全科教师的普适性问题,虽然在专业身份和社会职能上得到了合理的解释,但是否真正可以以"追求卓越"的教师形象普遍出现在小学中,以现状来看委实困难。小学教育的主流组织框架是"学科—课程—课时—教师",教师的专业职能本是多方面的,却成了轮流为每个学科服务的专业技术员。这种时间划分让学生很少有时间投入一项任务或计划的完成

中。课时的设置导致学生一直在"切换频道",不可能表现出创造性。[①] 目前多数小学虽已经认可核心素养导向的教育理念,但主流评价方式还未能褪脱学科导向,所以也难以开发跨学科融合课程,分科教师受用于当前需求,因此全科教师的培养则未成为非农村市场的正常需求。大学作为培养主体和教育研究机构应担当起小学教师教育的引领者角色,以正确的价值导向通过培养教师来引领小学教育从理念到行动快速转轨驶入"以促进儿童核心素养发展"道路。清华附小开展"主题教学"、上海多校开展"项目化学习"及已经发展较为成熟的 STEAM 教学等,这些成功的经验都可以证明小学全科教师培养的适用性和正确引领性。结合国情实际、借鉴国际经验培养出能够推动我国小学教育科学发展的卓越教师是大学教师教育义不容辞的责任。

Constraints and Breakthrough of Training Modes of General Subject Teachers in Elementary School

Zhiqiu Wang　Hongmin Xu

Abstract:The national orientation of the general subject teachers in elementary schools requires the university fostering teachers to clarity the key positions, such as the value of the elementary education and the professional status of teachers, the relationship of subject learning and the development of children. It also

---

① 窦桂梅:《让儿童站立在学校正中央——从"三个超越"到"成志教育"的升华之路》,《中国教育学刊》,2017 年。

calls for the university to clarify the connotation of general subject teachers and the professional characteristics, to realize shackles such as the limitations of the current objectives in cultivation, the fuzziness of the standards in quality, the low degrees of fusion in the content of cultivation and the shortage of motivation in cultivation. Teacher education in university should play a role in the guidance of value to the development of elementary education. The change of ideas in cultivation leads to the breakthrough of actions, highlighting the universality in professional status instead of the countryside – exclusive status. The structure of qualities sublates the permutation and combination of subject – oriented knowledge and abilities, leading to the formation of children's cross – subject ability from the perspective of the development of children. The participants of the cultivation, namely the elementary school and the local government, should break through the mode of liner task – based passive cooperation, to achieve a reciprocal benign interaction.

创新公费师范教育模式，促进基础教育均衡发展

——湖南第一师范学院乡村公费师范教育的改革与实践

刘志敏

湖南第一师范学院，教授

摘要：针对当前我国乡村小学教师培养过程中存在的问题，湖南第一师范学院在继承中师优秀教育传统的基础上，结合现代师范教育转型发展趋势，探索建立出"初中起点、六年一贯；综合培养、分向发展；三性融合、三位一体；实践导向，师德为先"的"初中起点六年制本科优秀小学教师培养一师模式"。"一师模式"有效解决了乡村教师"下不去、留不住、干不好"的问题，为湖南省培养补充了近万名高素质的优秀小学教师。为使公费师范教育成为一项可长期持续发展的事业和长期有效的乡村教师队伍培养补充机制，提出了鼓励乡村教师长期安心从教、乐教的政策建议。

关键词：一师模式；公费师范教育；政策

　　湖南第一师范学院是毛泽东、蔡和森、何叔衡、任弼时、李维汉等老一辈无产阶级革命家的母校，是中国共产主义运动和新民主主义革命的策源地。学校的前身城南书院始建于南宋 1161 年，1903 年始立为湖南师范馆，是中国现代师范教育的摇篮之一，素有"千年学府、百年师范"的美誉。毛泽东在学校学习、工作八个春秋。毛泽东称赞"一师是个好学校"，亲笔题写了"第一师范"校名，并立下"要做人民的先生，先做人民的学生"的校训。

116 年来,学校始终高举师范教育旗帜,坚守师范教育净土,是全国唯一举全校之力培养优秀小学教师的本科师范院校,形成了"培养小学教师,培训小学教师,研究小学教育,造就民族英才"的鲜明教师教育办学特色。学校目前是全国师范生比例最高的本科院校(80%),也是全国公费师范生比例最高、规模最大的院校(70%,11598 人),为湖南省乡村教育培养了近万名"下得去、留得住、教得好、有发展"的优秀小学教师。学校现为全国重点文物保护单位、全国爱国主义教育示范基地、国家教育体制改革试点单位、国家级骨干小学教师培训基地和国家卓越小学教师计划承担单位。

一、乡村小学教师队伍及教师培养中存在的问题

(一)乡村小学教师供给不足,结构失衡

目前,我国小学教师需求量仍然很大。据测算,不考虑流动性因素,我国小学教师每年平均需新增近 27 万人。小学教师尤其是乡村小学教师缺口较大,而且结构失衡。第一,学科结构失衡。英语、科学、音乐、美术、体育等方面的优质教师严重匮乏。第二,学历层次偏低。专任教师中具有本科及以上学历的比例偏低,且大多为自考或函授本科,全日制本科学历的教师很少,乡村小学教师中具有本科学历的比例更低。第三,年龄老化严重。据湖南省的一项调查显示,50 岁以上的小学教师约占 20%,有的小学甚至超过 50%,乡村小学教师年龄断层现象在今后几年将更加凸显。第四,师资流失严重。乡村基础条件差,农村教师发展空间有限,加之农村空心化严重,导致很多教师的职业认同感不强,不能安心在乡村从教,很多骨干教师频频流向城市或选择考公务员、转岗等。

(二)师范生源质量不高

过去的师范生源大多来自综合素质较高的优秀初中或高中毕业生,生

源质量较好。随着我国师范教育体制由三级走向两级,中师培养小学师资历史使命的终结,师范生免费培养、定向分配等优惠政策的取消及教师经济社会地位的削弱,近年来出现了师范专业生源质量普遍下降的问题。

(三)优质师资难以下到乡村小学

乡村小学尤其是一些偏远地区的小学条件艰苦、信息闭塞、交通不便,文娱设施缺乏,教学任务繁重,工资待遇偏低,住房及医疗服务难以得到有效保障,这些都导致乡村小学师资力量非常薄弱且得不到及时补充。即使在今日大学生就业日益艰难的情况下,愿意到乡村小学任教的师范生比例仍然很低,存在学生专业理想信念不牢固,"下不去、留不住、干不好"的问题。

(四)培养模式难以适应小学教育新要求

综合性是小学课程的突出特点,小学教师应具有广博的科学文化知识。而新进入本科层次的小学教师培养由于受中学教师培养模式的影响多采用分科培养,注重学科体系的构建,"重理论灌输,轻技能培养",致使培养出来的小学教师知识结构单一,知识面狭窄,教学基本功不扎实,学科融通能力欠缺,极大地影响了小学教育质量的提高。导致师范毕业生难以充分胜任小学教育要求,上不好课、带不好班,出现"小学教师的学历提高了,专业化水平反而下降了"的尴尬局面。

总体来看,我国乡村小学教师队伍普遍存在"年龄老化、结构失衡、素质不高、流失严重"的现状,以及小学教师培养过程中普遍存在的"生源质量不高、专业情意不牢、教学技能不强、学科知识不宽、就业机制不畅"等问题,我校不断探索创新,创造性地构建了特色鲜明的乡村小学教师培养补充机制,为湖南省乡村教育培养补充了大量优秀小学教师,在贯彻落实党中央、国务院《乡村教师支持计划(2015—2020年)》上走在了全国前列。

二、我校在乡村公费师范教育上的改革创新

我校从 2006 年起,在全国率先启动了"初中起点五年制小学教师公费定向培养计划";为适应小学教师学历逐步本科化的发展趋势,2008 年又启动了"高中起点四年制本科小学教师公费定向培养计划";针对初中起点五年制专科生源质量不够理想、理论基础不够扎实、学科水平不够高,以及高中起点四年制本科生综合艺体素质可塑性不够强、教师职业技能不够突出等问题,又于 2010 年在全国创造性地实施了"初中起点六年制本科层次农村小学教师定向培养计划"。2010 年,我校成为全国教育体制改革试点单位。2014 年,我校成为全国首批 20 所入选卓越小学教师培养计划的单位。

经过多年探索,在继承我校中师优秀教育传统的基础上,结合现代师范教育转型发展趋势,我校探索建立了"初中起点、六年一贯;综合培养、分向发展;三性融合、三位一体;实践导向,师德为先"的"初中起点六年制本科小学教师培养模式"。该模式以乡村小学教师队伍培养补充机制创新为核心,以小学卓越教师综合素质提升为主线,以师德规范养成为保障,已培养出近万名具有"四能四会"(能说会道、能唱会跳、能写会画、能教会研)"下得去、留得住、教得好、有发展"的高素质小学教师。

1. 传承中师优秀传统,创新教育学制,实施六年一贯制培养

六年制的招生对象为应届初中毕业生,学制六年,学历层次为本科,采用学籍管理"二·四分段"、培养过程"六年一贯"的方式进行培养。学生入学后的前两年注册为中职学籍,两年期满参加当年普通高校招生对口升学考试,招生计划纳入当年全省普通高校对口升学招生计划,考试成绩达到省当年划定录取控制分数线的,获得本科学籍并继续学习四年。本科修业期满,成绩合格者由培养学校颁发初中起点本科毕业证书和学士学位证书。

2. 严把招生入口,强化综合测试,确保师范教育优质生源

(1)报考基本要求:报考"初中起点六年制本科卓越小学教师"计划的考

生要求热爱祖国,热爱教育事业,品行良好,遵纪守法,志愿从事农村教育事业;中考成绩不低于当年当地省级示范性普通高中计划内招生录取控制分数线。

(2)招生过程管理按照"学生自愿报名→学校初审推荐→县市区教育局初选公示→市州教育局和培养学校综合测试→县市区教育局组织考生体检→市州教育局预录并公示→县市区人民政府与考生签订培养协议书→培养学校录取→省教育厅审核"的程序进行。

(3)实施综合测试,选拔优质生源。在考生初中毕业会考基础上,由培养学校对考生实施包括笔试、教师职业发展潜质测试和音体美专业技能测试在内的综合测试,确保选拔出具有良好培养潜力的优质生源。

3.按需招生、按需设编、公费培养、定向就业,畅通毕业出口

(1)按需招生。县市区教育行政部门根据本地区未来教师补充和课程建设需求,提出本年度小学教师培养招生需求建议计划并报当地政府审批后,向省教育厅申报招生计划;省教育厅对全省申报的招生计划进行综合平衡,编制全省六年制乡村小学教师培养项目预分计划,根据预分计划确定各县市区每年的公费师范生招生计划,实现按需招生。

(2)按需设编、公费培养。录取入学的公费师范生入校前,与地方政府、录取院校签订三方协议,由地方政府安排事业编制,学生带编入学,由省财政提供培养经费,免除学费、住宿费、军训费和教材费,在助学金奖学金方面与其他在校生享受同等待遇。

(3)定向就业。师范生毕业后,由县教育局根据三方协议将毕业生安排到乡镇以下乡村小学定向就业。

(4)定期服务。师范生回到生源地所在县市区乡村学校从事不少于六年的教育教学工作。

(5)退出机制。对定向培养期间学业成绩不合格者,不能按期取得教师资格证书者,予以留级或退学者;非正当原因退学者、毕业后不定向就业或定向就业时间不足者必须按协议退还培养费用并按培养费的 0.5 倍缴纳违

约金。

二、乡村公费师范生培养"一师模式"的优势

（一）生源质量好

本模式传承了中师优秀传统，确保了学校可以从初中拔尖学生中，提前选拔录取乐教适学、可塑性强的优秀生源。

（二）专业情意深

初中起点的学生可塑性强，一进校就受到"服务农村，扎根基层，献身教育"的职业理想教育与教师教育文化熏陶。学校特别注重学生的专业情意教育，充分发掘我校"千年学府，百年师范"的红色革命文化传统和深厚的教育文化资源，营造良好的校园文化氛围，给学生教师气质与人格精神的生成以多样化的、潜移默化的陶铸；通过观摩、演讲、校外辅导员、三下乡、义务家教、教书育人楷模进课堂、一线教师面对面等，如将我校的优秀毕业生党的十八大代表兰朝红、全国首届最美乡村教师吴金成等请进校园，这些形式多样、生动活泼、内容丰富、扎实有效的活动，将专业素质教育与理想信念教育相结合，确立德育为先的"现实落脚点"；将专业情意教育与校园文化建设相结合，精准文化育人的"最佳切入点"；将专业知识学习与实践能力提升相结合，抓住情意培养的"知行结合点"，筑牢了定向师范生的教师职业情意和教育理想。

（三）协同育人实

关起门来培养不出优秀小学教师。我校树立"开放培养、共享培养、衔接培养"的理念，进一步创新"高校—地方政府—小学"三位一体化协同培养优秀小学教师的长效机制。我校的"一体化"包括四方面：高等院校、地方政

府和基层学校机构合作的一体化;教师职前培养与职后发展衔接的专业发展一体化;大学教师、基础一线小学教师与师范生共同发展的人员一体化;以及师范专业招生、培养、就业等衔接环节的过程管理一体化。经过多年探索,打造出"共享培养资源、共拟培养规划、共商培养内容、共建实训基地、共育教学团队、共管实践运行"的协同培养机制,形成了"优势互补、合作共赢"的"高校—地方政府—小学"三位一体协同培养优秀乡村小学教师的长效机制。2016年学校与长沙市区60多所优质小学联合成立"小学教师教育联盟",与这些联盟校共建平台、共管实践、共享资源、共做研究和共育人才,成立"名师工作坊",组织开展"名师论坛""名师教学沙龙""名师示范课"等活动;开展"教学观摩课""教学研讨课""同课异构""合作开发小学校本课程""教学竞赛"等教学交流和研讨活动。"小学教师教育联盟"已逐渐成为一个培养培训协同、研究服务协同的合作共同体。双方在开展教学研究协作解决基础教育改革和发展中面临的关键问题、协同制定师范生专业培养方案、设计小学教师教育课程体系、改革教师教育课程内容及教学方法、开展小学教师职后培训、建设基础教育发展高校智库等方面进行了紧密的合作。

(四)教学技能高

一是按照"一体化、分阶段、有层级"的思路,构建六年全程开放的"TPRP"[理论(Theory)—实践(Practice)—反思(Reflection)—实践(Practice)]四阶螺旋渐进实践教学模式,即学校课堂理论学习→进入联盟校现场实践学习→回到学校开展反思学习→又回到联盟校实践检验学习,循环开展,促进师范生教师职业能力螺旋阶梯上升。TPRP模式包含了"见习—研习—实习—讲习"等环节,实现"拜师—学师—为师—出师"的实训实践过程。二是构建起全方位、全过程的实践教学体系。学校着力培养师范生的四种能力,即"育人育德能力""教育教学能力""反思实践能力""专业研究能力"。相应的培养策略是以高尚的情操提升育人育德能力,以丰富的实践知识提升教育教学能力,以深刻的教育领悟提升反思实践能力,以强烈的问题导向提升专业研究能力。为达到上述培养目标,学校精心设置实践课程,加大实践课程比例,改革实践教学方案,建构将高等教育共性,师范教育个性,小学教育特性及知识、能力与品行为一体的"三性一体"的实践教学培养方案。除了课内实践与职业技能训练之外,学生在前3年(本科学段)每一学年的第二学期都会有1周的时间进行教育见习。第五学期安排有为期6周的长沙市内实习。第七学期安排有为期18周的顶岗实习。在时间上做到集中与分散相结合,实践教学贯穿师范生学习的全过程。同时,在大教育实践观指导下,采取理论教学与职业技能训练相结合、教学实践活动与社团活动相结合、顶岗实习与教师培训相结合、教育实习与毕业论文工作相结合的方式,有序地组织师范生进行全方位、全过程的教育实践,引导师范生在实践中学习,在实践中感悟、在实践中体验、在实践中反思,有效地促进师范生的专业成长。三是优化课程体系,创新实践教学手段。根据学生身心发展和智力发展规律,利用初中起点学生可塑性强的特点,前置教学技能课程,在第一、二年级重点强化学生的音体美素质养成和三笔字、简笔画、普通话、教师口语等基本职业技能培养。按照"实践知识生成逻辑"的教学模式,灵活运用探究式、情景式、案例式、模拟式等方式组织实践教学,打破过去培养过程中"重理论灌输,轻能力培养"的窠臼,所有实践课程采取"听、观、思、研、议、行"六个维度与环节协同完成,即听教师引领、观示范案例、思教育行为、研小型课题、议收获成长、行教学实践,将课堂教学与案例分享相结合,考察观摩与反思共议相结合,案例交流与课题研究相结合,促进学生的理论与实践相融合、打造出以"自主合作、反思探究"为特征的实践教学课堂。四是实施小学教师教学基本技能测试认证制度,未能通过测试的学生不得毕业。

三、我校乡村公费师范教育取得的培养成效

我校探索创新乡村教师培养补充机制,有效解决了乡村教师"下不去、

留不住、干不好"的问题。成果荣获 2018 年国家高等教育教学成果奖二等奖,2019 年湖南省高等教育教学成果奖特等奖、一等奖、二等奖各 1 项。

一是高度契合国家精准扶贫战略,为大量贫困生提供了接受大学教育的机会,显著减轻了学生家庭的经济负担。公费师范生大多数来自贫困家庭,例如我校 2010 级首届初中起点公费定向生中,65.38% 的学生家庭月平均毛收入低于 2000 元,公费师范教育使这些家庭的优秀初中毕业生免于辍学,且一人学成就业,全家脱贫有望。

二是毕业生履约率和乡镇以下从教率高。我校公费师范生已毕业遍布三湘大地,目前我校已在全省 14 个市州 121 个县市区录取公费师范生 21275 人,毕业人数 9710。公费师范毕业生的平均履约率达 96.77%,9710 名毕业生中仍在教毕业生 9082 人,占比 93.3%,其中乡镇以下学校从教率达 90.40%,在一定程度上缓解了湖南省乡村教育师资紧缺的局面,有效地提升了乡村小学教师队伍的师资水平,提高了农村义务教育质量,促进了城乡教育公平。

三是毕业生综合素质高、发展潜力大,正迅速成长为乡村教育骨干。2011—2017 届到岗履约的 7298 名毕业生中已经有 553 人成为学校的中层以上干部,其中 2011 届毕业生任学校中层以上干部的比率达 18.65%。涌现出首届"寻找最美乡村教师"吴金成、"全国优秀乡村教师"喻文龙、"湖南省民族团结进步模范个人"蒲晴等典型代表。湖南省各县市区教育局普遍反映,湖南第一师范学院培养毕业的学生好用、管用、可以放心用。

四、公费师范教育存在的问题及建议

要使公费师范教育成为一项可长期持续发展的事业和长期有效的乡村教师队伍培养补充机制,必须解决卓越小学教师"下得去、留得住、干得好"的问题,为此,我们建议以特殊政策支持鼓励乡村教师长期安心从教、乐教:

第一,大力提高乡村教师的物质待遇。一是实行激励性岗位津贴制度,显著提高乡村教师的经济地位,对越是在边远贫困地区执教的教师,其岗位津贴越高。二是实行教龄累进工资制度,即教龄越长,奖励性工资的增长幅度越大,引导和鼓励乡村教师长期扎根乡村从教。三是完善乡村教师住房保障机制,建立多元化的乡村教师住房供给体系。四是进一步落实和完善乡村教师医疗、养老等社会保障制度,关心乡村教师的身心健康发展,努力提高他们的幸福指数。

第二,努力满足乡村教师的精神需求。一是实施职称评审政策性倾斜,优先支持乡村教师职称评定、评优评先。二是建立乡村教师终身从教国家功勋奖励制度,大力宣传乡村教师的优秀事迹,全社会营造尊师重教的好氛围。

第三,为乡村教师提供学历提升渠道和职业发展空间。6 所部属师范大学的公费师范生享有"农村学校教育硕士师资培养计划"和"服务期满特岗教师免试攻读教育硕士计划"等激励政策,而地方师范院校由于缺少教育硕士专业学位授予权,致使大量真正下到乡村基层的公费师范生在服务期内没有直接进一步学习深造、提高学历层次的机会。优秀教师在成长过程中,不仅需要物质待遇上的保障,更需要在专业发展和职业空间上不断提升,在履行国家使命的同时实现个人价值的提升和职业生命的升华,这样才能使他们安心长期从教、终身从教、乐于从教。据调查,2015 年湖南省有农村小学 7430 所,学生 375.4 万人,19.6 万名专任教师中研究生毕业的仅 265 人,农村小学严重缺乏高学历、高水平的课程带头人和教育教学骨干。因此强烈建议国家制订乡村基础教育硕士定向培养计划,由具备较强培养能力的地方师范院校承担培养任务,加大培养规模,培养大批乡村教育迫切需要的学科带头人、教研教改骨干和教育教学骨干,为乡村教育的持续稳定发展和乡村教育质量的不断提高奠定坚实的优质人力资源基础。

第四,建立地方高校公费师范生生均拨款奖补机制。公费师范生中的学前教育和小学教育都要求"全面发展、多能培养、注重实践",各培养高校在课程建设、教学团队、技能训练、教学实践等方面的经费投入事实上要比一般本科生的培养成本高出不少。目前,教育部部属师范大学公费师范生的生均拨款经费已达 3 万元以上,我校公费师范教育由省财政支持,目前生均拨款经费不到 2 万元,我们希望教育部充分考虑地方高校的办学困难和师范教育的公益性质,建立公费师范生培养经费奖补机制,使地方公费师范生培养经费逐步达到教育部部属师范大学的生均拨款水平,以改善办学条件,提高人才培养质量,实现公费师范教育的可持续发展。

第五,建立教师退出机制。受传统观念的影响和各种现实因素的制约,这一制度在全国范围内并没有很好地落实,真正意义上的教师退出机制并没有完全建立起来。其实教师退出应该常态化,企业职工早已打破"铁饭碗","能者上、庸者下"成为共识,教师作为一个职业,理应遵循职业进退的规则,不能有任何"特殊"。一些不合格的教师长期占据教师岗位,无法腾出编制补充新教师,"只进不出",导致一些地方教师队伍僵化,教育缺少活力;干多干少、干好干坏一个样,影响了广大教师的积极性,不利于教育质量提升,也引起了学生和家长的不满。建立合理有效的退出机制,能使教师群体提高竞争意识,使教师们感受到社会竞争的压力,从而激发起内在动力,提高他们的工作积极性,促使教师自觉地提升自身素养,进而提升学校教育质量与水平。一是建立一套科学的退出标准。建议从教育理念、专业知识、专业能力、师德师风、身心健康状态五个维度建立不合格教师的判定标准。建议国家应尽快出台判定不合格教师的标准,使退出机制做到有法可依。二是建立完整的教师退出程序。如提前发出解聘通知;教师有要求举办听证会的权利,在听证会上,学校和教师双方都可以聘请律师为自己辩护,出示有利于自己的证人证据;听证判决书要及时发送到相关教育部门、教师和学校手中;教师和学校如果对判决结果有异议,都可以提请上级教育部门审议或向法院上诉等。目前,我国教师解聘基本没有听证制度;教师解聘后寻求法律救济的渠道也不够完善,教师与校方发生的包括教师聘任在内的法律争议,目前是不能通过诉讼方式来解决的。因此需建立从定期评价、整改补救、下发解聘退出通知、举行听证会、到法律救济在内的一整套规范程序。

三是明确执行教师退出的权力主体。目前我国教师退出的权力主体并不清晰。在民办学校,学校校长可以直接解除聘用合同,辞退教师;如果教师不服,可以向地方教育主管部门提起申诉。有的地方,如实行"县管校用"教师管理体制改革的区域,一般由学校提出清退的不合格教师,然后经过上级教育行政部门审批,学校无权直接清退教师。因此,当前教师退出制度实施的最大障碍在于教师管理体制。目前教师的管理包括多方权力主体,教师的编制、工资等由人事部门负责、教师的培训和专业发展及评价由教师业务部门负责,不同管理部门各行其政,往往缺乏沟通和衔接,那么清退教师由谁来负责执行,必须明确权力主体。建议由教育部教师工作司(各地由所在教育管理部门)牵头,成立专门的教师退出管理机构,统一负责协调教师的聘用和退出问题。四是完善社会保障体系。将不合格教师退出之后,不能简单地将之推向社会,应该通过培训转岗、离职关怀,让其找到职业生涯新起点,尽可能降低改革的风险,保持社会和谐稳定。

Innovating the Model of Government – funded Normal Education to Promote Balanced Development of Basic Education
——Hunan First Normal University's Reform and Practice of Government – funded Normal Education for Rural Areas

Zhimin Liu

Hunan First Normal University

Abstract:In view of the problems existing in the cultivating process of rural primary teachers in China, on the basis of inheriting the excellent secondary normal education tradition, in combination with the development trend of modern normal education transformation, Hunan First Normal University (HFNU) explored and established the HFNU Model of cultivating junior middle school graduates into excellent undergraduates majoring in primary education, which is characterized by "enrollment from junior middle school graduates and six – year consistence in cultivation, comprehensive cultivation with multi – oriented development, tri – nature integration and trinity, practice – orientedness and firstness of teacher ethics". The HFNU Model has effectively solved the problem that teachers are not willing to go to the rural schools or stay there for long or teach well, cultivating and supplementing nearly 10,000 high – quality excellent primary teachers for Hunan rural areas. In order to make government – funded normal education a long – term career of sustainable development and a long – term effective supplementary mechanism for rural teacher cultivation, this paper puts forward some policy suggestions to encourage the rural teachers to devote themselves to teaching and enjoy teaching on a long – term basis.

Key Words: HFNU Model; government – funded normal education; policy

卓越小学全科教师培养方案的设计与实践①
——以重庆师范大学为例

林长春　路　晨

重庆师范大学

摘要：为促进城乡教育均衡发展,缓解农村学校教师短缺和结构性缺编问题,重庆师范大学于2014年开始定向农村培养卓越小学全科教师。在扎根乡村、协同培养、全面发展和实践取向的基本理念指导下,重庆师范大学确立了培养具有学、做教育家意识和追求卓越的高素质农村小学教师卓越人才的培养目标,在课程设计上采取"文科＋艺体""理科＋艺体"的选择模块和"1＋1＋N"课程层级模式。课程体系包括通识课程、专业核心课程、专业拓展课程和养成性教学实践课程。

关键词：卓越;小学全科教师;培养方案;"1＋1＋N"课程层级模式

近年来,在义务教育均衡发展的背景下,国内一些高师院校根据当地教育实际需求开始培养小学全科教师,小学全科教师的培养与发展也引起了学界的广泛关注。2013年,重庆市政府发布了《关于农村小学全科教师培养工作的实施意见》(下文简称《意见》),指出要定向培养一批"下得去、留得

---

① 本文系教育部卓越教师培养计划改革项目"基于UGIS联盟的卓越小学全科教师培养模式改革与实践(2014)的研究成果。

住、干得好"的本科层次小学全科教师。同年,重庆师范大学开始招收免费定向的小学全科师范生。2014 年,重庆师范大学"基于 UGIS 联盟的卓越小学全科教师培养模式改革与实践"又入选教育部卓越小学教师培养改革项目。目前,该项目已运行 6 年,对其设计理念、培养目标及课程方案设计等进行了初步的实践探索,对于卓越小学全科教师的培养取得了较好的成效。

一、卓越小学全科教师培养的基本理念

(一)扎根乡村

重庆师范大学卓越小学全科教师的培养植根于重庆市农村小学师资的现实需求。据统计,2013 年重庆市有村小 3472 所,教学办 14301 个,村小学生 39.3 万人,在编教职工 2.7 万人。现有的农村小学教师编制不足,乡村教师缺口较大,专业结构不合理,多数以语文、数学学科教师为主,同时兼任英语、艺体等学科教学,教学质量普遍不高,素质教育推进较难。[①] 因此,卓越小学全科教师培养致力于解决重庆市农村小学教师队伍整体素质不高及结构性缺编等问题。同时,在城乡义务教育均衡发展的背景下,通过卓越农村小学全科教师培养,提高农村教育质量,明显缩小城乡师资水平,保障教育公平。相应地,"扎根乡村"意味着卓越农村小学全科教师培养应加强师范生师风师德教育,鼓励他们热爱农村教育事业,引导他们富有社会责任感,到乡村学校任教,带动和促进乡村教师队伍整体水平提高,从而推动城乡一体化建设,促进教育公平。

(二)协同育人

重庆师范大学初等教育学院于 2013 年成立了"四位一体"的 UGIS 人才

---

① 重庆市教委:《重庆农村小学全科教师培养策略》,http://www.cqjw.gov.cn/Item/10345.aspx。

培养联盟,即由"高校(University)—区县教育主管部门(Government)—区县教师进修学院(Institute)—小学(School)"共同组成的协同创新型人才培养平台。这是重庆市的首个小学全科教师培养联盟。经过6年的发展,目前联盟成员涉及小学全科教师定向的17个区县教委及相应的乡镇小学。该联盟作为一种创新的教师培养模式,其工作覆盖小学全科教师的招生、录取、培养、就业全过程,建立了高校与定向区县及小学合作培养教师的新机制。首先,以地方需求为基础协同招生,由各区县根据自身教师队伍在4年后的需求情况提出招生计划,再由重庆市教育委员会根据重庆市的教师整体发展情况提出当年全市整体招生计划,体现招生工作以地方需求为基础。其次,地方政府深度参与小学全科教师人才培养的全过程,在人才培养方案的修订、学生年度考核、培养质量反馈、就业考核与激励措施、专业发展政策、小学教育研究、小学教师职后培训、学生教育实习基地建设等诸方面进行实质性合作,形成了教学、研究、实习、考核、就业、咨询、资源共享等优化培养模式。协同培养对于小学全科教师了解各定向区县的经济和教育现状,增强学生的使命感和责任感,让各定向区县了解学生的培养质量等均起到很好的作用,真正发挥高校、地方和小学对小学全科教师培养的协同作用。

(三)综合培养

教育部《基础教育课程改革纲要(试行)》明确提出课程结构要改变"过于强调学科本位、科目过多和缺乏整合的现状",小学阶段则应"以综合课程为主"。《小学教师专业标准(试行)》要求小学教师"适应小学综合性教学的要求,了解多学科知识","了解所教学科与社会实践、少先队活动的联系,了解与其他学科的联系"。全科教师本质上强调的是教师将多种学科知识进行综合,把关于生活与世界的完整知识传授给学生。[①] 相应的,重庆师范大学小学全科教师培养坚持围绕以"综合培养、全面发展"为中心。这就意

---

① 钟秉林:《积极探索小学全科教师的培养》,《中国教育学刊》,2016年第8期。

味着要突出培养小学全科师范生的综合素质,既具有良好的职业道德和文化素质,又要打破学科壁垒,使学科素养和教师专业素养高度整合,突出课程知识的"融合性",具备整合学科教学的意识和能力,适应小学综合性教学的要求,适应儿童发展的全面性和个性化需求。

(四)实践取向

教师教育最突出的特点就是实践性,教师的成长过程是一个专业化的实践过程,可以说,教师教育的实践取向既符合教师教育的本质特征,也是当前国内外教师教育改革的大势所趋。[①]《教师教育课程标准(试行)》也提出教师培养应坚持实践取向。重庆师范大学历来重视实践教学,将实践取向贯穿于小学全科教师培养过程中,建立了以创新意识与实践能力为核心的小学全科教师养成性实践教学体系,协同开展规范化实践教学,加强课程资源建设,注重培养能说会写、能唱会跳、能书会画、能教会导、能思会研的全科型师范生。同时,实践取向并不意味着忽视理论,或者将实践简单地等同于开设技能技巧性课程或者看作是各种教学技能的展示。重庆师范大学在卓越小学全科教师培养中,坚持理论与实践相结合,促进实践与反思的相互融合,通过在实践中不断反思,在反思中不断实践,体现"实践—理论—反思"(PTR)循环渐进的小学全科教师人才培养理念。

二、卓越小学全科教师培养的目标

基于教师专业化的发展趋势和基础教育对小学师资的需求,该专业目标定位在于立足重庆地区,为重庆市基础教育改革发展服务,培养具有良好的职业道德和文化素质,掌握学科基本理论、基础知识与基本技能,学科素养和教师专业素养高度整合,能够在定向服务区县的小学主教小学语文 +

---

① 张霞:《论教师教育实践取向的误识及其超越》,《中国教育学刊》,2017 年第 1 期。

小学英语或小学数学 + 小学科学,同时兼教小学音乐、美术、体育、道德与法治、综合实践活动、书法中的一到两门课程的教学与管理相关工作,未来 5 年能够成长为定向服务区县的小学骨干教师。

具体的目标预期由毕业生职业能力和毕业生职业成就预期构成。在毕业生职业能力方面,由五个方面构成:

第一,师德修养。这要求小学全科教师做到爱国守法,践行社会主义核心价值观,热爱小学教育事业,对教师职业有强烈的认同,爱岗敬业,关爱学生,为人师表,能够成为小学生健康成长的指导者和引路人。具有良好的教师职业道德,具有强烈的社会责任感。

第二,专业能力。要求小学全科教师能够形成综合的教育教学能力,具有较强的从事所担任 2 ~ 3 门学科课程的教学能力,包括学科课程标准与教材分析能力、教学设计与实施能力。具备教育教学组织与管理能力,能够熟练地综合运用专业知识和技能解决教学实践问题。具有设计、组织、指导小学生课外科技活动和艺体活动的能力,在教学中体现出改革创新意识。

第三,综合素养。要求小学全科教师熟悉国家有关教育法规和方针政策,具有良好的科学与人文素养、艺术修养、健康的审美观、体育与健康知识。具备小学生发展知识、教育教学知识,了解中国教育的基本情况,具有相应的自然科学和人文社会科学知识。熟练运用现代教育技术开展教学活动。

第四,反思学习。要求小学全科教师能够对教学活动进行持续深入的钻研与反思,不断改进教学工作。以问题和任务为导向,掌握中外文资料查询、文献检索能力,进行小学教育教学研究,指导学生开展探究性、合作性学习。终身学习能力强,能追踪我国与世界先进国家基础教育教学改革的新理念、新方法和新手段,提高自身教育教学水平,实现自我专业发展。

第五,合作交流。要求小学全科教师能够做到师生关系融洽,理解学生,引导学生学会与人交流、沟通。积极与同事、同行交流合作,分享教育教学经验和资源,与家长进行沟通合作,能指导家庭和社会教育机构等科学开展家庭教育与学科学习指导等,为引导乡村儿童健康成长发挥积极作用。

第六,社会责任。要求小学全科教师认真开展教育教学活动,并通过多种途径使公众认识到小学生学习特点和成长规律,教书育人,扎根乡村为区域义务教育均衡发展和提高乡村教育质量付出努力。在毕业生职业成就预期方面主要是由职业成就构成,要求小学全科教师通过深入钻研1~2门主干学科教育教学,成长为区域骨干教师,并结合学科教学实际问题组织区域教研,发挥辐射引领作用。能有效开展班级指导工作,有针对性地开展综合育人活动,自主规划专业发展。能通过有效沟通、运用反思和批判性思维方法等,紧跟国际国内小学教育改革发展动态,实现自身专业发展。

从具体的培养要素来看,包括知识要素、能力要素和情感要素。知识要素方面,要求涵盖小学生发展知识、学科知识、教育教学知识、通识性知识等;能力要素方面,要求小学全科教师具有良好的教学设计能力、教学组织实施能力、教学评价能力、班队管理能力、沟通合作能力、教育科研能力、反思与发展能力,以及说、写、教、作、弹、唱、跳、画等教学基本功;情感要素方面,要求小学全科教师热爱小学教育事业,具有坚定的专业理想和高尚的道德情操。从专业特质角度来看,要求小学全科教师能够把握国际基础教育改革动态,顺应国内基础教育改革方向,适应小学教育发展需求,胜任小学多学科教育教学需要,即为"情感的深厚性、专业知识的全面性、能力素质的综合性"。

三、卓越小学全科教师培养的课程结构设计

根据卓越小学全科教师培养理念和培养目标,重庆师范大学初等教育学院提出了卓越小学全科教师培养的"文科 + 艺体""理科 + 艺体"的课程选择模块和"1 + 1 + N"的课程层级模式。即小学全科师范生可以选择文科或理科为主修课程模块,再另外选择"艺体"为辅修课程模块。其中,"文科"包括小学语文和小学英语,"理科"包括小学数学和小学科学。"艺体"包括小

学音乐、小学美术、小学体育与健康。要求小学全科教师能够胜任语文或数学课程的教学工作,能够担任英语或科学课程的教学工作,可以兼任小学音乐或小学美术或小学体育与健康等课程的教学工作。具体课程结构分为通识课程、专业核心课程、专业拓展课程和养成性教学实践课程。

(一)通识课程

通识课程的设置是培养全面发展的高素质未来教师的内在要求。20世纪后半期以来,各国教师教育改革虽然注重对教师职业功能性训练,但一个明显的变化是转向了强调对教师作为完整的人的培育。[①] 卓越小学全科教师应具备广博的知识,养成良好的人文素养和科学素养,通识课程的开设有助于提升小学全科师范生的德性修养,引导他们建立学科之间的联系,同时又使其能够积极参与社会生活,成为有社会责任感的、全面发展的人。同时,通识教育还可以为专业教育铺垫宽厚的基础。因此,通识教育能够深化小学全科师范生对专业教育的理解,即在更高的水平上求得专业知识的融通。[②] 相应的,通识课程设置不仅涵盖人文社会科学领域、自然科学与技术领域、教师教育领域,而且针对重庆市农村小学师资发展的现实需要,还设计了艺术、体育与健康领域的相关课程来提升小学全科师范生的艺术素养,满足农村地区现实的教育需要。同时,通识课程设置充分体现了当前教师教育改革的发展趋势,在选修课中除上述领域外,还设计了创新创业系列、综合素质教育讲座和网络精品视频课程,满足小学全科师范生的多元化学习需求。

同时,由于学科交叉、课程内容繁杂等客观因素的存在,为了减轻小学全科师范生的学习负担,在通识课程设置上,对一些课程进行了整合,形成了一系列能够满足小学教育阶段对于教师"一专多能、全科发展"需要的课

---

① 朱旭东:《论当代西方教师教育思想》,《比较教育研》,2015年第10期。
② 刘小强、肖蓓:《地方本科师范生通识教育探析》,《内蒙古师范大学学报(教育科学版)》,2016年第9期。

程,如音乐与舞蹈、美术与书法、体育与健康等。

(二)专业核心课程

2012 年,《教育部关于全面提高高等教育质量的若干意见》提出,"鼓励高校开展专业核心课程教授负责制试点"。专业核心课程是指在人才培养过程中,为实现培养目标,对学生掌握专业核心知识和培养专业核心能力,对提高该专业核心竞争能力起决定作用的课程。[①] 卓越小学全科教师培养方案中的专业核心课程是该课程体系中的核心部分,是该专业主干课程中处于最关键位置的课程。它的制定以《小学教师专业标准(试行)》为指导,以小学教师职业能力培养为目标,是该专业的必修课程,关系到小学全科师范生能否达到培养目标的最基本要求。对于需要更"全"的知识的小学全科师范生而言,由于小学阶段课程设置中的学科数量和广度,要使专业核心课程设置在课程知识及学术要求与教学实践之间取得平衡是较困难的。"全"并不意味着不重视小学全科师范生的学科知识、教学技能及"教书育人"能力的获得,而是要从有利于小学全科师范生的综合素质培养出发,打破学科专业壁垒,注重小学全科师范生的知识整合能力培养。因此,在综合培养理念指导下,专业核心课程的设计采取"文科 + 艺体""理科 + 艺体"的培养模式,使小学全科师范生将来能够精通 1~2 门小学主干学科以满足教学工作需要,同时可以兼任小学其他学科的教学工作,引导小学全科师范生理解儿童成长的特点和差异,树立正确的教育观和学生观,支持小学全科师范生发展科研能力,同时能够运用现代教育技术手段进行教学,提升教育教学专业能力。方向课程由四个部分构成:教师教育类课程、文科方向课程、理科方向课程、艺体方向课程。其中,艺体方向包括音乐、美术和体育三个部分。小学全科师范生可以选择文科方向加艺体方向或者理科方向加艺体方向。在艺体方向的选择上,音乐、美术和体育选其一完成。可以说这种文科类或

---

① 岳爱臣:《专业核心课程的构建与实施》,《北京教育·高教》,2007 年第 3 期。

理科类与某一类艺体课程相结合的设置,既体现了培养模式的综合性和多学科之间的交融,又能兼顾多学科(主课两门且兼顾一门艺体课,注重音体美素质的培养)教学需要。① 具体设计详见下表:

卓越小学全科教师培养的专业核心课程

教师教育类课程	文科方向课程	理科方向课程	艺体方向课程(三选一)	
儿童发展	现代汉语	高等数学	音乐方向	钢琴基础
	古代汉语	解析几何		钢琴配奏
小学教育心理学	文学与写作	线性代数		声乐基础
	中国古代文学史	初等数论		合唱与指挥
初等教育学	中国现当代文学史	概率与数理统计		小学音乐课程与教学
	外国文学	小学数学研究	美术方向	素描基础
	朗诵艺术	自然科学基础		色彩基础
教育研究方法	英语精读	自然科学实验		国画基础
	英语语音	小学数学课程与教学		手工制作
小学课堂管理	英语听力与口语	小学数学课程标准与教材分析		电脑美术设计
				小学美术课程与教学
	英语翻译与写作	小学数学教学设计与技能训练	体育方向	田径、体操与武术教学与运动训练
现代教育技术	小学语文课程与教学			足球、篮球教学与运动训练
	小学语文课程标准与教材分析	小学科学课程与教学		排球教学与运动训练
小学综合实践活动设计	小学语文教学设计与技能训练			乒乓球教学与运动训练
	小学英语课程与教学	小学科学课程标准与教材分析		小学体育课程与教学
教师书写	小学英语课程标准与教材分析			

---

① 张虹、肖其勇:《全科教师培养:农村小学教师教育改革新动向——基于全科教师培养理念、培养目标和专业特质新探》,《教育理论与实践》,2015 年第 8 期。

(三)专业拓展课程

专业拓展课程是为了更好地提升卓越小学全科师范生的学科素养,在专业核心课程的基础上,以增强小学全科师范生的学科知识与课程整合能力为目标,从农村基础教育发展的实际需要而设计的选修类课程。小学全科师范生根据自身学习兴趣和专业发展需求来进行选择,这能够充分调动其学习积极性。鉴于专业核心课程的设计遵循"文科 + 艺体""理科 + 艺体"模式,专业拓展课程是以模块课程作为该部分的设计呈现的。模块课程是培养方案中不可或缺的一部分,从人才培养的质量与水平来看,"模块课程"的培养目标与其他课程模式的要求无异,均致力于小学全科师范生知识的扩展、能力的发展或素质的提高,具有一定的规格和标准。模块课程的设计不仅与当前经济社会发展的要求息息相关,同时,考虑了学习者的基本状态,符合学习者的身心发展特点和规律,与其知识、能力和素质等方面的发展需要相匹配。[①] 可以说,卓越小学全科教师培养方案中以模块课程作为专业拓展课程的表现形式,是符合当前教师教育发展趋势,满足卓越小学全科教师培养需要的。

具体而言,专业拓展课程分为文科模块、理科模块和艺体模块,学生需从中选修 16 学分,其中文科模块或理科模块选修 10 分,艺术模块选修 6 分。模块课程是对专业核心课程中各方向课程的拓展,课程设置见下表:

卓越小学全科教师培养的专业拓展课程

文科模块	理科模块	艺体模块
公文写作	数学思想史	音乐鉴赏
文学概论	数学思想方法	课堂乐器
美学	小学数学解题研究	自弹自唱

---

① 唐德海、甘鹏:《模块课程实现的若干原则性问题探讨》,《湖南师范大学教育科学学报》,2010 年第 3 期。

续表

文科模块	理科模块	艺体模块
儿童文学创作与欣赏	统计与测量	儿童舞蹈编排
文学批评与鉴赏	小学数学综合实践教学研究	装饰画
中国古代小学研究	高观点下的小学数学	儿童画技法与指导
小学作文教学研究	数学史与小学数学	水彩画技法
小学语文名师课例赏析	小学数学教育研究与写作	PS 图像处理
小学古代诗歌教学研究	小学数学名师课例赏析	简笔画与线描
英语经典名篇诵读	科技设计与制作	美术鉴赏
英美文学	STEM 课程设计与评价	行书技法
英语书写	科学技术与社会	隶书技法
小学英语教师口语	机器人设计与制作	
英语国家社会与文化	科学技术史	小学体育健康与安全指导
大学英语语法基础	科学探究与科学方法论	小学体育游戏设计与指导
小学英语课堂教学技能	青少年科技活动设计与指导	
思想品德与生活(社会)教学设计	小学科学名师课例赏析	

(四)养成性教学实践课程

重庆师范大学卓越小学全科教师的培养植根于我国农村基础教育均衡发展的现实需要,所以实践教学环节的设立必须深刻理解并紧紧把握当代小学教育实践的需求,坚持实践取向,秉承"四位一体"的培养模式,建构覆盖卓越小学全科教师培养全程的养成性实践教学体系,在 UGIS 联盟下,协同开展规范化的实践教学。养成性教学实践环节主要由校内实践创新能力培养和校外教育见习、研习、实习两大部分构成。

校内实践创新能力的培养主要针对小学全科师范生的语言、书写、美术、音乐、舞蹈、体育、写作、阅读、说课讲课、科技制作、教学课件及教学研究能力训练,主要通过课堂教学、早晚自习、课外活动、比赛项目、名师讲座等进行。一二年级侧重教师基本技能训练,三四年级侧重活动组织实施能力、教师教学教研能力培养。同时,通过整合第一课堂和第二课堂,使小学全科师范生除了获得相应学科知识、教育教学技能、教师道德修养理论知识外,还利用一系列浸润学生心灵的活动来塑造学生的未来教师气质,打造卓越小学全科教师成长和发展的特有育人文化,以此让全科师范生逐步从一种道德和情感的维度去认识和体会一名卓越小学全科教师所具有的情感特征和心理特征,形成一名卓越全科教师所必须具备的思维模式、行为特征和能力特点。

校外教育见习、研习、实习是独立实践教学环节,在设计和实践上充分发挥 UGIS 联盟优势,实行高校教师和小学教师、教研员共同指导师范生的"双导师"制,拓展教育实践内容,使学生将来能够真正胜任小学多学科教学,从事班主任工作、开展班队活动、进行班级管理等。独立实践教学环节中有两次见习、一次研习、一次实习,见习和研习时间均为 2 周,实习为 15 周,共 21 周。其中,一次见习和实习均安排在定向区县小学进行,其余在主城区小学进行。独立实践教学环节的安排与设计旨在让小学全科师范生了解重庆市小学教学改革特别是各区县开展素质教育的新形势,树立热爱教师职业、热爱学生、立志为小学教育事业,特别是为农村小学教育服务和奉献青春的高尚品德和情操,通过认真学习和了解小学教育教学工作的全过程,明确小学教师的基本工作内容,明确小学教育教学工作的一般特点和意义,熟悉从事小学教育管理、班主任、少先队和任课教师教学工作的全过程,学习先进的教育教学方法,提高教育教学和教学科研能力。在具体实践内容上包括四方面:学科教学工作、班主任工作、少先队工作等。对于教育实习工作,不仅要求全科生要试教语文、英语加一门艺术课,或者数学、科学加一门艺术课,共 3 门课,要求他们要试做班主任,以及要试教除了 3 门课以外的其余课程,从而培养全科师范生的多学科教学与课程整合能力,以及学生教育能力。

Program Design and Practice for Cultivating Prominent General Teachers of Primary Schools: Based on the Example of Chongqing Normal University

Changchun Lin　Chen Lu

Chongqing Normal University

Abstract: For the sake of promoting a balanced urban – rural development and relieving the teacher deficiency of rural schools, Chongqing Normal University started cultivating rural – targeted prominent general teachers of primary schools in 2014. Under the directions of the basic principles of rural – rooting, coordinating – cultivation, all – around development and practice orientation, Chongqing Normal University has established the education goal of cultivating high – qualified rural primary school teachers who are educators with the sense of learning and doing, 2019 International Conference on Elementary Teacher Education83 and pursue prominence. Thus in the curriculum design, the "Liberal Arts + Arts & Sports" and "Science + Arts & Sports" alternative module and "1 + 1 + N" curriculum layer mode are adopted. The curriculum system includes general education courses, major core courses, extended major courses and teaching practice – based formative education courses.

Key Words: prominence; general teacher; training program; "1 + 1 + N" curriculum layer

基于综合课程与活动课程的小学 全科教师培养实践

武启云

青海师范大学

摘要:全科型教师是小学卓越教师培养的基本路向,实践性知识与实践技能是教师教育课程的核心要素,发挥教育主体(教师、学生)的主体作用是教育改革的、成功的前提。人工智能和现代教育技术拓展了教师教育改革的空间,开辟了教师教育的新路径,教育改革一定要注重客观调查、科学设计、精细实施,面对社会的数据化特征,教育组织内信息的自由流动能够创造出无限的教育可能。西部农牧区特殊的地理、文化、教育生态,要求一支与之相适应的教师队伍。在西部农牧区全面普及九年义务教育的前提下,加强"全科型"教师培养,为有效解决西部农牧区广大小学普遍存在的学科教师"结构性缺编"这一瓶颈问题,推动区域内基础教育公平发展提供了一条新的思路。通过培养小学全科教师,为社会提供高水平教育资源,对提高基础教育质量,促进教育公平,尤其是维护西部农牧区社会稳定和发展,具有重要的现实意义和长远的战略意义。

教育部《关于实施卓越教师培养计划的意见》(教师〔2014〕5 号)指出:小学卓越教师培养"针对小学教育的实际需求,重点探索小学全科教师培养模式,培养一批热爱小学教育事业、知识广博、能力全面,能够胜任小学多学科教育教学需要的卓越小学教师"。《关于实施卓越教师培养计划 2.0 的意见》(教师〔2018〕13 号)进一步指出:"面向培养素养全面、专长发展的卓越小学教师,重点探索借鉴国际小学全科教师培养经验、继承我国养成教育传统的培养模式。"新课程改革强调小学阶段以综合课程为主,小学学科知识体系由分科走向综合,分科教师越来越难以适应小学阶段的新的教学要求。另外,在教育发达的国家,由 2 ~ 3 个教师教授一个班是小学教育的主流做法。青海师范大学针对西部农牧区小学教育实际,立足当前,面向未来,主动作为,综合改革,在探索西部农牧区全科型卓越小学教师培养方面取得了良好的成效。

青海师范大学小学教育(全科)专业主要针对西部农村和牧区地域辽阔,地形复杂,居住分散,小学点多面广且规模偏小,教师一人兼授多门学科等地域性特点设立的。广大农牧区小学,在现行的教师编制标准前提下,无法配置足够数量的单科教师(尤其是体育、音乐、美术等小学科教师),客观上要求每一位教师能够胜任多学科教学,有时还要求能够"包班"教学。现有小学教师除个别教师能够勉强胜任这一特殊的教学要求外,绝大部分教师确实无法有效完成。在专业建设中,学校立足区域实际,借鉴了发达国家小学教师培养由低学历向高学历、由分科培养向全科培养的成功经验。使人才培养既符合西部农牧区,特别是青藏高原地区基础教育发展的现实需要,也符合发达国家基础教育发展的基本趋势;既具有本土特征,也拥有国际视野。

小学教育(全科)专业按照"面向基层,全科培养,一专多能,学有特长,素质全面"的工作思路,突出"理念新、知识博、基础实、素质高、能力强、适应广"的特点,积极构建适应西部农牧区小学教学需求的教师教育课程体系和实践能力培训体系,探索"全科型"农牧区小学教师培养新模式。培养一批具有高尚的师德修养、扎实的专业基础、突出的教育教学实践能力、良好的教育教学理论素养、一定的教育研究能力和反思能力、能够胜任小学多学科教育教学需要的"下得去、留得住、教得好、有发展"的全科型教师。

小学全科型教师的知识和能力结构具体体现为"两基础、一专业、一特长",即每个学生系统学习小学英语和小学体育两个基础模块,在"语文与社会"或"数学与科学"中选一项学科模块作为主打方向,在音乐和美术模块中选修一项兴趣特长模块,通过四年的学习,系统掌握所选课程的专业知识体系,形成娴熟的学科教学技能,以满足小学多学科教学的需要。

在全科型小学教师培养中,加强师范生实践创新与实际应用能力培养,形成了"6514"实践教学体系。小学教育专业实践教学体系主要包括六个学期的系统的教学基本技能校内实训、五个学期的小学教育见习、一个学期的顶岗教育实习、四个学期两轮的毕业调查设计及调查报告撰写四部分。通过校内实训,着重培养学生的书写表达技能、教育信息技术技能和课堂教学技能;通过教育见习,重点了解小学教育概况、班主任工作、小学学科教学、小学课堂环节及小学管理的基本概况和一般流程;通过教育实习全面了解和把握小学的教育教学活动,深化教育教学技能;通过毕业调查设计及调查报告撰写,培养学生初步的发现教育问题、分析教育问题、解决教育问题的教育研究能力。

实行"双导师制"。从本科一年级开始,小教全科各班级配备校内导师、导师助理和校外实践导师。校内导师由具有学科教学论硕士研究生指导教师资格的校内教师承担,主要负责本专业学生的学科知识学习,并对学生的理念形成、行为规范进行引领。导师助理由研究生担任,主要负责校内教学技能实训的组织、检查和评价,校外见习的管理,各类资料的搜集整理及专业建设的理论研究。实践性导师由中小学特级教师或优秀的高级教师担任,主要负责相关专业学生实践性技能的训练与指导,承担学科教学法的教学,并根据课程安排的需要,组织课程见习。

2013年,小学教育(全科)专业成功入选教育部"教师队伍建设创新示范项目",承担该项目的师范院校全国只有11家。2014年,西部农牧区卓越小学全科型教师培养项目成功入选教育部"卓越教师培养项目",这两项都是青海省唯一一项入选的项目。2015年,小学教育(全科)专业纳入"青海省乡村教师支持计划（2015—2020）"。2017 年, 小学教育（全科）专业全面纳入青海省公费师范生培养计划。

青海师范大学小学教育（全科）专业, 拓展了政府、高校、小学"三位一体"教师教育协同培养模式, 创造性地构建了与地方经济社会发展密切联系的"教师教育发展先行试验区", 将大学的智力资源推向社会, 青海师范大学全面参与青海社会教育事业改革, 为青海社会教育改革的整体设计、具体教育教学模式创新、教师培训、教育评价提供智力支撑。同时, 高校人才培养主动将社会的优质实践资源引入大学, 青海社会力量在专业定位、人才培养、实践教育、教育评价等方面全面参与青海师范大学教师教育专业改革, 拓展教师教育的培养空间, 将传统上由"师范院校"独自承担的"小师范"转化为"高校、政府、中小学"协作培养的"大师范", 构建教师终身学习、终身成长的教师教育新体系。目前, 已建成教师教育先行发展试验区 1 个, 固定实践基地 12 个, 与 4 个地方教育局签订了人才协作培养协议, 与 30 多个地方教育行政部门签订了顶岗支教协议, 与 14 个一线小学建立了长期协作关系。师大内部积极挖掘小学教师教育资源, 形成了由教育学院牵头, 人文学院等 7 个院系共同参与的协同培养机制。

形成了非选择性全员培养模式。小学教育（全科）专业是在卓越教师理念下设计的。目前, 就全国来看, 卓越教师培养模式基本上有三个特点: 二次选拔, 从在校师范生中选拔有志于小学教育的学生, 专门进行培养; 激发潜能, 以激发部分有潜力学生的潜能为目标; 择优培养, 卓越教师是面向优等生的教育。青海师范大学小学教育（全科）专业依托教育部卓越小学教师培养计划——西部农牧区卓越教师培养项目, 形成了自己的特色。首先是非选择性全员培养, 本专业所有学生全部参加卓越教师计划; 其次是实践性取向, 培养方案制定、课程设置安排、课程教学实施、学业成绩评价等全部围绕实践性取向开展; 最后是无差别资源, 所有学生享受的教学条件和教学资源是无差别的, 我们的目的是通过该专业的实践, 探索教师教育改革的新模式。

构建了基于"学生发展共同体"和"教师成长共同体"的自主性发展模式。"学生发展共同体"是学生开展学习活动的基本单位,学生的学习、实训、展示、分享等各项学习活动基本上都是基于学生发展共同体而实现的。"教师成长共同体"是教师实施教学活动的基本依托,也是教师开展教育研究的基本依托,由高校教师、一线教师、研究生等组成。在教育实践和教育研究中实现教师自身的专业成长。

设置了实践取向的课程体系。实践知识缺乏,实践技能低是全国师范生的通病。在小学教育(全科)专业的培养中,青海师范大学将实践知识和实践技能作为师范生的核心素养来对待,建立了较为完善的实践教育体系。小学教育专业实践教学体系主要包括校内实训、实践基地见习、教育实习、毕业调查设计及调查报告撰写四部分。通过校内实训,着重培养学生的书写表达技能、教育信息技术及课堂教学技能;通过教育见习,重点了解小学教育、小学课堂教学及小学管理的基本概况和一般流程;通过教育实习全面了解和把握小学的教育教学活动,提升教育教学技能;通过毕业调查设计及调查报告撰写,培养学生初步的教育研究能力,以突出小学特征和实践特色。每学期安排由师范生基本技能、学科教学技能、现代教育技术技能组成的专项实践技能训练,具体内容包括:每天练习钢笔字、粉笔字、普通话。每周练习写教案、试讲,保证每个学生在校期间写出小学三、四、五年级《语文》《数学》《英语》的每篇课文和章节的教案,每节每篇课文和章节都最少讲一遍。将现代教育技术分解在每周的实训中,四年下来,保证每个学生都全部掌握基本的现代教育技术;从第二学期开始定期组织教育见习,教育见习做到精细化设计、精细化实施、精细化研究、精细化管理,增强教育见习的针对性和实效性,丰富学生的实践知识。这两个环节是小学教育(全科)专业投入时间和精力最多,收效也最为明显的环节。

探索了主体反思性行动评价模式。建构了以导师和学生构成的双主体评价机制,导师包括校内导师及助理、实践基地导师、实习基地导师,学生评价主要依托学习共同体进行。通过双主体评价,实现评价的全面性、综合性和发展性。实现了评价方式的多元化。校内实训的评价由校内导师及助理负责组织,以"书写、表达能力、教育技术能力、课堂教学能力"为主干内容,以实训记录、学生作业、学生教学设计、学生课件制作、各类教学竞赛的形式考核,由指导教师评定成绩并做好记载,按实践教学学时占总学时数的比例记入课程成绩。实践基地的见习评价由实践导师、校内导师及助理组织,以"小学教育概况、班主任工作、学科教学、教学环节、学校管理"为主干内容,成绩按优秀、良好、中、及格、不及格五级等次单独记入成绩档案。对学生参加教育见习的各个实践教学环节的效果提出严格要求,加强学生综合能力的考评,制定综合能力考评方案。教育实习评价由教育实习学校导师和学校带队教师组织,可通过评价学生的课堂教学、班主任工作、教务干事、德育干事等方面的工作实际,以观课、教学设计、说课、评课、实习报告等形式进行,可以由学院带队教师和顶岗实习学校联合考核,不仅考核学生的工作实绩,而且考核学生的素质和能力水平。毕业调查设计及调查报告评价由校内导师和实践导师共同负责组织,以调查方案、调查过程、调查报告为主要依据,进行综合评价。

"全科型"教师的基本特点是具有综合化的学科知识结构和思维方式,能够胜任多学科教学。西部农牧区特殊的地理、文化、教育生态,要求有一支与之相适应的教师队伍。在西部农牧区全面普及九年义务教育的前提下,加强"全科型"教师培养,为有效解决西部农牧区广大小学普遍存在的学科教师"结构性缺编"这一瓶颈问题,推动区域内基础教育公平发展提供了一条新的思路。通过培养小学全科教师,为社会提供高水平教育资源,对提高基础教育质量,促进教育公平,尤其是维护西部农牧区民族地区社会稳定和发展,具有重要的现实意义和长远的战略意义。

Practice of Elementary General – Subject Teachers Training Based on Comprehensive Curriculum and Activity – based Curriculum

Qiyun Wu

Qinghai Normal University

Abstract：The general – purpose teachers are the basic direction for the development of excellent teachers in primary schools. Practical knowledge and practical skills are the core elements of the teacher education curriculum. Play the main role of the educational subjects (teachers, students) is the prerequisite for successful education reform. Artificial intelligence and modern educational technology have expanded the space for teacher education reform, opening up a new path for teacher education. Education reform must focus on objective investigation, scientific design, and fine implementation. Facing the data characteristics of society, the free flow of information in educational organizations can create unlimited educational possibilities. The special geography, culture and education ecology of the western farming and pastoral areas require a team of teachers to be adapted to them. Under the premise of universally popularizing nine – year compulsory education in western agricultural and pastoral areas, strengthen the training of "general – based" teachers, and effectively solve the bottleneck problem of "structural lack of post" of the teachers in the primary schools in western agricultural and pastoral areas. This provided a new idea for promoting the fair development of basic education in the region By cultivating primary school teachers to provide high – level educational resources for the society , it has important practical significance and long – term strategic significance for improving the quality of basic education and promoting education equity , especially for maintaining social stability and development in the western farming and pastoral areas.

农村小学全科教师的"乡村属性"教学能力及培养路径①

肖正德　王振宇

杭州师范大学教师发展研究中心

摘要:农村小学全科教师是指热爱乡村教育事业,具有浓厚乡土情怀,掌握扎实的学科知识,拥有较高综合素质,能够承担农村小学多学科教学任务的教师。农村小学教学活动场域的特殊性,需要农村小学全科教师除了具备一般小学教师的教学能力外,还要具备浓厚"乡村属性"的特殊教学能力,即乡村教学情感动力、多学科教学能力、复式教学能力、跨学科教学能力、乡村综合实践活动教学能力和乡土教学资源开发与利用能力。农村小学全科教师的"乡村属性"教学能力培养,需要通过如下实践路径达成:确立信念,培育从事乡村教学情感动力;三位一体,突出全科教学能力协同培养;课程综合,重建覆盖全科知识模块课程;课程拓展,开发富有乡土文化特色课程;课堂创新,注重小学全科教学技能训练;实践浸润,构筑见习、实习、研习一体模式。

关键词:农村小学全科教师;乡村属性;特殊教学能力;培养路径

---

①　本文系国家社科基金教育学类一般课题"乡村振兴战略中的农村教师角色转型研究"(课题批准号:BHA180122)的阶段性成果。

农村小学全科教师培养是优化农村教师队伍结构、全面提高农村义务教育教学质量的主要举措。教育部在 2014 年《关于实施卓越教师培养计划的意见》中明确提出，针对小学教育的实际需求，重点探索小学全科教师培养模式，培养一批热爱小学教育事业、知识广博、能力全面，能够胜任小学多学科教育教学需要的卓越小学教师。2015 年，国务院办公厅颁布的《乡村教师支持计划（2015—2020 年）》中提出，鼓励地方政府和师范院校根据当地乡村教育实际需求加强本土化培养，采取多种方式定向培养"一专多能"的乡村教师。2018 年，《中共中央 国务院关于全面深化新时代教师队伍建设改革的意见》指出，鼓励地方政府和相关院校因地制宜采取定向招生、定向培养、定期服务等方式，为乡村学校及教学点培养"一专多能"的教师。同年，教育部等五部门关于印发《教师教育振兴行动计划（2018—2022 年）》的通知中又指出，通过公费定向培养、到岗退费等多种方式，为乡村小学培养补充全科教师。上述四个文件对农村小学全科教师培养提出指导性意见，为农村小学全科教师培养指明了方向。在农村小学全科教师培养过程中，其教学能力建设无疑是一项极为重要的内容。因为教学是教师的中心工作，教师教学能力对教学质量的高低、教学效果的好坏起着关键性作用。因此，探索与研究农村小学全科教师教学能力具有重要的价值意蕴。那么农村小学全科教师的教学能力究竟涵盖哪些方面？农村小学全科教师的"乡村属性"教学能力有哪些因素构成？如何培养农村小学全科教师的"乡村属性"教学能力？本文在对农村小学全科教师基本含义进行释义的基础上，对其"乡村属性"教学能力构成及培养路径这两个重要的问题进行初步探讨。

一、农村小学全科教师的含义阐释

要分析农村小学全科教师的教学能力结构，首先就要明晰什么是"农村小学全科教师"；要明晰什么是"农村小学全科教师"，就要了解什么是"全科教师"。阐释全科教师和农村小学全科教师的基本含义，是分析农村小学全科教师教学能力结构的逻辑前提。

（一）小学全科教师的基本含义

"小学全科教师"这一概念起源于西方国家。英国基于"人才培养的全面性、整体性策略"提出,在小学教育发展过程中实施全科教育,"培养教师跨学科教学的能力"[①]。但是他们并没有提出"小学全科教师"这一明确的学理化概念,仅仅是采用"全面""跨学科""整体"等一些较为模糊的术语。从逻辑上讲,全科教师是相对于分科教师提出的一个概念,因此全科教师必然具备分科教师所不具备的能力,以弥补分科教师在教学过程中的不足。众所周知,分科教师的弊端在于只关注单一学科内部的逻辑体系和客观知识,割裂了学科之间的有机联系,导致所传授内容与学生现实生活世界的背离。而全科教师的教学应当重构知识与生活的关联,将课堂上所学知识与学生的生活世界紧密联系起来,活化课本知识,激发学生的学习兴趣,扩展学生的学科视野。诚如西方要素主义流派学者所言:"教学应该打破了学科之间的界线,同时也打破了每门学科自身的逻辑组织,各门学科的讲授要有一定的次序,要组织成一个体系。"[②]小学全科教师的内涵与要素主义的观点不谋而合,获得了理论支撑。

"小学全科教师"这一明确概念是由我国学者经过吸收消化之后提出来的,但关于小学全科教师这一概念的内涵界定尚未达成一致。根据已有文献资料分析得出,我国学者对小学全科教师的内涵界定主要分为两大流派。其一认为,全科教师即具备多学科教学能力的教师。界定的着眼点在于教师应当担任的科目数量,认为作为全科教师应当能够胜任小学阶段全部科目的教学,类似于西方国家的"包班制"教师。持此种观点的学者指出,"全科型教师是由具备相应资质的教师教育机构专门培养的、掌握教育教学基

---

① 李其龙、陈永明主编:《教师教育课程的国际比较》,教育科学出版社,2006 年,第 25～26 页。
② 金传宝:《美国教育之要素主义的世纪回顾与展望》,《教育学报》,2005 年第 4 期。

本知识和技能、学科知识和能力结构合理、能承担小学阶段国家规定的各门课程教学工作、从事小学教育教学研究与管理的教师"①。此观点关注小学全科教师需要承担大量科目教学任务的特点，具有一定的合理之处，但是此观点同样存在误区。全科教师并非单纯的只会教所有科目的教师，这样的"多科教师"本质上和分科教师没有明显区别，传授的知识仍是割裂孤立的，没有突破学科的局限，本质上仍然是分科教学。因此以所教科目数量来界定是否是全科教师是存在问题的。此外，强行要求教师承担所有科目的教学任务将会给教师带来过重的负担，致使教学质量的下降。

其二认为，全科教师应该具有综合能力，拥有渊博的知识体系，能够对小学生进行整体化的、跨学科式的教学。此界定的着眼点在于教师的综合性能力，认为全科教师的核心应当是其综合能力。此观点的学者主张，"小学全科教师需要综合的能力素质，能力素质的综合性是指适应农村小学教育实际而具有的教育教学能力、活动指导能力、教育管理能力、教育研究能力、自我发展能力等多种能力"②。但此观点对全科教师的界定同样存在误区，"全科型"教师并非"通才"教师。通才即"通用之才"，其特点是融会贯通各学科的知识体系。杜威认为，假如存在"通才"型的全科教师，那么在日常教学中首先要充分深入了解每个学生的已有经验，然后自身掌握所教内容及其相关的全部知识，最后将这些内容以学生可以凭借自身经验理解的方式传授给他们。将这一假设摆在当前的班级规模和需要教授大量科目的背景下，杜威认为这基本上属于神话，即使存在这样的人物，那也应当是人类文明进程中的伟大领袖，而不是一名小学教师。因此单纯地要求教师是"通才"型人物是不现实的，全科教师并不是什么都懂、什么都会、各门学科均衡发展的教师。

尽管我国学界对小学全科教师的内涵界定还存在一定分歧，并未形成

---

① 周德义等：《关于全科型小学教师培养的思考》，《当代教育论坛》，2007 年第 9 期。

② 肖其勇：《农村小学全科教师培养特质与发展模式》，《中国教育学刊》，2014 年第 3 期。

一个普遍认可的、清晰的定义,但综上所述,我们可以获得对小学全科教师的一般性理解:小学全科教师是指热爱教育事业,知识广博,教育教学能力强,具有跨学科思维,能够进行跨学科教学,掌握好广博与精通之间张力的小学教师。

(二)农村小学全科教师的特殊含义

厘清小学全科教师这一上位概念的含义及人们对它的认识误区之后,农村小学全科教师的定义也就不难理解了。相比一般的小学全科教师,农村小学全科教师由于其身处教育教学场域的特殊性及其所面对学生的素质、规模的差异性,因而具有一定的特殊属性,即浓厚的"乡村属性"。首先,农村小学全科教师具有独特的教育情怀。农村小学全科教师的教育情怀是指他们始终保持一种激情,一种热爱,一种对农村教育的执着和追求。由于他们开展教学活动场域位于广袤的农村地区,其自然环境较为恶劣,经济发展较为落后,生活条件与教学条件均比较艰苦。在此特殊场域下从事教育教学,若是没有教育情怀是难以坚守的。

其次,农村小学全科教师要有针对不同班级规模因地制宜开展教学活动的能力。随着城市化进程的推进,大量的农村人口涌向城市,农村生源逐渐减少,农村学校办学规模日益变小,再加上"撤点并校"行动的推进,导致许多农村学校存在学生差异较大、各年龄段、各学段的学生数量参差不齐的境况。农村小学全科教师既有可能接手全是刚入学儿童的班级,也有可能接手所有年级学生都有的混合班级。一名合格的农村小学全科教师需要能够针对不同的学生规模合理地组织教学活动,确保教学活动的顺利开展。

最后,农村小学全科教师理应熟悉乡村、对乡村社会具有完整且深刻的认识。教学活动的开展不能只沉浸在书本当中,缺乏与现实世界的联系将会使所学知识变得枯燥无味,使学生逐渐丧失学习兴趣。农村小学全科教师的教学应当不单囿于课本,还应充分利用周遭环境,从丰富多彩的农村生活中汲取教学材料。若是农村小学全科教师能对当地的乡村风土人情、自然环境有完整且深刻的认识,那就便于他们开展乡村社会实践活动教学及对乡村教学资源的开发与利用,对于农村小学全科教师的"乡村属性"教学能力培养是大有裨益的。

基于上述的理解与认识,我们可将农村小学全科教师的特殊含义界定为:热爱乡村教育事业,具有浓厚农村情感,掌握扎实的学科知识,拥有较高综合素质,能够承担农村小学多学科教学任务的教师。其含义的特殊性可以从三个方面来理解:一是深厚的农村情感,即农村小学全科教师具有倾心于乡村教育、热爱乡村儿童的思想情感,是"下得去、留得住"乐教于乡村小学的教师。二是全面的专业知识,即农村小学全科教师专业理论深厚,学科知识宽广,是能适合农村小学多门学科教学的教师。三是良好的能力素质,农村小学全科教师是师德高尚、师艺突出、教学技能过硬、综合素质良好的教师。

二、农村小学全科教师"乡村属性"教学能力的构成分析

教学能力是指教师为达到教学目标、顺利从事教学活动所表现的一种心理特征。它是一位教师业务水平的体现,是决定教师作用和地位的核心因素,关系到学校的教育教学质量与水平。[①] 农村小学全科教师的教学能力是由一般能力和特殊能力组成。其一般能力是指作为一名小学教师首先要具备的完成一般教学活动任务所需的能力。其特殊能力是指农村小学全科教师具备的,在农村小学这一特殊的教学活动场域完成特殊的教学任务所需的具有浓厚"乡村属性"的专门能力。根据农村小学全科教师所处文化环境的特殊性、教学对象的特殊性及其国家对他们的特殊要求,决定了农村小学全科教师的"乡村属性"教学能力主要由如下六种特殊的教学能力构成。

---

① 申继亮等:《论教师的教学能力》,《北京师范大学学报(人文社科版)》,2000 年第 1 期。

（一）乡村教学情感动力

农村小学全科教师的乡村教学情感动力是指农村小学全科教师所具有的热爱乡村教育、热爱乡村儿童、倾心于乡村小学教学的思想情感层面的内在动力。它是农村小学全科教师的首要教学能力，因为丰富的学科知识和精湛的教学技能只有在深厚的乡村情感的熏染下才能在乡村小学教学中发挥最大作用。一位农村教师若是缺乏对乡村的深厚情感，没有坚守乡村的教育情怀，那么即使他教学能力再高、教学艺术再强也只是一个匆匆过客，难以长期扎根于乡村，不会乐教于乡村，无法持续为乡村教育做出自己的努力和贡献。情感是从事工作必备的感情基础，"即使有最完善的法案，最英明的指令，最好的教科书，而负责去实施的人没有饱满的热情，对自己的使命不是满腔热忱，对事业不付出激情和信仰……那么一切都是枉然的"①。缘此，农村小学全科教师应当具备热爱乡村生活、热爱乡村教育及热爱乡村儿童的一种"乡村感"，并在"乡村感"的催化下促使他们在教学中具有炽烈的情感和充沛的动力，将自己的心血、才智、温馨和激情凝聚在对乡村儿童的关爱中，点亮一双双呼唤未来的眼睛，塑造一个个美好、健康的心灵，引导乡村儿童学习知识、发展能力、健康成长。

（二）多学科教学能力

农村小学全科教师的多学科教学能力是指农村小学全科教师所具备的能够同时承担农村小学多门科目教学工作的能力。这一教学能力强调农村小学全科教师的全科属性，他们要从事小学语文、数学、英语、音乐、美术、体育、综合实践、信息技术、心理健康等多学科的教学。这是因为伴随我国城镇化进程的加快和人民对优质教育的渴望，大量农村学生通过各种方式"挤进"城市学校，乡村学校"自然小班化"。而目前教师数量是以师生比来配置

---

① 郭元祥：《综合实践活动课程设计与实施》，首都师范大学出版社，2001年，第48页。

的,这样显然无法保证农村小学所有科目均配齐相应的任课教师,绝大部分农村教师都需要"身兼数职"。此外,农村教师结构性不合理,语数学科教师相对富裕,音、体、美、英语、计算机等学科专任教师普遍紧缺。面对这样的现状,就亟须培养农村小学全科教师的多学科教学能力,以应对农村小学"自然小班化"和教师资源配置不足的"时代之需"。另一方面,农村小学生对世界的认识是整体化、生活化的,而这些来源于生活中包含着世界万物的各种自然现象实际上包含着各学科知识,他们需要从具备多学科知识的教师那里得到一个科学合理的解释和带来更多的知识享受。① 培养农村小学全科教师多学科教学能力,这既能解决农村小学师资数量不足及学科结构失衡的问题,又能针对小学生面对的完整的、统一的、不可任意分割的"生活世界",帮助他们逐步构建对这个世界的整体认识。

(三)复式教学能力

复式教学是指由一位教师在同一教室同时向两个或两个以上的不同年级施教的一种教学组织形式,它一般适用于学生少、教师少、基础设施落后的农村学校。② 农村小学全科教师的复式教学能力是指农村小学全科教师在同一教室同时向两个或两个以上的不同年级施教,针对不同的学生情况,合理地进行分组教学的能力。复式教学能力不仅仅是将学生分组的能力,更重要的是分组之后的课堂教学能力,复式教学不同于单式教学的是它具有"三多""两少"的特点,③即年级多、科目多、自主作业时间多;直接教学时间少、同一年级人数少。教师在课堂上需要对多个年级进行课堂讲解,意味着分配到每个年级学生的讲授时间就减少了,这需要教师具有很强的提炼总结能力,能够用尽量少的时间讲尽量多的知识点;当教师在给其中一个年级授课时,必然要给已授课的年级布置课后巩固作业,给未上课的年级布置

---

①　肖其勇:《农村小学全科教师培养特质与发展模式》,《中国教育学刊》,2014 年第 3 期。
②　刘冬梅:《中国近代复式教学研究》,陕西师范大学硕士研究生学位论文,2008 年。
③　吕晓虹:《复式教学在义务教育中的地位及前景》,《教育评论》,1999 年第 3 期。

课前预习作业,这就需要教师具有较强的布置作业能力;教学的年级多,学生年龄差异大,维持课堂纪律是一个难点,需要教师具备高超的课堂掌控能力;所教科目多,备课复杂,这就需要教师对各年级教材都有全面的认识。农村小学全科教师要具备复试教学能力,也是应对农村小学"自然小班化"和教师资源配置不足的"时代之需",也正是具备这一教学能力,才使农村小学全科教师更好地适应当前我国农村教育的现状,为农村教育发展发挥应有的作用。

(四)跨学科教学能力

农村小学全科教师的跨学科教学能力是指农村小学全科教师应当具有组织学生围绕一个话题,跨两门甚至更多学科进行主题单元教学的能力。跨学科主题单元教学具有传统分科教学所没有的优点:一是有利于培养学生的跨学科综合思维能力。设计主题教学单元,基于真实情境,解决真实问题,培养多角度综合思维能力和意识,培养多学科综合技能,激发学生的学习动力,在潜移默化中形成学生的跨学科综合思维能力;二是有助于促进学生的个性发展。跨学科主题单元教学的教学环节不是教师固定的,而是由学生来决定的,每个学生都会有独特的思考路径,用不同的方法来解决问题,有助于促进他们个性的独特发展;三是有利于加强课堂上的交流。在如此开放式的教学当中,交流是课堂组成的重要部分,师生之间的交流、生生之间的交流都占到较大的比重,在交流中促进学生发展人际交往能力、清晰表达能力和团队合作能力。跨学科的能力素养并非城市学生的特权,农村学生也应当具备这样的跨学科能力素养。农村小学全科教师有责任培养农村学生开阔的视野与跨学科的整体思维能力,为他们今后往更高层次发展打好基础。因此农村小学全科教师应该依据儿童兴趣,围绕儿童生活经验,以"学习主题"的形式实现课程的内在整合,[1]施行跨学科主题单元教学。

---

[1]　陶青等:《免费定向农村小学全科教师培养的必要性分析》,《教师教育研究》,2014年第6期。

(五)乡村综合实践活动教学能力

农村小学全科教师的乡村综合实践活动教学能力是指农村小学全科教师在乡村社会场域中带领学生开展综合实践活动的能力,即在具备课堂教学与常规管理能力之外,还要具备组织小学生进行劳动、社区服务、社会实践等教育性活动的能力。乡村综合实践活动是乡村学生沟通书本知识与乡村社会现实的重要桥梁。农村学校班级少,学生数量少,社会实践机会多,操作过程易于管理,恰好为综合实践活动的开展提供了良好的环境。这一教学能力主要是将学生的直接经验和兴趣作为基础,以与学生社会生活等密切相联系的各类综合性、实践性、现实性的问题为主要内容,以研究性学习的方式,培养学生的实践能力、创新精神及体现对知识的综合运用。[①] 综合实践活动对农村学生发展具有其独特的价值,它将学生从单一的以书本知识为内容,以讲授为主要形式的课堂教学中解放出来,学生通过亲自动手、体验和实践,增强他们的实践能力,培养他们的创新精神。乡村综合实践活动教学,有利于提高乡村学生的学习积极性,培养他们的探索兴趣,形成乐学的风气;有助于促进乡村学生的社会化,培养他们的实践能力;有利于乡村学生走进乡村社会,了解自己的家乡,培养热爱乡村的思想情感及未来建设乡村的责任感和使命感。所有这些,需要农村小学全科教师具备高强的乡村综合实践活动教学能力方能胜任。

(六)乡土教学资源开发与利用能力

农村小学全科教师的乡土教学资源开发与利用能力是指农村小学全科教师具备发掘乡村特有的教学资源,通过整合与编排,开发具有乡土特色的课程,或者整合与服务于已有课程教学的能力。在我国,农村地域辽阔,文化丰富多样,自然风光美不胜收,这些与城市截然不同的地方恰恰是乡村学

---

① 田慧生:《综合实践活动的性质、特点与课程定位》,《人民教育》,2001 年第 10 期。

校教学得天独厚的优势。在城市化进程加快的今天,尤其需要农村小学全科教师具备乡土教学资源开发与利用能力,传承乡土文化,健全乡村学生人格,复兴乡土文明,促进乡村文化与城市文化有机融合。① 农村小学全科教师具备乡村教学资源开发与利用能力,不仅可以弥补传统课堂教学的缺陷,丰富学生的知识,还可以将大自然搬进课堂里,将教学与小学生的生活实际联系在一起,激发他们的学习兴趣,让他们领略了乡村资源丰富、美不胜收的一面,同时又能传承乡土文化,培植他们的乡土情怀。

三、农村小学全科教师"乡村属性"教学能力的培养路径

上文所述的具有浓厚"乡村属性"的农村小学全科教师六种特殊教学能力,紧密结合、相互影响,构成了一个不断变化发展的有机体,共同推动农村小学全科教师教学能力发展。为此,我们要努力寻找农村小学全科教师"乡村属性"教学能力培养的有效路径,系统构建农村小学全科教师"乡村属性"教学能力的培养体系。

(一)确立信念,培育从事乡村教学情感动力

教育信念是教师行为实践背后的决定性力量,它影响着教师对职业的承诺与坚守,决定着教师的自我表现和工作成就。② 教育信念也是教师从事教育事业的灵魂和内核,对于处在农村场域的小学全科教师而言,教育信念最重要的一个组成部分是他们的农村教育情怀,只有一个对乡村、对乡村儿童有情怀、有情感的教师,才能自觉、自愿地投身乡村教育事业中,才能产生乡村教学情感动力,才能"留得住、教得好"。③ 那么如何确立农村小学全科

---

① 袁利平等:《乡土课程开发的文化价值与实践选择》,《中国教育学刊》,2018 年第 5 期。

② 邱德峰:《论乡村教师的教育信念——基于〈感动中国〉〈寻找最美乡村教师〉等素材的质性研究》,《当代教育科学》,2018 年第 2 期。

③ 朱纯洁等:《农村小学全科教师的特质结构及培养路径探析》,《教学与管理》,2015 年第 10 期。

教师的教育信念,培育他们的乡村教学情感动力呢?

第一,依托教师教育课程,培育热爱农村教育事业的职业情感。教师职业情感的产生要基于教师对自身职业的性质、意义有深刻而全面的认识。在农村小学全科教师培养中,通过在校学习期间开设教师教育类课程,把理想信念教育和乡村教学情感培育作为一项常规活动纳入课堂教学中,引导师范生对农村小学全科教师形成充分的认识与理解,增强职业使命感和责任感,进而坚定为乡村教育事业贡献青春、智慧和力量的信心。

第二,邀请小学名师走进大学课堂,发挥其对农村小学全科师范生的情感引导作用。乌申斯基认为,教师是学生的榜样,任何教科书、任何思潮、任何奖罚制度都无法动摇教师的地位,他对学生内心所产生的影响是独一无二的。教师的一举一动、一言一行深刻影响着学生的未来发展。因此在农村小学全科教师的培养过程中,邀请农村小学名师走进大学课堂,采取多种方式,让他们发挥对农村小学全科师范生的情感引导作用。如开办沙龙,与农村小学全科师范生们交流分享日常的乡村教育趣事,回忆年轻时的教育故事等。在潜移默化中促使农村小学全科师范生渐渐向往农村,热爱乡村,热爱乡村教育。

第三,组织农村小学全科师范生走进农村小学现场,培养热爱小学教育事业的情怀。分期组织农村小学全科师范生到农村小学进行教育见习和教育实习,以便充分了解与接触小学教育教学的实际,从而对自己将要从事的教师职业有更多的感性认识,以增强他们的职业意识。[①] 让他们在各类教育实践活动中感受到做乡村老师的快乐,体验到乡村教育的价值,从而确立献身乡村教育的信念,培育从事乡村教学的情感动力。

(二)三位一体,突出全科教学能力协同培养

农村小学全科教师教学能力培养不能单凭大学的孤军奋战,而需要大

---

① 何雪玲等:《基于岗位需求的农村小学全科教师培养策略探析》,《中小学教师培训》,2016年第 6 期。

学、地方政府与小学三者协同作战,以"全科"为核心,发挥各自的原生优势,构建大学、地方政府与小学"三位一体"协同培养机制。在"三位一体"协同培养模式运行过程中,三方的角色、任务、目标都需要向实现"全科"转变。

第一,大学、政府与小学要协同制定农村小学全科教师的培养目标。大学作为培养单位,要培养什么规格的农村小学全科教师,应从用人单位的需求出发,紧密联系农村小学实际,问道农村小学名师名校长,准确把握农村小学教学的真实需求,精准培养小学全科教师的教学能力。

第二,三者协同建立资源共享平台。在地方政府的统筹下,大学向农村小学开放网络教学资源,开展各类培训,更新农村小学教师的教育教学理念,提供最新的课程资源;反过来,农村小学向大学提供现场考察、见习实习的机会,为农村小学全科师范生带去大量的名师示范课,引领与加速他们向全科教师蜕变;地方政府提供优秀教研员为大学提供学术和政策资源。地方政府教研员和农村小学名师到大学兼职或学习与交流,实现名师互享。[①]

第三,三者协同建构全程化教育实践模式。农村小学全科师范生在校期间,合理分配教育实习任务,将理论与技能学习分为多个阶段,将教育实习穿插在各个阶段之间,使理论与实践多次交叉,有机结合,避免了传统的先学理论最后实习模式带来的弊端。同时,全程化实践模式延长了实践的时间,给农村小学全科师范生提供了大量的时间,锻炼他们的多学科教学能力、复式教学能力、跨学科教学能力、综合实践活动教学能力,在真实情境中不断体验、研究、观摩,积累教学经验,熟练乡村小学课堂教学技能,增长"乡村属性"教学能力。

(三)课程综合,重建覆盖全科知识模块课程

相比普通小学教师,农村小学全科教师强调一个"全"字,他们应当掌握

---

① 何雪玲等:《基于岗位需求的农村小学全科教师培养策略探析》,《中小学教师培训》,2016年第6期。

"全科知识",因此在课程的设置中应体现出全面与综合的特点。"全科知识"可以分为三类,科学文化知识、专业学科知识、教育理论知识。

首先,从传统课程设置来看,科学文化知识的获取一般是通过选修通识课来得到满足。但由于其选修的性质,存在着量少面窄的缺陷,不能保证全科教师的科学文化知识水平达到广博的程度。因此,在通识课程的设置上应当综合社会各个领域、各个学科,在每个领域均编制一定数量的主题模块课程,并要求农村小学全科师范生在每个不同领域修满一定学分,确保他们在每个领域都有所涉及,拓宽他们的知识面。

其次,专业学科知识也应当在相应的综合化课程中获得。普通小学教师的专业知识课程通常由一门主要的必修学科和一门次要的选修学科组成,主要学习该学科的基础知识和该学科的教材教法。这一做法割裂了学科之间的联系,而农村小学全科教师需要学习全部学科的基础知识及与之相匹配的教学法。同时,他们的教学能力并不是多门学科教学能力的简单叠加,跨学科的思维方式同样十分重要。而采用综合课程的方式学习专业知识,充分利用综合课程关注学科间的联系、具有整合性、统一性的特点,训练农村小学全科师范生的跨学科思维方式,增长他们的综合知识和综合技能。

最后,传统课程设置中教学理论知识一般由教育学和心理学两门课程来提供,理论知识的学习一般通过教师讲授学生记诵的方式进行,这种与教学实践相脱离的理论学习往往难以在日后的小学全科教师工作中发挥应有的作用,导致农村小学全科师范生产生教育学和心理学无用的想法。只有通过课程综合,将理论知识与实践体验联系起来,才能真正发挥教育理论知识指导教育实践的作用,从而更好地培养他们多学科教学能力和跨学科教学能力。

(四)课程拓展,开发富有乡土文化特色课程

农村小学全科师范生拓展性课程以开发农村小学全科师范生的潜能、

完善他们的知识结构、培养他们的特殊教学能力为旨归。农村小学全科教师的教学能力除了强调一个"全"字之外,还强调"乡村"二字,以培养农村小学全科教师的乡村教学情感动力和乡土教学资源开发与利用能力。因此,在农村小学全科师范生学习基础的通识课程、教育理论课程和专业课程之外还应进行课程拓展,开发具有浓郁乡土文化特色的拓展性课程。具有浓郁乡土文化特色的拓展性课程开发,既是对农村小学全科师范生进行乡土化教育的过程,也是教授他们如何发掘与活化乡土教学资源、编制乡土校本课程的过程。具有浓郁乡土文化特色的拓展性课程开发,既可以从特有的自然景观入手,也可以从独特的民俗文化出发;既可以从名人名家着手,也可以从社区文化活动开始。在具有浓郁乡土文化特色的拓展性课程学习中,农村小学全科师范生既受到乡村风土人情的熏陶,滋养"乡村属性",坚定扎根乡村的信念,激发乡村教学情感动力,又能促使他们的乡土教学资源开发与利用能力得到更好的培养。

(五)课堂创新,注重小学全科教学能力实训

农村小学全科教师的"乡村属性"教学能力培养应当"穿新鞋,走新路",要注重课堂教学创新,注重"乡村属性"教学能力的实训。一方面,进行课堂教学模式改革,实施"小学教师进大学课堂、大学生进小学课堂"的实践类课程教学改革模式,即"U—S—S"实践类课程"1 + 1 + 1"教学改革模式。"U—S—S"(大学—学校—学科)模式是指将大学课程直接搬到一线课堂,将一线农村小学名师请到大学课堂,具体通过"1 + 1 + 1"的创新教学模式来实现:大学教师负责课程约三分之一课时的理论部分教学和整体课程协调,小学对应的学科名师负责约三分之一课时的技能实训;农村小学全科师范生在小学课堂上实践练习约占三分之一课时。通过实践类课程教学模式改革,着力培养农村小学全科师范生的复式教学能力、综合实践活动教学能力和乡土教学资源开发与利用能力。另一方面,进行课堂教学方式创新。充分利用模拟课堂、现场教学、情境教学、案例分析等多样化的教学方式,激发农

村小学全科师范生的学习兴趣,着力提高他们的创新能力和实践能力。加强以信息技术为基础的现代教育技术开发与应用,将现代教育技术渗透、运用到教学中。充分利用信息技术变革农村小学全科教师教学方式、学生学习方式和师生互动方式,积极倡导在线学习、混合式学习等,提升农村小学全科师范生信息素养和利用信息技术促进教学的能力。概言之,通过课堂教学方式创新,努力提升农村小学全科教师的创新能力和实践能力,从而培养他们的多学科教学能力、跨学科教学能力和乡村综合实践活动教学能力。

(六)实践浸润,构筑见习研习实习一体模式

农村小学全科教师的"乡村属性"教学能力是一个多种因素紧密结合的有机体,它不是一成不变的,它会随着教师理论知识的充盈与实践经验的丰富而不断发展。农村小学全科教师的"乡村属性"教学能力培养必然要落到实践中去,在实践中验证教育理论,在实践中磨炼教学技能,在实践中培育教学能力。为此,需要为农村小学全科师范生构筑见习研习实习为一体的"浸润式"实践模式。见习、实习、研习这三个阶段是循序渐进、相互衔接的。其中,见习阶段指的是,农村小学全科师范生在积累了一定的教育理论知识以后,进入农村小学现场,进行观察、体验、感悟,为之后的教育实习与研习乃至从事农村小学教学工作做好心理准备,同时也触发"乡村属性"教学能力的萌生;研习阶段指的是,农村小学全科师范生通过校内外导师的指导,运用所学的教育理论知识,科学文化知识及专业知识,对农村小学教育教学过程中遇到的问题进行深入分析与研究,从而将理论与实践结合起来,培养他们的问题意识和研究能力,进而促进"乡村属性"教学能力的进步;实习阶段则指的是,农村小学全科师范生在见习与研习阶段完成的基础上,在导师的引导下深入了解农村小学教学工作的每一个细节,历练多学科教学能力、复式教学能力、跨学科教学能力、乡村综合实践活动教学能力、乡土教学资源开发与利用能力,加快由农村小学全科师范生到农村小学全科教师的身份转换。

Teaching Ability of "Rural Attribute" and Training Path of Multidisciplinary Teachers in Rural Primary Schools

Zhengde Xiao   Zhenyu Wang

The Center for Research on Teacher Development Hangzhou

Normal University

Abstract: Multidisciplinary Teachers in rural primary schools refer to teachers who love rural education, have strong homeland feelings, have solid knowledge of disciplines, have high comprehensive quality, and can undertake multidisciplinary teaching tasks in rural primary schools. The particularity of the teaching activity field in the rural primary schools requires that the multidisciplinary teachers in the rural primary schools not only have the teaching ability of the general primary school teachers, but also have the special ability with strong "rural attribute", i. e. rural teaching emotional motivation, multidisciplinary teaching ability, compound teaching ability, interdisciplinary teaching ability, rural comprehensive practical activity teaching ability and the ability to develop and utilize local teaching resources. In order to cultivate the teaching ability of "rural attribute" of multidisciplinary teachers in rural primary schools, the following practical path need to be constructed: Establishing belief and to cultivate the emotional force for engaging in rural teaching, Promote the co – cultivation of teaching ability through the cooperation among universities – local government – schools, Integrate the curriculum and rebuild the modular course covering the multidisciplinary knowledge,

Guide curriculum development and develop the curriculum with local cultural charactics, to innovate classroom teaching, Pay attention to the multi – subjects teaching skill training, Strengthen the practice and construct the integrated model of probation, practice and study.

Keywords: multidisciplinary teachers in rural primary schools; rural attribute; special teaching ability; training path

Elementary teacher training in Hungary: traditions and innovations

Csaba Csíkos

ELTE Eötvös Loránd University, Budapest, Hungary

Faculty of Primary and Pre-School Education

Abstract: State-sponsored elementary teacher training has a 150 year-long history in Hungary. Throughout the past 150 years our programs have continuously evolved to reflect the demands of a changing society while also striving to develop a professional, academic network that extends throughout the field of childhood education in both Hungary and abroad. The situation in Hungarian elementary teacher education seems to be similar to that of Chinese economy development in the twentieth century under the label of "walk on two legs". Tradition in elementary teacher education can be seen in the following factors: strong emphasis on field practice training from the very first semester; in-service mentor teachers take special care of the students entrusted to their support; and students are trained to teach each school subjects in grades from 1 to 4, and they can teach one subject as their chosen specialization in grades 5 and 6.

At the same time, university teachers from assistant professors to full professors are involved in scientific research under the Western maxim of "publish or perish". Consequently, the university courses have a twofold function: to provide support for pre – service teacher for their field training practice, and to share the latest findings from the international scientific discourse community they belong to. Elementary teacher educators have to be qualified in early childhood education and in their special content domain (e. g., Mathematics, Literature, Informatics etc.) as well.

Besides the challenges raised by "walking on two legs", there are current trends and problems we have to face: elementary teaching as a profession has currently not an outstanding prestige in Hungary. Consequently, high school students with the best academic achievement rarely choose the profession of elementary educator (however, there are notable exceptions!). However, pre – service elementary teachers are motivated to learn their profession.

When recruiting high school students I often ask them whether they know the name of the minister of education in the year they started to go school. Then the next question concerns their elementary teacher's name. The difference in the rate of answers strikingly indicates the importance of the elementary teacher's profession.

1. Brief historical background

State – regulated elementary teacher training has a 150 year – long history in Hungary. Throughout the past 150 years our programs have continuously evolved to reflect the demands of a changing society while also striving to develop professional, academic cooperation that extends throughout the field of childhood education in both Hungary and abroad.

In order to understand the processes that characterize elementary teacher ed-

ucation in Hungary and in other countries of the world, *Archer's* (1982) [1] semi-
nal work provides insights on three consecutive phases in the development of educational systems. According to her terminology, the first stage of development
called take – off is characterized by a competition between the state and the
church as school maintainers. The second phase can be described as rapid development in terms of quantitative and qualitative features in all stages of education.
In the second phase (growth) teacher training starts to move up one level, from
secondary to tertiary level. In the third phase of the educational expansion, inflation is characterized by an ever growing number of people having upper secondary
and tertiary degrees. In the third phase, teacher training is implemented almost
exclusively in tertiary education, and more and more in – service teachers have
doctoral degrees (Ph. D. or Ed. D.) directly connected to their professions.

In Hungary, the transitions in elementary teacher training took place as seen
below.

From 1869 to 1958, elementary teacher training in Hungary belonged to the
level of secondary schooling. Prospective elementary teachers were upper secondary school students. From 1958, the maturation exam (closing examination at the
end of upper secondary schooling) became an admission requirement for the three
– year – long tertiary level elementary teacher training. From 1995 and since
then elementary teacher training is of B. Ed. level and lasts four years. Due to the
challenges coming from knowledge – based societies, the idea of a master level elementary teacher training is on the table, i. e. is subject of discussions among professionals.

---

[1]　Archer, M. S. (Ed.), *The sociology of educational expansion: Take – off, growth and inflation in educational systems* (Vol. 27). Sage Publications, 1982.

2. "Walking on two legs": Theory and practice in elementary teacher training

The situation in Hungarian elementary teacher education seems to be similar to that of Chinese economy development in the twentieth century under the label of "walk on two legs". This metaphor refers to the fact that we necessarily rely on the traditions while we gradually introduce novelties and innovations.

Tradition in elementary teacher education can be seen in the following factors: strong emphasis on field practice training from the very first semester; in-service mentor teachers take special care of the students entrusted to their support; and students are trained to teach each school subjects in grades from 1 to 4, and they can teach one subject as their chosen specialization in grades 5 and 6. These traditions are further enhanced at ELTE, Budapest, by the fact that the practice school is only at one door distance (actually, not metaphorically) from the building of the Faculty of Primary and Pre-School Education. Traditionally, the Hungarian educational system has a 4 year long primary phase followed by the upper and lower secondary stages. Our elementary school teachers have a license to teach all school subjects in grades from 1 to 4, and they have one special subject to teach in grades 5 and 6.

Innovations in elementary teacher training come from several sources as well. First, in the 20th century, education became "big science" (as Solla – Price[1] would call it), i.e., educational science has research institutions, highly prestigious conferences and journals. Underneath the large umbrella of educational sciences both the topics on early childhood education and the topics of subject – spe-

---

[1] Price, D. J. *Little science, big science...and beyond.* New York: Columbia University Press, 1986.

cific didactics underwent a large increase in following the scientific standards. Consequently, the learning targets and the curricula of elementary teacher training is largely influenced by the latest cutting – edge research results. However, as pointed out by Darling – Hammond, teacher training is about 100 years behind medical education where doctors' training is led by conveying new knowledge in the university curricula and training.

3. Elementary teacher trainers

In elementary teachers training, an everlasting question may arise: Who are the best (or capable) trainers? Those who have several years of experience from educational practice as in – service teachers or those who have a massive publication background in early childhood education? (Other profiles are possible, of course.) It may be agreed upon that these two features should be joint in order to implement the best teacher training. However, the difficulties of being eminent in publishing and having ample practical experience are well – known. Many elementary teacher trainers become university staff member after 10 or even more years spent as in – service teachers. When being a university staff member they are usually obliged to obtain a scientific degree and to publish regularly. They have some kind of competitive disadvantage against those who could immediately start doctoral studies after obtaining their university degree. What is more, since elementary teaching is at the bachelor level in Hungary, those who would like to earn a PhD must complete their master's studies first in the field of education or other disciplines.

According to David Berliner (personal communication in 2005) the best university research teams in the field of education consist of two kinds of personalities. Those who earned their PhD rather early can enrich the community by their conceptual discipline and research methodological ideas. Whereas those who worked as in – service teachers before can enrich the research team by research questions that are instantly relevant and useful for the practice. There are numerous examples of research teams who exploit the benefits of different approaches coming from different personalities and lifelines.

University teachers from assistant professors to full professors are involved in scientific research under the Western maxim of"publish or perish". Consequently, the university courses have a twofold function: to provide support for pre – service teacher for their field training practice, and to share the latest findings from the international scientific discourse community they belong to. Elementary teacher educators have to be qualified in early childhood education and in their special content domain (e. g. , Mathematics, Literature, Informatics etc.) as well.

4. Pre – service elementary teachers

When recruiting high school students I often ask them whether they know the name of the minister of education in the year they started to go school. Then the next question concerns their elementary teacher's name. The difference in the rate of answers strikingly indicates the importance of the elementary teacher's profession.

Even though the prestige of being a teacher in Hungary is not so high nowadays, we can rightly claim that those who choose studies in elementary teaching are really motivated to learn, and they have the perseverance required by the profession. According to the latest statistical data, about 70% of the elementary teachers having obtained the degree starts working as in – service teachers. Many of them have further university studies or have family or parenting tasks that hinder or delay the start of working as a teacher. From international studies like the

TIMSS and PIRLS surveys we have ample evidence about the strengths of Hungarian elementary education. Children aged around 10 often perform surprisingly well in international comparison in the fields of mathematics and reading. (By means of surprisingly we mean two things: the PISA studies use to find our 15 year old students around or slightly below the OECD – average, and when comparing our students' results to the indexes of our economic and cultural life and health indicators, the strength of our educational system can be evidenced.

5. National and global challenges

Besides the challenges raised by "walking on two legs", there are current trends and problems we have to face: elementary teaching as a profession has currently not an outstanding prestige in Hungary. In this respect, a positive international example is Finland where teaching professions are among the most highly valued jobs in high – school students' views[①]. Consequently, in Finland high school students with the best academic achievement often choose the profession of elementary educator, in fact only one tenth of students who apply can start their teacher education program. In contrast, in Hungary we could admit much more pre – service elementary teachers than the number of applicants we currently have. Among the several reasons why the teaching profession has low prestige in Hungary is the relatively low salary teachers have. "Between 2005 and 2018, primary and lower secondary teachers' salaries increased by 9% , . . During this period, teacher salaries at these levels of education fell by approximately 30% between 2005 and 2013, but increased significantly between 2014 and 2018 to their

---

① http://ncee. org/what – we – do/center – on – international – education – benchmarking/top – performing – countries/finland – overview/finland – teacher – and – principal – quality/.

current levels. Despite the increases, teachers' salaries are still comparatively low."①(p. 4).

Teacher training (and especially elementary teacher training) is often thought to be a national endeavor. Since elementary teacher play their key role in developing their students' native language competence, a great proportion of the elementary teacher training courses deal with the theory and practice of how to foster native language competences. Even though – due to the internationalization of science in general – the majority of school subjects and the majority of the courses in elementary teacher training can have core elements worldwide, a significant proportion still should remain a national competence and effort. However, with the globalization processes of education, more and more students learn abroad either in exchange programs (like the Erasmus projects in Europe) or to obtain a degree. Elementary teacher education is not exceptional in this case, and both the exchange programs and the teacher diplomas obtained abroad will strengthen understanding between different cultures, nations and people.

6. Open questions

There are several dilemmas around elementary teacher education. From time to time, politicians, opinion leaders and professional discourse communities put a theme on the table. Do we need to keep tertiary elementary teacher training at the tertiary level of education (or upper secondary level would be just as fine)? To what extent the National Core Curriculum should detail the knowledge items students must learn in their early years of schooling (or it would be just enough to develop their key competences and basic skills)?

---

① https://www.oecd.org/education/education – at – a – glance/EAG2019_CN_HUN.pdf.

We aim to provide answers to these dilemmas in accordance with the tendencies and traditions described above. Our basic principle is that in the age of globalization the educational systems are more and more transparent and accountable, and the synergies between educational research and practical wisdom will conserve what is good and help to leave behind the elements of training that were present either because of a kind of adherence to traditions, or because of the attraction of scientific novelty.

匈牙利的小学教师师资培养:传统与革新

乔堡·西科斯

匈牙利罗兰大学初等教育和学前教育系,副院长

摘要:国家支持的小学教师培训在匈牙利已有150年的历史。在这过去的150年中,我们的课程不断发展,以适应不断变化的社会的需求,同时也努力建立一个遍及匈牙利和其他国家的儿童教育领域的专业学术网络。匈牙利小学教师教育的情况似乎与20世纪中国经济发展的情况相似,带着"两条腿走路"的标签。小学教师教育的传统可以从以下几个方面来看:从第一学期开始就非常重视实地实践培训;一线指导老师会给本科生需要的支持;学生经过培训,能讲授小学1至4年级的所有科目,并且可以教授5至6年级的一个科目作为自己的专业方向课程。

与此同时,大学教师从讲师到教授,都要按照西方的"不发文章,即灭亡"的准则进行科学研究。因此大学课程具有双重功能:为职前教师的实践培训提供支持,并分享其所属领域的国际最新研究成果。小学教师教育者还必须具备幼儿教育及其特殊学科领域(例如,数学,文学,信息科学等)的

资格。

　　除了"两条腿走路"带来的挑战之外,我们还必须面对当前的趋势和问题:小学教育作为一种职业目前在匈牙利尚无突出的声誉。因此学业成绩最好的高中生很少选择小学教育工作者这一职业(不过,也有个别的例外)。但是职前的小学教师都具有专业学习的积极性。

　　在高校招生时,我经常问学生是否知道自己开始上学的那一年的教育部长的名字。接着会问他们的小学老师的名字。回答率的差异明显表明了小学教师职业的重要性。

One Teacher – Seven Different Subjects: How can this be successful?

Esther Brunner

Thurgau University of Teacher Education, Kreuzlingen, Switzerland

Abstract: Swiss elementary teachers have to teach at least seven different subjects in their class. This profile is characterized as "the all – round teacher" and is common in Swiss elementary schools. The main idea behind this conception is that the teachers have the opportunity to build a strong social relationship and establish a learning community in the classroom with respect to social and content – related aspects. This places different demands on pre – service teachers and the school system in general and leads to specific consequences for elementary teacher education. The presentation first gives an overview of Swiss elementary teacher education and relates this outline to the Swiss education system. These explanations concerning the structural dimensions are followed by a description of the prerequisites that pre – service teachers are expected to fulfil and the kind of professional knowledge they have to acquire. In the third part, the example of the preparation for the teaching of mathematics, which is relevant to all elementary teachers, provides a concrete insight into elementary teacher education in Switzerland.

1. Swiss primary schools and their teachers

Swiss primary teachers are required and qualified to teach at least seven (sometimes even eight) different subjects during a longer period of at least two or three consecutive years in the same class. This profile is characterized as "the all – round teacher", which is common in Swiss elementary schools.

Elementary education concerns the Pre – K level of kindergarten and the Grades 1 to 6. The majority of the children complete their compulsory education at a state school in the municipality in which they live. The Canton[①] and the local municipality together finance 90 % of the total public expenditure on education (EDK, 2017). Only a few pupils—approximately 5%—go to a private school, which requires the parents to pay school fees, however. Schooling at state schools, by contrast, is free of charge. Compulsory education is organized in a three – level structure: Pre – K level (age 4 – 6), primary school (Grades 1 – 6), and lower secondary school (Grades 7 – 9). After this time, the pupils continue their education by entering a vocational or professional training programme or—if they had opted for a baccalaureate school (see below)—by going to university. These paths belong to the upper secondary and tertiary level.

In kindergarten and in primary school, the main profile of the teachers—as mentioned above—is the "all – round teacher" who teaches his or her class over a consecutive period of at least two or three years. This is not only common but also a reflection and manifestation of political and societal preferences and intentions. The basic idea behind this concept is that the teacher establishes a social class-

---

① The political structure of Switzerland is organized in 26 different Cantons. A Canton has a certain political and financial autonomy and is also responsible for running the schools that provide compulsory education.

room community in which all pupils can participate, irrespective of their social or cultural[①] and linguistic background, their gender, or their cognitive abilities. The prime responsibility for the 20 – 24 pupils lies with the all – round class teacher. Because classes of this size are often very heterogeneous, however, the class teacher is sometimes supported by an assistant teacher, teachers for a specific subject, or special – needs teachers.

An example might be helpful to characterize the profile of the " all – round teacher" more concretely. An elementary teacher, for instance, teaches one class from Grade 1 to Grade 3 in the subjects mathematics, first language, second language (English from the beginning of Grade 3), science, sports, music, and arts while another teacher works with this class only in technical and textile handicraft. Later on, in Grade 5, a third language (French, which is an official language in Switzerland), and media and computer science are taught by a specialist teacher while the seven or eight main subjects are still taught by an all – round teacher. Besides the teaching of the main subjects, the all – round teacher is responsible for all the duties that concern the class in general, for exchanging information and communicating with the parents, for social events and social activities, and importantly, for social learning and the promotion of soft skills in the class. For achieving the aims of the curriculum, the all – round teacher is granted a certain degree of autonomy: He or she is free in choosing suitable learning methods and materials to accomplish the objectives with all pupils. This degree of freedom implies a high extent of responsibility, however.

In the Swiss curriculum, education is understood as the open, lifelong and active developmental proces of each individual pupil (Amt für Volksschule des

---

① 32. 2 % of 15 – to 17 – year – old pupils in Switzerland have a migrant background (Wolter et al., 2018).

Kantons Thurgau, 2016). The general aim of education is that the pupils become independent and responsible individuals who are able to participate and to contribute autonomously and responsibly in the social, cultural, professional, and political context and thus to become reflective citizens (OECD, 2016, 2018). As in many other countries too, this is one of the core values in Swiss education because it is a prerequisite for the ideal of full participation in a democratic society. Achieving this objective implies the necessity of building a strong socially responsible community that cares for each child. Compulsory school, in particular kindergarten and primary school, is therefore expected to serve as a model and provide a context in which the pupils learn to establish such a community of responsible citizens who care for each other and their social environment.

The functions of school are manifold. Basically, there are four functions (Fend, 2008): 1) qualification of individuals, 2) selection of individuals for a specific task or a certain field, 3) allocation of individuals to a suitable educational path, and 4) integrating individuals into a social community. State schools play an important role in integration efforts. The ideal of integration of all children is another of the underlying ideas of the "all - round teacher". These core ideas place different demands on the teachers and the school system in general and lead to specific consequences for elementary teacher education.

2. Baccalaureate schools and access to higher – education institutions

Only approximately 20% – 30% of the pupils decide to continue school education after the compulsory completion of lower secondary school. This relatively small group of less than one third of all adolescents goes to a specialized upper secondary school or to a baccalaureate school. Baccalaureate schools prepare their pupils for tertiary education at a university, a university of applied sciences, or a university of teacher education while the other educational options at upper secondary level facilitate direct entry into the job market (EDK, 2017)①.

Pupils attending baccalaureate school have to graduate in twelve fields. These fields include the nine compulsory subjects (mathematics, physics, chemistry, biology, geography, history, first language, second language, third language) of the regular curriculum, plus an elective specialization subject and a second elective subject. Moreover, every pupil has to submit a baccalaureate thesis on a freely chosen topic. As for the weighting of the regular components, 30% – 40% of the time are allocated to languages, 25% – 35% to mathematics and natural sciences, 10% – 20% to the humanities and social sciences, and 5% – 10% to arts. The individual specialization subject, the second elective, and the thesis account for another 15% – 25% (Wolter et al., 2018)②. This system ensures that the pupils receive a broad education in a variety of subjects while, at the same time, they are provided with the opportunity to specialize in a specific part of the curriculum.

The baccalaureate degree is the necessary prerequisite for entering a higher – education institution (university, university of applied sciences, university of teacher education). Anyone who possesses the requisite qualification can, principally, enroll in the study programme of their choice at a freely selected university (EDK, 2017)③. At some universities, mostly internationally highly ranked technical universities, access is restricted but admission to universities of teacher education is always open.

---

① EDK, *The Swiss education system*, Retrieved: http://www.edk.ch/dyn/11586.php.

② Wolter, S. C., Cattaneo, M. A., Denzler, S., Diem, A., Hof, S., Meier, R., & Oggenfuss, C., *Swiss Education Report 2018*, Aarau: SKBF, 2018.

③ EDK, *The Swiss education system*, Retrieved: http://www.edk.ch/dyn/11586.php.

Since all university students have completed a baccalaureate school, prospective teachers who enroll at a university of teacher education are equipped with a solid and broad education in nine compulsory subjects. This educational background enables them to become competent all – round teachers. Building on this foundation, universities of teacher education can focus on imparting specific teaching – related and pedagogical knowledge and skills.

3. Teachers' professional knowledge and basic ideas of elementary teacher education

Teacher education starts after graduation at baccalaureate school at specialized universities. Primary school teachers acquire a bachelor's degree after a full – time study that covers a total of six semesters. Pre – service teachers spend approximately 20% of their study time at schools (Arnold et al.,2011) [1] where they learn to enact the teaching methods that they have dealt with at university in a real classroom setting. These practical courses are very popular and provide an authentic insight into the future profession as a primary school teacher. They are organized by the university in shared responsibility with local schools. While their time at school, the pre – service teachers receive support of schoolteachers as well as university lecturers and professors. After each practical course, the experiences are reflected on not only together with the schoolteacher but also at the university with the lecturers and professors.

At the university, the pre – service teachers acquire specific professional knowledge and methods in the seven or eight different subjects that they are ex-

①　Arnold, K. – H., Hascher, T., Messner, R., Niggli, A., Patry, J. – L., & Rahm., S., *Empowerment durch Schulpraktika: Perspektiven wechseln in der Lehrerbildung*, Bad Heilbrunn: Klinkhardt, 2011.

pected to teach. According to Shulman (1987) ,[1] different domains of professional knowledge can be deemed important for effective classroom teaching: content knowledge (CK) , pedagogical knowledge (PK) , and pedagogical content knowledge (PCK). CK is defined as a teacher's understanding of the structures of the subject or, in the words of Shulman (1986, p. 9)[2]: "the teacher need not only understand that something is so, the teacher must further understand why it is so. "PK relates to "knowledge with special reference to those broad principles and strategies of classroom management and organization that appear to transcend subject matter" (Shulman, 1986, p. 8)[3] whereas PCK consists in knowledge that serves "to make content comprehensible to others" (Shulman, 1986, p. 9). [4] These domains of professional knowledge combined with action – related and reflective skills (Lindmeier, 2011) [5]form the base of the study at a university of teacher education and thus provide the general structure of the courses in the different subjects.

Kunter et al. (2013)[6] elaborated Shulman's typology and adapted it to the school subject of mathematics. Figure Figure 1 illustrates the different facets of professional knowledge that, together with organizational and counseling knowledge and further aspects (beliefs, values, motivational orientations, and self – regulation), make up a teacher's professional competence. As Figure Figure shows, PCK encompasses at least explanatory knowledge, knowledge of the pupils' mathematical thinking and thus diagnostic knowledge, and knowledge of mathematical

---

① Shulman, L. S., Knowledge and Teaching: Foundations of the New Reform, *Harvard Educational Review*, 57(1), 1987, pp. 1 – 22.

②③④ Shulman, L. S., Those who understand: Knowledge growth in teaching, *Educational Researcher*, 15(2), 1986, pp. 4 – 14.

⑤ Lindmeier, A., *Modeling and Measuring Knowledge and Competencies of Teachers: A Threefold Domain – Specific Structure Model for Mathematics*, Münster: Waxmann, 2011.

⑥ Kunter, M., Baumert, J., Blum, W., Klusmann, U., Krauss, S., & Neubrand, M (eds.), Cognitive activation in the mathematics classroom and professional, New York: Springer, 2013.

problems. PK includes knowledge of pupil assessment, of the organization, fostering and initiation of learning processes in general, and of effective classroom management.

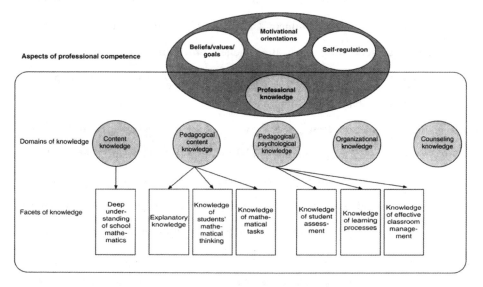

Figure: Professional competence with professional knowledge specified for the context of mathematics teaching (Baumert & Kunter, 2013, p. 29). ①

Pre-service teachers have to acquire knowledge in all these domains of professional knowledge in their study at the university. According to the constructivist paradigm, learning can be understood as an active, constructive, cumulative, reflective, and social process (Reusser, 2005)②. Lectures and professors facilitate this process by organizing, structuring, and teaching their subjects in a way that enables pre-service teachers to construct their professional knowledge actively.

---

① Baumert, J., & Kunter, M., The COACTIV model of teachers's professional competence, In M, 2013.

② Reusser, K. (eds.), Problemorientiertes Lernen – Tiefenstruktur, Gestaltungsformen, Wirkung. *Beiträge zur Lehrerinnen – und Lehrerbildung*, 23(2), 2005, pp. 159 – 182.

After entry into the profession, teachers are expected to participate in professional development activities in the course of which they constantly have to extend and improve the different facets of professional knowledge. This process stretches over their whole professional life.

4. The example of teacher preparation for mathematics education

In the following, the preparation for mathematics education at the Thurgau University of Teacher Education and the knowledge that pre – service teachers have to acquire on this subject shall serve as an example that is intended to illustrate the process of knowledge acquisition that has been outlined above in more concrete terms. In a first course, the pre – service teachers have to activate their mathematical CK (see above) and to use it to analyze the contents of elementary mathematics in the sense of Felix Klein as "Elementary mathematics from a higher standpoint" (Weigand, McCallum, Menghini, Neubrand, & Schubring, 2019) [1]. After this first course, a second course focuses on diagnostic knowledge as part of PCK. The goals are 1) to build up explanatory knowledge of important concepts of elementary mathematics, 2) to understand the children's mathematical development and thinking process, and 3) to become able to construct, change, and enrich a mathematical problem for pupils of Grade 1 to 6. The third compulsory course aims to combine the pedagogical knowledge that has been acquired in the courses in pedagogy with the specific objectives and characteristics of the learning and teaching of mathematics. This specific knowledge, in turn, is applied in the

---

[1] Kunter, M., Baumert, J., Blum, W., Klusmann, U., Krauss, S., & Neubrand, M (eds.), Cognitive activation in the mathematics classroom and professional, New York: Springer, 2019.

practical courses at school and afterwards again reflected on in the courses on mathematics education at the university.

What has been explained with reference to mathematics education, similarly applies to the preparation for the teaching of language and science subjects. The overall aim is that pre – service teachers who intend to enter a career as all – round teachers are equipped with the requisite professional knowledge and all its facets in each subject that they will have to teach.

5. Conclusion

The idea of an "all – round teacher" who is able to teach seven or eight different subjects in parallel requires pre – service teachers to acquire a solid and broad base of CK that enables them to understand the contents of primary school subjects in a comprehensive way and to analyze these contents from a "higher" standpoint.

There are some aspects, however, that put the ideal of an "all – round teacher" into perspective. First, a study of only six semesters hardly provides enough time to construct thorough knowledge in all the essential domains of knowledge in all of the seven or eight subjects that this type of teacher needs to be able to teach. Therefore, in – service training and professional development activities are vital. This implies that a study of this length is limited in scope; but it can nevertheless be seen as the important initial stage of a lifelong learning process as a reflective and responsible professional teacher. Second, the idea of an "all – round teacher" who acts as a social guide and facilitator in the pupils' knowledge acquisition at school requires a solid and strong foundation in pedagogical and psychological knowledge, which, in turn, contributes to the acquisition of content specific knowledge. Therefore, a close collaboration between lecturers and professors that goes beyond their own subject is absolutely indispensable. The professors for mathematics education have to know in detail what contents, which theories, and which concepts are taught in the lectures in pedagogy and psychology. Such a collaboration needs to be grounded in a shared understanding of both the overall aims of teacher education and the structure and the domains of professional knowledge that are to be acquired by pre – service teachers. This kind of inter – and transdisciplinary networking allows the lecturers and professors to plan and realize their lectures and courses in a mutually consistent way and thus to provide a rich and effective learning environment for prospective all – round teachers.

一名教师教七个不同科目的教学:如何成功?

艾斯特·布伦纳

瑞士图高教育大学,教授

摘要:瑞士的小学教师要求能够教授至少 7 门不同科目的课程。这种"全科教师"的情况在瑞士很普遍。这种思想源于瑞士的文化价值观,其主要思想是建立师生间牢固的社会关系,并创建与社会和学习内容相关的班级学习社区。这两种主要思想对师范生和学校制度有不同的要求,会产生不同的教师教育结果。

首先,基于瑞士学校制度对瑞士小学教师教育进行概述。其次,阐述小学教师教育的重要理念和主要目标是如何基于学习和教学的具体定义。最后,将以数学教育为例,对瑞士的小学教师教育进行更深层次的阐述。数学是所有教师的必教科目,因此数学教师教育具有代表性。

Humanistic Approach to Teacher Education at Soka University Based on the Philosophy of Soka Education

Masashi Suzuki

Soka University

Abstract：Tsunesaburo Makiguchi, a Japanese educator, initiated the theory of"Soka（Value – creating）Education"based on his long experience as a teacher and published The System of Value – Creating Pedagogy in 1930. His fundamental principles were the belief that every child has the highest potential and that the purpose of education is to make children happy by drawing out their inner abilities.

The philosophy was handed down to Makiguchi's desciple, Josei Toda, and to Toda's desciple, Daisaku Ikeda. Ikeda established"Soka School system"from Soka University to Kindergarten as an educational institution that carries out Soka education. These schools consistently provide education through learner – centered dialogue, and continually produce graduates who are willing to contribute to world peace and sustainable development.

Faculty of Education and the Graduate School of Teacher Education of Soka University conduct teacher training and teacher education based on Soka Education philosophy. We have established a strong cooperative relationship with the local community and over 7,500 school teachers have been sent to all over Japan since the foundation of Soka University. In particular, the teachers from Soka are highly appreciated for their attitude to snuggle up to troubled children and try to overcome the problems together with the children.

In Japan and globally, educational reforms are currently underway to increase proactivity and collaborativity of learners, which is exactly what Soka Education has promoted for many years.

1. History and Philosophy of Soka Education

The purpose of this article is to introduce the philosophy of Soka education, which is the foundation of education at Soka University, and to introduce the contents and achievements of teacher education at Soka University.

Soka education was initiated by Tsunesaburo Makiguchi (1871—1944), an educator, geographer, and Buddhist instructor, and was intherited to Makiguchi's desciple, Josei Toda (1900—1958), and then, to Toda's disciple Daisaku Ikeda (1928—   ). Soka education has been greatly developed by Ikeda and is now spreading to the world.

First, let me introduce the biography of its founder, Tsunesaburo Makiguchi.

1871, June 6 Born in Niigata Prefecture

1896 (25) Primary school teacher in Sapporo, Hokkaido

1901 (30) Moves to Tokyo to teach

1903 (32) Publishes The Geography of Human Life

1904 (33) Teaches geography to Chinese students as a lecturer at Kobun

Gakuin

1913（42）Principal at Tosei Elementary School, and subsequently served as principal of five elementary schools

1920（49）Meets Josei Toda

1930（59）Publishes The System of Value – Creating Pedagogy, Volume 1（4 of 12 are eventually published）and established Soka Kyoiku Gakkai

1943（72）Arrested for violation of security maintenance law and imprisoned

1944 November 18（73）Passed away at prison

Makiguchi, based on his long experience as a teacher for over 30 years, had the following thoughts on the purpose of "education".

（1）What is the purpose of life? If one were to express this in just a word, it would have to be "happiness." The purpose of education must therefore accord with the purpose of life.

（2）The aim of education is not to transfer knowledge; it is to guide the learning process, to equip the learner with the methods of research. It is not the piecemeal merchandizing of information; it is to enable the acquisition of the methods for learning on one's own; it is the provision of keys to unlock the vault of knowledge.

Next, I will introduce the biography of Makiguchi's desciple, Josei Toda.

1900 February 11 Born in Ishikawa Prefecture, moved to Hokkaido at the age of 2 and eventually becomes an elementary school teacher

1920（20）Meets Makiguchi in Tokyo on a trip, and decides to become his disciple

1923（23）Established a private prep school Jishu Gakkan

1930（30）Publishes A Deductive Guide to Arithmetic and other study materials

1943（43）Arrested with Makiguchi as a thought criminal

1945（45）Prison release；dedicates his life to peace and happiness of all people through individual empowerment and life philosophy

1947（47）meets Daisaku Ikeda

1951（51）The Seikyo Shinbun is launched，and the novel Human Revolution begins.

1957（57）Expounds" Declaration calling for the Abolition of Nuclear Weapons"

1958 April 2（58）Passed away

Makiguchi invented the word"Soka"with his disciple Toda. "Soka"is an abbreviation for"value − creation"in Japanese，and it incorporates the following ideas from Makiguchi.

（1）Humans cannot create matter：what we can create，however，is value and value only. When we praise persons for their " strength of character ，" we are really acknowledging their superior ability to create value.

（2）Soka education means the knowledge system of how to train humans who can create the value of life.

（3）The state exists only because its citizens exist；society exists only because of individuals. The growth and development of individuals brings the flourishing，fulfillment and growth of the national society.

（4）The purpose of education is to cultivate the ability to create value for the well − being of the whole society，along with the well − being of the educat-

ed person who is an element of the social group.

In other words, in Makiguchi's idea, every human being has the unlimited intrinsic power to create value and the purpose of education is to "enhance the ability to create value". This is also an idea that leads to the Buddhism philosophy that Makiguchi believed. On the extension, it can be said that he envisioned "social change through education" in which not only the people who increase their value by receiving education become happy, but also the whole society becomes happy.

Therefore, "Soka Education" has the following characteristics.

(1) Teachers believe in the "value creation potential" of all learners and aim to let them enhance their values

(2) Interactive teacher – learner relationship is built through the education centered on dialogue rather than one – way teaching

(3) Learners not only increase their own value but also find the purpose of life from the viewpoint of contributing to enhance the value of others and to make the society happy

(4) As a result, the global citizenship that respects the dignity of life and pursues peace is nurtured

Makiguchi had the concept of establishing schools that practice this educational philosophy he initiated, but he was arrested during World War II for criticism of militaristic politics and died in prison. However, his concept was certainly handed down to his disciple Toda and further entrusted to Ikeda.

2. Soka Education System Established by Daisaku Ikeda

It was Daisaku Ikeda, the disciple, who inherited Toda's will. First of all, let's introduce a brief history of Daisaku Ikeda.

1928 January 2 Born in Tokyo to family that harvested edible seaweed

1947 (19) Meets Toda and decides to follow and learn from him

1960 (32) The third president of Soka Gakkai

1964 (36) Starts writing novel The Human Revolution

1968 (40) Proposal for the normalization of Japan – China relations

1975 (47) President of Soka Gakkai International (SGI)

1981 (53) Receives the title of "poet laureate" from the World Academy of Arts and Culture

1993 (65) Begins writing the novel The New Human Revolution (completed in 2018)

Ikeda is not only a Buddhist leader, but also an educator and a poet, and has established numerous cultural organizations and a political party. In addition, he has talked with many experts around the world to promote the internationalization of Soka Gakkai and has received honorary titles from over 380 academic institutions around the world so far.

This article will shed light on Ikeda's aspect as an educator. The educational institutions that practice Soka education, envisioned by Makiguchi, have become reality as "Soka education system" that covers from kindergarten to university through the effort of Ikeda. First, in 1968, Tokyo Soka Junior and Senior High School (also called Soka Gakuen) was opened, and in 1971, Soka University opened in Hachioji, Tokyo where Toda hoped. After that, Soka schools opened one after another and they are still spreading to the world as shown in the table below.

1968 – Soka Junior and Senior High School = "Soka Gakuen" (Tokyo)

1973 – Soka Women's Junior and Senior High School (Osaka)

1976 – Sapporo Soka Kindergarten

1978 – Tokyo Soka Elementary School

1982 – Kansai Soka Elementary School (Osaka)

1982 – Soka Women's High School becomes Kansai Soka High School (Osaka)

1985 – Soka Women's Junior College

1992 – Hong Kong Soka Kindergarten

1993 – Singapore Soka Kindergarten

1994 – Soka University Los Angeles Branch (Currently Graduate School of SUA)

1995 – Malaysia Soka Kindergarten

2001 – Soka University of America

2001 – Brazil Soka Kindergarten

2003 – Brazil Soka Elementary School

2008 – South Korea Happiness Kindergarten

2017 – Brazil Soka High School

In Soka education system, Makiguchi's Soka education philosophy is realized in the following concrete forms.

(1) Every human being has unlimited potential power to create value

> Soka education system is based on intrinsic development of inner pow-

er , not teaching from outside. The emphasis is placed on teacher – learner dia-
logues and learner – learner dialogues , rather than talks by teachers.

(2) The purpose of education is happiness of learners

＞ Soka education system creates safe learning environment for children
and creates a network of teachers to watch over each child and solve problems
together.

(3) The growth of teachers is the key to the growth of children

＞ As it is said that " teachers are the greatest educational environment " ,
children grow up by looking at the teachers and feeling their personalities.
Therefore , enhancing teacher 's own inquiring mind , sincere attitude toward
learning , and personality is essential for the growth of children.

(4) Education is not only for the happiness of learners , but also for the
well – being of the society as a whole.

＞ Learners who feel the power of value creation will find the same power
among others. It leads to consideration for others and contributive attitude to
the society.

Students who receive this kind of education will soon look at the society surrounding them and then the world and want to contribute to solving problems such
as peace and environmental issues. Young people with such a mind have been
continually produced from Soka education system.

3. Founding Principles of Soka University

Soka University was founded by Daisaku Ikeda in 1971 and will celebrate its
50th anniversary in 2021. Soka University also started as an educational institution that realizes Soka Education and its philosophy is accurately expressed in the

following"Founding Principles". Ikeda put the ultimate goals of Soka University into three statements at its establishment.

(1) *Be the highest seat of learning for humanistic education.*
(2) *Be the cradle of a new culture.*
(3) *Be a fortress for the peace of humankind.*
(*https://www. soka. ac. jp/en/about/philosophy/mission*)

These three statements have been the fundamental goals of Soka University since the day of its establishment and the students studying at Soka University have always kept these statements in their minds for half a century. Let us consider the relationship between these three statements and Soka Education.

The first statement"Be the highest seat of learning for humanistic education" is that the foundation of education at Soka University is humanistic education, that is, education that nurtures humans holistically. Conversely, it is also an assertion that the purpose of education is not just the transmission of knowledge and technology.

This is the spirit that inherited Makiguchi's words, "Education is for learners ´happiness" and "Education is a way to teach people how to create value". This spirit is the core philosophy of Soka University, which leads to "University for Students" advocated by Soka University, or "Discover your Potential" which is the current slogan.

Next, the second statement, "Be the cradle of a new culture," incorporates the founder Ikeda's ideal on university. Ikeda has insisted in various speeches and lectures as follows: "Study is for the people. Historically the university was originally established by the people, and the university should not be a tower of research isolated from the public. "It is also true that there are such aspects in academic researches that have adversely affected humanity and have disparaged the dignity of life, such as war and environmental destruction. "A new culture" in this second statement means a culture that leads the entire human beings to peace and happiness based on the dignity of life. This principle embodies Makiguchi's words, "The purpose of education is to cultivate value – creating ability for the sake of the happiness of the society as a whole."

Finally, the third statement "Be a fortress for the peace of humankind" is the conclusion of Soka Education. Those who have the power to create their own values will be able to recognize the same power in others and sympathize with each other. In other words, being aware of one's own dignity will also make it possible to respect the dignity of others. Even if we use the phrase "respect for diversity", it is difficult to achieve it unless we put basis on this practical philosophy. It can be said that Soka Education = Value Creation Education advocated by Makiguchi is essentially an education that fosters people who seek peace.

4. Global Development of Soka University

As suggested by the conclusion of the previous section, Soka Education advocated by Makiguchi originally has an aspect of global education, since when put into practice, Soka education enables learners to naturally turn their eyes to the outside world. For this reason, globalization including peace education and environmental education has been progressing at Soka University in recent years. Here are some examples.

(1) Top Global University

In 2014, the Ministry of Education, Culture, Sports, Science and Technology (MEXT) launched the "Top Global University Creation Support" project, which selected subsidized universities for 10 years to promote the globalization of Japanese universities. Soka University is one of 37 universities that were selected from 109 universities that applied from all over Japan.

This project has a number of numerical targets. For example, (a) Increase the number of international students from 313 to 1215 per year, (b) Increase the number of students going to study abroad from 557 to 1260 per year, (c) Increase the number of students with excellent English proficiency from 296 to 1500 per year, and (d) 10% of all classes will be taught in English. Currently, the numbers are steadily approaching the target, and so Soka University successfully got the top rating "S" in the 2018 mid – term evaluation. Meanwhile, Soka University newly established the Faculty of International Liberal Studies and the Graduate School of International Peace Studies. In this way we are playing a role of leading the globalization of Japanese universities.

(2) Private university research branding project

In 2017, Soka University acquired a new subsidy project, "Private university research branding project" from MEXT. This is a project for private universities that gives a five – year subsidy to a university – wide project that works as a brand of the university.

Soka University is engaged in international contribution activities set in Ethiopia, which consists of the following four steps. (i) Eliminate the water hyacinth that grows in Lake Tana, the largest lake in Ethiopia, and obtain energy and fertilizer by methane fermentation. (ii) Culture spirulina, one of the phytoplankton, using the obtained energy and fertilizer. (iii) Produce healthy food including spirulina with high nutritional value and improve the health condition of Ethiopian people by having them ingest the food. And then establish companies that sell food products to make Ethiopian people also economically independent. (ⅳ) Advance entrepreneur education and environmental education through this business. (https://www. soka. ac. jp/en/research/branding/) The project is now in its third year and is entering step (ⅲ).

(3)Initiatives for the SDGs

Soka University will celebrate its 50th anniversary in 2021. For this reason, we have decided to work on commemorative projects throughout the year of 2020, and one of the major programs  is an event called"Value Creation x SDGs". Needless to say, the SDGs are"sustainable development goals" promoted by the United Nations, consisting of 169 goals across 17 fields. As a result of Soka Education, Soka University has many teachers and students who want to do their best to contribute to the society and to the world. Many faculty seminars and club activities have various initiatives related to SDGs. The"private university research branding project" mentioned above is also a project that spans many areas of the SDGs. Based on these specific achievements, Soka University is ranked 101 – 200 in the world and 4th among Japanese universities in the"World University Impact Ranking" announced by THE (Times Higher Education) in April this year.

(https://www. soka. ac. jp/en/topics/2019/04/10297/)

It is important to remember that this trend of globalization of Soka University has not emerged recently. As already mentioned, global education is inevitably derived from Makiguchi's philosophy of Soka education, and the"founding principles" that embodied the philosophy in terms of university education. In this sense,

Soka University has always aimed for global education since its founding in the year 1971.

One indication of this was the acceptance of six first – time government – sponsored international students from New China in 1975. Soka University, which had just founded, was the first to accept international students from China that other universities were reluctant to accept, based on the judgment of Ikeda, the founder of the university. As a result, all six were involved in some form of friendship project between Japan and China, and one of them, Mr. Cheng Yonghua, served as the Chinese ambassador to Japan for nine years until this year.

In this way, under the spirit of Soka Education and Ikeda's leadership, Soka University has consistently conducted educational and research activities open to the international societies since its foundation.

5. Teacher Education at Soka University

Tsunesaburo Makiguchi, and his disciple Josei Toda were both educators. Makiguchi was the first president of the buddist organization Soka Gakkai, but at the beginning it was an educator group called Soka Kyoiku Gakkai (Soka Education Organization). In addition, Daisaku Ikeda considers education as "the final and most crucially important undertaking of my life." In this sense, in Soka University founded by Ikeda, the Faculty of Education and the Graduate School of Teacher Education have a central significance in terms of nurturing practitioners of Soka Education.

Of course, MEXT imposes detailed instructions and requirements to qualify teacher training institutions and no universities in Japan can train teachers without following them. However, what MEXT demands are the "minimum requirements", and just following them will not necessarily assure that excellent teachers are au-

tomatically nurtured. What kind of teachers are actually nurtured depends on ??
the ideal image of teachers that each institution aims to train.

Like other schools of Soka education system, the Faculty of Education at Soka University conducts educational activities in accordance with the principles of
Soka Education described so far. In addition, the Graduate School of Teacher Education is practicing more specialized and deeper teacher education. Since the
Graduate School of Teacher Education will be introduced in detail in another session, here I would like to concentrate on Faculty of Education and introduce some
unique efforts of the undergraduate teacher education from the viewpoint of Soka
education.

(1) Three courses in the Department of Education

The Faculty of Education at Soka University has two departments, the Department of Education and the Department of Child Education. The Department of
Education is mainly for students aiming to be junior and senior high school teachers and academically explores pedagogy and psychology. There are three courses
that can be selected according to the student's future aspirations: Education
Course, Psychology Course and International Education Course.

In every course, on the premise of the philosophy of Soka education that "all
children have the ultimate power to create value", the students consider the questions such as "What is education?", "What does it mean that humans educate
humans?", "How does a human mind grow?" Through these considerations and
discussions, we are striving to develop human resources who can practice Soka education in all fields of society, not just teachers.

(2) Two approaches of the Department of Child Education

The Department of Child Education is mainly for students who want to become teachers at elementary schools and kindergartens. The goal is to learn basic theories of pedagogy and psychology based on the philosophy of Soka Education, as well as to acquire solid practical skills to be able to take charge of classes at actual educational sites.

However, the practical skills of a teacher in charge of actual children cannot be acquired simply by studying at university. In addition to the subjects obligated by MEXT such as "teaching practicum", Department of Child Education prepares various programs that I will introduce below and strives to nurture practitioners of Soka education.

(3) School internship

School internship is an attempt that Soka University started in 2000 ahead of other universities in Japan. Students in the second and third years go to elementary and junior high schools in Hachioji city basically once a week for class support and after – school class activities. This is an opportunity for students to experience the school work directly to learn about the teachers' actual work and to know their aptitude for teachers before going to teaching practicum. By participating in this school internship, each student earns 2 credits every semester.

School internship is at the same time greatly appreciated by neighboring schools for community contribution activities. Makiguchi, who was also a geographer, advocated "Local Studies" as a subject that integrates all the subjects of elementary school and stated that "It is easy for everyone to start from local studies and then expand the learning to the world". It can be said that the practice of school internship that values the local community is exactly what Makiguchi aimed for.

(4) Education using art museum

The Tokyo Fuji Art Museum is adjacent to the Soka University site, which is a rare and valuable environment for universities. Taking advantage of this location, we offer a class called "Education at Museum" that utilizes the art museum. This is an attempt of "school internship" set in the museum.

Before starting this class, students must learn about the intentions and methods of painters and sculptors for the works in the museum. Then children from nearby elementary schools are invited and students try to provide art appreciation education by explaining how to view the art works to the invited children. Children can experience first – class authentic artworks that cannot be seen in textbooks and in their schools and students who want to become teachers can gain experience of actual contact with children. This attempt is highly regarded as one of the local contributions by university, and was introduced on television by local TV stations.

(5) Collaboration with local communities in English education

English education has begun as an official subject in Japanese elementary schools. In order to enable our students to conduct foreign language experiences and English classes at elementary schools, the Faculty of Education offers a class called "Special Course of Teaching English".

In this class, students actually go to an elementary school and conduct an

English class in cooperation with nearby elementary schools in order to have a practical experience of teaching English. On the other hand, elementary school children are invited to the Christmas party at Soka University.

Through this kind of interaction, students will not only improve their English teaching skills, but also develop a spirit of valuing the local community and, above all, a spirit of Soka education that hopes for the happiness of children.

(6) Global education

Every semester the Faculty of Education invites a lecturer from abroad to teach pedagogy or psychology in a class called "Special Lecture on International Education". English education has now been introduced to elementary schools, and many children from overseas have come to study at Japanese elementary schools. So school teachers are required to have international perspectives and language skills so that they can cope with such an environment.

So far, more than 10 lecturers have been invited from Canada, USA, Germany and China to conduct classes. Knowing educational issues, philosophy of education, and methods of teaching subjects of foreign countries will be an opportunity for students to foster their minds to be human resources that respect diversity and contribute to world peace, regardless of whether they become school teachers or not.

(7) Environmental education

In 2018, the Faculty of Education and the Graduate School of Teacher Education joined an inter-university network that supports UNESCO associated schools. UNESCO Associated Schools Network is a world-wide school network that promotes ESD (education for sustainable development) led by the United Nations. From kindergarten to university, if the school's own ESD efforts are approved by UNESCO headquarters in Paris, they can call themselves as "UNESCO Associated Schools". Currently, there are about 11,000 UNESCO associated schools around the world and over 1000 in Japan.

Currently Soka University provides support for seven nearby schools to become UNESCO associated schools. The spirit that "since wars begin in the minds of men, it is in the minds of men that the defences of peace must be constructed" in the preamble to the UNESCO Constitution has many points in common to the Founding Principles of Soka University. It has many similarities and resonates strongly with the Soka Education philosophy.

(8) Hidden curriculum

In addition to the explicit curriculum, Soka University is said to have a "hidden curriculum" that might be somewhat more effective. In fact, few of the courses at Soka University actually deal with "Soka Education" as their main themes. Although many of the courses, including the examples introduced so far, are based on the spirit of Soka education, the class titles themselves are quite normal. However, they are supported by the "hidden curriculum", that is, the spiritual atmosphere among students that Soka University has cherished since its foundation.

More specifically, as clearly shown in the Founding Principles, Soka University was established with the ultimate goal of realizing world peace through humanistic education. In addition, Soka University was built on the hill where nothing originally existed, supported by the trust of many people who believed us. Students studying there have a sense of security supported by the trust of their surroundings, which creates a stable educational environment. This sense of trust and the philosophy of realizing world peace through valuing each person form the "hidden curriculum".

Furthermore, Soka University originally has the philosophy of "teachers and learners together" and "university for students". There is no vertical relationship between professors and students and both have a common recognition that universities should be constructed by professors and students together. Teacher education at Soka University is carried out in this atmosphere, creating a lot of teachers who want to realize the philosophy of Soka Education in school education.

6. Japanese Education Reform and Soka Education

Like other countries in the world, Japan is currently making major educational reforms. In school education, "one – way teaching" from teachers is eliminated and "interactive learning" that incorporates dialogue and group discussions is being introduced. In other words, this reform is "From teacher – centered to learner – centered". MEXT expresses this in terms of "proactive, interactive and deep learning (so – called active learning)". All schools in Japan, from elementary schools to high schools, are now making effort to realize "proactive, interactive and deep learning. "

On the other hand, new perspectives are also taken into the "academic competence" gained through such learning as below.

---

3 elements of academic competence by MEXT of Japan

(1) Knowledge / Skills: What you understand and what you can do?

(2) Thinking, judgment, and expressiveness, etc.: How you can use your knowledge and skills

(3) Ability to learn, humanity, etc.: How you engage with society and the world for a better life

---

This view of academic competence stems from the reflection that no matter how much "currently – known knowledge and technology" you remember in the ever – changing world, it will be useless in the real world decades later. Ability of taking on new challenges independently, thinking with their own power, persuasively expressing what they have decided, and flexibly solving new problems while cooperating with others: such ability is the academic competence required in the future.

In other words, it is the view that although the knowledge given from outside will soon become outdated, you can positively tackle new problems if you have strong power from inside.

This is nothing other than the goal of Soka Education. It can be said that the society in the 21st century needs and approaches to the education based on the belief and trust that "everyone and the surrounding society can seize happiness by demonstrating the power of value creation inherent to everyone and applying the power to the society." that Makiguchi aimed at 90 years ago.

Soka University wants to continue to produce many teachers who can inherit the tradition of Soka Education, apply it into the future society, and contribute greatly to building a better world.

基于创价教育哲学的创价大学人本主义取向的教师教育

铃木将史

日本创价大学副校长,教授

摘要:牧口常三郎,日本教育学家、地理学家、佛教领袖,拥有多年小学从教经验,于 1930 年创建了创价教育的体系。创价教育的核心理念是相信每个孩子都有自己独特的发展潜能,教育的目的是通过激发他们的内在潜能,让每位儿童快乐成长。

牧口先生萌发了创立一所大学的想法,以宣扬自己的教育哲学。后来池田大作先生继承了创价教育的理念,实现了牧口先生的初衷。池田先生于 1971 年建立了创价大学,并建立了从幼儿园到高中的体系,以贯彻牧口先生的教育哲学。

创价大学及其集团学校的教师教育都将重点放在人本主义教育上。目前已经培养了七千多名教师。他们将继续致力于提高日本的教师教育水平。

第三编　小学教师教育质量保障

PART Ⅲ : Quality Assurance of Elementary

Teacher Education

小学教育专业认证下自我评估
改进内部质量保障体系探究

唐　斌

首都师范大学初等教育学院

摘要:小学教师教育内部质量保障体系的改进迫切且重要,小学教育专业作为小学教师教育外部质量保障体系的构成,为改进小学教师教育内部质量保障体系创建积极环境,以外促内,能推动其发展。小学教育专业认证中的自我评估是专业认证的基础,专业自我评估关联内外质量保障体系,助推内部质量保障体系改进,并以对"质量保障"的自评自建来改进内部质量保障体系,应充分发挥专业自我评估效能在完善内部质量保障体系中的作用。

关键词:小学教育专业认证;内部质量保障体系;专业自我评估

教育质量是教育发展的永恒主题,教育质量保障的健全与改进是时代赋予这个主题的重点。小学教师教育发展亦然。在大力实施师范类专业认证制度、健全教师教育质量保障体系的新时代,探究以小学教育专业认证促进小学教师教育质量保障体系改进,是深化我国小学教师教育综合改革、推动我国小学教师培养质量的内涵建设的必然要求。

一、内部质量保障体系改进之迫切与重要

2018 年 1 月,中共中央、国务院印发的《关于全面深化新时代教师队伍建设改革的意见》指出,新时代"人民对公平而有质量的教育的向往更加迫切",但"师范教育体系有所削弱",应"大力振兴教师教育","提升教师培养质量"。2018 年 2 月,教育部等五部委联合印发的《教师教育振兴行动计划(2018—2022 年)》,以提升教师教育质量为核心,以加强教师教育体系建设为支撑,明确了包括教师教育质量保障体系构建行动在内的十大行动。2018 年 9 月颁布的《教育部关于实施卓越教师培养计划 2.0 的意见》提出了"经过五年左右的努力,办好一批高水平、有特色的教师教育院校和师范专业……教师教育质量文化基本建立"的目标要求,"构建追求卓越的质量保障体系"是实现目标的重要举措之一。2019 年 2 月,中共中央、国务院印发的《中国教育现代化 2035》部署的战略任务中明确提出:"发展中国特色世界先进水平的优质教育","建设高素质专业化创新型教师队伍",强调"完善教育质量标准体系","建立全过程、全方位人才培养质量反馈监控体系"。

密集出台的一系列重要政策文件,均指向或突出了教师教育和教师队伍高质量建设,不仅有对现实的重要判断,更有鲜明的态度、有效的原则和有力的举措,增强了整个社会对"提升教师培养质量""夯实师范人才培养质量保障体系"等工作的高度关注和热切投入。构建并逐步完善与小学教师教育改革发展相契合的小学教师教育质量保障体系,是实现我国小学教育专业人才高质量培养的关键,势在必行,且迫在眉睫。

教师教育质量保障体系通常是指为确保职前教师培养达到一定的质量标准,在生源、认证、评估、投入等方面采取的系统性的教师教育政策措施。从主体来看,可分为由政府或者专业组织开展的标准发布、专业认证、资格认证等组成的外部质量保障体系,以及由教师教育机构开展的机构设置、专

业评估等组成的内部质量保障体系①,回顾历史,放眼整个高等教育,20 世纪中叶之前,高等教育质量属于大学内部事务,大学依靠内部管理保障着大学教育质量。随着高等教育规模日益扩大,其教育质量逐渐受到社会的广泛关注,社会及其个人对高等教育的有效性和优质性需求不断增加,外部监控由此介入高等教育质量保证过程,高等教育质量不再只是属于大学的内部事务。内部管理与外部监控相结合的高等教育质量保证体系成为必要②,产生了高等教育质量保障体系的外部质量保障和内部质量保障两个部分。来自不同主体的质量保障活动的结合既是顺应历史的潮流,也是教育发展的自觉。

质量保障体系源于大学内部对教育质量的关注;当内外质量保障体系并存时,质量保障体系在外部质量保障体系的助推下,通过内部质量保障体系运动而发生变化。所以内部质量保障体系是质量保障发展的起点,具有基础性和根本性的作用。

改进小学教师教育内部质量保障体系,关系到小学教师人才培养的质量,关系到中国特色世界先进水平的优质小学教师教育发展。作为培养小学教师的专业,是教育活动实施的主体,同时也是内部质量提升的主体,建立健全小学教师教育内部质量保障体系责无旁贷。

二、内部质量保障体系改进之认证驱动

师范类专业认证是专门性教育评估认证机构依照认证标准对师范类专业人才培养质量状况实施的一种外部评价,旨在证明当前和可预见的一段时间内,专业能否达到既定的人才培养质量标准③。国外教师教育经过多年

---

① 王薇:《国际教师教育质量保障体系的构建及其启示》,《教师教育研究》,2017 年第 9 期。
② 胡建华:《高等教育质量内部管理与外部监控的关系分析》,《高等教育研究》,2008 年第 5 期。
③ 教育部教师工作司、教育部高等教育教学评估中心:《培养新时代大国良师——普通高等学校师范类专业认证工作指南(试行)》,2018 年。

的尝试、探索,已经建立了较为成熟的教师教育认证制度。并且通过教师教育认证积极实施教学及管理改革,专业内部质量保障体系不断完善,有效保障教师培养的质量。比如,美国的师范专业认证历史悠久、方式科学、经验成熟,认证已经成为美国师范专业建设质量控制、内涵建设和改进完善等方面的关键点①。这自然涉及对内部质量保障体系的构建。

2017年10月,教育部颁布了《普通高等学校师范类专业认证实施办法(暂行)》,出台了配套的认证标准,开启了我国师范专业认证的新局面。根据师范类专业认证的指导思想,小学教育专业认证以"全面贯彻党的教育方针、落实立德树人根本任务"为根本,以"构建中国特色、世界水平的小学教师教育监测认证体系"和"培养高质量的小学教育专业人才"为目标,通过"以评促建""以评促改"和"以评促强"三项任务,致力于实现"为培养造就党和人民满意的高素质专业化创新型小学教师队伍提供有力支撑"的目的。

师范类专业认证以"学生中心、产出导向、持续改进"为基本理念②。在小学教育专业认证中,强调遵循小学教师成长成才规律,以小学教育专业学生的学习效果和个性发展为中心,合理配置教育资源和安排教学活动,建立质量保障体系,将学生和用人单位满意度作为小学教育专业人才培养质量评价的重要依据。产出导向,强调聚焦学生受教育后"学到了什么"和"能做什么",明确学习产出标准,对接社会需求,以学生发展成效为导向,对照毕业生核心能力素质要求,反向设计课程体系与教学环节,配置师资队伍和资源条件,评价小学教育专业人才培养质量。持续改进,强调聚焦小学教育专业核心能力素质要求,对人才培养活动进行全方位、全过程跟踪与评价,并将评价结果用于教学改进,形成"评价—反馈—改进"闭环,建立持续改进的小学质量保障机制和追求卓越质量文化,推动小学教育专业人才培养能力

---

① 龙宝新:《美国师范专业认证工作对构建我国师范专业认证工作框架的启示》,《教师发展研究》,2018年第2期。

② 教育部:《普通高等学校师范类专业认证实施办法(暂行)》,http://www.moe.gov.cn/srcsite/A10/s7011/201711/t20171106_318535.html。

和质量的不断提高。

小学教育专业认证强调工作中遵循统一体系、高校主责、多维评价等原则，认证实行三级递进监测认证体系，应对照科学认证标准，进行规范认证工作程序，合理使用认证结果。这些无不在强化高校在小学教育专业质量建设中的主体责任，无不聚焦于建立以内部保障为主、内部保障和外部评价相结合的教师教育质量监测保障制度。特别值得关注的是，在小学教育认证标准指标中专门设置了独立的"质量保障"指标，从保障体系、内部监控、外部评价、持续改进四个方面对"评价培养目标是否达成及持续改进"提出了具体要求；在"课程与教学""合作与实践"部分均设置了"评价"二级指标，在"师资队伍"部分设置了"持续发展"二级指标，要求专业建有的各种机制、制度和措施，最终都要落实到执行、跟踪、评价与改进。

小学教育专业认证创建了利于小学教师教育机构建立健全内部质量保障体系的积极环境，以外促内，内外结合，极大地增强了小学教师教育机构在质量提升上的主体性，推动小学教育专业形成"持续改进"的发展机制，推动内部质量保障体系建设，实现从质量控制向质量提升转变。这体现了小学教育专业认证的根本价值。

三、自我评估改进内部质量保障体系之思考

教育中的自我评估，其主体是从事或实施教育评估活动的人，客体是主体的教育行为及其结果①。在高等教育范畴，谈自我评估，多指学校自我评估，但不止于此，专业认证中就要求专业进行自我评估。

（一）自我评估关联内外助推内部质量保障体系改进

一般来说，自我评估是外部评估的基础，小学教育专业的自我评估是小

---

① 王行晖、王行甫：《浅谈自我评估及其作用》，《教育与现代化》，1996 年第 4 期。

学教育专业认证的基础。一是,参评的小学教育专业依据认证标准开展专业自我评估,形成自评报告,才能有后续的审核及现场考查。进行专业自我评估是参加小学专业认证的前提。二是,小学教育专业认证作为外部评估,最后形成结论的正确与否,与小学教育专业发展的客观现实的逼近程度,取决于所收集到信息的真实与可靠性。按照认证要求所做的专业自我评估,是专业认证的第一手资料,现场考查专家组开展自评报告审阅、进校现场考查及认证结论审议,均以自评报告作为重要依据。专业认证的结论是在专业自我评估的基础上,进行现场综合考查后形成的。现场考查的主要目的是核实自评报告的真实性和准确性,并了解自评报告中未能反映的有关情况。自我评估是做好小学教育专业认证工作的基础。

从主体上来看,专业认证属于外部质量保障体系,自我评估属于内部质量保障体系。小学教育专业认证以规范的专业自我评估为基本前提和重要依据,使内外质量保障体系产生丰富的关联和互动,外优内强,充实内部质量保障体系,助推内部质量保障体系改进。

(二)自评自建"质量保障"改进内部质量保障体系

专业自评要求小学教育专业根据认证标准要求,根据专业办学特点,通过举证方式,详细说明小学专业围绕人才培养目标和毕业要求达成所开展的具有自身特色的教育教学实践与取得的成效。也就是说,从培养目标、毕业要求、课程与教学、合作与实践教学、师资建设、条件支持建设、人才培养质量保障、学生发展与人才质量等方面对照标准对小学教育专业进行系统审视,客观描述各项达标情况,发现主要的问题后,提出针对性改进措施。可以发现,"质量保障"是独立的指标,如前文所述,在这个维度要从保障体系、内部监控、外部评价、持续改进四个方面,就"评价培养目标是否达成以及持续改进"进行自评。根据认证的要求,不仅要自评,还需要自建,加之"常态监测与周期性认证"方法的采用,对"质量保障"检视和再建,就是内部质量保障体系的迭代。

（三）充分发挥自我评估效能优化内部质量保障体系

自实施小学教育专业认证以来，自我评估在帮助小学教育专业自我发现、自我改进等方面发挥了重要作用。小学教育专业都很重视专业的自我评估。需要注意的是，开展自我评估是师范类专业认证制度的基本要求，由于这是来自外部的要求，自我评估的实施，难免具有被动性、服从性，从而掩盖了自我评估本应具有的主体性和能动性。此外，自我评估是处于专业认证链条中的一个环节，也使其带有一定的流程化、程序化的色彩。

针对上述问题，自我评估应强调主体性，倡导自觉、自省、自律的自我评估，强化持续改进理念下的自我诊断、自我改进和自我激励。如此，才能充分发挥自我评估效能，优化内部质量保障体系。

An Exploration of Professional Self – Assessment to Improve the Internal Quality Assurance System in the Context of Professional Accreditation in Elementary School Teacher Education

Bin Tang

School of Elementary Education, Capital Normal University

Abstract: It is urgent and important to improve the internal quality assurance system of elementary school teacher education. As an external quality assurance system for elementary school teacher education, professional accreditation in elementary school teacher education creates a positive environment for improving the internal quality assurance system of elementary school teacher education. The external quality assurance system acts as a catalyst for the internal quality assurance system. Meanwhile, professional self – assessment in elementary school teacher education is the basis for professional accreditation in elementary school teacher education. Professional self – assessment is considered linked to the internal and external quality assurance systems to improve the internal quality assurance system and improve it through professional self – assessment and self – construction of "quality assurance". The effectiveness of professional self – assessment should be fully leveraged to improve the internal quality assurance system.

Key words: Professional Accreditation in Elementary Education; internal quality assurance system; Professional self – assessment

教师的教育惩戒伦理及其规范研究①

蔡连玉　李　琴

浙江师范大学教师教育学院

摘要:教师的教育惩戒权在学界已取得肯定性共识,教育惩戒立法正在推进中,但法律本身具有简约性,教师在教育实践中拥有较大的教育惩戒自由裁量权。为确保教育惩戒被合理运用,教师应具备教育惩戒相关的伦理素养;教育惩戒伦理是教育惩戒立法的思想基础和功能补充。从不同伦理思想出发探究可知,教育惩戒的善在于其教育性,即促进全体学生在学业维度和社会性的可持续成长。实践中教师的教育惩戒伦理风险有"放弃使用""错误使用"和"过度使用"三种类型,这三种错误都有悖于伦理性。基于对教育惩戒善的理论探讨及对教师教育惩戒伦理风险的实践分析,可以构建出教师教育惩戒伦理的 1 阶和 2 阶规范,包括教育惩戒的教育性、不被放弃,以及方法、时机、场合、程度与范围的合理性等内容。教师应通过理论学习和实践反思来提升教育惩戒伦理素养。

关键词:教育惩戒;惩戒伦理;伦理风险;伦理规范

在我国教育现代转型过程中,传统的"棍棒教育"被摒弃,这是社会文明

---

① 基金项目:教育部人文社会科学研究规划基金项目《小学教师德育素养的结构要素与培育机制研究》(19YJA880023)。

进步的体现。然而实践中教育惩戒被"因噎废食",在"少子化"社会的当下,导致了受社会广泛关注的教育困境。从学理上分析,教育是一种特殊的社会活动,教师应被赋予作为公权力的教育惩戒权。① 当前教育惩戒权在学界已取得肯定性共识,相关立法也在推进之中。然"徒法不足以自行",法律自身具有简约性,面对纷繁芜杂的教育实践,教师拥有较大的教育惩戒"自由裁量权"②,教师的教育惩戒伦理修炼是其教育惩戒行为"合善"的基础。从伦理学、教育学角度厘清教育惩戒的善性标准,分析实践中教师教育惩戒的伦理风险,并在此基础上构建教师教育惩戒的基本伦理规范,能为教师的教育惩戒伦理修炼提供思想资源,具有理论与实践价值。

一、教师的教育惩戒伦理及其价值

教育惩戒,是学校或教师为避免失范行为再次发生以达到教育目的,依法对学生的失范行为进行否定性评价的一种教育手段,可分为纪律惩戒与学业惩戒两类。③ 教育惩戒作为一种"必要的不幸"④,如同奖励与表扬一样,是教育中不可或缺的部分,换言之,没有惩戒的教育是不完整且责任缺失的教育。⑤ 这是教师思想意识中的一种并不难以达成的共识,但不得不承认的是,在教师行使教育惩戒权的实践过程中存在着各种伦理问题,困扰着大众对教育惩戒的价值判断,也影响着广大教师对教育惩戒权的规范运用。

---

① 程莹:《论教师惩戒行为的正当性:惩戒德性之异化与回归》,《教育科学研究》,2014 年第 3 期。

② Kenneth Culp Davis, *Discretionary Justice: A Preliminary Inquiry*, Louisiana State University Press, 1969.

③ 任海涛:《"教育惩戒"的概念界定》,《华东师范大学学报(教育科学版)》,2019 年第 4 期。

④ Tim McDonald, *Classroom Management: Engaging Students in Learning*, Oxford University Press, 2010.

⑤ 陈兰枝、夏豪杰:《把教育惩戒权还给教师:访全国人大常委会委员、中国教育学会副会长、华中师范大学教授周洪宇》,《教师教育论坛》,2019 年第 6 期。

一般认为,伦理是指基本的人际关系及其所应遵循的道德原则。[1] 伦理和道德与人的行为准则密切相关,但前者着重强调具有客观社会性的道德法则,后者则侧重于个体性。[2] 由此可以推论,教师的教育惩戒伦理是指教师对学生的失范行为进行否定性评价及采取教育措施时所应遵循的道德准则与行为规范。

教师的教育惩戒伦理是教师专业伦理的重要组成部分。教师专业伦理是指教师作为具有专业性的职业在教育工作中所应遵循的道德准则。[3] 教师的专业伦理是教师从事教育专业活动时所应遵循的伦理规范,而教师所从事的教育专业活动就包括了教育惩戒行为,人类社会只要存在教育活动,就存在教育惩戒,教育惩戒是教育活动的重要组成部分。教书育人作为一项专业的教育事业,就应该恰当地履行教育职责,根据专业的教育判断和伦理基础,对学生实施适当形式和恰当程度的惩戒,以纠正失范行为,使学生有更好的学业发展,形成良好的规则意识,能更好地社会化与成长,这一点在"少子化"社会的当下尤为重要。教育惩戒是教师专业教育活动的重要组成部分,所以教育惩戒伦理就是教师专业伦理的一部分。譬如实践中,教师在教育学生时有意免除教育惩戒以规避教育惩戒所可能带来的"麻烦",或者将教育惩戒与体罚混为一谈都是不可取的,[4]因为这些行为都违背了教师的教育惩戒伦理,没有体现教师对学生的关爱,没有为学生的成长担责,从而也就违背了教师的专业伦理。

相较于教育惩戒法律,教育惩戒伦理蕴含着独特的价值。首先,教育惩戒伦理与教育惩戒法律相异,前者是后者的思想基础。伦理与法律相异,从约束形式来看,伦理主要通过个体的内心信念与社会舆论来起作用,是一种间接、温和的"软约束";而法律主要是根据明确的法律条例、通过强制性的

---

[1]　朱贻庭:《伦理学小辞典》,上海辞书出版社,2004 年。
[2]　檀传宝:《教师伦理学专题:教育伦理范畴研究》,北京师范大学出版社,2003 年。
[3]　檀传宝等:《教师专业伦理基础与实践》,华东师范大学出版社,2016 年。
[4]　卢世林、胡振坤:《教师伦理学教程》,华中科技大学出版社,2012 年。

力量给予制裁,是一种直接、刚硬的"硬约束"。① 所以,教育惩戒的伦理与法律一样都对人的行为起约束作用,但是约束方式与强度有异。另外,伦理是立法的思想基础,即教育惩戒立法需要有相应的伦理思想基础,教育惩戒立法不能违背教育惩戒伦理规范。

其次,教育惩戒伦理是教育惩戒法律的功能补充。社会有了从外部"令行禁止"的法律还不足以形成良好的社会秩序,因为法律制裁针对的只是犯罪行为,轻微细小的失范行为不在其管辖范围内。那些严重程度较低的错误或者不当言行举止需要伦理的约束和道德的谴责,以制止与纠正。对教育惩戒而言,相关法律以刚性的方式约束着教师的惩戒行为,防止严重和原则性的教育惩戒失范行为发生,但教育惩戒法律因其简约性难以对教育实践中的所有细微方面进行规范,这时需要教育惩戒伦理进行功能上的补充。具体的,因为教育惩戒法律具有法律的简约性,所以在教育实践中教师在行使教育惩戒权时拥有较大的自由裁量权,"徒法不足以自行",只有教师具有较高的教育惩戒伦理素养,才能更好地行使教育惩戒权,在教育实践中更好地自由裁量,从而有利于全体学生的身心成长。

在教育实践中,由于教师教育惩戒伦理素养的缺失,教师职业所赋予其的教育惩戒权遭遇"放弃使用""错误使用"和"过度使用"的现象屡见不鲜。教师从事的教育教学实践活动纷繁复杂,与整个社会紧密关联;教师所面对的学生千差万别,学生具有不同的生理基础,学生早期家庭教育也各不相同,而且学生是成长中的个体,一方面作为人,学生具有精神性,另一方面学生还处在成长过程中,理性不成熟,具有犯错逾矩的可能性。教师承受着社会性的教育焦虑和"少子化"社会家庭对孩子过度关爱的压力,面对具有差异性、成长性和精神性的学生,在这样的工作情景中,即使有了教育惩戒的立法,教师在运用法律所赋予的教育惩戒权和面对相关的自由裁量空间时,只有具备了较高的教育惩戒伦理素养,才能减少实施教育惩戒时的失当,如

---

① 何怀宏:《伦理学是什么》,北京大学出版社,2002 年。

此则特别地彰显了教育惩戒伦理的价值。

二、教师教育惩戒中的善与教育性

教师教育惩戒伦理具有独特的价值,所以教育实践中的教师应有相应的修炼以获致教育惩戒的伦理素养。然而当前学界对教师教育惩戒伦理规范的探讨语焉不详,而这一学术努力的基础是从学理上追问教师教育惩戒的"善"的标准是什么。

从伦理的角度来看,教师在教育实践中实施教育惩戒,追求的理应是"善"。这一点容易形成共识,关键是到底什么是教育惩戒中的"善",而这一探究应设定在"教育"这一特定情景中来。《说文解字》从词源上解读"善"为:"善,吉也,从言从羊,此与义、美同意";另外,通过对儒家思想的分析,还可以认为,"己所不欲,勿施于人"为"善"。[①] 在西方伦理思想史上对"善"的理解更是聚讼纷纭,快乐主义认为只要让人快乐就是"善",德性主义认为只要符合美德就为"善",功利主义则要仔细计算各种功利得失,并根据功利的"量"的多少来判断是否为"善",康德的"义务论"则认为要符合道德的"绝对命令"才为"善"。这些伦理思想可能是"目的论",抑或是"效果论",它们展示了伦理分析的两个传统维度。除此之外,罗尔斯的正义论也值得关注,他的理论核心在于构建一个公平的程序,以实现正义。[②] 所以程序正义为"善",而程序正义是一种"过程论"。以上对什么是"善"的纷争的梳理并不一定能让我们通约获取一个对"善"的一般性理解,但是从中可以明确出讨论"善"的三个维度:"目的""过程"与"效果",这三者就是一个伦理事件的"发生学"逻辑。基于此,讨论教育惩戒这一发生于教育场域的事件的善性标准时,我们也应该相应地从教师实施教育惩戒的"动机""过程"和"结果"

---

① 蔡连玉:《信息伦理教育研究:一种"理想型"构建的尝试》,中国社会科学出版社,2011 年。
② 林火旺:《伦理学入门》,上海古籍出版社,2005 年。

三个维度来展开。

　　从理论上看,在教育场域中教师的每一教育活动都应具有教育性,这是由教育的根本旨趣所决定的。这里的教育性具有"个体本位"和"社会本位"双重属性。教育惩戒是众多教育活动之一,所以教育惩戒也应具有教育性。有学者把教育惩戒分为"教育性惩戒""非教育性惩戒"和"反教育性惩戒"三类,①这是一种有益的学术努力,但其着眼点主要是在教育效果上。而且问题的关键是,我们对何谓"教育性"需要有全面深入的理解。思考"教育性"的内涵,首先要做的是探究何谓真正的教育。② 就此学界古今中外的叙说丰富,但归根到底真正的教育就是要促进学生的成长,而且强调是每一个学生的成长。这里就回到了个体本位的思路。就学生个体而言,其成长有当下的成长和未来的成长之分,具有教育性的教育显然是兼顾当下和未来的成长,偏重于应试的教育以学生的想象力、创造性和求知欲望为代价,来追求当下的考试分数,显然是教育性不足。从横向来看,学生个体的智力是多元的,每个学生都是不同智力的组合,基于学生不同智力组合的全面发展的教育,以及追求学生学业成绩与社会性发展并重的教育更具有教育性。总之,"纵向有序、横向丰裕"地促进学生成长的教育具有教育性。而且教育要面向全体,部分学生的成长不能以忽视另外一部分学生为代价,能促进所有学生的成长的教育才具有教育性。再从社会角度来审视,具有教育性的教育必须是促进社会整体文明发展的教育,而不只是培养"精致的利己主义者"③或者鼓励学生"原子式生存"的教育。④ 综上所述,教育的教育性体现在这种教育能够促进学生个体当前和未来的成长,能够促进学生个体基于其自身多元智能组合的全面成长,能够促进所有学生的成长,能够促进社会整体福祉提升的成长。

---

　　① 　蔡辰梅:《论教师的惩戒之善及其实现》,《教育伦理研究》,2017 年第 0 期。
　　② 　曹永国:《道德教育必须坚守教育性》,《现代大学教育》,2017 年第 2 期。
　　③ 　钱理群:《中国教育的血肉人生》,漓江出版社,2012 年。
　　④ 　许敏:《美国中产阶级"协作培养"家庭教育方式的伦理风险》,《道德与文明》,2014 年第 1 期。

教育惩戒发生在教育场域和学生的教育生活之中,所以其善的判断标准理应就是教育惩戒行为是否具有如上所讨论的教育性,但是可不可以认为只要教育惩戒具有教育性,就达到了善?学校只是整个社会的一个子系统,在社会大系统中存在诸多的"善"或者"德目",如果特定的教育惩戒具有教育性,它就应该也必然符合社会大系统中的善。所以不需要在教育性之外另用其他伦理标准来判断教育惩戒的善。也正是基于此,我们可以断定,教育性就是教师教育惩戒的善性追求。而且根据上文的探讨,我们在审视特定的教师教育惩戒行为是否具有教育性时,不能单一地局限于结果维度,而应综合全面地审察教师实施教育惩戒的动机、过程和结果三者是否都具有教育性。教育实践中存在诸多以"为学生好"的教育惩戒动机善遮蔽教育惩戒方法、场合和时机(过程)选择不当的恶的现象,也存在以学生考试分数高(结果)来为自己恶的教育惩戒辩护的教师。而且单一的效果论对教育而言难有定数和说服力,因为教师教育实践的好或坏的结果具有滞后性和迷散性,所以在判断教师教育惩戒行为的善性程度时需要从"动机""过程"和"结果"三个维度来综合考察其是否具有教育性。教师的教师惩戒在"动机""过程"和"结果"三个维度都具有教育性,是教师教育惩戒伦理的最高位的规范,这一认识也是制订教师教育惩戒基本伦理规范的基础之一。

三、教师面临的教育惩戒伦理风险

教育惩戒之善在于惩戒的动机、过程和结果均具有教育性,即对全体学生的学业与社会性成长都有益。然而在实践中教师的教育惩戒未必都能达到这种善,对每一个教师而言,在教育惩戒行为上都存在不同程度的伦理风险。伦理风险,意味着不确定性,且这种不确定性极可能致使在做出道德选择后产生不良效应。[1] 在教育惩戒中,教师所面临的伦理风险是指教师在选

---

[1] 张彦:《价值排序与伦理风险》,人民出版社,2011 年。

择教育惩戒行为时可能带来的伦理层面的负面后果。通过对教育实践中教师教育惩戒行为细致观察与梳理,可以发现,教师面临的教育惩戒伦理风险主要有"放弃使用""错误使用"与"过度使用"三种类型。

(一)教育惩戒的"放弃使用"

教育惩戒的"放弃使用"是指教师没有对学生的行为失范实施应有的教育惩戒这一现象,弃用教育惩戒又分为"有意识放弃"与"无意识放弃"两种。在教育实践中,一些教师明知道学生行为失范,更好的帮助学生成长的方式是实施相应的教育惩戒,然而因现实社会层面原因,教师不去惩戒学生,久而久之教师甚至形成了不愿惩戒学生的习惯,此为有意识放弃教育惩戒。教师有意识放弃教育惩戒,很大程度上是出于现实和社会性的考量,是趋利避害的人性所致。当前,我国"少子化"社会的格局已形成,家庭对孩子的过分呵护具有普遍性,再加上不当教育观念的流行,导致学校教育中教师应有的教育惩戒权被虚化。现实中,教师因管教学生而引发"校闹"事例屡见不鲜,教师轻则名誉受损、受处分,重则遭受人身伤害,甚至生命威胁,这样的教育环境让教师即使认为应当惩戒,也不敢惩戒学生。另外,也有教师在应当惩戒学生的情境下却不自知,没有实施应有的教育惩戒行为,此为教师无意识放弃教育惩戒。教师无意识放弃使用教育惩戒,主要是由于教师专业理性不足或对教育惩戒的认知不当。譬如,"学生插队,教师无动于衷"之类现象的发生,可能是因为教师认为"插队"等只是小事情,无须惩戒和引导纠正。这种情况下,教师不是因为不敢管或不想管,而是没有意识到这些"小事"属于应当被教育惩戒的范围,也就不会采取举措进行制止。

无论是有意识还是无意识,教师对教育惩戒的"放弃使用",都与教师的专业理性包括教育惩戒伦理修炼不足有关。教育惩戒的放弃使用,最终的受害者是学生。教师没有对学生的失范行为实施合理惩戒,这种对学生成长教育的不作为,会让学生不能认识到自己的错误所在,也就失去了纠正的机会,教师也就难以帮助学生学业成长和社会性发展。所以本质观之,合理的教育惩戒是学生成长的需要,[1]而教师不因教育目的放弃教育惩戒实质上是教师对学生成长没有真正担责,从而不具教育性。

(二)教育惩戒的"错误使用"

教师对教育惩戒的"错误使用"体现在教师惩戒学生所运用的方法、所选择的时机与场合的不当上,相应的,教育惩戒的"错误使用"就有"方法错误""时机错误"和"场合错误"等主要类型。教师教育惩戒的方法错误,意指教师实施教育惩戒时没有学生个体的针对性,具体的就是没有考虑学生的年龄、性别、个性等的差异而"因人施戒"。在实施教育惩戒时,有的教师不管是对低年级的学生还是高年级的学生,都采用同样的惩戒措施,而事实上对处于叛逆期的学生来说,以更为尊重的方式进行教育惩戒会更有效果,更具教育性;有的教师不管行为失范的是男生还是女生,都毫不留情地进行同样的惩戒,而没有顾及学生性别的差异;有的教师没有考虑学生的性格内向或外向等个性特质,而实施同样的教育惩戒。在现实中有较多的案例表明,心理敏感、抗压能力差的学生易因受方法不当的教育惩戒而走极端,甚至酿成悲剧。

教育惩戒的时机错误,意指教师实施教育惩戒时时机选择不正确。教育惩戒的时机与学生对惩戒的接纳程度紧密相关,而教师是否准确把握惩戒时机会产生云泥之别的教育效果。譬如,有教师观察到学生在教室里情绪激动地打架,如果这时教师严厉地指责正处情绪中的学生,学生肯定难以听进教师的言说,甚至会顶撞教师。所以这时的教育惩戒效果往往不佳,只有当学生心平气和后,才可能接纳批评惩戒,这时的教育惩戒才可能触及学生的灵魂。

教师教育惩戒的场合错误,意指教师实施教育惩戒时所处的场合不当。例如,有教师因为班上有一位学生多次迟到,便让该生举着检讨书站在校门

---

① Don Fuhr, *Effective Classroom Discipline: Advice for Educators*, NASSP Bulletin, No. 1, 1993.

口示众。这种场合不当的教育惩戒存在双重风险：一是对被惩戒学生。作为有生命的个体，学生的自尊心在众人面前受到打击，这可能会让学生陷入自卑或者产生愤怒甚至怨恨情绪，对学生的人格发展带来伤害；二是对旁观的其他学生。教师是学生的榜样，尤其是对"向师性"强的中小学生，教师的一举一动都会对其产生潜移默化的影响。教师对被惩戒学生的严苛同样也会印刻在旁观学生心中，这不仅在学生与教师之间增添了隔阂，学生"不亲其师"也就"难信其道"，教师教育的效果也会不彰。而且从长远来看，这种严苛的教育惩戒会让学生无意间习得刻薄与不宽容，从而难以在学生心中播下温暖与关怀的种子。

如上三类教育惩戒的"错误使用"之所以发生，主要是因为教师专业素养包括教育惩戒伦理素养的不足。作为专业的教师，不应只是凭着直觉与感性实施教育惩戒，因为不充分考虑学生差异、方法与场合选择不当的教育惩戒，不利于学生的成长，缺失教育性。

（三）教育惩戒的"过度使用"

教师对教育惩戒的"过度使用"涉及惩戒实施的程度与范围，教育惩戒实施时在程度和范围上应有"度"的限制。对行为失范学生的惩戒超过了其所犯错误的严重程度，此为教育惩戒在程度上的"过度使用"；教师本应对失范者学生个体实施惩戒却波及班级或小组全体，这是教育惩戒在范围上的"过度使用"。从惩戒严厉程度上来看，教师的教育惩戒总容易与体罚或变相体罚混为一谈，而在现实中的确存在较多教师对学生的惩戒过度现象。有教师因为班上学生不遵守课堂纪律对其动辄辱骂，还有教师因学生背诵课文不过关，罚其抄写课文上百遍。从教育惩戒的范围来看，教师教育惩戒对象的扩大化在现实中也时有发生。譬如，某小学教师因班上几名学生犯错，惩罚全班学生在烈日下晒1小时。教师意在通过惩罚全班的方式让犯错的学生及其他学生知道错误的严重性，教师甚至有这样一种想象：犯错的学生因为自己拖累其他同学受罚会心生愧疚，便不会再犯。此惩戒行为可能达到阻止犯错者及其他同学的类似错误行为的效果,为此教师不惜对无辜学生一同惩戒。但事实上,教师扩大教育惩戒对象,虽然其动机是好的,但过程中没有正确对待不相关的学生,所以这种方法缺失教育性。从惩罚效果来看,这样会导致无辜学生受到不公正对待,他们可能会因此对教师甚至学校产生不满心理,这种不满往往伴随着疏远与敌视感,甚至可能出现破坏性行为。[①] 教师的教育惩戒行为,无论是程度上还是范围上的过度使用,都缘起于教师专业理性包括教育惩戒伦理素养不足。过度的教育惩戒行为都不具教育性和伦理上的合理性。

总而言之,教师在履行教育惩戒权时存在"放弃使用""错误使用"和"过度使用"三种伦理风险,这三种情况也是实践中较多存在的教师教育惩戒问题。究其因,都在一定程度上与教师专业理性和教育惩戒伦理素养不足相关。但是以上分类并不是绝对和非此即彼的,现实中存在教师的教育惩戒行为具有类型上的交叉性,譬如,教师的某些情绪性惩戒,可能是不考虑方法、场合的教育惩戒"错误使用",又是超出了学生犯错程度和范围的教育惩戒"过度使用"。

四、教师教育惩戒伦理的基本规范

对教师教育惩戒所应遵循的善的探讨,以及教育实践中教师实施教育惩戒时所面临伦理风险的分析,是研究提出教师教育惩戒伦理基本规范的理论基础和思想来源。在构建教师教育惩戒伦理规范的方法论上需要进一步阐明的是,教师教育惩戒行为所面临的情境具有复杂性,而教育惩戒行为本身也是多样复杂的,所以教育惩戒伦理的规范在微观层面是零碎和细节化的,而且还会因为社会情景的变化甚至新技术在教育领域的应用而变化

---

① ［美］肯尼思·斯特赖克、乔纳斯·索尔蒂斯:《教学伦理》,洪成文、张娜、黄欣译,教育科学出版社,2007 年。

发展。基于此,我们这里主要从宏观和中观层面来构建教师的教育惩戒伦理规范,并且把最上位宏观层面的教育惩戒伦理规范称为"1 阶伦理规范",而中观层面则是"2 阶伦理规范"。

教师的教育惩戒最上位的"1 阶伦理规范"是:教师的教育惩戒行为应是善的,即教育惩戒的动机、过程和结果都应具有教育性。某一项活动具有教育性,简单地说就是具有正面和积极的教育价值。对教师的教育惩戒而言,其教育性也就是它对全体学生的成长具有教育意义。这里的个体成长,包括了学生个体的学业成长和社会性成长,学业成长体现在学习动机、学习习惯和学习成绩等方面,社会性成长包括其美好品德的塑造等方面。而且学生个体成长的教育性还体现在成长不只是当下的,而且是可持续的。教育惩戒的教育性还要求惩戒是追求全体学生成长的,而不只是少数和部分学生的成长。另外教师教育惩戒的教育性不只是对全体学生个体成长的追求,而且还应具有提升社会整体福祉的旨趣。需要强调的是,判断教师教育惩戒行为是否具有教育性和善,需要对教师教育惩戒行为的动机、过程和结果进行综合判断,而不只是单一向度的考察。作为 1 阶伦理规范,这一伦理规范是处于最高位的,用它可以宏观地判断现实中具体的教师教育惩戒行为是否合乎伦理,它也是审察中观层面的教育惩戒 2 阶伦理规范合理性的依据。

教师教育惩戒中层的"2 阶伦理规范"依从于"1 阶伦理规范",来源于研究对实践中教师教育惩戒伦理风险的观察分析,可以细分为三条。2 阶伦理规范一是:教师不应无故放弃对失范学生的教育惩戒。这里的"无故"指的是"没有符合教育性的原因",也就是说,如果教师放弃了对失范学生的教育惩戒,其原因应是放弃教育惩戒与实施教育惩戒在动机、过程和结果的综合考量上,放弃更具教育性,即更有利于全体学生的成长,否则就是"无故"放弃教育惩戒。在教育实践中,有诸多教师放弃教育惩戒的现象,而其原因有很大一部分是因为教师基于现实个人利益的考虑,如避免为自己招来"麻烦""多一事不如少一事"等,还有教师是"不自知"、无意识地放弃教育惩戒,这些现象都属于无故放弃教育惩戒。教师无故放弃教育惩戒行为,不利于需要纠正失范行为、培育美德的学生的成长,从而最终损害了学生的长远利益,所以有违教育性。

2 阶伦理规范二是:教师实施教育惩戒时应选择适当的方法、时机和场合。教师针对学生的行为失范实施教育惩戒时,即使动机是为了学生的成长,如果实施具体教育惩戒的方法、时机和场合选择不合理,也难以从结果上有教育收获。学生之间有年龄、性别差异,这些是自然分布的不同;另外,学生的差异一般地还来源于学生的生理基础与早期教养,不同的基因组合和相异的家庭教养形成了学生迥异的个性与气质特征。无论是学生自然分布的不同,还是个性气质的差异,都需要教师实施教育惩戒时选择相匹配的方法。接受教育惩戒的学生不是没有思维的"物",而是具有主观动机、会思考的精神性个体,所以教师只有选择合适的时机和场合才有可能让学生"悦纳"教育惩戒,教育惩戒才能触动学生的灵魂,也才会有教育效果,具备教育性。

2 阶伦理规范三是:教师实施教育惩戒时应注意程度与范围的合理性。从学理上讲,教师对学生失范行为进行惩戒,其程度应与学生失范行为的严重性相匹配,当然还要考虑失范行为学生的个性、气质等个体差异。从程度上来看,过重或过轻的教育惩戒带来的教育效果都不佳,甚至会产生负面教育效应,因而不具备教育性。从范围来看,缩小和扩大教育惩戒的范围,因公平性欠缺等原因,也不具备应有的教育性。所以教师实施教育惩戒时,追求合乎伦理,就应充分考虑惩戒的程度与范围的合理性。如上三条中层教师教育惩戒 2 阶伦理规范,上承 1 阶伦理规范,下接更为细致、更为具体的教师应遵循的教育惩戒伦理细则。

研究通过理论探讨与实践观察,构建了教师实施教育惩戒时应遵循的上位的 1 阶和中层的 2 阶伦理规范。教育惩戒的伦理规范外在地看是一种客观的社会存在,它应成为一种思想共识,起到约束教师教育惩戒行为的作用;内在地看,教育惩戒伦理规范要深入教师的思想意识中去,才能发挥无形的约束作用,使教师面对行为失范学生时合乎伦理地去应对和施教。教师获致教育惩戒的伦理素养需要经由理论学习和实践反思两条路径。研究分析构建出的教育惩戒伦理规范是教师理论学习的应有内容,对其研习能够加深教师对什么是善的教育惩戒的认知,在中观层面能够指引教师的教育惩戒行为。当然,理论学习的内容还应包括"迷恋他人成长的学问"教育学。① 另外,教师还应根据伦理学理论特别是所构建的教育惩戒伦理规范,以及教育学相关理论对教育惩戒的案例和自己已经历、正在经历的教育惩戒事件进行"事上磨炼"②。理论学习与实践反思是提升教师教育惩戒伦理修养的两条必要路径,提升教师教育惩戒伦理修养是规避相关伦理风险,更好地引导全体学生成长的基础。

On the Ethics of Teachers' Education Disciplining & Its Norms

Lianyu Cai　Qin Li

College of Teacher Education, Zhejiang Normal University

Abstract: A positive consensus on the right of teachers' education disciplining has been reached academically, and the legislation of education disciplining is being advanced. In view of the generality of the law itself, however, teachers will have relatively great discretion in education disciplining practice. In order to ensure that the right of education disciplining is used rationally, teachers should

---

① ［加拿大］马克斯·范梅南:《教学机智:教育智慧的意蕴》,李树英译,教育科学出版社,2001 年。

② 孙培青:《中国教育史》(第 2 版),华东师范大学出版社,2000 年。

have the ethical literacy related to education disciplining, and the ethics of education disciplining is the thoughts basis and functional supplement of education disciplining legislation. From different ethical ideas, the "goodness" of education disciplining lies in its education nature, that is, to promote the sustainable growth of all students both in academical and social dimensions. In practice, there exists ethical risks in teachers' education disciplining, including "abandoned use" "wrong use" and "over use", which are contrary to its education nature. Based on the theoretical discussion of education disciplining and the practical analysis of the ethical risks of teachers' education disciplining, the first – level and second – level ethical norms of teachers' education disciplining can be constructed. Besides the educational nature and not being given up of educational disciplining, the norms involve the rationality of methods, timing, occasions, degree and scope. Teachers should improve their own ethical literacy of education disciplining through theoretical study and practical reflection.

Keywords: Educational Disciplining, Disciplining Ethics, Ethical Risks, Ethical Norms

普通高考生与"三位一体"生专业成长的差异性比较研究
——以浙江师范大学 2013 级小学教育专业为例①

李志超　王　佳

山东师范大学教育学部，浙江湖海塘小学

摘要："三位一体"招生制度是完善高校自主招生制度，建立起分层、分类选拔人才的重要方式之一。人才的选拔跟人才的培养与发展紧密联系，通过对浙江师范大学 2013 级小学教育专业学生进行为期四年的跟踪调查，以专业知识学习、专业能力发展和专业理念养成等维度为观察点，发现"三位一体"生的专业成长显著好于普通高考生。因此，综合素质人才的培养，需要学生具有良好的角色认知、合理的课程学习和有效的反思性实践。

关键词："三位一体"生；普通高考生；专业成长比较

一、研究缘起

"三位一体"招生制度是对教育部提出的"要努力形成分类考试、综合评

---

①　基金项目：本文系浙江省高等教育"十三五"第一批教学改革研究项目"从实践环节到实践课程：小学教育专业教育见习重构研究"阶段性研究成果之一。

价、多元录取的考试招生制度"①的一次尝试。浙江省采用"三位一体"招生选拔的方式,打破高校"一考定终身"的招生录取方式,将"高中学业水平考试、综合素质考试和高考成绩"有效结合,选取综合素质人才。2011 年,浙江工业大学、杭州师范大学完成招生的试点任务。随后几年,浙江省参加"三位一体"招生制度的高等院校不断增加,试点范围逐步扩大,省外的 985、211 大学(如上海交通大学、中国科技大学等)逐步参与其中。"三位一体"招生人数也从 2011 年的 260 人逐步上升为如今的近 6000 人。

2012 年,浙江师范大学首次将"三位一体"综合评价制度纳入招生工作范畴,以小学教育、学前教育两个本科专业作为主要试点招生专业;不久,逐渐扩展到思想政治教育、特殊教育、汉语言文学等专业。2019 年,浙江师范大学"三位一体"招生共覆盖 7 个专业,招生人数扩展到 301 人。

从历年的招生报名情况可以看出,"三位一体"招生模式日渐受到家长和考生的热捧,第一批提前批的志愿填报率甚至高达 1020%。"三位一体"综合评价体制将学生的在校学业与能力特长紧密联系,注重学生专业爱好和专业潜质的挖掘,打破了"一考定终身"对学生发展的禁锢。

火热的报考局面引来的思考是,通过高考分数划档统招(以下称"普通高考生")和"三位一体"综合评价选拔的学生(以下称"三位一体"生),他们在大学的表现是否有明显差异?有的话,主要表现在哪些方面?一般认为,高考生在高考成绩上比"三位一体"生更有优势,三位一体生则以优秀的综合素质脱颖而出,这种"先入之见"是否会影响他们在高校的学习?两种不同选拔类型进入高校的学生,应该怎样做到互相帮助、互相学习,实现共同发展?

带着这些问题,我们对浙江师范大学教师教育学院 2013 级小学教育专业的普通高考生与"三位一体"生进行了为期四年的跟踪调查研究,希望能够从中获取与两者发展紧密相关的宝贵信息,从而为不同类型的学生在高

---

① 教育部副部长杜玉波 2011 年 3 月 28 日在国新办举行的新闻发布会上的讲话。

校得到更好的发展,提供一定的建议。

二、研究设计

　　研究者以浙江师范大学教师教育学院 2013 级小学教育专业学生为研究对象,采用跟踪调查的方式,对普通高考生与"三位一体"生的专业成长进行系统的比较分析。从生源基本情况来看,当年浙江省文科一本录取分数线为 617 分,国家任务统招计划上来的小学教育侧文方向最高投档分数线为 649 分,最低投档分数线为 629 分,平均分为 636 分,超一本线 19 分;当年浙江省理科一本录取分数线为 619 分,国家任务统招计划上来的小学教育侧理方向最高投档分数线为 662 分,最低投档分数线为 631 分,平均分为 641 分,超一本线 22 分。相比而言,国家任务"三位一体"计划的小学教育侧文方向最高投档分数线为 631 分,最低投档分数线为 587 分,平均分为 614 分,低于一本线 3 分;国家任务"三位一体"计划的小学教育侧理方向最高投档分数线为 643 分,最低投档分数线为 608 分,平均分为 625 分,超一本线 6 分。(具体如下表所示)

浙江师范大学小学教育专业 2013 级生源情况结构分析表

年级	重点线 (文/理)	批次	最高分 (文/理)	最低分 (文/理)	平均分 (文/理)	平均分 - 重点线 (文/理)
2013	617/619	第一批	649/662	629/631	636/641	19/22
		三位一体	631/643	587/608	614/625	-3/6

　　我们设计了学生专业成长调查问卷,分别在 2014 年 2 月和 2017 年 2 月进行两次问卷发放。2014 年 2 月,作为一个时间节点,是考虑到大学生有一定的高校学习生活适应期;节点计算到 2017 年 2 月,主要是第八学期,同学们需要应聘工作、顶岗实习、完成毕业论文等,课业学习已在此之前基本完成。研究样本剔除了高水平运动员、浙师大附中直升班、新疆预科班和丽水

定向生等"干扰信息",先后于 2014 年 2 月和 2017 年 2 月,发放问卷 130 份。2014 年,有效回收问卷 111 份,其中"三位一体"生 37 份,普通高考生 74 份;2017 年,有效回收问卷 116 份,其中"三位一体"生 40 份,普通高考生 76 份。

在问卷编制过程中,以国家提出的"有理想信念、有道德情操、有扎实学识、有仁爱之心的"的"好教师"标准为参考,同时吸取"自我发展力是教师专业成长的核心动力,它由教师对教育的信仰力、对学科知识的学习力和对教学变革积极适应的转换力三股力量构成"的相关观点①,从专业知识学习、专业能力发展和专业理念养成三方面进行设计,考察学生的专业成长情况。

就"专业知识学习"这一部分,我们主要采用李克特 5 点量表式计分,内部一致性检验发现,总的信度系数为 0.794,各个问题的信度系数位于 0.739~0.803。一般认为,问卷的信度系数在 0.70~0.80 间相当好,在 0.80~0.90 之间非常好。总体而言,问卷的信度较高。就"专业能力发展"和"专业理念养成"来说,更多的是通过访谈法、参与式观察法等,获得第一手资料,为研究开展提供重要的信息。

三、研究结果与分析

(一)专业知识学习

专业知识是学生能够站好讲台、站稳讲台的基础,是成长为一名人民教师的核心要素。马云鹏认为教师的专业知识包括"教育理论知识、课程知识、学科知识、学科教学法知识"等方面②。这些可以通过学生在校期间的学习成绩给予一定的显性化体现。在此,我们通过比较普通高考生与"三位一体生"初入校时的分数的不同;经过专业学习之后,彼此之间又产生了怎样的变化,予以说明。

---

① 姚新瑜等:《自我发展力:教师专业成长的内核动力》,《教育发展研究》,2015 年第 15 期。
② 马云鹏等:《教师专业知识的测查与分析》,《教育研究》,2010 年第 12 期。

从下表中发现,高校录取的"三位一体"生与普通高考生是有高考成绩差异的。"三位一体"的平均高考成绩为 619.5,高考生则为 638.5。普通高考生的高考分数显著高于"三位一体"生。或许我们会得出这样的结论,学生在大学期间的学习状况将是入学差距的延续。

"三位一体"生与普通高考生在高考成绩上的 t 检验

类别	M	SD	t
三位一体生	619.5	13.00	−11.04 ***
高考生	638.5	6.44	

注:* 表示 p<0.05,** 表示 p<0.01,*** 表示 p<0.001,下同

然而研究发现,经过四年的专业学习,两类学生之间的成绩差距正逐渐减弱,甚至"三位一体"生实现了反转。从大学第四年的平均绩点看,"三位一体"生的绩点均值要高于普通高考生,并且差异性显著(见下表)。

"三位一体"生与普通高考生在平均绩点上的 t 检验

类别	M	SD	t
三位一体生	3.60	0.20	.28 *
普通高考生	3.50	0.25	

面对大学培养方式的综合化,以往过分注重"成绩论英雄"的学生缺少学业优势发展的可持续性,在某些方面甚至表现出潜力不足,这跟"高考成绩与师范生培养不存在显著性相关"的既有研究是相吻合的①。知识,不再被认为是确定的、不可改变的规则、命题、原理。知识正在从"命题性知识"向"能力性知识"转化②。大学中,课程设置走出了"坐而论道"的窠臼,注重

---

① 张天雪:《如何让"差生"走向"卓越"——"三位一体"小教师范生养成的个案研究》,《教师教育研究》,2016 年第 6 期。

② [美]路易斯·P. 波伊曼:《知识论导论》,洪汉鼎译,中国人民大学出版社,2008 年。

实践与应用、综合与创新。例如,小学教育专业的专业课程中不仅涵盖"教育学""心理学""课程与教学论"等理论课程,也包括"微格教学与教学诊断""演讲与口才""素描基础与色彩基础""小学科技活动设计"等实践性课程。

当然,大学期间的学业绩点无法反映一个人专业知识学习的全貌,还需要学生具有专业学习的主观评定。大学与高中最大的区别是,大学更加强调学生学习的自主性、自觉性,这也就要求学生们能够具有良好的学习适应度、有针对性地制定学习计划、确定学习目标、总结学习方法,甚至做好清晰的职业发展规划,这样才能保证自己完成从高中学习模式到大学学习模式的转变,从而更好地适应新的学习环境。

问卷调查显示,"三位一体"生在专业学习主观评定的均值得分比高考生高,这一差距在大一时并未达到显著性,但在大四时已经达到显著性水平,两种类型学生的差距随着时间的推移正在增加(如下表所示)。"三位一体"生表现出了更多的主动、积极、自觉、饱满之情。

"三位一体"生与普通高考生在专业学习主观评定上的 t 检验

类别	项目	大一	大四
三位一体生	M	3.31	3.65
	SD	0.62	0.64
普通高考生	M	3.08	3.39
	SD	0.61	0.65
显著性	Sig.	0.068	0.009 **

具体来说,"三位一体"生和普通高考生在"我觉得上大学后,对职业生涯规划更加清晰"出现显著差异。这说明经历过综合选拔的"三位一体"生,能够更好地进行自我评估。他们不仅了解自己的优缺点和兴趣爱好、能力性向,而且能够根据自己目前所处的专业发展水平和层次做出较为合理的分析判断,确定自我进一步发展的规划,以及相应的行动方案。

专业学习的主观评定的另一个显性化方面就是学生的课堂参与情况。相比普通高考生,"三位一体"生的课堂参与更好一些。"三位一体"生自身的演讲、口才方面的优势,以及活泼开朗、积极主动、勤于思考、善于表现的一面,使他们在课堂上"爱表现""敢表现",能够在一定程度上提出质疑、发表自己的观点。这可以从他们在课堂上能够勇于发表个人观点、积极参与学习讨论的数量和质量中看出。

(二)专业能力发展

教育部颁布的《小学教师专业标准(试行)》将"能力为重"作为合格小学教师的基本理念之一,将之具体化为:"把学科知识、教育理论与教育实践有机结合,突出教书育人实践能力;研究小学生,遵循小学生成长规律,提升教育教学专业化水平;坚持实践、反思、再实践、再反思,不断提高专业能力。"[①]反映到学生培养中,集中于学生的教学能力、研究能力和其他实践能力等方面。

教学能力,是教师的心理素质、教态仪态、言语表达、思维品质、教学设计、组织与实施等方面在课堂教学中的综合体现。在此,我们选取教师资格证通过率和师范技能大赛获奖率两个指标,作为观测点。教师资格证考试作为达标性考核,是师范生走向专业教师的"门槛",是检验学生教学能力发展的重要维度。调查发现,"三位一体"生的教师资格证一次通过率为92%,要高于普通高考生78%的通过率。师范技能比赛,作为选拔性评定,是以赛促练的方式,助力师范生教学能力的进一步提升。在师范技能比赛中,我们施行"班级、学院、学校"三种选拔方式,在"人人参与"的基础上,选优、择优。结果接受问卷调查的40位"三位一体"生中,有10人在院校以上师范技能大赛中获奖;76位普通高考生中,仅有1人在院校师范技能比赛中获奖。

两种类型群体之所以出现如此差异,首先来自"三位一体"生强大的心

---

① 中华人民共和国教育部:《小学教师专业标准(试行)》。

理自信。这种心理优势的形成,一方面是之前的综合素质考察对他们的能力特长给予的认可;另一方面是通过高校《儿童发展心理学》《小学生行为观察与指导》《课堂教学行为训练》等课程学习,在培养他们向"善"的品质中,具有与个性特点相匹配的"机智"。这种机智,"表现为克制,对孩子的体验的理解,尊重孩子的主体性,'润物细无声',对情境的自信和临场的天赋"①。内在的心理自信转化到行动上,便形成强大的驱动力。自信心的养成,带来的是学生强大的自我效能感,形成鲜活的教学个性。相比较而言,"三位一体"生更加注重知识的活学活用。学习就是我们在课堂内外建立起的有机联系,对知识不断结构和建构的意义生成的过程。"在大学学习中,我们的生活体验、知识视野,真的很重要。大学注重的是'应用'而不是'纸上谈兵'。因为你永远不知道试卷上和老师会提什么问题,根本没有办法提前准备,一张试卷里我做到了各种类型的题目,时事政治、文学常识、逻辑推理、甚至还有法律问题……"这是"三位一体"生在考试后的真实感叹;普通高考生则更善于用"我没复习过,知识点超纲"之类的表达进行总结。

师范生要成长为一名教师,就要有所思、有所行,做"教学研究者",学会研究课堂、研究学生、研究自身,而不是做技工型的"教书匠"。师范生科研素养的提升,需要从科研意识、方法和能力等方面进行锻炼,课题则是科研素养培养的最好途径。2013 级学生在大一下学期接受的问卷调查显示,参与课题研究的"三位一体"生和普通高考生分别占同类型人群的 59% 和 50%;到了大四上半学期,比例变为 90% 和 80%。"三位一体"生表现出较好的研究倾向,并在做的过程中,表现出一定的问题意识、研究能力和团队协作能力。

除了教学和科研,诸如学生组织能力、文体活动能力等,也是学生综合素质应用的实践场。相比较普通高考生,"三位一体"生更希望通过加入学

---

① ［加拿大］马克斯·范梅南:《教学机智——教育智慧的意蕴》,李树英译,教育科学出版社,2014 年。

生组织来锻炼自己、提升自己。这批学生中,有89%的"三位一体"生在大一时报名参加学生会干事;普通高考生中报名参加的却只有47%。之后,从能够当上学院或学校副部及以上学生工作职位的人数分布构成来看,"三位一体"生和普通高考生各占各自群体的48%和28%。在各项文体活动和比赛中,大一时,平均每位"三位一体"生参与了3项院、校级比赛和活动,获得1.9项荣誉或奖项;平均每位普通高考生参与了2.4项院、校级比赛和活动,获得1.5项荣誉或奖项。大四时,平均每位"三位一体"生参与了8.3项院、校级比赛和活动,获得7.3项荣誉或奖项;平均每位普通高考生参与了3.8项院、校级比赛和活动,获得3.4项荣誉或奖项。

(三)专业理念养成

良好的专业理念是师范生专业成长的主要"内驱力"。学生的专业理念越强,发展的目标越明确,在专业学习中的主动性和积极性也就越强。专业理念背后渗透的专业情感可以通过专业满意度和职业信念来衡量。

专业满意度是师范生对自己专业的认可。四年以来,不同层次、不同类型的学生在自己的学习过程中,由最初的招生宣传对小学教育专业的间接认知,转变为一名参与专业学习过程中的亲历者,感受着自己的成长。总体而言,大家对于大学阶段包括的课程设置、师资配备、教学方式等方面还是满意的(如下表所示)。这从总体上反映了我们现在的高校招生中更多地依据办学定位和人才培养目标选择考生;学生也可以在某种程度上选择自己心仪的学校和专业,而不像以前那样过多地受到分数的羁绊所表现出的无奈和被动。在学生和学校的双向选择中,有利于增加学生对专业的认同感,激发起学生的学习积极性和主动性;同时,高校选拔了更符合专业培养和规格要求的学生,能够集中更多优质资源集中到学生的培养中,提升了教育教学效率,进一步促进学生的成长和发展。

"三位一体"生与高考生的专业满意度比较

年级	学生类型	很满意	比较满意	始终不满意	开始不满意，后来满意	开始满意，后来不满意
大学一年级	"三位一体"生	10.8% 8.1%	73% 60.8%	10.8% 10.8%	5.4% 13.5%	0 6.8%
	普通高考生	12.5%	75%	0	5%	7.5%
大学四年级	"三位一体"生	9.2%	69.7%	9.2%	9.2%	6.6%
	普通高考生					

　　信念是"主体对于自然和社会的某种理论原理、思想见解坚信无疑的看法，是人们赖以从事实践活动的精神支柱，是人们自觉行为的精神力量，决定着一个人的行为的原则性、坚定性"[1]。师范生的职业信念是在专业学习过程中形成的对教师职业的认识和选择。在下表中，我们不仅看到了师范生整体而言所表现出的较高的职业信念；也看到相比高考生，"三位一体"生的"向师""从师"的职业信念更强一些。这主要是基于学生自主专业选择的基础上，我们通过《小学教育专业导论》《大学生职业生涯规划与就业指导》等课程的开设，榜样示范的引领作用，创新性实践活动的开展，使学生对教育有了深刻的认识，明确自己的发展方向，增进对教师职业的热爱之情。

"三位一体"生与高考生的职业信念比较

年级	学生类型	一定会	可能会	一定不会
大学一年级	"三位一体"生	45.9%	54.1%	0
	普通高考生	44.6%	52.7%	2.7%
大学四年级	"三位一体"生	60%	40%	0
	普通高考生	61.8%	36.8%	1.4%

---

① 林传鼎等：《心理学词典》，江西科学技术出版社，1986 年。

四、思考与讨论

从以上研究结果看,"三位一体"综合评价选拔的学生在专业发展的优势的确明显。透过 2017 年浙江省高考改革新方案,人才选拔的专业化是一大趋势。浙江新高考放弃了文理分科,实行了 3 门必考和 3 门选考的模式(3 + 3),旨在鼓励人才培养的多样性。与此同时,高校的招生也更具自主性和灵活性,高校可以根据自身的办学定位和每个专业的不同培养目标,分专业确定选考科目,考生只需要有一门选考科目在专业要求的范围之内,就可以报考这个专业。除此之外,高校还可以将考生的高中阶段综合素质评价作为录取参考。考生在填报专业时,也从"学校 + 专业"的模式改为"专业 + 学校"的模式,这些高考制度的改革都是为了人才选拔能够更符合专业培养的要求。

新型的高考制度改革和招生模式打破"一考定终身"的局面,促进了人才选拔的专业化,实现了学生多元化发展,但高校的人才培养是否完全适应这一招生模式?对于两者在专业发展中出现的差异和学生专业发展中存在的问题,培养单位应该怎么做呢?

(一)"我是谁"——师范生专业成长的"角色认知"

根据当前的招生模式,我们小学教育专业主要通过统一高考招生和"三位一体"招生两种方式进行。两种类型的同学,在入学之初往往被动地贴上了"角色标签",按照人们期望的和自己想要做的方面发展。当"角色标签"外显到行为方式中,就会导致学生在专业学习中出现"自卑"或"自负"倾向。"自卑"表现在学生在学习生活中,不愿意积极地投入到知识学习和能力锻炼中;"自负"则是学生以"超然的优越感"审视自己。

专业的人才培养方式就是要在最大程度上弱化"角色标签"给学生带来的消极影响。教师尽可能减少"先入为主"带来的"有色眼镜",给每位同学提供平等发展、共同参与的机会。学生的情感培育融入组织学习中，需要学生承认"他者"的存在，学会看到每一个人的"成功"。这就需要教师鼓励并正确引导两种类型的学生学会"赏识"彼此，形成并建立"学习共同体"，在相互学习、激励中，实现共同进步，营造"以文化人"的学习型文化。

（二）"我要做什么"——师范生专业成长的"有效给养"

在师范生从"走向讲台"到"走上讲台"的过程中，专业化的培养必不可少，课程建设显得尤为关键。课程体系架构不仅要符合学生的身心特点和兴趣爱好，集中反映一线学校教育的基本诉求；还要折射"冰山之下"的育人理念、指导思想，形成"人—制度—内容—环境"四维一体的培养机制。即以"教师专业成长"为目标，以"面向生活、面向实践的学与教的理论"为核心内容，以"问题与情境、分享与交流、整合与内化"为过程特征，通过校内外导师相结合的"双导师制"，加强课堂内外的互通联动，在以见习、实训、考核、实习、研习为经，以短课程、短学期、达标考核、竞赛提升等实践教学形态改革为纬的"三习一训一考核"的协同创新的实践教学体系中，提升师范生的综合素质，尤其是普通高考生这一大群体。

此外，我们身处互联互通的网络时代，这就意味着这是一个泛在学习的时代。这是当今师范生培养中不可忽视的重要时代特征。在师范生培养过程中，采用虚拟和现实、"线上"和"线下"紧密结合的方式，有机融入系统化、协同化、可视化的"微"元素，实现学习可以在任何时间、任何地点的泛在进行，使师范生的课堂在个性化订制的基础上更加富有互动性和趣味性。师范生的专业成长中，也会改变学习就是枯燥无味的累人之事，学习就是在校读书、教师教学生学的传统认知；形成新的学习观，即将学习视为一种体验、一种乐趣，学习就是促进人不断发展的动力机制。

（三）"我该怎么做"——师范生专业成长的"蜕变过程"

师范生的专业成长过程是理论和实践对话的过程，是在"理论知识实践化”和“实践知识理论化”的互动过程中,促进学生成长的过程。一方面,师范生需要思考如何将学习的理论知识运用到实践中去,增强发现问题、分析问题和解决问题的能力;另一方面,又需要在“做”的过程中,积累经验,不断修正、重组或保持理论知识。这一过程又被视为反思、实践、对话的过程。反思意味着学生的学习是投入身心的、积极主义的、持续的能动过程。实践强调的是“做中学”“知行合一”的过程。“对话”则是师生之间建立起平等沟通的人际关系,在倾听和交流、参与互动中进行理论重构的过程。

我们不仅需要关注师范生在他们的成长过程中做了什么,还要聚焦他们是否具有“向师”的职业信念,培养并使他们养成教师应当具有的人格特征与核心素养。大学教师需要担当起“引路人”的角色,真正发挥“学高为师,身正为范”的作用,帮助师范生祛除功利性、浮躁化和私利化,加强自律、自觉、自为意识,做到为人坦诚、秉持责任意识和创新意识,不断走向“卓越”。

A Comparative Study on the Difference of Professional Development between Average Candidates for College Entrance Examination and Students for "Trinity" Enrollment System of Comprehensive Assessments

Zhichao Li   Jia Wang

College of Teacher Education, Zhejiang Normal University,

Zhejiang Hu hai – tang Primary School

Abstract: The "Trinity" Enrollment System of Comprehensive Assessments is one of the important ways to improve the system of university autonomous enrollment with classified examination and layered selection. Since there is a close relationship between the selection and cultivation of talents, this research conducted a four – year tracking studies on the students of grade 2013 from primary school education major of Zhejiang Normal University. The analyses include the perspectives of professional knowledge learning, the development of professional ability and the cultivation professional concept with the research result that the students selected through the "Trinity" Enrollment System of Comprehensive Assessments are better than the average candidates for college entrance examination from the perspective of professional development. Hence, this research comes to the conclusion that the good role of cognition, the reasonable course learning and effective reflective practice are the elements of cultivation of comprehensive quality talents.

Keywords: Students for "Trinity" Enrollment System of Comprehensive Assessments; Average Candidates for College Entrance Examination; Comparison of Professional Development

新疆地方普通高校师范生劳动价值观
与从教意愿现状调查

——以 Y 大学为例

王晓芳

摘要: 劳动价值观不仅影响着师范生的素质水平,更在一定程度上影响着师范生的职业选择。基于 120 名师范生调查数据,采用定量研究方法对劳动价值观、择业观、从教意愿等方面的相互关系进行了分析。结果发现:师范生的劳动价值观整体呈积极导向。其中,愿意从教的学生拥有更高的劳动美德观;师范生的劳动价值观与择业观显著相关。其中,"自主保障"择业观人群的劳动心智观与学业参与最高;师范生的职业锚以稳定型、独立型、生活型三种类型为主,且与劳动价值观密切相关。基于研究发现,提出了师范生劳动教育的实施策略。

关键词: 师范生;劳动价值观;从教意愿;择业观;职业锚

一、问题的提出

2018 年 9 月 10 日,习近平总书记在"全国教育大会"上深刻指出:"要努力构建德智体美劳全面培养的教育体系,形成更高水平的人才培养体系,培养德智体美劳全面发展的社会主义建设者和接班人。"为传达教育大会精神及落实教师教育振兴行动计划,教育部于 2018 年 9 月 17 日发布《关于实施卓越教师培养计划 2.0 的意见》,该意见明确了培养造就一批教育情怀深厚、专业基础扎实、勇于创新教学、善于综合育人和具有终身学习发展能力的高素质专业化创新型中小学教师的总目标。① 同时,随着"一带一路"倡议的大力推进,西部农村基础教育也迫切需要综合素质高、教育情怀深厚、适应能力强的高劳动素养的师范毕业生。具体表现为:在认知上以教书育人为首选职业;在情感上对教师职业有自豪感、向往感;在意志上不畏艰难、自觉抵制物质诱惑;在行为上投入精力学习教育理论与专业技能。②

目前国内劳动价值观研究主要以中小学、职业院校及高校大学生为对象,主题涵盖劳动教育的内涵、劳动教育实施的现状和存在的问题、开展劳动教育的途径等,且以思辨类研究居多。③ 实证研究则相对较少,其中,徐海云(2019)经问卷调查后发现大学生对劳动的积极意义认同度高、劳动的工具理性明显、对劳动创造美好生活的信心偏低、劳动吃苦精神不足等现状;④ 李珂(2019)则从"劳获之间"和"行不及义"两个方面,分析了大学生劳动价值观的现状、问题及原因,并提出了新时代加强劳动教育的实施体系。⑤ 这些实证研究主要以频率统计来呈现大学生劳动观的特点,对于劳动价值观的维度划分并没有十分清晰的界定。

---

① 《教育部关于实施卓越教师培养计划 2.0 的意见》,http://www.moe.gov.cn/srcsite/A10/s7011/201810/t20181010_350998.html。

② 乔晓华:《地方综合性大学师范生从教意愿现状研究——以 Y 学院为例》,《运城学院学报》,2018 年第 3 期。

③ 徐长发:《劳动教育是人生第一教育——对习近平总书记"以劳动托起中国梦"重要思想的学习体会》,《中国农村教育》,2015 年第 10 期;周秀平:《劳动教育就是素质教育》,《中国教育报》,http://www.jyb.cn/zgjyb/201811/t20181109_1260107.html;曲霞、刘向兵:《新时代高校劳动教育的内涵辨析与体系建构》,《中国高教研究》,2019 年第 2 期;班建武:《"新"劳动教育的内涵特征与实践路径》,《教育研究》,2019 年第 40 期。

④ 徐海云:《新时代大学生劳动价值观转型与嬗变研究》,《未来与发展》,2019 年第 5 期。

⑤ 李珂:《嬗变与审视:劳动教育的历史逻辑与现实重构》,社会科学文献出版社,2019 年。

　　从教意愿作为特定主体对专业认知或职业认同显性的、综合的表现形态,①是个体从事或者准备从事教育事业的态度与行为倾向。② 现有影响师范生从教意愿的因素研究主要从个人背景及职业观两方面展开。就个人背景因素来说,家庭收入较低、居住在乡村和家长为专业技术人员对学生毕业后和一生从教意向的正面影响较强;③就职业观念而言,教师收入低、工作环境差、强度高、压力大成为导致师范生不愿从教的主要原因,而教师职业所具有较长假期及相对稳定性成为师范生愿意从教的直接影响因素,④同时,看重教师职业内在价值的师范生更愿意从教,学习动力也更积极。⑤ 在愿意从教的人群中,师范生对于去农村从教的积极性和意愿远远低于师范生去城市学校从教的意愿,个人未来发展因素、生活条件因素、教学条件因素、婚姻问题因素对师范生的农村从教意愿具有显著影响。⑥

　　综上所述,能够投身西部基础教育事业并"下得去、留得住、教得好"的师范生需具备较高的劳动素养和专业素质,换言之,需要具备"在劳力上劳心"的特质。针对现有研究空白,关注地方普通高校师范生劳动价值观、择业观及从教意愿,探讨师范生劳动教育的开展实施,对于预测未来地方中小学教师队伍的质量具有十分重要的意义和价值。

---

　　① 蒋亦华:《本科院校小学教育专业学生从教意愿的调查研究》,《教师教育研究》,2008 年第11 期。

　　② 乔晓华:《地方综合性大学师范生从教意愿现状研究——以 Y 学院为例》,《运城学院学报》,2018 年第 3 期。

　　③ 付卫东、曹青林:《高校师范类学生就业需求与师范生免费教育政策调整——基于全国 6 所部属师范大学和 30 所地方院校的调查》,《华中师范大学学报(人文社会科学版)》,2013 年第 11 期;徐国兴、谢安邦、刘海波:《师范毕业生的从教意向及其影响因素研究——以 X 大学为例》,《教师教育研究》,2015 年第 9 期。

　　④ 蒋亦华:《本科院校小学教育专业学生从教意愿的调查研究》,《教师教育研究》,2008 年第11 期;安蕾、刘晓军:《地方师范院校毕业生从教意愿及职业价值观调查》,《当代教育论坛》,2010 年第 8 期。

　　⑤ 丁钢、李梅:《中国高等师范院校师范生培养状况调查与政策分析报告》,《教育研究》,2014年第 11 期。

　　⑥ 刘佳、方兴:《我国师范生农村从教意愿及影响因素的实证研究》,《教师教育学报》,2015 年第 10 期;付卫东、付义朝:《地方师范生享受免费教育及农村从教意愿的影响因素——基于全国 30所地方院校的调查》,《河北师范大学学报(教育科学版)》,2015 年第 1 期。

二、研究对象与测量工具

（一）研究对象

研究采用问卷调查的方式,对新疆 Y 大学人文与自然两个学科的 120 名高年级阶段的本科生(即大三和大四本科生)进行调查,具体专业包括英语、数学、艺术。选取高年级学生的主要原因在于高年级学生有着更加丰富的课程经历,能够较为全面地评价自己的学习经历。同时,高年级学生对待职业选择,是否从教的看法相对成熟。对这部分学生施测有助于客观地分析师范生劳动价值观、择业观、学习经历、从教意愿的现实情况。本次调查共发放和回收问卷 120 份,剔除机械作答及填答率过低问卷 15 份,有效回收问卷 105 份。从性别分布来看,男生占比 15.4%,女生占比 83.8%;在年级分布上,大三年级占比 20%,大四年级占比 77.1%;在学科专业分布上,人文学科占比 80%,自然科学占比 20%。

（二）测量工具

本研究采用统计软件 SPSS 21.0 对师范生在《中国大学生劳动价值观量表》《大学生择业观量表》《大学生学习经历量表》[①]中的测量结果进行信效度检验、单变量的描述统计、聚类分析、轮廓分析(Profile Analysis)、双变量的相关分析等。其中,聚类方法的本质是根据数据间的"亲疏程度"进行样本的聚合和分组,展示各个分组的聚合因素和差异特征[②];轮廓分析是一种对不同群体进行多变量关系的整体分析技术,它试图对不同群体所具有的多

---

① 《中国大学生劳动价值观量表》《大学生择业观量表》《大学生学习经历量表》三大量表均在南京大学教育研究院吕林海教授指导下,由 18 级学术型博士生研究团队自主改编开发,量表的信效度均达到检验标准。

② 吕林海、郑钟昊、龚放:《大学生的全球化能力和经历:中国与世界一流大学的比较——基于南京大学、首尔大学和伯克利加州大学的问卷调查》,《清华大学教育研究》,2013 年第 4 期。

个变量进行整体的差异检验,目的是发现不同群体之间的轮廓差异。[1] 各量表测量均采用6分李克特量表,用于师范生群体测量后,依然具有一定的一致性和稳定性。

《中国大学生劳动价值观量表》中的"劳动"指大学生花费时间、付诸心力,并且能对自己、他人和社会产生影响与贡献的身心投入过程,包括体力劳动和脑力劳动。量表包含劳动美德观、劳动心智观、劳动功利观、"劳动不勤"观四个维度。其中,劳动心智观指在劳动中能积极思考,运用自己的专业知识和能力进行创造性劳动的态度和行为倾向。如,我会在各种劳动活动中发挥创造力、敢于创新;"劳动不勤"观指对不愿意身体力行从事体力劳动的态度和行为倾向。如,我觉得体力劳动是吃苦受罪,并且尽量不去干体力活。《大学生择业观量表》包括有自主择业观、有保障择业观、有回报择业观三个维度。其中,有自主择业观可解释为:今后的工作能符合自己的兴趣、能实现自己的理想、能做出创造性的成就。如,我毕业后的工作要能符合自己的兴趣爱好。《大学生学习经历量表》由学业参与、活动参与两个维度构成。学业参与主要指在课堂表现、课后讨论、自主学习等方面的参与程度;活动参与主要指在校园文体活动、社团活动、担任干部等方面的参与程度。

三、研究与发现

(一)现状分析

1. 师范生劳动价值观现状与聚类人群特点

通过均值比较可见师范生劳动价值观总体情况及各维度差异。下表中总体分值为4.6414,说明师范生劳动价值观整体较为成熟。其中,劳动美德

---

① Tabachnick, B, Fidell, L. *Using Multivariate Statistics*, Boston: Pearson, 2007.

观分值最高,反映出师范生对中国传统文化中"吃苦耐劳是一种美德""劳动没有贵贱之分"等说法持认同态度;"劳动不勤"观最低则表明师范生并不完全排斥体力劳动。

劳动价值观各维度均值

维度	劳动美德观	劳动心智观	劳动功利观	"劳动不勤"观
单项均值	5.0693	4.6825	4.6089	2.7917
总体均值	4.6414			

　　为了进一步了解师范生在劳动价值观四个维度中的分布特点,笔者对人群进行 K–Means 聚类,共得到四类群体(见下图)。第一类群体人数为17 人,该群体在劳动中功利心强且不愿意付出劳动,属于功利且"四体不勤"型;第二类群体人数为37 人,这类学生更愿意发挥美德,创造性的劳动,属于美德心智型;第三类群体人数为41 人,这类群体在四种劳动观点中得分均为正值,说明他们在劳动中综合具备四类价值观,属于"融合"型;第四类群体人数为2 人,这类学生在"劳动不勤"观中得分最高,其他三观均为负值,说明他们持有消极抵抗劳动的态度,属于单纯"四体不勤"型。总计有效样本量为97 人,缺失8 人。为保证聚类结果具有合理性,采用判别分析对师范生劳动价值观的四类人群进行检验。检验结果为:对初始分组案例中的97.9% 进行了正确分类,对交叉验证分组案例中的93.8% 进行了正确分类,表明聚类人群合理。

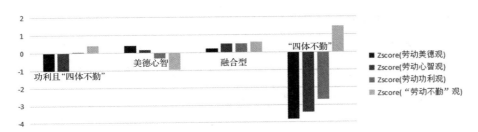

四种劳动价值观的聚类人群

由各群体人数比例可以看出,"美德心智"及"融合型"人群总人数为 78 人,反映出大部分师范生的劳动价值观较为成熟,这与上表总体分值偏高结果一致。功利且"四体不勤"及单纯"四体不勤"人群总数为 19 人,虽占少数比例,但消极劳动观念背后的原因值得深入探究。

2. 师范生择业观现状及聚类人群特点

下表中总体均值反映出师范生价值观在择业问题上的倾向与偏好。各维度得分由高到低依次为有保障择业观、有自主择业观、有回报择业观。"有保障"这一需求仍是师范生最为看重的职业需求,这与当今大学生择业时不仅注重个人发展,同时也看重经济收入的特点一致。①

择业观各维度均值

维度	有保障择业观	有自主择业观	有回报择业观
单项均值	4.8857	4.5524	4.1046
总体均值	4.5142		

为了解师范生在择业观中的人群分布特点,进行 K – Means 聚类后,共得到三类学生群体(见下图)。第一类群体人数为 42 人,在三类择业观上的得分均为负值,说明他们在对待择业持有一种随意的态度,属于"低要求"型,第二类群体人数为 44 人,这类群体在三类择业观上的得分均为正值,说明他们对择业抱有积极的态度,属于"高要求"型,第三类群体人数为 16 人,该类群体在保障和自主择业观上得分高,说明他们在择业中的回报并不是其关注的首要条件,属于"自主保障"型。总计有效样本量为 102 人,缺失 3 人。同时采用判别分析检验劳动价值观四类人群聚类是否合理。经检验对初始分组案例中的 94.1% 进行了正确分类,对交叉验证分组案例中的 92.2% 进行了正确分类,表明聚类人群合理。

---

① 朱春红、杜学元:《中国大学生择业价值观的变迁及启示》,《青海社会科学》,2007 年第 5 期。

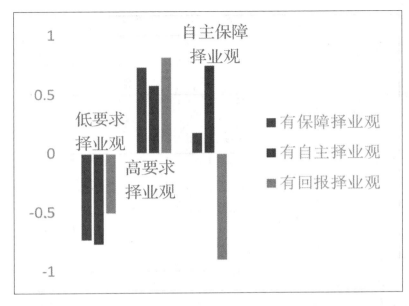

三类择业观聚类人群

3. 不同择业观群体的轮廓分析

择业观在很大程度上受劳动观的影响。为了更好地解释三种择业观人群的特点，采用"轮廓分析"对三类人群在劳动价值观、学习经历等 5 个轮廓变量上的表现进行分析，了解其背后可能存在的深层现象。其中，"高""低"描述均以三组群体互为参照。

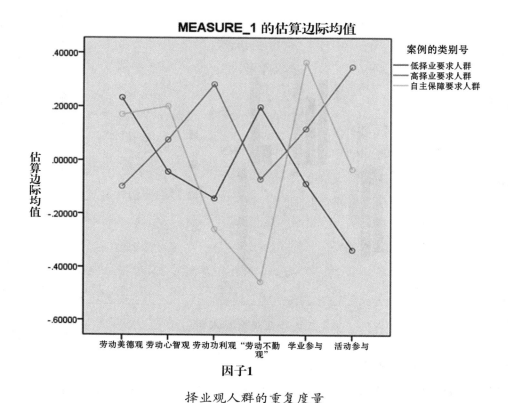

因子-1

择业观人群的重复度量

　　上图展示了轮廓分析的图示结果。"低要求"择业人群比例较大,占总人数的41%。究其背后的原因可能存在"好学"与"混学"群体。"好学"的学生并没有毕业后求职的打算,而是将重心放在备考研究生或出国留学上;"混学"学生属于高校的游离人群,存在上课玩手机、睡觉,陷入网络游戏无法自拔等问题,对就业规划毫无方向,甚至把读书阶段看作是职业生涯开始前的痛苦煎熬。但无论是"好学"还是"混学",低要求择业观整体呈现"劳动不勤"观最高、学业与活动参与最低的特点;"高要求"择业人群比例占总人数的43%,对择业的标准为有保障、有自主、有回报。这部分学生的劳动功利观与活动参与最高,劳动美德观最低;"自主保障"择业人群所占比例较低,仅占总人数的16%。这类群体对工作回报要求不高,在保障的基础上,希望选择符合兴趣爱好的职业、并能在工作中实现自己的理想、能做出富有创造性的成就。这部分群体的劳动心智观与学业参与最高、"劳动不勤"观最低,说明这类学生在学习中投入最高,并愿意在工作中通过自己的努力去创造性的劳动,体现出"以劳创新"的本质即创新始于劳动。①

通过对比分析三类择业观人群在劳动价值观及学习经历上的特点,"自主保障"择业人群具有"高素质、专业化、创新型"教师的特征,最符合卓越教师的标准,最适合成为教师队伍的储备力量。因此高校应对该类人群给予更多的关注和支持,从而不断提高其实践操作、敢闯会创的能力,以期更好地为完成到 2035 年"教师综合素质、专业化水平和创新能力大幅提升,培养造就数以百万计的骨干教师、数以十万计的卓越教师、数以万计的教育家型的教师"这一宏伟目标打下人才基础。

(二)从教意愿背后的现象

1. 师范生从教意愿人群聚类

调查问卷中的从教意愿题干表述为"您目前从事教师职业的意愿是怎样的?"选项为意愿程度,采用 5 点李克特量表计分方式,"1"代表非常不愿意,"5"代表非常愿意。该题有效样本量为 103 人,缺失 2 人。为了解不同从教意愿的师范生在劳动价值观、择业观、学习经历上的差异,首先对从教意愿结果进行了人群聚类。通过采用 K-Means 聚类,师范生的从教意愿结果被分为两类人群:愿意从教人数为 69 人,均值为 4.19;不愿从教人数 34 人,均值为 2.00。

2. 两类从教意愿群体的轮廓分析

本部分利用轮廓分析对比两类从教意愿群体在劳动价值观、择业观、学习经历、主观家庭经济状况等 10 个轮廓变量中的特点与差异。其中,"高""低""好""差"等描述均以 2 组群体互为参照。

---

① 徐长发:《新时代劳动教育再发展的逻辑》,《教育研究》,2018 年第 11 期。

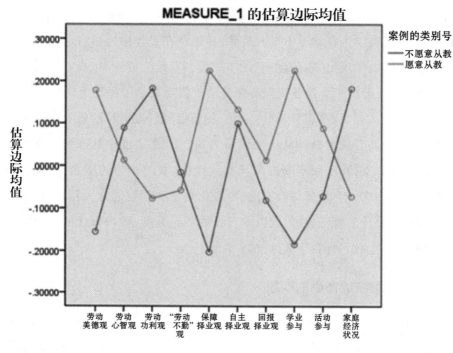

两类从教意愿群体的重复度量

由上图两类从教意愿群体的特征来看,群体差异主要反映在劳动美德观、劳动功利观、保障择业观、学业参与及家庭经济状况 5 个方面。具体来说,相较于不愿从教群体,愿意从教群体的劳动美德观高、劳动功利观低、有保障择业观高、学业参与高、家庭经济状况差,而教师职业的特殊性恰好需要有奉献、吃苦耐劳精神、在学业参与中更加积极投入的后备力量。这些差异中,愿意从教人群的有保障择业观明显高于不愿从教群体,反映出物质保障依然是师范生愿意从教的前提条件,这与已有研究结论相吻合,即当教师薪酬比其他职业更有竞争力时,更容易吸引教师从教,①教师起薪和工薪的

①　Loeb S, Beteille T. Teacher quality and teacher labor markets, https://cepa. stanford. edu/content/teacher – quality – and – teacher – labor – markets.

不断增长是吸引和留住教师的重要因素,[①]同时,经济条件越差的人群越需要有一份稳定的、有保障的职业,更倾向于接受补偿性工资的激励,选择去乡村任教。[②] 因此在吸引优秀师范生进入教师队伍时,要切实保障其待遇问题。

(三)相关分析

1. 劳动价值观与择业观的相关分析

大学生的劳动价值观不仅直接影响其大学阶段学习生活的方方面面,更关系到走向工作岗位后的价值取向、就业倾向、社会责任等方面的精神特质。[③] 为进一步解释师范生劳动价值观与择业观各维度之间的关系,特对两者进行了双变量相关分析。由下表可见有保障择业观及有回报择业观均与劳动功利观呈显著正相关,这说明通过劳动获得高回报的价值观越明显,师范生在择业时越会选择高保障和高回报的工作;有自主择业观与劳动美德观、劳动心智观呈显著正相关,与"劳动不勤"观呈显著负相关,说明有自主择业观的学生愿意在兴趣的促使下,积极发挥创造力,即使付出辛苦努力也不过多计较回报。

劳动价值观与择业观相关分析

维度	劳动美德观	劳动心智观	劳动功利观	"劳动不勤"观
有保障择业观	—	—	.227[*]	—
有自主观择业观	.202[*]	.269[**]	—	.236[*]
有回报择业观	—	—	.251[*]	—

注:* P<0.05 , ** P<0.01 , *** P<0.001

---

① Loeb, S., & Beteille, T. (2009). Teacher quality and teacher labor markets. In G. Sykes, B. Schneider & D. N. Plank (Eds.), Handbook of Education Policy Research, pp. 596 – 612.

② Adamson F, Hammond L D. Funding disparities and the inequitable distribution of teachers: evaluating sources and solutions, Education Policy Analysis Archives, 2012(37):1 – 46.

③ 刘向兵、李珂:《论当代大学生劳动情怀的培养》,《教育与研究》,2017 年第 4 期。

事实上,美国著名人力资源专家施恩(Schein)(1985)在其职业锚理论(career anchors theory)中就明确提到价值观、动机、个人能力三者之间的相互关系。当一个人不得不做出选择的时候,他无论如何都不会放弃的职业中的那种至关重要的东西或价值观就是这个人的职业锚。[①] 通过表2、表3数据特征,我们可以认为在施恩所列出的技术型、管理型、创造型、自主与独立型、稳定型、服务型、挑战型、生活型八种类型职业锚中,师范生的职业锚以稳定型(追求工作中的安全与稳定感)、独立型(追求能施展个人能力的工作环境,最大限度地摆脱组织的限制和制约)、生活型(平衡并结合个人、家庭和职业的需要)三种类型为主,而每一种职业锚均与特定的劳动价值观密切相关。

2. 从教意愿的相关影响因素

经相关分析发现师范生的从教意愿与有保障择业观、学业参与、学习经历和学习收获满意度、学科专业兴趣程度均呈显著正相关;与家庭经济条件呈显著负相关,经济条件越好从教意愿越低;从教意愿与劳动价值观的四个维度均无显著相关(参见下表)。

从教意愿、有保障择业观、学业参与、学习经历与收获满意度的相关矩阵

变量	1	2	3	4	5
1. 从教意愿	1				
2. 有保障择业观	.196*	1			
3. 学业参与	.246*	.243*	1		
4. 学习经历和学习收获满意度	.348**	—	.344**	1	
5. 学科专业兴趣程度	.229*	—	.309**	.301**	1

注:$*P<0.05$,$**P<0.01$,$***P<0.001$

---

① Schein E. H. *Career anchors: Discovering your real values*, San Diego, CA: University Associates, 1985.

从职业观角度来看,在三种择业观中,仅"有保障"择业观与从教意愿显著相关。现有研究中也发现职业价值观能有效预测师范生的从教意愿,师范生职业价值观中的"家庭维护"维度能够有效预测其从事教育工作的主观意愿,即越看重职业的"家庭维护"价值,师范生的从教意愿越高。[1] 而该研究中的"家庭维护"主要指减轻家庭负担,凸显了马斯洛需求层次理论的低级别需求——"安全需求",愿意从教的师范生更加看重教师职业的稳定性,以此来改变家庭经济状况。

从学习过程来看,从教意愿、学业参与、学习经历与学习收获满意度、学科专业兴趣之间均存在显著相关关系。专业兴趣驱动下越积极投入学业的学生,其学习经历和学习收获的满意度越高。已有研究也表明在高考填报志愿时依个人兴趣主动填报专业的师范生100%愿意从教;依父母要求而被动填报专业的占30.6%愿意从教,其他原因填报本专业的51.2%愿意从教。[2] 本研究再次验证了专业兴趣与师范生从教意愿的相关性。

综上所述,本研究调查结果可归纳为三点:首先,师范生的劳动价值观整体呈积极导向,师范生拥有较高的美德观与心智观,体现出"德才兼备"的劳动素质,愿意从教的学生则拥有更高的劳动美德观;其次,师范生的职业选择一定程度上受劳动价值观的影响,并以稳定型、独立型、生活型职业锚为特征。其中,"自主保障"择业观人群的劳动心智观与学业参与最高,这类学生愿意在工作中通过自己的智慧与努力进行创造性的劳动,具备"农夫的身手""科学的头脑"及"改造社会的精神"的专业素质;最后,愿意从教人数虽占总人数的67%,表明大部分学生愿意选择教师职业,但整体教师队伍储备情况并不乐观。高校应对持有消极劳动观念及择业观的特殊群体予以更多的关注。

---

[1]　安蕾、刘晓军:《地方师范院校毕业生从教意愿及职业价值观调查》,《当代教育论坛》,2010年第8期。

[2]　蒋亦华:《本科院校小学教育专业学生从教意愿的调查研究》,《教师教育研究》,2008年第11期。

四、对策建议

　　师范生对于"得""失"的判断在本研究中具体反映在对劳动价值观、择业观及从教意愿的判断上。如何帮助师范生正确看待"功利"与"奉献"之间的博弈是摆在高师院校面前的重要问题,不仅要培养师范学生的劳动美德,懂得如何辛勤劳动和欣赏劳动,还需要培养其劳动心智,懂得如何进行创造性劳动。基于研究发现,本文将从地方高校、政府、师范生角度提出对策建议。

(一)地方高校需明确劳动教育目标,优先解决"培养什么样的人"

　　第一,师范生劳动价值取向决定了未来教师队伍乃至整个国民教育的价值取向。在师范生培养中,需要确立以劳动美德观与劳动心智观为主体的劳动价值观主体地位。高师院校可尝试增加劳动价值导向课程或组织丰富多彩的活动,例如,定期观看优秀教师劳动模范视频并开展讨论、举办"我心中的劳模"主题团日活动、组织"大学生如何践行劳动价值观"为主题的辩论赛,通过系列活动让"劳动最光荣、劳动最崇高、劳动最伟大、劳动最美丽"深入每一位师范生的心中。

　　第二,"培养什么样的人"是教育的首要问题,高校只有明确"什么样的人最适合从教"才能开展"如何培养人"的具体措施。定期掌握学生劳动价值观、择业观、学习参与等方面的特征,通过辨识不同特征群体,使劳动教育更加精准化。高校可给予具有"高素质、专业化、创新型"卓越教师特征的"自主保障"群体更多的"量体裁衣"式的教育支持,通过开展学科交叉融合、搭建创新创业平台等方式提高其实践操作、敢闯会创的能力。同时,也要对"低要求""高要求"择业人群进行"查漏补缺"式教育,尤其对实习冲击所导致的从教流失问题予以关注,为该人群提供心理疏导及积极的教育引导,以保障教师储备队伍的稳定供给。

（二）政府需使经济保障取得显著效果，完善高考志愿筛选机制

第一，影响师范生从教意愿的诸多因素中，最凸显的是经济保障问题。愿意从教人群的有保障择业观明显高于不愿从教群体，且研究结果也表明愿意从教的师范生家庭经济条件相对较差。因此在高校大力培养师范生劳动美德及教师情怀的基础上，政府应采取措施使西部农村教师政策的倾斜性取得显著效果，使教师的待遇达到真正意义上的"有保障"，打消愿意从教学生的经济顾虑，踏踏实实地将教学热情倾注在其所热爱的教学事业中。

第二，从教意愿与专业兴趣显著相关。第一志愿报考师范专业的学生学习目的性更加明确，学习动机也更强，对师范专业的选择有着更多的自主性。① 因此，完善高考志愿填报的相关筛选机制，在高考"入口"多下功夫，有助于选拔专业兴趣度高、更容易融入当地文化的本土生源，降低因地域、风俗习惯差异造成的"水土不服"型从教流失。

（三）师范生需培养专业兴趣，全方位体悟教师职业的特殊性

专业兴趣是师范生学习投入的最大驱动力。师范生在专业学习中应发挥主观能动性，在教学实践中切身体悟教育的意义与价值，始终保持自我认同、职业认同与价值认同的一致性。具体而言，低年级学生应随着对所学专业的深入了解，主动培养专业兴趣，打牢专业基础，做到勤于学习，敏于求知；对高年级学生而言，则需要更多地在各类实践教学中有效地掌握教学技能、培养吃苦耐劳的精神、在"被需要"的实习环境中深刻体悟教师职业的特殊性及内在价值，做到善于实践，勇于创新。

当然，本研究的不足之处还有待改进，如样本局限性使研究结论具有一定的地方特殊性，今后可提高样本的代表性，进而掌握我国师范生整体劳动

---

① 周海林：《师范生专业承诺和学习投入的现状及关系研究——以福建省6所高校为例》，《淮北师范大学学报（哲学社会科学版）》，2018年第1期。

价值观现状，探索劳动价值观与择业观的影响关系，考查学生个体特征或学校类型等情景因素是否影响劳动教育的结果等，这些方面将在后续研究中加以考虑。

The Survey on Labor Values and Teaching Intention of Normal Students in Local Colleges and Universities in Xinjiang

Xiaofang Wang

Abstract：Normal university students are the reserve force of primary and secondary school teachers, and labor values affect their career choice to some extent. Based on the survey data of 120 normal university students, a quantitative research method was adopted to investigate the labor values, vocational values, teaching intention, learning experience. The results show that: first, in the analysis of the status quo, there are differences in the group characteristics of their willingness to teach, which is manifested in the group's high concept of labor virtue, low concept of labor utility, high concept of guaranteed career choice, high academic participation, and poor family economic status. Second, in the correlation analysis, the labor values of normal university students are significantly correlated with their vocational values, and their willingness to teach is significantly positively correlated with their guaranteed vocational values, academic participation, learning experience and satisfaction with learning gains, and their degree of interest in subjects and majors, while negatively correlated with their family economic conditions. Based on the above findings, this paper puts forward the training counter-measures of normal university students´labor education.

Keywords：normal students；labor values；vocational values；learning experience；teaching intention

自主学习变革课堂教学与教师专业发展

刘 鹤

澳门化地玛圣母女子学校

怎样的课堂是高效的课堂？课堂中如何培养学生的兴趣？如何提高学生的积极性？如何提升教师的专业发展？针对这些问题，本校积极实施课程改革，通过"请进来，走出去"的交流学习，不断提升教师的专业发展。在实践过程中，我们始终坚持将"自主学习"融入课堂教学中，不断提高学生自主学习的能力。老师们共同探讨，一起研究，形成学习共同体，推动课程的改革与发展。

一、课堂教学的变革

（一）提高兴趣的课堂

兴趣是最好的老师，兴趣是推动学习的内在动力。在数学教学过程中，要注意激发学生的学习兴趣，抓住能引起学生兴趣的知识点，让学生在兴趣中学习。例如，在教学六年级《圆的面积》这一课时，以往的教学都是教师拿着教具，将圆分成若干份后，拼成近似的长方形，带领学生将图形转化，再推导出计算圆面积的公式。通过学习，学生虽然能掌握计算圆面积的方法，但这样的课堂，教师成了主演，学生只是观众。实施课程改革后，我让学生自己将圆剪拼成近似的长方形,自己观察前后两个图形之间的关系,再引导学生推导出计算圆面积的公式。虽然两种教学方法都是推导圆面积计算的公式,但改革后的教学,不仅提高了学生的学习兴趣,还让学生真正参与到课堂中,让学生成为课堂的主人,感受知识的形成过程。类似的例子在教学中还有很多,只要教师在备课中善于挖掘,就一定能找到学生感兴趣的素材。

(二)创设情境的课堂

数学来源于生活,又服务于生活。新课程标准明确指出:"数学教学,要紧密联系学生的生活实际,从学生的生活经验和已有的知识出发,创设生动有趣的情境。"基于这样的标准,教师们在教学改革的过程中,将新的数学知识从学生的已知经验出发,并创设情境,将数学知识与生活紧密联系起来。例如,魏老师在教学五年级"平行四边形的面积"这一课时,就创设故事情境,故事讲述了两位同学在争辩两块地(一块是长方形,一块是平行四边形)面积的大小而发生争吵的故事,为了帮助这两位同学解决问题,老师引导学生自主探究平行四边形的面积。吕老师在教学一年级"分类与整理"这一课时,为了提高学生的探究欲望,她特意创设老师开生日会的情境,并将这一情境贯穿于整堂课中,通过让学生帮忙分一分气球、饮料等情境,让学生在玩中学、学中悟,并在轻松愉悦的情境教学中感受数学知识的形成过程。

实践证明,创设充满激情的学习情境,可以激发学生自主探究的学习兴趣与热情,起到事半功倍的学习效果。

(三)以学生为主的课堂

"最好的教,就是让学生学会学习;最好的学,就是让学生给别人讲"。在实施自主学习的教学过程中,适当地教授一些学习方法,引导学生有效地获取知识,凸显学生的主体的教学是非常重要的。例如,陈老师在教学三年级上册"三位数加法(1)"中,教师创设情境,让学生通过观察情境图,自主收集信息、自主提出问题、自主解答。为了让学生搜集到有用信息并提出有效的问题,教师这样引导学生:"你发现了一些怎样的数学信息?""老师也有一个相关的数学问题,你能不能也提出一个类似的问题呢?"黄老师在教学四年级下册"四则运算(括号)"这一课时,她引导学生通过自学课本第9页的内容,让学生自己去寻找带括号的四则运算的法则,之后让学生分享,起到良好的效果。

在实施新的课改后,教师们通过不断的引导,无形中教会学生搜集有效信息和主动掌握研究问题的方法,为学生能更好地自主学习打下了坚实的基础。

二、教师专业发展

(一)交流研讨促进步

通过不断的实践我们发现,提高教师与教师之间的交流、教师与学生之间的交流,都能提升教育教学的质量。不同学校教师之间的交流可以让老师们了解不同学校之间的经验,相互学习,取长补短。同科不同级教师之间的交流,能够让教师更好地了解知识之间的相互联系与衔接,以便能更好地开展教学,为新知识打下坚实的基础。同级教师之间的交流,能够让老师更全面地掌握同一阶段孩子的学习能力和水平。教师与学生之间的交流能够让老师更好地了解学生所需,让老师能更好地因材施教。

(二)教研活动促提升

通过集体备课、听评课活动、专家讲座与培训等教研活动,让老师们形成了一个强大的"学习共同体"。老师们相互学习、一起讨论、共同备课,互帮互助,建构起相互合作、学习的关系。教师们通过协同学习来提高教学质量。实践证明,作为一个学科的引领者,要将"学习共同体"继续坚持下去,并且还要开创一些新的教研活动,使整个团队都能凝聚在一起,共同进步,提升整个教研团队的专业发展。

（三）开拓创新促发展

作为团队的引领者，要勇于开拓创新，不断探索新的方向。我校数学科就在不断地优化教学，如，改革学生的功课，要求每一位老师每天只能布置1项功课，关键要求教师提高课堂40分钟的效率，而不搞题海战术。改革测考卷，将本学科的测考卷全部规范题型，统一评分标准、难易程度等。通过一系列的改革，我们发现学生慢慢地对学习产生了兴趣，测考成绩有了显著的提升，不合格人数明显下降。实践证明，只有不断探索才会有真的进步；只有为老师们指明了方向，才能让大家一起前行；只有将团队的成员凝聚在一起，才能创造出最大的效能。

Elementary Teachers Education in Japan: focusing on quality assurance

Yasuyuki Iwata

Professor, Deputy President

Director, Gakugei International Student Exchange Centre,

Tokyo Gakugei University

Abstract: In Japan, there has been a continuous over – production of teachers' license holders since 1970s. This phenomenon is caused by two major factors – the 'Open System' and the expansion of higher education in post – war Japan. The 'Open System' means that any institute with approved courses for can provide initial teacher training (ITT) programme. Now we have approximately 600 universities with ITT programme of BA level in Japan. However, due to the government policy to control the quantity of pre – service education programme for several kinds of profession including elementary teachers, ITT providers for elementary teachers has been relatively closed. Most of traditional ITT providers are national universities with their origin of former normal schools and their status have been pretty high. As 'Deregulation' policy has been widely introduced after the millennium in Japan, quantity control for elementary teachers has also been abolished. Then lots of private universities have started to provide ITT programme for elementary teachers. Though the aim of this policy is to raise the quality level of teachers in Japan through the expansion and competition among ITT providers for elementary teacher education, now Japan has some serious problems/challenges for teachers' quality assurances. In this paper, the author would like to introduce some policies on quality assurances for teacher education in Japan and show some challenges on elementary teachers in Japan.

1. Elementary School Teachers and Their Pre – service Education in Japan

1.1 Elementary School Teachers in Japan

Unlike China, elementary school teachers in Japan usually teach all the subject in classroom. They are allocated to handle one certain classroom (maximum 35 pupils in P1 & P2, 40 in P3 and above, according to Japanese government standard). As in(Figure 1), single license for elementary school teacher allows to teach all 10 subjects.

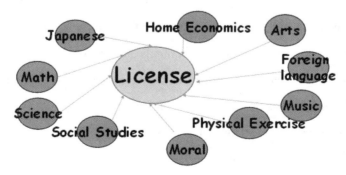

Figure 1   Elementary SchoolTeachers' License in Japan

So, they are usually called ' classroom teacher'. In some schools, several extra teachers for specified subjects (PE, HE, Arts, etc.) can be allocated according to each local governments' regulation. However, in recent years, as children's number has been decreasing, the average size of elementary school is getting smaller. Actually, most popular size of elementary school is 7 classrooms (one in each grade and one for children with special needs) with approximately 200 – 300 pupils.

1. 2 Teacher Education System in Japan: Two Major Principles

It is a well – known fact that the two major principles of teacher education in Japan are "Teacher Education at/by Universities" and "Open System for Teachers' License".

"Teacher education at/by Universities" been established after the argument of Post – War Education Reform on the late 1940s. There has been a harsh criticism against previous pre – service teacher training for elementary school teachers at Normal Schools (3 – years vocational school after secondary education, specified to grow elementary school teachers) and their graduates (Kimura & Iwata, 2007)[1]. For example, pre – war elementary school teachers are so – called 'with narrow – perspective', 'without academic wisdom' and/or 'only know the obedience to imperialism', etc. That is the background of new principle of 'Teacher Education at/by Universities' – all kinds of teachers (including elementary school teachers) should be trained at universities based on liberal arts (wide range of general education) and academic wisdom.

However, elementary school teachers' pre – service education at universities (undergraduate, Bachelor level) in Japan has started the earliest among East Asian Regions.

---

[1] Kimura, H., Iwata, Y., The Historical Trend of Teacher Identity in Japan: Focusing on Educational Reforms and the Occupational Culture of Teachers, *Hitotsubashi Journal of Social Studies*, Vol. 39 – 1, 2007.

1.3 Traditional Conflict between Universities and Normal Schools

On the other hand, there has been a traditional conflict between 'universities' and 'Normal Schools' as in Hayhoe's (Table1) below (Hayhoe, 2002)[①].

Table 1　Conflicts between University and Normal Schools

University	versus	Normal school
Theory	versus	Practice
Specialized disciplines of knowledge	versus	Integrated learning areas
Value neutral approaches to knowledge	versus	Morally directive approaches to knowledge
A relatively impersonal environment	versus	A nurturing environment with strong mentorship ties between teachers and students
The liberal pursuit of all questions/intellectual curiosity	versus	Action oriented and field-based knowledge
Academic freedom and autonomy	versus	State control and professional accountability
An orientation to deep-level understanding and long-term change	versus	A craft orientation towards high standards of practice

Particularly in the case of elementary school teachers in Japan, the conflict has been harder than those of secondary school teachers because they are basically required to handle all the subjects and it becomes more difficult to find an academic core in pre-service education in universities. Therefore, though 'Teacher Education at/by Universities' has become a major principle in post-war Japan, there have been only a few universities that provide pre-service teacher education course for elementary teachers besides former Normal Schools.

---

① Hayhoe, R., Teacher Education and the University: a comparative analysis with implications for Hong Kong, *Teaching Education*, Vol. 13, No. 1, 2002.

2. 'Open System' and 'Deregulation' Policy after 2000s

2.1 'Open System' in pre – service teacher education in Japan

'Open System' in Japan means that any universities – private, provincial (municipal) and national funded – with approved programme (by the Ministry) can provide pre – service teacher education. In other words, there are no priority for licensing or employment among universities with pre – service teacher education programme. At the beginning of the 'Open System', there were a shortage of secondary school teachers due to an expansion of compulsory education in Japan (from 6 years to 9 years, including junior secondary). In addition, a baby – boom in Japan during post – war Japan (1946 – 1949) has increased further requirement for new teachers. So, this principal has had a meaning of a solution for the quantity matter. On the other hand, the principal also has been a solution for recruiting new teachers with various academic basis.

According to the popularization of higher education in Japan after 1960s, more and more universities have come to provide pre – service teacher education programme of undergraduate level. Now approximately 700 universities are providing certain kind(s) of teacher education program(me).

Generally speaking, there are two types among the universities with teacher education courses as follows.

Type A: Specified Universities and Faculties of Education (48 organizations)

Before 1949, each Japanese province (prefecture) had its own Normal School(s) which were specialized for the training of elementary school teachers. Graduates of these Normal Schools had to get teacher's license and be primary school teachers for several years. These Normal Schools has turned into national universities which have BA degree course since 1949 and they are now called"Universities and/or Faculties of Education". Only these universities and faculties have special course for teacher training, whose students have to get at least one kind of teachers' license for elementary or secondary schools. But graduates of these universities and faculties no longer have duties to be teachers.

Type B:Other Colleges and Universities (600 + organizations)

Besides the (Type A), there are many national, private and provincial (municipal) higher education institutes (colleges and universities) with optional courses to get teachers' license. Students of these colleges or universities are not necessary to get the license, and this is the point of deference from (Type A). Most of these organizations provide teacher education programme for secondary school teachers.

Under the 'Open System' among popularized higher education in Japan, there has been a continuous over − production of teachers' license holders since 1970s.

2.2 Elementary Teacher Education as an Exception

However, as mentioned above, the number of pre − service teacher education providers in Japan had been relatively small. On 2004, total number was 94 − 47 of(Type A) and 47 of (Type B). There are two reasons as follows.

Under the 'Open System' principle, any universities with approved programme can provide pre − service teacher education. But there are some differences for the approval by the Ministry. To set up some pre − service secondary teacher education programme, the regulation is relatively free − any department, any course can provide an optional licensing programme for secondary school teachers. While, setting up the programme for elementary school teachers, specified organization for elementary teacher education such as faculty of education, department of elementary education, childhood studies, infant studies, etc.

In addition, after 1980s when higher education in Japan has been pretty pop-ularized, Ministry has introduced a new policy to control the quantity of pre – service education programme for five kinds of profession – medical doctors, den-tists, veterinarians, sailors and elementary school teachers. So, no new providers for pre – service education for the five professions have been allowed for 20 years from 1980s.

Thus, at least until 2004, it can be said that the system for pre – service edu-cation for elementary school teachers in Japan has been relatively closed. Most of traditional providers are (Type A) and their status and reputation have been rela-tively high.

2. 3 "Deregulation without Sanctuary" Policy after 2000s

During KOIZUMI Jun – Ichiro's Cabinet, 'Deregulation' policy has been widely introduced at all fields (as in his word 'without sanctuary'). The aim of this policy was to make public services better through the introduction of market – theory with competitive environment.

According to the 'deregulation' policy, quantity control of pre – service edu-cation for the five kinds of profession had to be re – considered. In this context, quantity control for elementary teachers has also been abolished from FY2005. Then lots of private universities have started to provide pre – service teacher edu-cation programme for elementary teachers as in (Table 2) (Figure 2).

(Table 2　'Deregulation' Before & After)

Established	Type	Funding	Number
Before FY2004	Type A	National , Municipal	44
		Private	3
	Type B	National , Municipal	9
		Private	38
FY 2005 – 2017	Type A	National , Municipal	0
		Private	1
	Type B	National , Municipal	4
		Private	144
Total			243

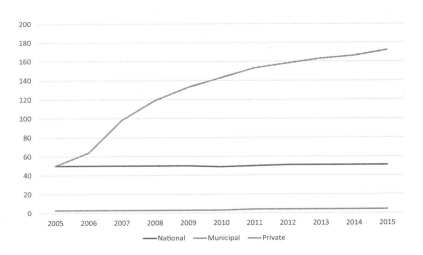

Figure 2　Pre – service Teacher EducationProviders for Elementary Teachers in Japan

Majority of these new providers of pre – service teacher education programme are in large city are like Tokyo and Osaka, and most of them are also facing with difficulties to intake students of enough quantity up to their capacities. Thus, entrance examinations for those kinds of new providers are not so competitive in general – so – called 'border – free' universities (Murasawa,2015)[①]. Prospective teachers for elementary school after 2010s have pretty diversified – in other words, contain lots of young teachers with less competency.

3. Quarilty Assurances for Elementary School Teachers

3.1 Government Control for Prospective Teachers: both national an provincial

The 'deregulation' policy has made serious effects upon qualities of new teachers: basic knowledge, teaching skills, academic wisdom, etc.

Facing with this phenomenon, Ministry of Education (MEXT) in Japan has tightened the government check for approved programme among various universities under the 'Open System'. Each syllabus of approved programme has to be checked one by one, all the teacher educators in approved courses (faculty professors) have come to be required specified paper(s) related to the subject(s) they teach, all the organizations with approved course(s) for teacher education have to recruit and allocate a certain amount of full – time faculty staff independently. These kinds of tightening policy have made a partial success to keep new provider's quality, though they have not made any remarkable effect to raise up prospective teachers' competency directly. Moreover, these kinds of policy have some negative effects upon traditional providers – invading academic freedom and universities' autonomy.

Some local(provincial) governments also have started or tightened their administrative procedure as in Tokyo since there have been lots of new providers (2

---

① MURASAWA, Masataka, 'Characters of ITE Providers for Primary School', 2015.

national and 34 private) in Tokyo Metropolitan Prefecture. Tokyo Board of Education has started some new experiments to intake new elementary school teachers with high competency as follows.

1) New recruiting system of elementary teachers (with specialized training course for the final year students in undergraduate and postgraduate courses among universities in Tokyo area).

2) Guideline for undergraduate curriculum of pre – service teacher education for elementary school teachers in Tokyo.

3) Guideline for teaching practice (including evaluation form for universities' management of teaching practice).

4) Make up an original evaluation form of teaching practice in local schools in Tokyo and asked universities to use it.

These new experiments by local government also have made a partial success to keep qualities of new providers as well as new teachers, though they do not have enough grand – design for elementary school teachers for the future – just an 'emergency evacuation'. Moreover, these 'emergency evacuation' can be extra (and unnecessary) pressures upon teacher education programme conducted by old providers – universities with long tradition an high reputation.

3. 2 Challenges of New – Providers

New provides are facing with challenges for producing new teachers of elementary schools. Unlike the traditional (Type A) universities from former Normal Schools, they cannot easily attract students with high motivation as prospective and, most of the students of these universities do not have enough basic skills nor academic achievement of secondary (or even elementary) school education. Some new students of these new providers even have experiences of adjustment disorders and/or developmental disorders. Some of these kinds of students may become excellent teachers with good sympathy with pupils who feel stumble or difficulty to keep their school life. However, it takes politer care for those new prospective teachers than those of traditional (Type A) students.

In this situation, lots of teacher educators working in new providers are tenaciously taking care of their students – providing supplementary lessons for remedial, giving drills for employment test, having plenty chances to engage nearby schools as intern, etc. Of course, these new providers usually recruit teacher educators with rich experiences as teachers and/or education administrators.

4. Discussion

4. 1 Findings

As shown above, ' deregulation' policy introduced in elementary teacher education in Japan has not been working well. We have to admit that it's not successful to recruit new teachers with better competency than before. On the other hand, the power balances – especially between the local governments and university (TE providers) has been changed and universities' autonomy has been in crisis. This might be because of the uniqueness of quality assurance system of pre – service education in Japan as in (Table 3)

Table 3　Quality Assurances of Teacher Education among East Asian Region

	Japan	China, ML	Taiwan	Korea
Quantity Control of Prospective Teachers	None	Partially	Partially	**Strict**
Control for Pre-service TE Programme	**Strict** (curricula, credits, contents, etc.)	Partially (curriculum standard without compulsory)	Partially	None
Control for Pre-service TE Providers	[in trial]	[preparing]	**Strict** (periodical evaluation by government agency)	**Strict** (periodical evaluation by government agency)
National Exam for New Teachers	None	**Strict** (nation-wide exam for teachers' certificate)	**Strict** (nation-wide exam for teachers' certificate)	None

As in（Table 3）, Japanese system of quality assurances basically relies on programme approval by the Ministry. This kind of approval is only for teacher education providers（universities）and there have been almost no direct control by the government for prospective teachers' individuals.

4.2 Points of Arguments for Further Development

Through the findings above, some points of arguments can be seen as Japan's challenges for promoting elementary teachers' competency.

At this point, we have to re-consider about the basic and traditional question 'what is crucial for new elementary school teachers?' As some emphasize on their academic wisdom or their competencies based on liberal arts while others put premium on their practical skills, there have been no common understandings until now.

After getting a solid image for new teachers' competency, we should face with the next questions:'what kind of government control is effective others put premium on to keep new elementary school teachers? – quantity,quality,or else?' and 'how should we conquer the conflict between universities and teacher education,especially those for elementary schools in Japan?'

Of course,these questions are not easy to find suitable answers. However, teacher educators in Japan cannot avoid to tackle with these challenges.

日本小学教师教育的发展:聚焦质量保障

岩田康之

日本东京学艺大学校长助理,教授

摘要:自 20 世纪 70 年代以来,日本教师资质持有者持续过剩。造成这一现象的原因主要有两个:一是"开放体制",二是战后日本高等教育的扩张。"开放体制"是指任何拥有经过批准的课程的院校都可以提供教师职前培训(initial teacher training,ITT)项目。目前在日本大约有 600 所高校开设了本科层次教师职前培训课程。然而由于日本政府对包括小学教师在内的几种职业的职前培训进行数量上的政策管控,小学教师的教师职前培训项目提供院校相对封闭。传统的教师职前培训项目提供院校多为前身是师范院校、地位很高的国立大学。千禧年后,日本广泛推行"去监管化"政策,小学教师的数量控制也随之废除。之后,许多私立院校开始向小学教师提供教师职前培训项目。这一政策旨在通过增设小学教师职前培训项目提供院校并加强它们之间的竞争来提高日本教师的素质水平,但目前日本在教师质量保障方面仍然存在一些问题与挑战。本文介绍了日本教师教育质量保障的相关政策,以及日本小学教师所面临的一些挑战。

The Changing Paradigms in Digital Education: Influence of Self – Efficacy on Faculty in Higher Education

Q. Y. Wang   Ryter D.   Vasinda S.   & Hathcock S.

Oklahoma State University, Fort Lewis College

Abstract: Remote learning and mobile devices have become part of everyday experience in education. In higher education settings, research indicates that pre-service teachers' understandings of how to integrate technology into their classrooms are dependent upon experience in their university methods courses and in their field placements. These findings place a new responsibility on teacher educators for modeling effective integration of technology into methods courses. In our previous study (Vasinda, Ryter, Hathcock, & Wang, 2017), we discovered that access to technology is not sufficient for faculty to integrate mobile technology such as iPad use in their courses. Faculty's self – efficacy impacted the extent to which they integrated mobile technology. Data was collected via auto – ethnographical writings, audio recorded meeting notes, and subsequent expanded auto – ethnographical writings. Time for exploration, experimentation, and practice as well as professional support is needed to enhance self – efficacy of using available technologies.

1. Purposes of the Study

With the pervasiveness of mobile devices (laptops, tablets, smartphones, mobile phones and so forth), and all the classrooms are moving online, it is necessitate for K − 12 schools to explore and implement mobile devices to increase learning opportunities for students. This disruption, or rapidly changing nature, of mobile technology provides new challenges for teacher educators as we currently prepare teachers for teaching and learning environments that neither we, nor they experienced as teachers or learners. Traditionally, methods courses in teacher preparation programs serve to build pedagogical knowledge for teaching specific disciplines, such as science, mathematics, social studies, and reading/language arts. Teacher educators often find that they are still supporting stronger disciplinary content knowledge while addressing pedagogy. Schulman (1986) identified this specific type of teacher knowledge as Pedagogical Content Knowledge (PCK). Teachers and teacher educators are now expected to have new knowledge that includes Technological Knowledge (TK) that intersects with PCK. This new integration forms a new teacher knowledge referred to as Technological Pedagogical and Content Knowledge, or TPACK (Figure 1; Koehler & Mishra, 2005; Mishra & Koehler, 2006).

Many faculty members are aware of the opportunities of integrating technology that are available for instructional purposes, but are often hesitant to capitalizing on the opportunity these tools may afford. Researchers attribute underutilized technology to teachers' lack of self − efficacy in incorporating such resources into their classrooms (Kellenberger & Hendricks, 2003). Not surprisingly, educators who feel uncomfortable using technology are unlikely to incorporate it because of the fear associated with using something with which they have limited experience.

Previous studies have identified several factors that may play a role in teachers' decisions to integrate technology into their classrooms, self – efficacy being one of those factors (e. g., Kellenberger & Hendricks, 2003; Teo, 2009; Wang, Ertmer, & Newby, 2004). However, studies that attempt to identify teacher educators' levels of technology self – efficacy are scarce.

2. Who We Are

At the time of this study, the four of us were content area faculty members interested in technology integration at a land grant university in the U. S. Midwest. Dr. Sheri Vasinda is a literacy faculty with over 20 years of K – 12 experience as a classroom teacher and literacy specialist in U. S. public schools. She was considered an innovator in both school reform and technology integration in her K – 12 school district. Dr. Di Ann Ryter, a social studies faculty, started her 20 – year teaching career as a Peace Corps Volunteer in Jamaica. She continued to teach social studies in American and International Baccalaureate accredited high schools abroad in the United Arab Emirates, Japan, and Tanzania. She began working in higher education as a teacher educator in 2008. In this role she consciously considered how to incorporate appropriate technology in my social studies methods courses, which included both content and pedagogy. Dr. Stephanie Hathcock, a science faculty, spent 8 years as a classroom teacher in the Midwest and eastern United States. In her teaching career, she has always welcomed the use of technology. She was often the first adopter of a new technology within her building and experienced successful results doing things like blogging with students and using probeware. She sees both the need and desire for her preservice teachers to integrate technology into their teaching and view herself as a catalyst to their increased knowledge, awareness, and appropriate use. Dr. Qiuying Wang is also a literacy faculty who was born in China and educated in China, Great Britain and the United States, her view of education was shaped through her interaction with people from different perspectives, and through experience by navigating between the clash of Eastern and Western values in education. She is open – minded, cutting edge and a chance – taker with the innovation in education. With recent and ever – growing numbers of mobile devices in K – 12 classrooms, she feels that it is imperative that future teachers learn and teach with the same tools.

3. Perspective(s) and theoretical framework

Self – efficacy has a theoretical foundation grounded in social cognitive theory developed by Albert Bandura (2001). Bandura (2001) defines self – efficacy as one's beliefs in one's capabilities to organize and execute the courses of action required to produce a given outcome. Using this definition, self – efficacy plays a role in classroom decision making. If a teacher believes s/he is incapable of performing a particular action, then s/he may not attempt to carry out said action. Bandura has identified four general sources of self – efficacy, which include performance accomplishments, vicarious experiences, verbal persuasion, and physiological states (Crittenden, 2009). Although these general sources of self – efficacy are known and help to inform those attempting to influence self – efficacy, Henson (2002) emphasized that it is valuable to examine self – efficacy within a specific context because self – efficacy is contextually situated. Therefore, focusing specifically on faculties' technology knowledge self – efficacy is meaningful and valuable and leads to the new teacher knowledge identified by Mishra and Koehler (2006), TPACK (Figure 1) and Bandura's (2001) Four Sources of Self – Efficacy (Figure 2).

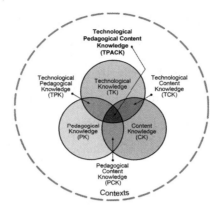

Figure 1：Technological Pedagogical Content Knowledge（TPACK）

（Mishra & Koehler,2006）

Figure 2：Four Sources of Self – Efficacy（Bandura,2001）

The TPACK model（Mishra & Koehler,2006）（Figure 1）offers a frame-work for understanding the complexities of teaching and learning with technology and can help educators choose technological tools that enhance student under-standing and are aligned with effective pedagogy. Therefore, the TPACK model was used as a conceptual framework for university faculty as they planned lessons for their respective students. We also used the TPACK framework to consider how developing our TK developed the other intersections of this model as we developed our TPACK. As new technology devices, applications and programs released, we all found, and find, ourselves in continual development of TPACK. As we develop TPACK, we found ourselves in different stages of technology adoption.

To describe ourselves in terms of our levels of mobile technology adoption and integration, we used part of Rogers' (1995) Diffusion of Innovation model. Rogers (1995) categorizes adopters of an innovation into five group – based sequence of adoption: Innovators, Early Adopters, Early Majority, Late Majority, and Laggards. Adopters consider the following characteristics when considering adopting an innovation: 1) Relative Advantage, 2) Compatibility with Existing Values and Practices, 3) Simplicity and Ease of Use, 4) Trialability, and 5) Observable Results (Rogers, 2003). Innovators, described as visionary and imaginative, are willing to put forth lots of time and energy on an innovation they have identified and evaluated as better than what is currently being done or used. Early Adopters join the Innovators as soon as benefits become apparent. Early Majority are more pragmatic and join an innovation once there is established proof of value and complications have been worked out. These three categories are more prone to adopt an innovation. Rogers' (2003) last two categories, Late Majority and Laggards, are more prone to resist an innovation. Since we embarked on this self – study, we all fall into the three categories prone to adopt.

4. Methods, techniques, or modes of inquiry

Collaborative autoethnography (CAE) is a qualitative research method that builds upon concurrent autobiographical ethnographies in the context of a collaborative group (Chang, Ngunjiri, and Hernandez, 2012). "Researchers who embark on autoethnographic research methods have agreed on the importance of 'data on the self' as relevant in social inquiry" (Chang, Ngunjiri, and Hernandez, 2012, pg. 18). Data for this study included our auto – ethnographical writings, audio recorded discussion notes during our bi – monthly meetings, and subsequent expanded auto – ethnographical writings. These personal stories and reflections focused on our technology integrations, and times when we hesitated or chose not to integrate, in the methods courses we taught became data through the unique lenses of self. Additionally, we pooled our stories together to find commonalities and differences and then wrestled with these stories to discover their meaning in relation to our sociocultural context and the impact on our teaching practices. The CAE approach started as a research method, but also became a community of practice. It allowed us to socially construct our perceptions of self – efficacy.

Data sources, evidence, objects, or materials

Data for this study included faculty auto – ethnographical writings and audio recorded meeting notes and subsequent expanded auto – ethnographical writings. We met bi – monthly during Fall semester and weekly during Spring semester to share, examine, and probe our auto – ethnographical writings often resulting in assigning ourselves expanded writings on a particular discovery. Ethical considerations were part of our collaborative discussions, which emphasized that the research and writing focused on us faculty/instructors, not our students. These reminders were necessary because in our reflection as effective practitioners in our methods classes we often think about the experiences of our students, instead of ourselves. Initially, we used open – coding (Corbin & Strauss, 2015) to explore the data. We read and coded our own and each other's journal entries to capture the meanings line by line. Then we looked for patterns of similarity and difference in the data. This process of open coding allowed us to further reflect on our experiences of how, why and when we used, or did not use, technology in our methods courses. It allowed us to question the data as well as notice commonalities and

differences of experiences or thinking. A second round of coding, axial – coding
(Corbin & Strauss, 2015), was conducted to developed categories or focus codes.
Focus codes were identified by classifying related open codes. These initial two
steps were completed manually – either on paper hard copies or digitally in elec-
tronic documents numbering lines for easy references depending on the researcher's preference. Coding each other's journals helped establish validity and
trustworthiness of our identification of open and axial codes of our data. After this
manual process, we moved our data into Dedoose, a web application for qualitative
and mixed methods research, and is the successor to EthnoNotes (https://www.
dedoose. com). Dedoose allowed us to work collaboratively in analyzing our code
and categories and to identify the frequency or "totals" of the code co – occur-
rence. This resulted in 60 analytic codes which were then collapsed into categories
or focused codes. Focused codes were beneficial because they help to sort large a-
mounts of data (Charmaz, 2000). We wanted to use both manual coding and Dedoose to compare the identified codes and to ensure qualitative validity.

We then used three recursive, nonlinear processes to help interpret our codes
and categories: data organization, analysis, and interpretation (Chang, Ngunjiri,
and Hernandez, 2012). We used a web – based mind – mapping tool for this
process (https://bubbl. us). The mobility of this process allowed for reorgani-
zation and identification of larger categories. These categories helped us assess the
patterns in the data and identify themes that addressed issues of self – efficacy in
developing a technology infused teacher preparation program (Braun & Clarke,
2006). We also used Dedoose's WordCloud feature to further validate themes we
identified. We created a codebook to identify representative quotes to support a
particular code, which helped to facilitate the identification of our themes. Dedoose also allowed us to select passages from our narratives to support our
themes.

Summary of Steps in data analysis

(1) Open and axial – coding (Corbin & Strauss, 2015)

(2) We coded each other's journals to establish trustworthiness of open and axial codes of our data.

(3) Analyzed codes in Dedoose. Resulted in 60 analytic codes and categories.

(4) Created a codebook to identify representative quotes to support a particular code.

(5) Recursive, nonlinear processes: data organization, analysis, and interpretation (Chang, Ngunjiri, & Hernandez, 2012) resulting in identify themes (Braun & Clarke, 2006).

Results and substantiated conclusions

Both faculty and students lack sufficient experiences in technology – rich classroom environments as either teachers or learners. With our limited knowledge, we were charting new territory and had feelings of inadequacy. The purpose of this study was to examine faculty's technology knowledge self – efficacy in order to identify specific factors and dispositions that influenced their classroom implementation in order to create learning environments that model high – quality technology integration. Multiple factors influenced our technology knowledge self – efficacy were discovered. Our attitudes toward technology, and fears about using technology, knowledge of available instructional technology apps, limited knowledge of full integration of apps (beyond just using the app to issues of sharing in class and posting digital products), few professional development opportunities, available personal time used to learn about technology, and the amount of time available during class for practice technology integration, all played a role in influencing faculty's technology knowledge self – efficacy.

Our level of self – efficacy impacted whether we were eager to experiment with technology or waiting for someone to show us what to do. We found that time to explore and learn about various apps was needed, yet we struggled with finding the time to learn and play, above our job expectations of teaching, research and service. Moreover, we found that we had to be more comfortable with failure and technology glitches. Our confidence and level of efficacy influenced whether we ventured out with new technology and were willing to face the possibility of technology not working or experience glitches while instructing our methods courses. Furthermore, being on the forefront of this integration left us with few guiding resources resulting in the need to explore, which highlighted our limited knowledge and, again, requires more time.

5. Scholarly significance of the study

The latest statistics from Apple report sales of more than seven million iPads to schools in the US, with most of those sold in the last two years (Hoffelder, 2014). According to latest report from Project Tomorrow's Speak Up survey (Blackboard, Inc., 2013), preservice teachers report that they learn about educational technology integration from what they observe their university professors doing and using as well as their what they learn in their field experience. Since research suggests that preservice teachers appeared to be dependent upon faculty for each knowledge domain and their intersections, research addressing university faculty technology integration in methods courses is much needed (Vasinda, Kander, & Sanogo, 2015). Examining the self – efficacy and dispositions of faculty in teacher preparation programs gives us insight in how to support thoughtful technology integration. Using a framework such as TPACK (Mishra & Koehler, 2006) to match technology use to pedagogical beliefs is wise, as is examining and linking technology self – efficacy dispositions to Roger's Diffusion of Innovation model (Rogers,2003). Faculty needs time for experimentation and collaboration, as well as professional development to enhance faculty self – efficacy toward the inclusion of mobile technology to model the possibilities of technology – rich learning.

Qiuying Wang is Professor in the School of Teaching, Learning, and Educational Sciences at Oklahoma State University. Her work focuses on cross – cultural and cross – linguistic comparative perspectives on literacy education.

Di Ryter is an Associate Professor in the Department of Teacher Education at Fort Lewis College in Durango, CO. Her experiences and interests are in social science education with a focus on awareness and concern for diverse learners, multiculturalism, social justice, and global connections.

Sheri Vasinda is Associate Professor in the School of Teaching, Learning, and Educational Sciences at Oklahoma State University. Her research interests include the intersections of literacy and technology and teacher educators' integration of technology.

Stephanie Hathcock is an Associate Professor of Science Education in the School of Teaching, Learning, and Educational Sciences at Oklahoma State University. Her work focuses on outdoor learning, creativity, and professional identity.

数字化教育范式的变迁:自我效能感
对高校教师的影响

王秋颖　迪·莱特　谢莉·沃辛塔　斯蒂芬妮·哈斯考克
美国俄克拉荷马州立大学教育学院
刘易斯堡大学

摘要:本文旨在探讨高校教师在培训准教师以提升科技在教学中应用的高效性所起的作用。随着科技的进步,电子新产品的不断涌现与更新,在线教育越来越普及。在高等教育教培领域,有科研表明准教师对如何将科技有效融入教学的理解与他/她们实践的效果和他/她们在学校教的教法课及实践课息息相关。因此,高校的教法课及实践课教师有责任在教学中融入相关内容。在我们之前的科研中发现,高校教师需不断学习,提升自身能力,才能与时俱进。只是为高校教师提供科技产品(比如,艾派德)供他/她们在教学中使用并不够。高校教师的自我效能感影响他/她们全面发挥在教学中数字技术的优势。本文的四位作者都是美国高校准教师和在职教师培训专家。通过自我分析,我们发现高校教师在研究如何在教学中高效融入科学技术方面,投入的时间、自我学习与提升,还有学校和行业的支持都是提升高校教师自我效能感的关键因素。

Preparing Teachers to Support Children with Learning Difficulties Using Databased Individualization

Kristen L. McMaster

University of Minnesota, Minneapolis, MN, U. S. A.

Abstract: Many teachers are challenged to meet the needs of children who experience learning difficulties and for whom high – quality core instruction is not sufficient. Databased Individualization, or DBI, provides a framework within which teachers use assessment data to individualize instruction for children with significant learning needs. DBI is a systematic process whereby teachers (a) establish students' current performance levels, (b) set long – term goals, (c) implement high – quality instruction with fidelity, (d) monitor students' progress, (e) examine students' progress and used decision rules to determine whether instructional changes are needed, (f) develop hypotheses about what instructional changes are needed, and (g) implement those changes and continue the process. Researchers have shown that, when teachers implement this process, students' academic outcomes improve, especially when teachers receive training and support. In this presentation, I will describe the DBI process, share examples from research and practice illustrating its effectiveness, and discuss implications for teacher education.

Many teachers are challenged to meet the needs of children who experience learning difficulties and for whom high – quality core instruction is not sufficient. This problem is significant in U. S. contexts：national assessment data show that, year after year, many children experience difficulty learning to read and write. For example, the National Assessment of Educational Progress（https：//www. nationsreportcard. gov/reading_math_2017）shows that about one third of fourth – grade students perform below basic levels in reading—and this percentage has been stable for over a decade. Similarly, in writing, over half of eighth – grade students perform at or below basic levels. Unfortunately, students who struggle to reach proficiency in literacy are likely to struggle throughout their education and employment（Snow, 2002）. Thus, there is an urgent need for teachers to address the needs of students who struggle to learn to read and write as quickly and effectively as possible.

One approach to supporting children with significant learning difficulties is called Databased Individualization. Databased Individualization, or DBI, provides a framework within which teachers use assessment data to individualize instruction for children with significant learning needs. DBI relies on the following assumptions：First, to provide effective individualized instruction, educators should implement instructional approaches that are evidence – based. However, it is impossible to predict whether these approaches will meet the unique needs of each individual student. Rather, we can only hypothesize that a given instructional approach will work for an individual student；thus, we must test whether it is effective for that student. To do so, we can collect ongoing assessment data and use it as evidence to determine whether an instructional approach is working for an individual student.

DBI is not a single assessment, intervention, or curriculum；rather, it is a systematic process whereby teachers (a) establish students' current performance levels, (b) set long – term goals, (c) implement high – quality instruction with fidelity, (d) monitor students' progress, (e) examine students' progress and used decision rules to determine whether instructional changes are needed, (f) develop hypotheses about what instructional changes are needed, and (g) implement those changes and continue the process. To illustrate, let's look at a case example of a teacher named Mrs. Lewis and her student, Molly.

Molly is an 8 – year – old student who is struggling to learn to read and write. Mrs. Lewis is trying to find a way to provide Molly with the support she needs to be successful in school. She decides to use DBI to identify Molly's needs in writing and provide her with individualized instruction. The first step is to establish Molly's current level of performance in writing. To do so, Mrs. Lewis administers a writing assessment that has been shown in research to be reliable and valid for measuring the performance and progress of young children. She uses a picture – word prompt, which is a 3 – minute timed assessment in which the student is presented with pictures and corresponding words, and is asked to write a sentence for each word. The student's response is then scored for correct word sequences, a quantitative scoring procedure that accounts for correct spelling, punctuation, and grammar. Mrs. Lewis administers three prompts and takes the median score, and plots this score on a graph to show Molly's current level of performance—or baseline (see Figure 1; the baseline score is the red diamond).

The second step is to set a reasonable but ambitious long – term goal. This goal represents Molly's expected level of performance by the end of the school year. The goal could be based on normative data for students who are the same age as Molly, or a more individualized goal based on what can be reasonably expected for her to grow in one year. Mrs. Lewis plots this goal on the graph (see Figure 1; blue star). She also draws a line from baseline to the goal. This line is

Molly's "goal line," representing the rate of progress Molly will need to make to reach her goal.

The third step is to implement high - quality writing instruction with fidelity based on Molly's individual needs. To do so, Mrs. Lewis constructs a writing instructional plan that incorporates research - based instruction that aligns with Molly's specific needs (for example, instruction focused on spelling and sentence construction). Mrs. Lewis shows that instruction has begun by drawing a vertical line on the graph after the baseline data point, and labeling the next section "Intervention 1." She then implements the writing instructional plan.

Fourth, while Mrs. Lewis is implementing the writing instruction, she monitors Molly's progress toward her goal. To do so, she administers different forms of the picture - word writing assessment once per week, and plots Molly's scores on the graph. Once she has about 8 data points, she draws in a trend line to determine Molly's overall progress (see Figure 1). Fifth, Mrs. Lewis uses decision rules to evaluate Molly's progress and the effectiveness of instruction. The decision rules that she uses are as follows: (a) if the trend line is steeper than the goal line, then increase the goal; (b) if the trend line is even with the goal line, then continue with the current instruction as - is; and (c) if the trend line is flatter than the goal line, then change instruction. In Figure 1, it is clear that the trend line is flatter than the goal line, so Mrs. Lewis will need to make an instructional change.

The sixth step is to generate hypotheses to individualize instruction. This means that the teacher becomes like a scientist: she needs to develop hypotheses about why Molly is not making sufficient progress, and test her hypotheses to see what will work best for Molly. To do so, Mrs. Lewis will ask herself the following questions: Were the early writing lessons delivered as intended? Did the student participate in all of the planned lessons, and did I implement the intervention with fidelity? If the answer to any of these questions is NO, then Mrs. Lewis should first make sure that she implements the writing lessons as they were intended to be used. If the answer is YES, then Mrs. Lewis should ask additional questions, such as, does the student need changes to the content or delivery of the lessons. From there, she can explore additional ideas of what types of changes might be helpful. For example, she might hypothesize that the student needs more time in intervention, or that she needs to break the instruction into smaller steps, or provide more modeling and practice, and so on.

After developing a hypothesis, Mrs. Lewis then makes an instructional change to test the hypothesis. For example if her hypothesis is that Molly needs more time in instruction, she might increase the intervention time from 20 to 30 minutes per day. She would then implement this change, and continue to monitor Molly's progress using the picture - word assessment. She would repeat this process, periodically looking at the data and making additional changes, until Molly reaches her goal.

As part of the Early Writing Project, my colleagues and I have developed supports for teachers to facilitate their success in using DBI to improve student outcomes in writing. The Early Writing Project includes tools (assessments, evidence - based mini - lessons & materials, decision - making tools), learning modules (face - to - face workshops on how to use data to individualize instruction), and coaching (ongoing, personalized support) that teachers can access while they are implementing DBI with students who are struggling to learn to write.

We hypothesize that, when teachers receive these supports, their knowledge, skills, and self - efficacy improve, which in turn improve teachers' fidelity of DBI implementation, leading to improved student outcomes. We tested this "theory of change" in a small randomized control trial in which 20 teachers and their students were assigned randomly to either receive support to implement DBI or to serve as a control group. We pretested all teachers and students on a variety of teacher – and student – level measures. Then, teachers either implemented DBI for 20 weeks, or conducted their usual instruction. We then posttested all teachers and students, and then provided all the training and materials to the control teachers.

Our findings revealed that teachers who received support to implement DBI outperformed controls in their knowledge, skills, and personal efficacy. Their fidelity of implementation varied, with fidelity to the assessment procedures being relatively high, and fidelity to the decision – making process being relatively low. Students whose teachers implemented DBI showed a pattern of higher performance on early writing measures, though differences were not statistically significant. Thus, we are undertaking additional research with a much larger sample of teachers and students to better understand the effects of DBI and the supports that we provide.

Preliminary findings suggest the following implications for teacher preparation: Teachers benefit from receiving support to develop knowledge and skills related to DBI, including an understanding of how literacy skills develop, how to assess literacy skills using reliable and valid measures, how to identify and implement high – quality instruction matched to student needs, and how to examine students' data to determine if instruction is effective. Such support should also help teachers to develop self efficacy; that is, they should believe that they can make a difference in children's learning. Support should also help teachers implement DBI with fidelity, including administering assessments and instruction as designed, as well as making timely and appropriate decisions.

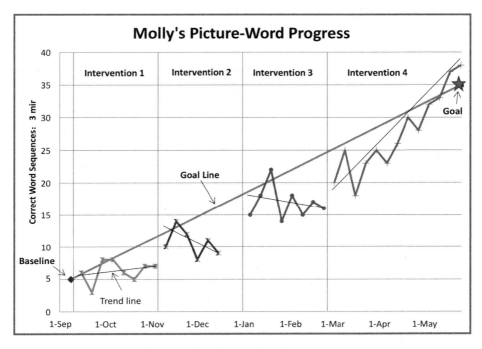

Figure 1　An example of a student's progress during the
Databased Individualization process.

运用个性化数据库支持教师辅导学习困难儿童

克里斯汀·麦克马斯特

美国明尼苏达大学教育学院,教授

摘要:许多教师在满足学习困难儿童需求时面临挑战。对于这些儿童,
高质量的核心课程不能满足他们的需求。数据库个性化或 DBI,提供了一个
框架。在这个框架下,教师使用评估数据为有重大需求的儿童提供个性化

教学。DBI 是一个系统化的过程。在这个过程中,教师①建立学生的当前表现水平;②设定长期目标;③实现高质量的精准教学;④监控学生进步情况;⑤检查学生进步情况,并使用决策规则确定是否需要改进教学;⑥提出教学改进假设;⑦实现教学改进,并继续这个过程。研究人员发现,当教师实施这一过程时,特别是当教师接受培训和教学支持时,学生的学业成绩会提高。在这次演讲中,我将描述 DBI 过程,分享来自研究和实践的例子来说明它的有效性,并讨论其对教师教育的启示。

附　录

Appendix

一、会议日程

Ⅰ：Conference Agenda

2019 小学教师教育国际会议
会议日程

2019 年 10 月 23 日　全天			
08：00-22：00	会议报到		
2019 年 10 月 24 日　上午			
时间	内容	主持人	地点
08：30-09：00	开幕式致辞 首都师范大学校长　孟繁华 教育部教师工作司司长　任友群	李小娟 首都师范大学 副校长	国际文化大厦 南二楼报告厅
09：00-09：10	参会者合影		国际文化大厦 楼前
主论坛：国际视野			
09：10-09：40	迎接未来的教育 顾明远 北京师范大学，资深教授	刘慧 首都师范大学 初等教育学院 院长	
09：40-10：10	多元化世界背景下小学教师教育的批判性想象 彭恩霖 美国密歇根州立大学教育学院副院长，教授		
10：10-10：40	小学教师教育的未来发展趋势 白淳根 韩国首尔国立大学教育学院教学系主任，教授		
10：40-10：50	茶歇		国际文化大厦 南二楼报告厅
10：50-11：20	日本小学教师教育的发展：聚焦质量保障 岩田康之 日本东京学艺大学校长助理，教授	蔡春 首都师范大学 教育学院 院长	
11：20-11：50	面向小学教育多样性的师范生培养：以芬兰的跨文化教师教育为例 文德 芬兰赫尔辛基大学，教授		
11：50-12：20	构建 U-D-S 教师教育共同体，培养高质量专业化教师 孟繁华 首都师范大学校长，教授		
12：20-14：00	午餐与午休		

2019 年 10 月 24 日 下午			
主论坛：中国经验			
时间	报告内容	主持人	地点
14：00-14：30	论一流小学教师教育体系重构 朱旭东 北京师范大学教育学部部长，教授	王智秋 首都师范大学 初等教育学院 教授	国际文化大厦 南二楼报告厅
14：30-15：00	"本硕一体·全科·融通"卓越小学教师培养模式的实践探索 刘学智 东北师范大学教育学部初等教育学院院长，教授		
15：00-15：30	厚实学养 聚焦能力 ——天津师范大学小学教育专业 20 年发展回顾 杨宝忠 天津师范大学教育学部，教授		
15：30-15：50	讨论、提问与回应		
15：50-16：10	茶歇		
16：10-16：40	创新公费师范教育模式 促进基础教育均衡发展 ——湖南第一师范学院乡村公费师范教育的改革与实践 刘志敏 湖南第一师范学院副校长，党委副书记，教授	惠中 上海师范大学 教育学院 教授	
16：40-17：10	"1+X 主辅学科、全程知行合一"的小学教育专业培养模式 ——南京晓庄学院小学教育专业培养模式变化之我思 曹慧英 南京晓庄学院教师教育学院，教授		
17：10-17：40	"精准扶教"提升乡村学校薄弱学科教师素养的创新探索 李中国 临沂大学社会科学处处长，教授		
17：40-18：00	讨论、提问与回应		
18：00-20：00	晚餐		

2019 年 10 月 25 日　上午

	论坛一：小学教师培养理念与模式		
时间	报告内容（每人报告 15 分钟）	主持人	地点
8：30-10：00	**从同课异构看国际型素质的小学教师培养** 董芳胜 日本创价大学，副教授 长野修一、嶺井勇哉、渡辺優 日本创价大学，研究生 **小学教育、学校转型与全纳：欧洲的变与不变** 雷吉斯·马莱 法国波尔多大学教育研究院副院长，教授 **基于整合模式培养职前教师的实践性知识** 魏戈 首都师范大学初等教育学院，博士 **一名教师教七个不同科目的教学：如何成功？** 艾斯特·布伦纳 瑞士图高教育大学，教授 **点评、提问与回应** **主持人颁发证书** **（30 分钟）**	傅添 首都师范大学 初等教育学院 教育教研室 主任	国际文化大厦 南二楼报告厅
10：00-10：20	茶歇		
10：20-11：50	**胜任与超越：我国卓越小学教师职前培养再思考** **——基于在职小学优秀教师核心素养构成视角** 庞国彬 大连大学师范学院院长，教授 **农村卓越小学教师培养模式的构建与实践** **——以陇南师范高等专科学校为例** 张永明 陇南师范高等专科学校初等教育学院院长，教授 **我国小学教师培养中儿童研究的缺席与回归** 王丽华 浙江师范大学教师教育学院教育学系主任，副教授 **首都师大小学教育专业人才培养的目标定位、课程体系** 孙建龙 首都师范大学初等教育学院副院长，副教授 **点评、提问与回应** **主持人颁发证书** **（30 分钟）**	司成勇 天津师范大学 教授	
11：50-14：00	午餐与午休		

论坛二：未来小学教师教育发展路向			
时间	报告内容（每人报告 15 分钟）	主持人	地点
8：30-10：00	**超深／超广：跨领域美感创意教学之探究** 高震峰 中国台北市立大学视觉艺术学系，教授 **新时代卓越教师培养两个维度——师德与教育实践** 肖冬民 高等教育出版社教师教育事业部小教学前教育分社，社长 **小学教师的教育惩戒伦理研究** 蔡连玉 浙江师范大学教师教育学院，副教授 **小学教师德育专业化：愿景与进展** 李敏 首都师范大学初等教育学院，教授 **点评、提问与回应** **主持人颁发证书** **（30 分钟）**	赵丹妮 洛阳师范学院 教育科学学院 副院长	国际文化大厦 南楼东侧八层 多功能厅
10：00-10：20	**茶歇**		
10：20-11：50	**以素养导向为核心之小学阶段师资培育：从美感的价值谈起** 赵惠玲 中国台湾师范大学艺术学院院长，教授 **智能教育与教师角色转变** 朱永海 首都师范大学初等教育学院，副教授 **自主学习变革课堂教学与教师专业发展** 刘丽妹 中国澳门化地玛女子学校，校长 梁政妍、刘鹤、郭丽君、陈丽珠 中国澳门化地玛女子学校，教师 **21 世纪素养教育的重新定位：范式的变迁** 王秋颖 美国俄赫拉荷马州立大学教育学院 **点评、提问与回应** **主持人颁发证书** **（30 分钟）**	朱萍 连云港师范高 等专科学校 初等教育学院 院长	
11：50-14：00	**午餐与午休**		

论坛三：小学教师教育质量保障			
时间	报告内容（每人报告 15 分钟）	主持人	地点
8：30-10：00	理论与实践结合的创价大学教职研究生院的小学教师培养： 成果与课题 铃木词雄 日本创价大学，副教授 濱佳子、原田秀满、山本美纪 日本创价大学，研究生 师范认证背景下小学教育专业以自我评价为核心的 内部质量保障体系改进 唐斌 首都师范大学初等教育学院，副教授 小学教师培养质量保障体系建构探索 ——以延边大学小学教育专业为例 崔梅花 延边大学师范学院小学教育系主任 运用个性化数据库支持教师辅导学习困难儿童 克里斯汀·麦克马斯特 美国明尼苏达大学教育学院，教授 点评、提问与回应 主持人颁发证书 （30 分钟）	张志坤 首都师范大学 初等教育学院 副院长	国际文化大厦 南楼二层 第六会议室
10：00-10：20	茶歇		
10：20-11：50	研究型全科小学教师培养模式探索 易晓明 南京师范大学小学教育系主任，教授 农村小学全科教师的"乡村属性"教学能力与培养路径 肖正德 杭州师范大学教师发展研究中心，教授 基于综合课程与活动课程的小学全科教师培养实践 武启云 青海师范大学教师发展中心主任，教授 卓越小学全科教师培养方案设计与实践 ——以重庆师范大学为例 林长春 重庆师范大学初等教育学院院长，教授 点评、提问与回应 主持人颁发证书 （30 分钟）	林李楠 沈阳师范大学 学前与初等 教育学院 副院长	
11：50-14：00	午餐与午休		

2019 年 10 月 25 日　下午			
主论坛：多元共享			
时间	内容	主持人	地点
14：00-14：30	**中国小学教师培养模式探析及未来展望** 刘慧 首都师范大学初等教育学院院长，教授	刘立德 人民教育出版社教育编辑室主任	国际文化大厦南二楼报告厅
14：30-15：00	**匈牙利的小学教师师资培养：传统与革新** 乔堡·西科斯 匈牙利罗兰大学初等教育和学前教育系，副院长		
15：00-15：30	**面向全球公民教育的小学教师教育** 默瑞·普林特 澳大利亚悉尼大学教育与社会工作学院教育系主任，教授		
15：30-15：50	茶歇		
15：50-16：20	**基于创价教育哲学的创价大学人本主义取向的教师教育** 铃木将史 日本创价大学副校长，教授	田国秀 首都师范大学教师教育学院院长	
16：20-16：50	**冰岛教师教育中的认知暴力** 扬·卡亚兰 冰岛大学教育学院，教授		
16：50-17：20	**智慧教育与教育智慧：新时代新技术环境下教师专业发展的人文视域** 李树英 中国澳门城市大学教务长，教授		
17：20-18：00	**闭幕式总结** 王智秋 教育部高等学校小学教师培养教学指导委员会秘书长 杨志成 首都师范大学副校长	韩梅 首都师范大学国际合作交流处处长	
18：00-20：00	晚餐		

2019 International Conference on Elementary Teacher Education Agenda

October 23，2019	
8：00-22：00	Registration

Morning，October 24，2019			
Time	Programs	Chair	Venue
08：30-09：00	**Opening Ceremony Speech** MENG Fanhua，President，Capital Normal University REN Youqun，Director-General，the Department of Teacher Education， Ministry of Education	LI Xiaojuan Vice President of Capital Normal University	Lecture Hall， Second Floor， South Building of International Cultural Plaza
Main Forum：International Perspectives			
09：00-09：30	**Education for the Future** GU Mingyuan Distinguished Professor，Beijing Normal University	LIU Hui Dean of College of Elementary Education， Capital Normal University	Lecture Hall， Second Floor， South Building of International Cultural Plaza
09：30-10：00	**Critically Imagining Elementary Teacher Education for a Pluralistic World** Lynn Paine Associate Dean，Professor，College of Education，Michigan State University，U.S.A.		
10：00-10：30	**The Future Development Directions for Elementary Teacher Education** Sun Geun Baek Chair，Professor，Department of Education，Seoul National University，South Korea		
10：30-10：45	Tea Break		
10：45-11：15	**Elementary Teachers Education in Japan：Focusing on Quality Assurance** Yasuyuki Iwata Deputy President，Professor，Tokyo Gakugei University，Japan	CAI Chun Dean of College of Education， Capital Normal University	
11：15-11：45	**Preparing Student Teachers for Diversity in Elementary Education：an Example of Intercultural Teacher Education from Finland** Fred Dervin Professor，University of Helsinki，Finland		
11：45-12：15	**Building a U-D-S Teacher Education Community to Cultivate High-Quality Professional Teachers** MENG Fanhua President，Professor，Capital Normal University		
12：15-14：00	Lunch and Noon Break		

Afternoon，October 24，2019			
Main Forum：Chinese Experience			
Time	**Programs**	**Chair**	**Venue**
14：00-14：30	**On the Reconstruction of First-Class Elementary Teachers Education System** ZHU Xudong Dean，Professor，Faculty of Education，Beijing Normal University	WANG Zhiqiu Professor， College of Elementary Education of Capital Normal University	Lecture Hall， South Building of International Cultural Plaza
14：30-15：00	**Practical Exploration on the Training Mode of Excellent Primary School Teachers of "Integration of Undergraduate and Postgraduate Education，Whole Subject and Integration"** LIU Xuezhi Dean，Professor，School of Primary Education，Faculty of Education，Northeast Normal University		
15：00-15：30	**Boosting Knowledge and accomplishment；Focusing on Abilities -- Review of 20 Years of Development of Elementary Education Programs in Tianjin Normal University** YANG Baozhong Professor，Faculty of Education，Tianjin Normal University		
15：30-15：50	Discussions，Questions and Answers		
15：50-16：10	Tea Break		
16：10-16：40	**Innovating the Model of Government-funded Normal Education to Promote Balanced Development of Basic Education ——Hunan First Normal University's Reform and Practice of Government-funded Normal Education for Rural Areas** LIU Zhimin Vice President，Professor，Hunan First Normal University，Deputy Secretary of the Party Committee	HUI Zhong Professor， College of Education， Shanghai Normal University	
16：40-17：10	**"1+x" Primary and Secondary Courses System with Unity of Knowing and Doing---On the Training Modal of Elementary Teacher Education in Nanjing Xiaozhuang University** CAO Huiying Professor，College of Teacher Education，Nanjing Xiaozhuang University		
17：10-17：40	**Innovative Explorations through a "Targeted Teaching Support" Project to Improve the Qualities of Rural School Teachers in Weak Subjects** LI Zhongguo Director，Professor，Social Science Department，Linyi University		
17：40-18：00	Discussions，Questions and Answers		
18：00-20：00	Dinner		

Morning，October 25，2019			
Forum 1：Ideas and Modes of Elementary Teachers Education			
Time	Programs (15 Minutes for Each Presentation)	Chair	Venue
8：30—10：00	**Research on Training of Primary School Teachers with International Quality from Heterogeneous Forms for Same Lesson** DONG Fangsheng Associate Professor，Soka University，Japan Yuya MINEI，Yu WATANABE，Shuichi NAGANO Graduate Student，Soka University，Japan **Elementary Education，School Transitions and Inclusion in Schools：Variations and Continuities in Europe** Regis Malet Vice-Head，Professor，Graduate School of Education，University of Bordeau，France **Developing Pre-Service Teacher Practical Knowledge through an Integrative Training Model** WEI Ge Ph.D.，College of Elementary Education，Capital Normal University **One Teacher-Seven Different Subjects：How Can This Be Successful?** Esther Brunner Professor，Thurgau University of Teacher Education **Comments，Questions and Answers** **Chair Issuing Certificates** **(30 Minutes)**	**FU Tian** **Head of Department of Educational Research College of Elementary Education，Capital Normal University**	**Lecture Hall，Second Floor，South Building of International Cultural Plaza**
10：00-10：20	**Tea Break**		
10：20-11：50	**Qualifying and Excelling：Rethinking about Pre-service Education of Outstanding Elementary Teachers in China from the Perspective of Core Competencies of In-service Excellent Elementary School Teachers** PANG Guobin Dean，Professor，Teacher College of Dalian University **Construction and Practice of the Education Mode of Outstanding Elementary Teachers in Rural Areas** **--Taking Longnan Normal College as an Example** ZHANG Yongming Dean，Professor，Department of Elementary Education，Longnan Normal College **The Absence and Recurrence of Studies on Children in Elementary Teacher Education in China** WANG Lihua Director，Associate Professor，Education Department，Teacher Education College of Zhejiang Normal University **The Goal Orientation and Curriculum System of Elementary Education Programs in College of Elementary Education of Capital Normal University** SUN Jianlong Deputy Dean，Associate Professor，College of Elementary Education，Capital Normal University **Comments，Questions and Answers** **Chair Issuing Certificates** **(30 Minutes)**	**SI Chengyong** **Professor，Tianjin Normal University**	
11：50-14：00	**Lunch and Noon Break**		

Forum 2: Future Development Direction of Elementary Teacher Education			
Time	Programs(15 Minutes for Each Presentation)	Chair	Venue
8：30—10：00	**Deepening and Expanding: Exploration of Innovative Cross-Disciplinary Aesthetic Teaching** GAO Zhenfeng(KAO Cheng-Feng) Professor，Visual Arts Department of University of Taipei，China **Two Dimensions of Outstanding Teachers Education in the New Era: Teacher Morality and Educational Practice** XIAO Dongmin Director，Elementary and Preschool Education Branch，Teacher Education Department of Higher Education Press **Research on Elementary School Teachers' Ethics of Educational Punishment** CAI Lianyu Associate Professor，College of Teacher Education，Zhejiang Normal University **Professionalism of Elementary School Teachers' Moral Education: Vision and Progress** LI Min Associate Professor，College of Elementary Education，Capital Normal University **Comments，Questions and Answers** **Chair Issuing Certificates** **(30 Minutes)**	ZHAO Danni Deputy Dean of School of Educational Science，Luoyang Normal University	Multifunction Hall，South Building of the International Culture Plaza (the 8th Floor，East Side)
10：00-10：20	**Tea Break**		
10：20-11：50	**Cultivation of Elementary School Teachers with Competencies Orientation: Beginning with the Value of sense of Aesthetics** ZHAO Huiling(CHAO Huei-Ling) Dean，Professor，Art College of Taiwan Normal University，China **Intelligence Education and Change of Teachers' Roles** ZHU Yonghai Associate Professor，College of Elementary Education of Capital Normal University **How Self-Directed Learning Changes Classroom Teaching and Teacher Professional Development** LIU Limei Principal，Macau Fatima Girls' School LIANG Zhengyan，LIU He，GUO Lijun，CHEN Lizhu Teachers，Macau Fatima Girls' School **Redefining Literacy Education in the 21st Century: the Changing Paradigms** WANG Qiuying Professor，College of Education of Oklahoma State University，U.S.A **Comments，Questions and Answers** **Chair Issuing Certificates** **(30 Minutes)**	ZHU Ping Dean of Department of Elementary Education，Lianyungang Normal College	
11：50—14：00	**Lunch and Noon Break**		

Forum 3：Quality Assurance of Elementary Teacher Education			
时间/Time	Programs (15 Minutes for Each Presentation)	Chair	Venue
8：30—10：00	Achievements and Challenges of Soka University Graduate School of Teacher Education Aiming at Interaction between Theory and Practice Norio SUZUKI Associate Professor，Soka University，Japan Yoshiko HAMA，Hidemitsu HARADA，Miki YAMAMOTO Graduate Students，Soka University，Japan Improvement of Internal Quality Assurance System of Elementary Education Programs with Self-Evaluation as the Core under the Background of Accreditation of Teacher Education TANG Bin Associate Professor，College of Elementary Education，Capital Normal University Exploration for the Construction of Quality Assurance System of Elementary Teacher Training -- with Elementary Education Programs of Yanbian University as an Example CUI Meihua Dean，Primary School Education Department，Normal School of Yanbian University Preparing Teachers to Support Children with Learning Difficulties Using Databased Individualization Kristen L.McMaster Professor，University of Minnesota，Minneapolis，MN，USA. Comments，Questions and Answers Chair Issuing Certificates (30 minutes)	ZHANG Zhikun Deputy Dean of College of Elementary Education，Capital Normal University	Second Floor，Conference Room 6，South Building of International Cultural Plaza
10：00-10：20	Tea Break		
10：20-11：50	Exploration of the Training Mode of Research-Oriented General-Subject Elementary School Teachers YI Xiaoming Dean，Professor，Elementary Education Department，Nanjing Normal University The Rural-Based Teaching Competence of General-Subject Teachers in Rural Elementary Schools and Its Training Path XIAO Zhengde Professor，Education College of Hangzhou Normal University Practice of Elementary General-Subject Teachers Training Based on Comprehensive Curriculum and Activity-based Curriculum WU Qiyun Director，Professor，Teacher Development Center，Qinghai Normal University Design and Practice of Training Program for Outstanding Elementary General-Subject Teachers -- Taking Chongqing Normal University as an Example LIN Changchun Dean，Professor，School of Primary Education，Chongqing Normal University Comments，Questions and Answers Chair Issuing Certificates (30 minutes)	LIN Linan Deputy Dean of College of Preschool & Primary Education，Shenyang Normal University	
11：50-14：00	Lunch and Noon Break		

Afternoon，October 25，2019			
Main Forum：Pluralist Sharing			
Time	Programs	Chair	Venue
14：00-14：30	Analysis of Elementary Teacher Training Modes in China and Its Prospects LIU Hui Dean，Professor，College of Elementary Education，Capital Normal University	LIU Lide Director of Teacher Education Branch， People's Education Press	Lecture Hall，Second Floor，South Building of International Cultural Plaza
14：30-15：00	Elementary Teacher Training in Hungary：Traditions and Innovations Csaba Csikos Associate Dean，Faculty of Primary and Pre-School Education，Roland University，Hungary		
15：00-15：30	Elementary Teacher Education for Global Citizenship Education Murray Print Chair，Professor，Faculty of Education & Social Work，University of Sydney，Australia		
15：30-15：50	Tea Break		
15：50-16：20	Humanistic Approach to Teacher Education at Soka University Based on the Philosophy of Soka Education Masashi Suzuki Vice President，Professor，Soka University，Japan	TIAN Guoxiu Dean of Teacher Education College，Capital Normal University	
16：20-16：50	Epistemic Violence in Teacher Education in Iceland Jón Ingvar Kjaran Professor，School of Education，University of Iceland		
16：50-17：20	Wisdom Education and Educational Wisdom：Humanistic Perspective on Teachers Professional Development in the New era and New Technological Environment LI Shuying Professor，Provost of Macau City University，China		
17：20-18：00	Closing Ceremony WANG Zhiqiu Secretary- General of the Teaching Steering Committee for Elementary Teacher Traning at Higher Education Institutions，Ministry of Education of the People's Republic of China YANG Zhicheng Vice President of Capital Normal University	HAN Mei Director of Office of International Cooperation and Exchange，Capital Normal University	
18：00-20：00	Dinner		

二、多元·智慧·素养
Ⅱ：Diversity，Wisdom，Competency

2019"首届小学教师教育国际会议"摘要集

小学教育、学校转型与全纳：欧洲的变与不变

雷吉斯·马莱

法国波尔多大学教育研究院副院长，教授

摘要：近 20 年来，教育中的公民意识与包容性一直作为欧洲政策的核心，促进了社会凝聚力、对世界的开放心态和"共享生活"精神等积极的价值观的培育。

这个基本主题将是我演讲的核心。事实上，除公认意向性议题和最具前瞻性的欧洲政策之外，教育、公民意识和整合等概念在整个欧洲范围内，国家与国家之间的差异非常大。这些不同是建立在国家教育体系模式的不同、对儿童概念不同，以及不同文化与教育背景下教师和教育者使命的不同之上的。

我们认为在教育领域，这些历史累积的变化依然强势且明显，可以从教育体系中看出，也可以从学校如何从小为孩子规划并评估孩子的体系中看出。尤其是在孩子成长发展及社会化的过程中，教师及师范教育所充当的

角色,家庭教育所充当的角色。

我们将从公民教育和学校全纳教育的角度,识别并讨论这些变化以及越来越多的混合模式、内容和特征,这一系列特征可在欧洲和其他地区观察到,并在全球范围内考察公民教育、教学和学校教育的效果。

Elementary Education, School Transitions and Inclusion in Schools: Variations and Continuities in Europe

Régis Malet

Professor, Vice – Head of Graduate School of Education,

University of Bordeau, France

Abstract: Citizenship and Inclusion in education have been at the heart of European policies for at least two decades, promoting positive values of social cohesion, openness to the world and "living together" ethos.

This essential topic will be at the core of our presentation. As a matter of fact, beyond a consensual discourse of intention and most proactive European policies, the conceptions of education, citizenship and integration vary a lot through the European space, from one country to another. These variations are related to the modes of construction of the national education systems, to the conceptions of the Child and to the missions of teachers & educators in contrasted cultural & educational settings.

We suggest that these historically built – up variations are still strong and vivid in educational spaces and are readable in the very structures of the systems and in the way children are conceived and recognized in schools from an early age, which is readable through the role given to teachers as well as teachers educators, families in the process of education, and in children's development and socialization.

We will identify and discuss these changes and more and more hybrid models, content and features that can be observed in the European area and beyond, in terms of citizenship education and inclusive education in schools, and consider the consequences for citizenship education, teaching and schooling at the global scale.

多元化世界背景下小学教师教育的批判性想象

彭恩霖

美国密歇根州立大学教育学院副院长,教授

摘要:小学教师教育正处于关键时期,虽然培养小学教师的传统如今已经采用了许多不同的模式,但是解决理论与实践之结合中所固有的困境依然是一个挑战。以改革为导向的教师培养模式为新入职教师的能力发展提供了完全不同的思路,这些方法要求教师教育传统中惯常的安排和实践都要发生关键性变化。基于教师教育之现状所面临的挑战,教师教育的课程也必须要做出改变,以反映小学生学习目标的新变化。教育和技能的新理念要求初等教育的革新,这意味着新一代的教师需要发展一系列高标准、多样化的能力。本文批判性地审视全球范围内常见的支撑教师教育未来发展的新理念。

Critically Imagining Elementary Teacher Education for a Pluralistic World

Lynn Paine

Professor, Associate Dean of College of Education,

Michigan State University, U. S. A

Abstract: Elementary teacher education is at a critical juncture. While traditions of preparing elementary teachers have drawn on a range of different models, the persistent dilemma of combining theory and practice remains a challenge. Reform – oriented models of teacher preparation offer sharply different notions of how beginning teachers can develop competence. These approaches require significant change in the institutional arrangements and practices of teacher education. On top of this challenge to teacher education's status quo, the curriculum for preparing teachers must also change to reflect new goals for elementary students' learning. New frameworks for education and skills call for innovations in elementary teaching; this means that the next generation of teachers has a much more demanding and diverse set of competences it must develop. Together, the call for new models and new curricula offer threats and opportunities for teacher education. This presentation critically considers globally circulating reform ideas that can support the development of promising approaches to teacher education.

冰岛教师教育中的认知暴力

扬·卡亚兰

冰岛大学教育学院教授

　　摘要：在过去的几十年中，冰岛与北欧许多国家一样，由于移民的增加，变得更加文化多元和多样化。冰岛总人口 33 万，移民占总人口的 10%，如果包括第二代移民，则占 12%。人口异质性的增加对学校系统的学生构成产生了影响，如今的移民学生约占义务教育和中学教育的 12%。这些变化在许多方面反映在最新的《国家课程指南》中，该指南于 2011 年生效，适用于义务教育和高中教育。教育的重点是包容性，学校应迎合不同的身份类别，例如种族、性别和性取向。但是教师的教育和培训计划并未紧随其后。提供的课程很少专门针对多元性，而且当前的教学方法可再现霸权价值观和文化。因此在本文中，我们的目的是讨论认知暴力的概念，以及在评估冰岛的师范教育时如何应用认知暴力，在过去的几十年中，认知暴力又是如何发展的。G. 斯皮瓦克（G. Spivak）（1994）认为，认知暴力是占主导地位的知识体系对边缘群体施加影响而造成的。保罗·弗索尔（Paulo Freire）（1996）将认知暴力视为一种"文化入侵"，这种入侵是由占主导地位的群体强行施加"他们的世界观于被入侵者，并通过遏制他们的思想表达来抑制其创造力发展"。在我们的分析研究中，我们将借鉴批判种族理论，该理论可以为教师和研究者提供理论框架和多元的观点，以期应对不断的变革。同时，可以启发教师转变教育方式，以满足所有学生的需求。在教育教学情境下，上述内容十分重要。因为在这种情境中,占主导地位的价值观往往会被复制或是强加于"他人"。换言之,教师经常是主导地位文化价值观的一部分。因此在教师教育或培训过程中,着眼批判种族理论是很重要的,这样才能在教育教学中应对认知暴力。

Epistemic Violence in Teacher Education in Iceland

Jón Kjaran

Professor, School of Education, University of Iceland

Abstract: During the last decades Iceland, as many other countries in Northern

Europe, has become more multicultural and diverse due to increased immigration/migration. Today (im)migrants comprise 10% of the total population of and 12% if second generation of (im)migrants is included. This increased heterogeneity of the population has influenced the school system in terms of composition of its students and today (im)migrant students make up around 12% of compulsory and secondary schools. In many ways these changes are reflected in the latest National Curriculum Guide, which came into force in 2011, both for compulsory and upper secondary schools. There the emphasis is on inclusion and that schools should cater to different identity categories such as ethnicity, gender, and sexuality. However, teacher education and training programs have not followed suit. Few courses are offered which specifically address diversity and current pedagogical approaches reproduce hegemonic values and culture. Thus, in this paper our aim is to discuss the concept of epistemic violence and how it can be applied when evaluating teacher education in Iceland and how it has developed during the last decades. Epistemic violence is as G. Spivak (1994) has argued, inflicted towards marginalized groups through the dominant knowledge systems. Paulo Freire (1996) refers to epistemic violence as "cultural invasion," in which the dominant group imposes "… their own view of the world upon those they invade and inhibit the creativity of the invaded by curbing their expression". In our analysis we will also draw on critical race theory which can provide a theoretical framework and perspective both for teachers and researchers in order to bring about changes; to transform education to serve the needs of all students. This is particularly important within educational contexts where the values of the dominant class and culture are often reproduced and forced upon the "other". In other words, teachers are agents and often part of the dominant culture and therefore it is important to include in their education and training critical race awareness in order to work against epistemic violence in education and teaching.

面向全球公民教育的小学教师教育

默瑞·普林特

澳大利亚悉尼大学教育与社会工作学院教育系主任,教授

摘要:作为一个工业和贸易大国,同时拥有大量的外国游客和留学生,中国需要接受全球公民的概念并且承担相应责任。全球公民身份不是人们的天然属性,相反对许多人来说,它是一种与人们普遍理解的国家公民身份大相径庭的观念。

有人认为,人类社会要想在 21 世纪生存下去,每一个个体的一思一行都需要更多地从全球化的角度出发,而非局限于一国。既然全球公民不是人类生来就有的属性,那么人们要如何成为"全球公民",小学教师教育又可以在这一过程中发挥什么作用呢?

本文探讨了基础教师教育中全球公民教育(GCE)的理论和实践,主要提出了两个问题:什么是全球公民教育(GCE)?我们可以从相关的国际研究中学习到什么来应用于首都师范大学的教学实践,同时也为小学教师教育发展的讨论提供新思路。

Elementary Teacher Education for Global Citizenship Education

Murray Print

Professor, Chair of Faculty of Education & Social Work,

University of Sydney, Australia

Abstract: As a major industrial and trading country, with vast numbers of tourists and students studying abroad, China needs to address the concept and responsibilities of global citizenship. Global citizenship is not a natural condition for people. For many it is a contrarian position to the commonly understood construct of national citizenship.

Yet it may be argued that for the world to survive the twenty – first century individuals will need to think and act more globally and less nationally. If global citizenship is not natural how do people become ' global citizens ' and what role can elementary teacher education play?

This presentation examines theory and practice of Global Citizenship Education (GCE) in elementary teacher education. It asks – What is GCE and what can be learnt from international research that can apply to Capital Normal University and raise issues for discussion in elementary teacher education.

智慧教育与教育智慧：新时代新技术环境下教师专业发展的人文视域

李树英

中国澳门城市大学教务长，教授

摘要：教育的颠覆性新技术不断创新涌现给传统意义上的教师定位带来巨大挑战和冲击。新技术的显著特征是"智慧"，由此在教育行业带来了新的话语，诸如"智慧校园""智慧教室""智慧课堂""智慧学习"之类的"智慧教育"已逐渐见诸中小学的教育之中。研究智慧教育的文献纷至沓来，而智慧的教师研究为学者们所忽略。《卓越教师计划2.0计划》提出了应对新时代新技术环境中的教师教育改革和教师专业发展，其中一个重要的概念就是"智慧教师"。本文从教育现象学的行动研究视角阐述了"智慧教师"所具备的特质，即对学生主体、个体的关注，一种关注他人的体验和敏感性、一种独特的教育智慧。研究提出了新技术环境下教师教育和教师培训的重点路径，即对"教育智慧"养成的发展方式。

Wisdom Education and Educational Wisdom: Humanistic Perspective on Teachers Professional Development in the New era and New Technological Environment

Shuying Li

Professor, Provost of Macau City University

Abstract: Disruptive technology in education has brought drastic challenge and impact on the roles of a teacher. One of the outstanding features of these technologies is "smartness", which, therefore, has coined a new language in education sector, such as "smart campus", "smart classroom", "smart lesson", "smart learning". These terms have been frequently used in various school practices. Studies on "smart education" are pouring out in literatures. However, studies on pedagogical thoughtfulness and wisdom are largely neglected. "Outstanding Teacher Project 2.0" proposed by the Ministry of Education of China requires innovative teacher education and teacher professional development. One of the key ideas in this government document is "teachers' pedagogical thoughtfulness and tact". This presentation elucidates the major qualities of teachers' pedagogical thoughtfulness and tact, that is, the type of unique attention to the uniqueness of the individuals, the sensitivity to the lived experience of the other, the unique pedagogical wisdom. By showing a series of lived experience descriptive anecdotes, the presentation proposes a new model for teacher professional development, the cultivation and development of the teacher's pedagogical thoughtfulness.

人工智能之于小学教师专业发展

朱倩楠

山西师范大学教育科学学院

摘要：人工智能的出现，预示着教育与 AI 的融合将成为必然趋势，但是人工智能在教育界的出现，尤其是出现在小学课堂，对小学教师来说既减轻了教学负担，同时也带来了一定的挑战。人工智能的出现意味着教师要转变传统的教师角色，这需要教师提升扩充自己的专业知识与能力，同时也应更加注重对学生的情感、道德素质教育。因此小学教师应正确认识并且灵活地将人工智能与教学融合起来，更加专注对学生心灵世界的关怀。有了人工智能的辅助，教师可以利用更多的时间参与教育教学的研究与创新，并不断更新自己的知识库，做一个终身学习者，从而促进教师的专业发展，提升教学质量。

关键词：人工智能；小学教师教育；专业发展

Artificial Intelligence in the Professional Development of Primary School Teachers

Qiannan Zhu

Education Science College of Shanxi Normal University

Abstract:The emergence of artificial intelligence indicates that the integration of education and AI will become an inevitable trend. However, the emergence of artificial intelligence in education, especially in primary and secondary school classes, not only reduces the teaching burden, but brings some challenges to primary school teachers. The emergence of artificial intelligence means that teachers should change the traditional role of themselves, which requires teachers to upgrade and expand their professional knowledge and ability, and at the same time pay more attention to the emotional and moral quality education of students. Therefore, primary school teachers should correctly understand and flexibly integrate artificial intelligence with teaching, and pay more attention to caring for students´ spiritual world. With the help of artificial intelligence, teachers have more time to participate in the research and innovation of education and teaching, and constantly update their knowledge. As lifelong learners, teachers should promote their professional development and improve teaching quality.

Keywords:Artificial Intelligence; primary school teachers; professional development

从同课异构看国际型素质的小学教师培养

董芳胜

日本创价大学副教授

长野修一、岭井勇哉、渡边优

日本创价大学研究生

摘要: 国际化的发展已经是我们任何一个国家都无法预测的,承担培养未来社会主人公的小学教师如何培养未来型人才已经是各个国家的紧要课题。中国的首都师范大学初等教育学院和日本的创价大学教育学院早在十年前就从国际化的视野中把培养未来志向的国际型教师作为一个共同关心的课题进行了多年的探讨,其中"同课异构"的实践交流已经取得了一些成效。第一,国际型教师的素质能力受课堂主体和课堂形式的影响。课堂主体把握可以增强国际型教师对教育对象、课堂意义的深层理解。第二,不同文化背景对象的学生能提高教师国际型素质的自身能力。教师的国际型素质能力可以通过不同文化背景的学生进而扩大自己文化认识的视野。第三,国际型教师的素质能力有其动态性的和静态性的性质。动态性的性质是指教师国际型素质能力的内化过程,这一内化过程是在不同文化背景下的交流中得以形成和推进的;相反静态性的性质是指教师原有的知识技能等,并且能维持这个状态的性质。

Research on Training of Primary School Teachers with International Quality from Heterogeneous Forms for Same Lesson

Fangsheng Dong

Associate Professor, Soka University, Japan Yuya MINEI,

Yu WATANABE, Shuichi NAGANO

Graduate Student, Soka University, Japan

Abstract: The trend of internationalization cannot be predicted by any country. It is a critical issue for all countries to investigate how to train teachers, especially primary school teachers who are responsible for cultivating the future social protagonists. As a common concern, the Elementary Education College of Capital Normal University in China and the Faculty of Education of Soka University in Japan have been discussing on the training of teachers who are future – oriented from the perspective of internationalization for more than a decade.

Among these discussions, the practice of the heterogeneous forms for same lesson (Tongkeyigou) has already achieved some results. (1) The quality of an internationalized teacher is affected by classroom subject and form. The mastery of the classroom subject and form can enhance their understanding of the students and the significance of the classroom. (2) Students with different cultural backgrounds can improve the international quality of teachers, hence broaden their horizon on cross – cultural understanding. (3) The nature of teachers' international quality is both dynamic and static. The dynamic nature refers to the inner process of teachers' international quality, which is embodied and promoted in classroom communication with students of different cultural backgrounds. Meanwhile, the static nature refers to the original knowledge and skills of teachers, and the property of maintaining this status.

以素养导向为核心之小学阶段师资培育:
从美感的价值谈起

赵惠玲

台湾师范大学艺术学院院长,教授

摘要:进入 21 世纪后,"素养"成为世界各国进行教育政策策划时,最为关注的问题之一。小学阶段为每一个体成长过程中至关重要的基石,如何为小学阶段的儿童培育其终生受用的素养与态度,是小学阶段教师的当代责任。素养意指每一个体适应复杂多变的外在环境时,所应具备的知识、能力与态度,因此素养导向的课程设计与以往视学科知识为主要目标之概念不同,转而关注个体学习与日常生活面向的联结,以及学习历程的构筑。在此时代趋势下,小学阶段的师资培育课程亦须有所转向。鉴于在全球化瞬息万变的脉络中,"创新"被视为教育的基本精神,而能展现整合力及创新能量的"美感素养"(aesthetic literacy)则跃升为当代公民的重要核心素养,认为竞争力构筑在新时代学习者丰富的美感相关创造力之上,本文尝试提出以美感价值为核心的小学阶段师资培育,着眼于透过艺术领域具弹性的实践力,以及创作、鉴赏、展演等机制,为不同学科领域酝酿多元思维与做法的可能性。

Cultivation of Elementary School Teachers with Competencies Orientation: Beginning with the Value of sense of Aesthetics

Huiling Zhao

Professor, Dean of Art College of Taiwan Normal University

Abstract: Since entering the 21st century, the development of "literacy" has become one of the main focal points of many of the world's education system policy makers. Primary school education is the cornerstone of each individual's growth process. The cultivation of life – long literacy and mindsets among primary school students is a prime responsibility that all modern primary school teachers should bear. "literacy" refers to the knowledge, ability and attitude that each individual should possess when adapting to the complex and ever – changing external environment. Therefore, literacy – based curriculums diverge from previous concepts which emphasize the attainment of factual knowledge; and instead focuses more on both the connection between individual learning and everyday life as well as the construction of a cohesive learning process. Under this trend, training methods for pre – service primary school teachers must also be adjusted. In the context of the ever – changing globalization, "innovation" is regarded as an essential aspect of education; and "aesthetic literacy", which is embodied by the assimilation of various fields of knowledge and innovation, has become an essential core – literacy of modern citizens. Holding a firm belief that, for modern generation learners, competitiveness is built upon the richness of their aesthetic creative capacities, this article seeks to present a method for pre – service teacher training in elementary schools that focuses on the strengthening of aesthetic values. With a particular emphasis on the substantial applicability of the field of art, as well as through various mechanisms such as the creating, appreciation, and exhibition of art, this article further seeks to explore the possibilities for multi – leveled thinking and methods in different disciplines.

超深/超广:跨领域美感创意教学之探究

高震峰

台北市立大学视觉艺术学系,教授

摘要:全球化及都市化的快速发展对今日学校内的艺术教育起了深远的影响,艺术学科本身涵盖创作及鉴赏的内涵,以及跨学科的本质精神,原本就是一门专业并具挑战的教学科目。网络社群媒体与各式新兴教学科技(如 AI、VR、AR 等),冲击了艺术教学场域的疆界,以及视觉艺术教师的专业知识。美感素养与创新解决问题的能力,则为新时代学童的教育目标,同时在 STEAM(Science、Technology、Engineering、Arts、Math)教育理念的兴起下,更着重探究艺术如何融合于美与世界之窗的课程中,因此艺术学科在其中扮演了重要的角色。在视觉艺术教师教学与学童实践的场域当中,如何关注学童自身的视觉文化与跨文化诠释权,不断地就跨域统整相关议题进行师生对话,以共构一个超深/超广的视觉艺术教学实践典范,应是艺术教育界一个重要的课题。

Deepening and Expanding: Exploration of Innovative Cross – Disciplinary Aesthetic Teaching

Zhenfeng Gao

Professor, Visual Arts Department of University of Taipei

Abstract: The rapid development of globalization and urbanization has had a profound impact on the art education in today's schools. The art discipline encompasses the elements of both creation and appreciation of arts, while also maintaining a cross – disciplinary philosophy, making it an inherently professional and challenging teaching subject. Internet social media and various newly developed teaching technologies (such as AI, VR, AR, etc.) have challenged the boundaries of the art teaching field and the professional capacities of visual art educators. Aesthetic literacy and innovative problem – solving skills have become the educational goals for new generations of students. Meanwhile, the rise of STEAM (Science, Technology, Engineering, Arts, Math) educational concepts has made it common to integrate arts into all fields of study, giving the art discipline an essential role in the modern classroom. In terms of the teaching and learning of both teacher and student in the field of visual arts, it is essential to construct an environment which respects and encourages the freedom to actively discuss and define one's own visual – cultural and cross – cultural identity. Achieving this will bring us closer to constructing a visual arts education that is truly Comprehensive and complete in both its content as well as value; a goal that all members of the art education field should pursue.

三、卓越·全科·乡村

Ⅲ：Excellence，Multidisciplinary，County

2019"首届小学教师教育国际会议"摘要集

"本硕一体·全科·融通"卓越小学教师
培养模式的实践探索

刘学智

东北师范大学教育学部初等教育学院院长，教授

摘要：东北师范大学有着小学教育研究的深厚底蕴。20世纪50年代伊始，我校汇聚了吴杰、马云鹏等国内外有影响力的小学教育研究者。1998年教育部在我校首批设置小教本科专业。2004年、2009年获小学教育专业硕士、教育博士学位授予权。2008年被评为国家级特色专业，2014年列入国家首批卓越教师培养计划。面向新时代，确立了东北师范大学小学教育专业建设的新目标，即国内领先、国际有一定影响力的小学教育人才培养示范基地。为中国基础教育培养师德高尚、理论扎实、教学实践能力强，具有研究能力、创新能力和国际视野的小学卓越教师和未来教育家，为小学教育研究培养拔尖创新人才。基于这样的使命，我校全面探索"本硕一体·全科·融通"卓越小学教师培养模式。其内涵包括：确立尚师德养成、精专业理论、

厚实践能力、强研究创新,作为本硕人才一体化培养的共通目标;构建全专结合、本硕衔接的全科型课程体系;构建理论—实践循环往复有机融通的教学体系。同时,在大学 U—G—S 高平台建设基础上,以全国有影响力的附校集团为主要实践基地,创新大学、教育行政部门和小学三位一体(U—A—S)协同育人机制,从而实现我校小学教育专业的高品质建设和人才的高质量培养。

Practical Exploration on the Training Mode of Excellent Primary School Teachers of "Integration of Undergraduate and Postgraduate Education, Whole Subject and Integration"

Xuezhi Liu

Professor, Dean of school of Primary Education, Faculty of Education, Northeast Normal University

Abstract: Northeast Normal University's primary education research has a profound foundation. Since 1950s, Wu Jie, Ma Yunpeng and other influential primary school education researchers both here and abroad are gathered in our school. In 1998, the Ministry of Education set up the first batch of undergraduate majors in our school.

In 2004 and 2009, our school obtained a master's degree in primary education and a doctoral degree in education. In 2008, it was rated as a national – level specialty. In 2014, it was included in the first batch of excellent teacher training programs in the country. Facing the new era, the new goal of the construction of primary education in Northeast Normal University has been established, That is the domestic leading and internationally influential primary education demonstration base for talent training. For the basic education in China, we will train outstanding teachers and future educators with high academic abilities, solid theoretical skills, strong teaching and practical ability, research ability, innovative ability and international vision, and cultivate top – notch innovative talents for primary education research. Based on such a mission, our school comprehensively explores the cultivation mode of excellent primary school teachers of "integration of undergraduate and postgraduate education, whole subject and integration". That includes: Establish the cultivation of teachers´ morality, refinement of professional theory and practical ability, strengthen research and innovation as the common goal of the integrated training of undergraduate and master talents; Construct the teaching system of theory – practice circulation and reciprocation. At the same time, on the basis of the U – G – S high platform construction of the university, with the influential affiliated school group as the main practice base, the university, the education administration department and the primary school are innovative in the trinity education mechanism (U – A – S) , Thereby achieving the high quality development of the primary education major and the high quality training of talents.

"1+X 主辅学科、全程知行合一"的小学教育专业培养模式

——南京晓庄学院小学教育专业培养模式变化之我思

曹慧英

南京晓庄学院教师教育学院，教授

摘要：南京晓庄学院自办小学教育专业本科以来，培养模式进行了多次改变，从综合培养到"2+2"模式，再从分科模式到"1+X"模式。影响培养模式选择的因素有很多，教师教育政策导向、社会对小学教师招考要求、毕业要求和学科建设均对培养模式的选择有巨大影响，培养模式的选择又决定了课程结构、课程设置、教学方式、师资变化和硬件设施。南京晓庄学院目前选择的"1+X 主辅学科、全程知行合一"的小学教育专业培养模式，顺应了地方对小学教师的需求，也符合小学教师培养的规律，取得了一定的成效。

"1 + x" Primary and Secondary Courses System with Unity of Knowing and Doing: On the Training Modal of Elementary Teacher Education in Nanjing Xiaozhuang University

Huiying Cao

Professor, Secretary of the Party Committee of the College of Teacher Education,

Nanjing Xiaozhuang University

Abstract: Nanjing Xiaozhuang University established the undergraduate major of Primary Education 20 years ago, and the cultivating mode has changed eight times from then on – from cultivating comprehensive abilities to "2 + 2" mode, and from departmental mode to "1 + X" before the professional accreditation period. The reasons of changing are including special background and thinking each time. There are many factors greatly affect the change of cultivating mode, such as education policy, recruiting examination policy, cultivating objective, graduation requirement, and subject construction, etc. On the other hand, the choice of cultivating mode also determines the curriculum structure, curriculum design, teaching method, faculty variation, and equipment facilities. Comply with the demand of local primary schools, and accord with the rules of cultivating primary school teachers, Nanjing Xiaozhuang University chose the "1 + X main – supplement subjects, full internship in four – year length study" cultivating mode of Primary Education currently, and has got some achievements.

"精准扶教"提升乡村学校薄弱学科教师素养的创新探索

李中国

临沂大学社会科学处处长，教授

摘要：教育扶贫、教育精准扶贫、乡村教育精准扶贫是当下中国教育改革发展中的重要议题和重点领域。精准施教助推精准扶贫，针对培训乡村教师存在的目标定位精准不高、培训准备不足、培训模式不适宜、培训内容错位等诸多问题，山东省创新开展了教育志愿者共同体"送教下乡"扶教活动，通过"省级统筹、校地协同、问题导向、对接课堂、强化实践"的精准扶教机制，取得了明显成效。万名乡村薄弱学科教师的教学素养明显提升，学生学习的积极性和主动性明显增强，"协同发展、合作育人"模式业已形成。

Innovative Explorations through a "Targeted Teaching Support" Project to Improve the Qualities of Rural School Teachers in Weak Subjects

Zhongguo Li

Professor, Director of Social Science Department, Linyi University

Abstract: Targeted education support can promote targeted poverty alleviation. Nowadays, there are many problems in rural teachers training, such as inaccurate location, insufficient training preparation, unfit training models and lack of communication in training contents. In order to solve the problems, an assigning teachers to the remote areas activity was created by an educational volunteer community to support the education in Shandong province. The activity adopted a targeted education support mechanism through provincial coordination, collaboration between schools and local government, problem – oriented, docking classroom, lasting for one year and strengthening practice. Now the innovation of precision support mechanism of has achieved remarkable results.

农村卓越小学教师培养模式的构建与实践

——以陇南师范高等专科学校为例

张永明

陇南师范高等专科学校初等教育学院院长,教授

摘要:卓越小学教师培养问题目前是我国教师教育研究的热点之一,陇南师范高等专科学校作为全国承担"卓越小学教师培养计划"唯一一所师范专科院校,在实施"卓培"计划五年中,立足西部农村小学教育,研究西部农村小学教育,不断创新人才培养体系,积极探究卓越小学教师的"本土化"培养。初步构建了以"课堂育人""活动育人""环境育人"为中心的师德养成体系;"综合+1专+1特"课程体系;"全流程"协同育人体系;"贯穿全程"的实践教学体系;"注重能力"的技能考核体系。

Construction and Practice of the Education Mode of Outstanding Elementary Teachers in Rural Areas: Taking Longnan Normal College as an Example

Yongming Zhang

Professor, Dean of the Elementary Education Department,

Longnan Teacher's College

Abstract: The training of Excellent primary school teachers is currently one of the hot topics in the research of Teacher Education in China. Longnan Teachers' College, as the only one junior college undertaking the "excellent primary school teacher training program" in the whole country, has based on the western rural primary school education and studied the western rural primary school education for five years of implementing the training program, constantly innovating the talent training system and actively explore the "localization" training of excellent primary school teachers. Preliminarily constructed the Teachers Moral Cultivation Systems centered on "classroom education", "activity education", "environment education", "comprehensive + 1 discipline + 1 specialty" curriculum system, and the "whole process" collaborative education system, the "throughout the whole process" practical teaching system, "ability – oriented" skills assessment system has been preliminarily constructed.

研究型全科小学教师培养模式探索

易晓明

南京师范大学小学教育系主任,教授

摘要:"热爱小学教育事业、知识广博、能力全面、能够胜任小学多学科教育教学需要的卓越小学教师"是我国小学教育培养的方向。基于南京师范大学的办学定位和生源特点,我们提出培养"研究型全科小学教师"的培养目标。我们将与大家分享我们对"研究型""全科教师"内涵的理解,以及围绕培养目标,从培养机制、课程设置、课堂教学等多个方面所进行的理论思考和实践探索。

Exploration on the Training Mode of Research – oriented General – Subject Primary School Teachers

Xiaoming Yi

Professor, Dean of Elementary Education Department,

Nanjing Normal University

Abstract:"The excellent primary school teachers who love primary education, with broad knowledge, comprehensive ability, and the ability to be qualified for multidisciplinary education in primary schools" is the direction of primary education training in China. Based on the orientation of Nanjing Normal University and the characteristics of students, we propose the goal of training "research – oriented general primary school teachers". We will share with you our understanding of the connotation of "research – oriented" and "general – subject teacher", as well as our theoretical thinking and practical exploration around the training goal, from the aspects of training mechanism, curriculum design, classroom teaching and so on.

胜任与超越:我国卓越小学教师职前培养再思考

——基于在职小学优秀教师核心素养构成视角

庞国彬

大连大学师范学院院长,教授

摘要:基于教师专业发展视角,卓越小学教师职前培养模式亟待重构。职前培养阶段是卓越小学教师培养的起点。职后卓越教师的特质是卓越小学教师职前培养的重要依据。卓越小学教师培养要注重职前与职后协同培养的逻辑关照。卓越小学教师职前培养要立足核心素养的共性追求,要基于职后优秀小学教师的核心素养构成。

第一,我们初步认为,卓越小学教师是一个动态发展的概念,是一个追求的理想与目标。卓越小学教师的形成,需要经历职前培养、入职适应、在职发展等多个阶段。每一个阶段的基本任务和发展目标各不相同。

第二,详尽探索职前培养阶段对于卓越中小学教师的形成与发展,到底起到了什么样的作用。我们初步认为,目前,在高校教师教育职前培养阶段,存在着一定的办学误区。对高校职前培养阶段的目标没有真正厘清,职前培养任务没有完全落实到位。与教师在职发展阶段的目标和任务衔接不够,同时存在一定的错位现象。

第三,具体设计基于一线卓越中小学教师核心素养的实证调查,揭示带有一定普适性的卓越小学教师核心素养指标体系,并进一步探索核心素养与其他素养的关系问题。我们初步认为,卓越小学教师核心素养有其共性特征,有其不同于其他职业群体的独特性特征,需要在职前培养阶段有针对性地进行培养。同时,小学教师核心素养与非核心素养对于一个卓越教师都是非常重要的,需要全面揭示与探索。

第四,针对性提出我国职前培养卓越小学教师若干对策和建议。我们初步认为,要真正培养出我国高水平的卓越小学教师,要处理好适职期的胜任与以后发展的超越、卓越发展目标问题。要科学有序改进现行职前小学教师培养机制、模式和课程体系,全方位探索建立职前卓越小学教师培养对策非常重要,已经刻不容缓。

Qualifying and Excelling: Rethinking about Pre – service Education of Outstanding Elementary Teachers in China

——From the Perspective of Core Competencies of In – service Excellent Elementary School Teachers

Guobin Pang

Professor, Dean of Normal College of Dalian University

Abstract: Based on the perspective of teacher professional development, the pre – service training model for outstanding primary school teachers needs to be reconstructed urgently. The pre – service training stage is the outset for the training of outstanding primary school teachers. The quality of excellent post – service teachers is an important basis for the pre – service training of excellent primary school teachers. The training of excellent primary school teachers should pay attention to the logical care of pre – service and post – service collaborative training. The pre – service training of excellent primary school teachers should be based on the common pursuit of core literacy and the composition of core literacy of excellent post – service primary school teachers.

Fristly, We initially believe that excellent primary school teacher is a concept of dynamic development and an ideal and goal to pursue. The formation of outstanding primary school teachers requires multiple stages of pre – service training, on – job adaptation and in – service development. Each stage has different basic tasks and development goals.

Seandly, What role does pre – service training play in the formation and development of outstanding primary and secondary school teachers. We preliminarily believe that there are some mistakes in running a school in the pre – service training stage of college teachers´education at present. The goal of pre – service training stage in colleges and universities is not really clear, and the pre – service training task has not been fully implemented. There is not enough connection with the goals and tasks of teachers in the in – service development stage, and there is a certain dislocation phenomenon at the same time.

Thirdly, The specific design is based on an empirical investigation of the core literacy of frontline excellent primary and secondary school teachers, revealing a certain universality of the core literacy index system of excellent primary school teachers, and further explores the relationship between core literacy and other literacy. We preliminarily believe that the core literacy of excellent primary school teachers has its common characteristics and unique characteristics different from other occupational groups, which requires targeted cultivation in the pre – service training stage. At the same time, both the core and non – core qualities of primary school teachers are very important for an excellent teacher and need to be fully revealed and explored.

Fourthly, Targetedly put forward several countermeasures and suggestions for pre – service training of excellent primary school teachers in our country. We preliminarily believe that in order to truly cultivate high – level and excellent primary school teachers in our country, we should deal with the problems of competency in the appropriate period and transcendence and excellent goals for future development. To scientifically and orderly improve the current training mechanism, mode and curriculum system of pre – service primary school teachers, it is very urgent to comprehensively explore and establish training countermeasures for pre – service excellent primary school teachers.

首都师范大学小学教育专业人才培养的
目标定位、课程体系

孙建龙

首都师范大学初等教育学院副院长,副教授

摘要: 中国有广大的农村地区,同时也处于快速的城市化进程中,这带来了基础教育发展及对教师需求的差异性、发展性特征。"产出导向"的"小学教育专业"建设应满足不同地区基础教育发展对小学教师素养的需求。首都师范大学的小学教育专业,其人才产出的服务对象主要为北京,因此带有极强的都市化特征。"国际视野、本土实践、尊重历史、面向未来"是本专业的办学理念,"综合培养、发展专长、注重研究、全程实践"为其办学模式。基于这样的理念与模式,并通过相应的课程设计与教学实施,以产出适应城市发展需要的具有如下品质的卓越小学教师:师德优秀、儿童为本、素养综合、创新思维、国际视野、终身学习。为实现上述培养目标,该专业设计了以"通识"类课程、"儿童研究"类课程、"教育理解"类课程、"学科方向"(主教、兼教)类课程、"实践反思"类课程为主要模块的课程结构。在此基础上,以学科研究为支撑,进行课程群建设,以达成对培养目标的有效支撑。

The Goal Orientation and Curriculum System of Elementary Education Programs in College of Elementary Education of Capital Normal University

Jianlong Sun

Associate Professor, Deputy Dean of College of Elementary
Education, Capital Normal University

Abstract: China has vast rural areas, and meanwhile it is in the process of rapid urbanization. Such a fact presents differentiation as well as development potential to basic education and teacher training. The "Product – Oriented" elementary education program construction carried out by College of Elementary Education of Capital Normal University is supposed to satisfy the demands of basic education development for elementary teachers' literacy in different areas. The elementary education program of Capital Normal University is aimed at cultivating talents to serve Beijing, hence its strong urban features. The principles of our college's program include "international vision, native pragmatism, grounded in history, oriented toward the future" with the following education mode encompassing "comprehensive cultivation, specialty development, research emphasis, and whole – course practice. "Based on those principles and education mode, we have set the education objectives concerning cultivating excellent teachers with the following qualities so that they can satisfy the needs of the city development: excellent morality, children – orientedness, comprehensive literacy, creative thinking, international perspectives, life – long learning. To achieve those education objectives through curriculum design and teaching practice, a curriculum framework covering these five modules is constructed: general courses, children studies courses, educational understanding courses, discipline specific courses (first courses and secondary courses), and practice and reflection courses. Based on the framework and supported by discipline studies, we have explored the curriculum group construction that helps to attain the education objectives.

新时期卓越教师培养的两个维度

——师德养成与教育实践

肖冬民

高等教育出版社教师教育事业部小教学前教育分社社长

摘要: 本研究依据我国当前有关教师队伍建设精神要求,立足卓越教师培养新精神,谈新时期教师培养的两个重要维度,即师德养成和教育实践,以及重要实践路径即信息技术的运用。为此,本文将结合过去 5 年来研究者自身在帮助数所高校开展专业建设的成果,总结出抓好这两个维度,贯通学科专业建设的信息技术建设+学科建设+人才培养模式改革+教师教育队伍建设这个专业发展模式。

Two Dimensions of Outstanding Teachers Education in the New Era: Teacher Morality and Educational Practice

Dongmin Xiao

Director of Elementary and Preschool Education Branch, Teacher Education Department of Higher Education Press

Abstract: Based on the current requirements of the spirit of building a contingent of teachers in China, and the new spirit of training excellent teachers, this study discusses two important dimensions of teacher training in the new era, namely, the cultivation of teachers´ professional ethics and educational practice, as well as the application of information technology, an important practice path. Therefore, based on the achievements of the researcher in helping several universities to carry out professional construction in the past five years, this paper sums up a professional development model by the two dimensions, namely, information technology construction + discipline construction + personnel training model reform + teacher education team construction.

我国小学教师培养中儿童研究的缺席与回归

王丽华

浙江师范大学教师教育学院教育学系主任,副教授

摘要:儿童研究的先行者和倡导者的研究都表明,儿童研究是教师培养不可或缺的根基之一。从我国小学教师培养院校的人才培养方案来看,尽管有些院校的人才培养方案关注儿童,但儿童研究基本缺席,具体表现在人才培养方案的培养目标和课程设置中。我国小学教师培养中儿童研究缺席的主要原因在于:其一,多数院校的人才培养方案基于职前教师学习的接受观;其二,多数院校人才培养方案中的培养目标和课程设置基本建基于静态的教师知识观——即"给教师的知识"(实践性知识尽管有些许体现,但其后隐含的仍然是"给教师的知识");其三,缺乏相应的课程设置。根据信息时代小学教师培养的需要,我国小学教师培养中儿童研究回归的关键在于,重建职前教师学习观,重构职前教师的知识基础,开设并实施促进小学职前教师儿童研究能力提升的课程。

Absence and Return of Child Study in the Preparation of Primary School Teachers in China

Lihua Wang

Associate Professor, Director of the Education Department, College of Education, Zhejiang Normal University

Abstract: The research of the pioneers and advocates of child study shows that child study is one of the indispensable foundations of teachers' preparation. From the primary school teachers' preparation programs of normal colleges and universities in China, although some normal colleges and universities pay attention to children, child study is basically absent, which is embodied in the preparation objectives and curriculum settings of the programs. The main reasons for the absence of child studyin primary school teachers' preparation in our country lie in the following: firstly, most primary school teachers' preparation programs of normal colleges and universities are based on the acceptance view of pre – service teacher learning; secondly, the preparation objectives and curriculum settings in those programs are basically based on the static teacher's knowledge view, namely "knowledge for teachers". However, some of them embodied practical knowledge, but the implicit assumption behind the program is still "knowledge for teachers". Thirdly, there is a lack of corresponding curriculums. According to the needs of primary school teachers' preparation at the information age, the key to the return of child study in primary school teachers' preparation in our country lies in rebuilding the learning concept of pre – service teachers, rebuilding the knowledge base of pre –

service teachers, and setting and implementing courses to promote the improvement of pre – service teachers'child study ability.

我国小学教师培养的发展历程与模式变迁

晋银峰

洛阳师范学院

摘要：我国小学教师培养，经历了中师培养的发端阶段、专科培养的提升阶段、本科培养的主流阶段及全科培养的缓解短缺四个阶段。因培养目标、培养规格等差异，小学教师培养呈现不同模式："胜任为本、一专多能"的中师模式，"分科培养、学有专长"的专科模式，"综合培育、专项发展"的本科模式，"跨科培养、融合发展"的全科模式。

The Development Process and Model Changes of Primary School Teacher Training in China

Yinfeng Jin

Luoyang Normal University

Abstract：Primary School Teacher Training in China has experienced four stages：the beginning stage of specialized high school training，the promotion stage of junior college training，the mainstream stage of undergraduate training，and the lack of links in general training. Due to differences in training objectives, training specifications, etc., primary school teacher training presents different models: a specialized high school model with competence – based, one – specialized and multi – skilled training; a junior college model with division of discipline and good at specialized discipline training; an undergraduate model with comprehensive training and special development; a general model with cross – discipline training and integrated development.

基于"知情行合一"的素养目标理念

—— 全科性小学教师培养范式探索

杜　娟

南通师范高等专科学校

摘要:本文首先考察小学教师"知情行合一"素养培育目标的生成之理,通过对教育改革不同情境下的专业素养、全科性素养和核心素养等"前见"话语分析,阐释其内涵逻辑和演进理路,进而提出"知情行合一"理念在小学教师培养中具有目标统贯性和范式统整性的价值功能。基于素养目标理念呈现新时代小学教师教育诸多问题视点,据此提出建构型课程、情境化教学、共同体教育和统整性发展的教师教育形态,为培养全科性小学教师提供系统性范式参照。

Exploration on the Training Paradigm of General Primary School Teachers

Juan Du

Nantong Normal College

Abstract: Firstly, the paper examines the generating principle of primary school teachers 'cultivation goal of "integration of knowledge, feeling and practice". Through the analysis of "foresight" discourse of professional accomplishment, general practice accomplishment and core accomplishment in different situations of educational reform, it explains its connotation logic and evolution path, and then puts forward that the concept of "integration of knowledge feeling and practice" has unity of objectives and paradigm in primary school teachers 'cultivation. Based on the concept of literacy goal, this paper presents the viewpoint of many problems in primary school teacher education in the new era, and puts forward the teacher education form of constructive curriculum, situational teaching, community education and integrated development to provide a systematic paradigm reference for the training of general primary school teachers.

基于全科理念的小学教师职前教育
2+2培养模式探索

侯彦斌　海存福

兰州城市学院教育学院

摘要: 步入21世纪以来,探索借鉴国际小学全科教师培养经验,致力于培养素质全面、专长发展的卓越小学教师,继承我国养成教育传统的培养模式,是小学教师教育人才培养的基本任务。其中,追求卓越是人才培养的质量要求,素质全面、专长发展是人才培养的规格要求,而基于全科理念借鉴国际经验、继承养成教育传统是当前小学教育专业人才培养的基本途径。这为"2+2"培养模式提供了理论依据,并且成为该模式的总体设计思路。

Exploration on The 2 + 2 Training Mode of Pre Service Education For Primary School Teachers Based on The Concept of General Education

Yanbin Hou   Cunfu Hai

College of Education, Lanzhou City University

Abstract: Since entering the new century, it is the basic task of primary school teacher education talent training to explore and learn from the training experience of international primary school general teachers, devote to cultivating excellent primary school teachers with comprehensive quality and professional development, and inherit the training mode of cultivating educational tradition in China. Among them, the pursuit of excellence is the quality requirement of talent training, comprehensive quality and expertise development are the specification requirements of talent training, and the basic way of talent training for primary education majors is to learn from international experience and inherit and develop educational tradition based on general – subject concept. This provides a theoretical basis for the "2 + 2" training mode, and becomes the overall design idea of the mode.

"全科性小学教师"培养模式实践探索

—— 以兰州城市学院为例

李晓梅　侯彦斌　秦积翠　蔡兆梅

兰州城市学院教育学院

摘要: "全科性小学教师"已经成为培养卓越小学教师的主要趋势。小学教育对象的特点、小学教育的特质、小学课程综合化、小学教师培养实践构成了"全科性小学教师"培养的学理依据。兰州城市学院小学教育专业顺应时代发展的趋势和社会需求,在培养卓越小学教师的背景下确立了"全科性小学教师"的培养目标,立足师德为先、儿童为本、综合培养、学有专长、学会发展的具体目标与要求,采取"2+2"的培养模式,创建了富有特色的人才培养体系,其人才培养模式的有效实践探索,为其他师范学院小学教师培养提供了可资借鉴的思路和方法。推广有效经验并反思问题以期寻求更好的发展是本文的旨归。

Practical Study on General – Subject Primary School Teacher Training Model
——A Case Study of Lanzhou City College

Xiaomei Li　Yanbin Hou　Jicui Qin　Zhaomei Cai

College of Education, Lanzhou City University

Abstract: "General – subject primary school teacher" has become the main trend of cultivating excellent primary school teachers, which depends on the characteristics of primary education objects, the characteristics of primary education, the integration of primary curriculum and the practical training of primary school teachers. In Education School of Lanzhou City College, "General – subject primary school teacher" training target is set up, conforming with the trend of era development and social demand, under the background of developing excellent primary school teachers. The School presents the concrete goals and requirements of "virtue – first, child – centered, comprehensive training, know – something, learn to be, adopts the training mode of "2 + 2" and creates a distinctive talent training system. Such moves provide the referential ideas and methods for training other Normal College primary school teachers. The purpose of this paper is to popularize effective experience and reflect on problems in order to seek better development.

兼济彼此 共襄变革

——构建卓越教师人才培养的职前教育语文学科教学课程共同体

刘　春　靳涌韬　宋英智

大连大学教育学院

摘要:大学与中小学合作伙伴的建立是教师职前教育人才培养模式的创新探索形式之一。"U—S"学习共同体为语文学科教学课程提供了革新范式;反之,语文学科教学课程又为"U—S"学习共同体创设了成长载体。鉴于此,"U—S"学习共同体下的教师职前教育语文课程体系,应该遵循关联性、整体性和现实性的基本原则,以"理论与实践相结合"为主导目标,促进"U—S"合作交流,构建学习共同样态的教师职前教育语文学科教学课程体系模式,向着"卓尔不凡"的境界不断超越。

Based on the Training of Excellent Teachers of Curriculum System Construction of Chinese Teaching for the Teachers´ Pre – service Education

Chun Liu　　Yongtao Jin　　Yingzhi Song

College of Education, Dalian University

Abstract: The establishment of partners of university and primary and secondary school is one of the innovative exploration forms of the pre – service education personnel training model. The learning community of University & School provides a new paradigm for the Chinese subject teaching courses; on the contrary, the Chinese subject teaching courses has created a growth carrier for the learning community of University & School. In view of this, the Chinese subject teaching courses for teachers' pre – service education under the learning community of University & School, the construction of Chinese subject teaching courses should carry out the basic rules of relevance integrity and reality, follow the goal of "theory into practice", promote cooperation and exchange between universities and base schools, build the teachers' pre – service education Chinese subject teaching courses system model of style of learning community and to go beyond more superior state constantly.

探析基于两个对接的"2+X"为指向的
人才培养模式

郑艳斐

上饶幼儿师范高等专科学校

摘要：纵观35年来我国小学教育专业的人才培养模式，有分科型、综合型和中间型之说，或曰"全科型教育""大全科型教育""小全科型教育"之分，继而与其匹配的课程体系设置也就呈现出多样化的局面。小学教育专业如何规划课程体系，归根到底是由人才培养目标、规格与定位等确定的。作为专科三年制小学教育专业，从当下的形势看，人才去向更多的是到乡村小学就业，故三年制大专小学教育专业的课程体系的构成与课程设置必须对接满足乡村小学对教师队伍建设的诉求。同时，还要对接学生的智能合理构建课程体系。实践以"2+X"为指向的人才培养模式是必要的，也是可行的。

Analyze the Talent Training Mode Based on Two "2 + X"

Yanfei Zheng

Shangrao Preschool Education College

Abstract: Throughout the past 35 years, the talent training mode of primary education specialty in China has been divided into subject type, comprehensive type and intermediate type, or "general subject education", "large general subject education" and "small general subject education". The matching curriculum system presents a diversified situation. How primary education majors plan the curriculum system is determined by talent training objectives, specifications and positioning. As a three – year junior college's primary education major, from the current situation, talents go to rural primary schools for employment. Therefore, the composition and setting of the curriculum of primary education major in three – year colleges must meet the demands of the construction of teachers in rural primary schools. At the same time, we should connect students´intelligence and build a reasonable curriculum system. It is necessary and feasible to practice the talent training mode directed by "2 + X".

四、多样·评价·提升
Ⅳ : Multiplicity , Assessment , Improvement

2019"首届小学教师教育国际会议"摘要集

面向小学教育多样性的师范生培养：
以芬兰的跨文化教师教育为例

文　德

芬兰赫尔辛基大学教授

摘要:在芬兰的教师教育中,关于多元文化的论题无处不在,给人的错觉是人人都知道如何应对多元文化。然而芬兰教师往往缺乏在课堂上教授多元学生的意识和技能。毫不夸张地说,迄今为止,芬兰的教师教育未能教给这些未来老师如何具备教授多元化学生的能力。在本演讲中,我将举例说明我如何与赫尔辛基大学的研究者和教师团队一起,为实习教师提供高质量、具有思辨和反思性的技能,让他们具备在未来课堂上跨文化交流的能力。由于欧洲学者在讨论多元文化时,大多使用以北美为中心的理论与案例,亚洲地区常被主流讨论所忽视。我将从思考教师教育的多样性和跨文化意义入手,与参会者讨论我们是如何通过对中国及其他国家的关注,丰富了小学教师培训中与跨文化相关的理论和方法。我将提出如何培训未来教师应对多元化学生的新观点，举出具体案例并做出评估。

Preparing Student Teachers for Diversity in Elementary Education: an Example of Intercultural Teacher Education from Finland

Fred Dervin

Professor, University of Helsinki, Finland

Abstract: Diversity – talk is now omnipresent in Finnish teacher education, giving the impression that everybody knows how to deal with interculturality. However Finnish teachers often lack an awareness of it and skills for teaching so – called diverse students in the classroom. It would not be an exaggeration to say that Finnish teacher education has failed until now to equip them properly to do so. In my talk, I will provide examples of how I have tried with my team of researchers and teacher educators at the University of Helsinki to provide student teachers with quality, critical and reflexive skills to do interculturality in their future classrooms. I will start by interrogating the meanings of diversity and interculturality for teacher education. I will then share with the audience how we have enriched theories and methodologies related to interculturality in the training of teachers for elementary education by looking towards China and other parts of the world, which have often been ignored in discussions of interculturality and diversity in Europe, scholars preferring to use North American – centric knowledge. Concrete examples of how this renewed perspective on how to train future teachers for dealing with diverse students will be presented as well as evaluated.

理论与实践结合的创价大学教职研究生院的
小学教师培养:成果与课题

铃木词雄

日本创价大学副教授

滨佳子　原田秀满　山本美纪

日本创价大学研究生

摘要: 日本的教职研究生院已经发展了 12 年。教职研究生是专职研究生院,是培养具有高度专业性和实践能力的教师培养机构。其关键就是注重"理论和实践相结合"。创价大学教职研究生院是在日本教职研究生院制度建立之初时创立的。创办人池田大作先生在创价大学原有的:"成为人间教育的最高学府""成为新大文化建设的摇篮""成为保卫人类平和的要塞"的三个建校精神理念的基础上、为教职研究生院提出了更新的人类观、教育观、发展观、方法观来培养具有高度专业性和实践能力的教师培养目的。本研究就是通过介绍我们研究生院现行课程,还有通过在职研究生、本科生、在职教师等学生们的教职课题研究、实习研究,还有教职课题研究的情况,探寻我们教职研究生院的成果和课题。

Achievements and Challenges of Soka University Graduate School of Teacher Education Aiming at Interaction between Theory and Practice

Norio SUZUKI

Associate Professor, Soka University, Japan Yoshiko HAMA,

Hidemitsu HARADA, Miki YAMAMOTO

Graduate Students, Soka University, Japan

Abstract: It has been 12 years since graduate schools were established in Japan. Graduate school of teacher education is positioned as one of the professional graduate schools and it is an institution that nurtures teachers with advanced expertise and practical skills. The keyword is "interaction between theory and practice". Graduate School of Teacher Education at Soka University was established at the same time that the system of graduate school of teacher education launched in Japan. It aims to nurture teachers with advanced expertise and practical skills while renewing the innovative views of humanity, education, development, and method through academic researches and education based on the philosophy of "humanistic education". This philosophy is common to the founding principles of Soka University by the founder Daisaku Ikeda, "Be the highest seat of learning for humanistic education", "Be the cradle of a new culture", and "Be a fortress for the peace of humankind". In our talk, we introduce our curriculum that is developed to achieve our educational philosophy, objectives, and goals and then take up three courses: international on – site research, teaching practicum training, and thesis research. These courses present learning to the master students who just graduated from undergraduate course and the in – service teacher students. Then we discuss the achievements and challenges of Graduate School of Teacher Education, including the current situation of the graduates.

小学教师培养质量保障体系建构探索

——以延边大学小学教育专业为例

崔梅花

延边大学师范学院小学教育专业主任,副教授

摘要:建构和完善高校小学教师培养质量保障体系,提高人才培养的质量,既是提升高师院校办学水平的客观要求,又是培养高素质小学教师教育人才的有效途径,对促进区域基础教育发展有着重要意义。

延边大学小学教育专业经过近年来办学的持续探索,逐渐形成了特色鲜明的"综合培养、突出专长、强调能力、注重实践"一体化教师培养模式。以培养具有创新精神、实践能力和跨文化素质,能够胜任小学教育、教学工作的卓越教师为目标,形成"以小学教育专业文化为引领,突出培养学生的综合素质、实践素质和创新素质"的专业特色和"创新意识与创新能力培养"的专业优势。

为提升学生的综合素质、创新能力和实践能力,小学教育专业在办学过程中始终围绕确定专业特色进行探讨、改革、凝练,逐渐形成人才培养目标与人才培养质量保障的特色与优势。

第一,打造优秀的专业文化。本专业把小学教师优秀品质纳入专业文化建设内容中,树立了"爱、责任、奉献"的专业精神。与此同时,根据小学教师职业技能训练特点,把对学生职业技能的要求融入专业文化的建设内容中,使学生长期在专业文化的熏陶中得到成长和蜕变。此举收到了明显的

育人效果,学生的责任感、使命感得到加强,综合素质得到广泛提升,专业文化建设成果得到国内同行的高度评价,许多高校前来学习借鉴。

第二,整合第二、第三课堂,建立完整的实践教学体系。本专业非常重视学生职业技能的训练,书写能力、口语表达能力、才艺表现能力、教学能力、课堂组织能力、班级管理能力等都需要在 4 年的学习时间里得到提升。为此,本专业把第二课堂、第三课堂与第一课堂进行了有机整合,按照小学教师的技能要求,设计一个个展示平台,让学生在快乐的实践中自主地学习实践,收到了显著的效果。学生在全国历次书法、诗画比赛和省级大赛中屡获佳绩。

第三,深化课堂教学方法改革,效果突出。对于侧重能力培养的课程,采用了案例教学、探究式教学、工作坊、混合式教学等教学模式,使同学们在学习实践中实现了要我学向我要学的转变,学生学习热情高、学习效果好。

第四,打造能研究、善服务教师队伍,实现良性互动。本专业主要开展基础教育课堂教学、学生教育、家庭教育、教师发展和学校管理等五个方面的研究与社会服务,72% 的教师主持省级或省级以上研究课题,68% 的教师承担小学教育培训与指导服务工作。通过研究与指导服务,一方面扩大了社会影响,另一方面实现教学、科研、社会服务的良好互动。

第五,注重双创教育和就业教育,成效显著。专业建立了全员开展双创教育的良好局面,学生创新课题立项 50 项、发表论文 39 篇,其中国家级 3篇;学生参加国内外竞赛获奖达 110 多项。建立了"全员、全程、全方位"的就业教育体系,2016 年首届毕业生就业率 100%(考研率 28.57%)、2017 届毕业生就业率 93.02%(考研率 39.53%)、2018 届毕业生就业率 84%(考研率 28%)、2019 届毕业生就业率 90.4%(考研率 52.4%)。

今后,我校将进一步调适专业发展定位,依据小学教师人才培养服务面向和人才培养定位,为延边地区和吉林省的教育事业服务,为地方经济建设和社会发展服务,培养具有良好的思想道德品质、扎实的学科知识和较强的教育教学能力,能够在小学从事教育、教学和管理工作,具有创新精神、实践能力和跨文化素养的复合型人才,使小学教育专业特色和优势更加明显。

Exploration on the Construction of Primary School Teacher Training Quality Assurance System: Take the primary education major of Yanbian University as an example

Meihua Cui

Associate Professor, Dean of Primary School Education Department,

Normal School of Yanbian University

Abstract: Constructing and perfecting the quality assurance system for the training of primary school teachers in universities and improving the quality of talents training is not only an objective requirement for improving the level of running a higher normal college, but also an effective way to cultivate high – quality primary school teachers to educate talents. It has an important significance for promoting the development of regional basic education.

After the continuous exploration of schooling in recent years, the major – Primary Education(PE) in Yanbian University has gradually formed a comprehensive teacher training model with distinctive characteristics of "integrated training, outstanding special, emphasizing ability, and practice – oriented". With the goal of cultivating excellent teachers who are innovative, practical and cross – cultural with capable of teaching primary school, we will form professional features of "primary education professional culture as the guide and highlight the comprehensive quality, practical

quality and innovative quality of students" and professional advantages of "innovation awareness and innovation ability training".

In order to improve the comprehensive quality, innovative ability and practical ability of students, the Primary Education major has been discussing, reforming and consolidating in determining the professional characteristics in the process of running the school, and gradually formed the characteristics and advantages of talents training objectives and quality assurance of talents training.

Firstly, creating excellent professional culture. This major incorporates the excellent quality of primary school teachers into the content of professional culture construction, and has established the professional spirit of "love, responsibility and dedication". At the same time, according to the characteristics of primary school teachers´ vocational skills training, the requirements for students´ professional skills are integrated into the construction content of professional culture, so that students can grow and change in the professional culture for a long time. This move has obviously educated effect. The sense of responsibility and mission of the students has been strengthened, the comprehensive quality has been widely improved, and the achievements of professional culture construction have been highly evaluated by domestic counterparts, which many universities have come to learn from them.

Secondly, integrating the second and third classrooms and establishing a complete practical teaching system. The major paid more attention on the training of students´ professional skills. The writing ability, oral expression ability, talent performance ability, teaching ability, classroom organization ability, class management ability, etc. need to be improved in the four years of study stage. To this end, the major integrated the second classroom, the third classroom and the first classroom organically. According to the skills requirements of primary school teachers, designing a display platform to allow students to learn and practice independently in the happy practice, which received significant effects. The students have won many awards in the national calligraphy, poetry and painting competitions and provincial competitions.

Thirdly, deepening the reform of classroom teaching methods has achieved outstanding results. For the courses focusing on ability development, the use of case teaching, inquiry teaching, workshops, mixed teaching and other modes, make students in the study and practice to achieve the changes "I want to learn" from "Let me learn" with highly learning enthusiasm and great learning effect.

Fourthly, building a teacher team that is good at researching and serving and achieving benign interaction. This major mainly conducts research and social services in five aspects: basic education classroom teaching, student education, family education, teacher development and school management. 72% of teachers preside over provincial or provincial research projects, and 68% of teachers undertake educating, training and mentoring services for primary school. Via researching and guidance services, on the one hand, it expanded social influence; on the other hand, it achieved good interaction among teaching, researching and social services.

Fifthly, paying attention on dual education and employment education, and it has achieved remarkable result. The major has established a good situation for all employees to carry out dual education. The students created 50 projects and published 39 papers, including 3 national papers; The students have won more than 110 awards in domestic and international competitions. By establishing a "full – staff, full – time, all – round" employment education system, the employment rate of the first graduates in 2016 was 100% (the postgraduate entrance rate was 28. 57%), the employment rate of the 2017 graduates was 93. 02% (the postgraduate entrance rate was 39. 53%), and the employment rate of 2018 graduates is 84% (the postgraduate rate is 28%), and the 2019 employment rate is 90. 4%

（the postgraduate rate is 52.4%）.

In the future, we will further adjust the orientation of professional development, provide services for the education of Yanbian region and Jilin Provinces, serve the local economy and social development, cultivate integrated talents with good ideological and moral quality and solid foundation of subject knowledge and strong educational and teaching ability, which are able to engage in education, teaching and management in primary schools, with a combination of innovative spirit, practical ability and cross – cultural literacy, make the characteristics and advantages of primary education more obvious.

师范生生源质量的影响因素及提升路径

乔璐瑶

山西师范大学教育科学学院

摘要：师范生生源质量是教师教育质量的重要决定因素之一。目前我国师范生生源质量堪忧，主要表现在师范院校招生录取分数线普遍低于同层次的综合性大学和师范生缺乏教师职业认同感等方面。教师职业吸引力不具有明显的竞争力、师范生的招生选拔方式单一且专业性考察不足、国家对师范生的支持性优惠政策力度不够，以及一流大学和高水平综合性大学参与度较低等因素都在一定程度上影响着师范生生源质量。为此，应从提高教师社会经济地位、改革招生制度、增加政策供给、吸引高水平非师范院校参与师范生培养等方面着手，保障和提高师范生生源质量，为国家教育事业的发展提供人才保障和动力源泉。

Impact Factors and Improvement Path of the Student Source Quality of Normal University Students

Luyao Qiao

College of Educational Science, Shanxi Normal University

Abstract: The quality of normal students is one of the important determinants of the quality of teacher education. At present, the quality of the source of normal students in China is worrying, which is mainly reflected in the fact that the admission scores of normal colleges are generally lower than those of comprehensive universities at the same level and normal students lack a sense of teacher professional identity. The less competitiveness professional attraction of teachers , the single enrollment and selection method of normal university students and the insufficient professional investigation, the lack of national supportive preferential policies for normal university students and the low participation of first – class universities and high – level comprehensive universities all affect the quality of normal university students to a certain extent. Therefore, we should improve the social and economic status of teachers, reform the enrollment system, increase policy supply, attract high – level non – normal colleges to participate in the training of normal university students and other aspects, to ensure and improve the quality of normal university students, and provide talent guarantee and power source for the development of national education.

情境学习视角的教育实习过程分析

徐爱杰

首都师范大学初等教育学院

摘要：教育实习是教育现场中的情境学习，实习生遇到的困难主要是对环境的适应与利用有关的关系建立、沟通合作、参与等问题。提升教育实习过程的科学性与有效性应遵循情境学习的相关规律，在过程设计中把教育实习看作一种特殊的社会实践，重点在环境融入、经验积累与反思、完善实习生、指导教师、同伴三者的合作机制、推动充分参与教育实践等方面做好规划。

An Analysis of Educational Practice Process from the Perspective of Situated Learning and Suggestions for Improvement

Aijie Xu

College of Elementary Education, Capital Normal University

Abstract：Educational practice is a kind of situated learning in the field of education. The difficulties encountered by the interns are mainly the establishment, communication, cooperation, participation and other problems related to the adaptation and utilization of the environment. To improve educational practice process, we should follow the relevant rules of situated learning, regard educational practice as a special social practice in process design, and focus on the integration of environment, experience accumulation and reflection, improvement of the cooperation mechanism of interns, guidance teachers and peers, and promotion of full participation in educational practice.

论师范教育专业见习的层级性特征

李金泽

合肥幼儿师范高等专科学校

摘要: 教育见习是师范教育专业实践教学的重要组成部分,承载着一定的教育价值功能,即通过对教育活动进行观察和感悟,帮助师范生体验、认知教育和教学的外在呈现形态和内在运行规律,认知教师职业特征,积累从感性认知到理性认知的教育教学经验。教育见习的价值功能具有内在层级性,包括职业感知、教育对象认知和课堂教学认知三个层级。教育见习价值功能的层级性决定了教育内容设置的层级性和教育见习时序的层级性。教育见习的层级性对有效组织教育见习活动具有重要的理论指导意义。

The Hierarchical Characteristics of Internship in Normal Education

Jinze Li

Hefei Preschool Education College

Abstract: Educational internship is an important part of the practical teaching of normal education. It carries a certain educational value function. Observation and perception of educational activities can help normal students experience and recognize the external appearance and internal operation law of education and teaching, recognize the professional characteristics of teachers, and accumulate education and teaching experience from perceptual cognition to rational cognition. The value function of educational internship has internal hierarchy, including professional perception, cognition of educational objects and cognition of classroom teaching. The hierarchy of educational internship value function determines the hierarchy of educational content setting and the hierarchy of educational internship time sequence. The hierarchy of educational internship has important theoretical guiding significance for the effective organization of educational internship activities.

中美农村小学教师队伍建设对比探析

夏　蕾

山西师范大学教育科学学院

摘要：教师质量反映教师实际教育教学业务水平与能力，是决定教师队伍整体内涵的关键因素，农村教师队伍质量关系着农村教育水平高低，也关系着我国特色教师教育体系构建。首先介绍高质量农村教师队伍建设的重要性；其次分别介绍中美两国农村教师队伍建设困境、梳理相关政策举措；最后通过对比研究，道出两国农村教师队伍建设的共同之处和不同之处，及美国农村教师队伍建设于我国农村教师队伍建设的启示。以期建设一支高水平农村基础教育教师队伍，提高农村基础教育质量，促进教育公平，实现基础教育整体水平质的提升。

A Comparative Analysis of the Construction of Rural Primary School Teachers between China and the United States

Lei Xia

College of Educational Science, Shanxi Normal University

Abstract: Teachers′ quality reflects teachers′ actual educational and teaching professional level and ability, which is the key factor of the overall connotation of teachers. The quality of rural teachers is not only related to the level of rural education, but also related to the construction of teacher education system with Chinese characteristics. Firstly, this paper introduces the importance of the construction of high – quality rural teachers; Secondly, it introduces the difficulties in the construction of rural teachers in China and the United States, and introduces the relevant policies and measures; Finally, through the comparative study, it shows the similarities and differences of the construction of rural teachers in the two countries, and the enlightenment of the construction of rural teachers in the United States to the construction of rural teachers in China, in order to build a high – level rural basic education teacher team, improve the quality of rural basic education, promote educational equity, and realize the improvement of the overall level and quality of basic education.

农村小学教师教学信念的现状与发展

——以粤东地区学校为例

严　权　王晶晶

广东省韩山师范学院

摘要：教学信念是指教师因个人特质、文化环境、专业知识、经验积累、教学场景等因素，对教学相关的课程、方法、学生、师生关系等方面持信以为真的观点。通过对广东省粤东地区 768 名农村小学教师进行调查，表明农村小学教师教学信念总体呈进步取向，但不同年龄、不同职称教师教学信念差异显著。建议从政府、学校、社会等宏观层面，教师集体、教师个体等微观层面出发，共同发展农村小学教师教学信念。

The Present Situation and Development of Teachers´ Teaching Beliefs in Rural Primary Schools
—A Case Study of Schools in the Eastern Region of Guangdong Province

Quan Yan   Jingjing Wang

Hanshan Normal University

Abstract:Teaching beliefs refered to teachers´beliefs about teaching – related courses, methods, students, teacher – student relationships, and other aspects, which were believed to be true due to factors such as personal characteristics, cultural environment, professional knowledge, experience accumulation, and teaching scenes. The survey of 768 rural primary schools teachers in the eastern region of Guangdong province showed that the teaching beliefs of rural primary school teachers were generally progressive, but there were significant differences among teachers of different ages and professional titles.

平面 立体 灵动:浅析后课改时代
学生素养发展与评价

张长征

郑州师范学院初等教育学院

　　摘要:在中国共产党领导下全面建设现代化的百年大计中,教育目的的实现应植根于全体学生的发展。本文所及"核心素养"是从学生自我经验连续性视角出发,来窥探"后课改"条件下的学生全面发展中的阶段性"活化"问题的应然境遇:主体性全面明确、合法性立体有力与合理性能动适切,且由此厘清素质教育"源头活水"的"灵动",成就师生精致共生,乃至"创新能力"和"实践能力"获得其强国境遇。

Strain · Stereo · Smart: Analyzations on the Development and Evaluation of Student Literacy in the Post – New Round Curriculum Reform Times

Changzheng Zhang

School of Elementary Education, Zhengzhou Normal University

Abstract: Under the leadership of the party, the PRC have been doing great efforts on the country building modernization, and the realization of educational goals should be directly grounded within all students ' development. The "core literacy" mentioned, in this paper, is based on the continuity of students' self – experience, to explore the situation of the stage "Reflected" in the comprehensive development of students in the "post – course reform": the subjectivity is comprehensive and clear, and the legitimacy is sound and abound, and reasonable performance is suitable and fit, so as to get the "intelligence force" of quality education "source of living water", to achieve the symbiosis between teachers and students, and to obtain its strong country powers on "innovative abilities" and "practical abilities".

后　记

　　办人民满意的小学教师教育，发展中国特色世界先进水平的优质小学教师教育，是中国小学教师教育人的中国梦。中国小学教师教育人用理论、用实践，也用对话来铸就中国梦。2019 年，首都师范大学、中国教育国际交流协会教师教育国际交流分会在北京成功举办了"首届小学教师教育国际会议"，通过交流与互动，书写出具有里程碑意义的新诗篇。

　　自本科层次小学教育专业设置以来，小学教育领域的国际研讨会在多所院校召开过。如，2016 年 6 月 12 日至 13 日，在上海师范大学召开的"卓越小学教师培养"国际论坛，由教育部小学教师培养教学指导委员会和全国教师教育学会小学教师教育委员会主办，上海师范大学和南京晓庄学院共同承办，主题为"面向教育国际化的卓越小学教师培养"。参会学者来自中国、美国、英国、澳大利亚和日本。2017 年 4 月 14 日至 16 日，湖南第一师范学院召开主题为"小学教师教育的难点问题、核心问题"的"首届小学教师教育国际论坛"。参会学者和一线工作者来自中国、美国和英国。2018 年 3 月 15 日至 16 日，在南京晓庄学院召开"与儿童一起成长的卓越小学教师之路"国际学术论坛，由教育部高等学校小学教师培养教学指导委员会主办，南京晓庄学院和上海师范大学共同承办，南京大学出版社协办。有来自中国、美国、日本和澳大利亚 120 多位专家学者参会。2018 年 7 月 9 日至 10 日，由宁波大学主办、宁波大学教师教育学院承办的"核心素养背景下的卓越小学教师培养国际会议"，以"卓越小学教师培养的全球做法"为主题，中国、澳大利亚、罗马尼亚的 80 余位学者参加了此次会议。

　　"首届小学教师教育国际会议",有来自中国、澳大利亚、芬兰、法国、匈牙利、冰岛、日本、韩国、瑞士、美国 10 个国家 102 个不同单位(其中包括 78 所大学)300 余位专家学者参加,是国内乃至国际小学教育界的盛举。国内外知名学者共聚一堂,围绕"走近·对话·共享——多元取向小学教师教育理论与实践"主题,以小学教师教育的理念、模式及质量保障为议题,分享理论,交流经验,探讨困惑,展望未来。本书汇集了国内外学者的智慧与经验,记录了全球化视野下中国小学教师教育人追梦的精彩步伐。本书的出版,提供了一份互通理论创新和实践创新成果、并促进世界小学教师教育多元发展的思想大餐,相信随着时间的推移其积极意义和价值会更加凸显。

　　本书由刘慧负责全书的构架,唐斌、魏戈、杨天和鲁华夏负责统稿和校对工作。付梓在即,一是感谢与会学者,各位学者的热忱参与及智慧贡献成就了本书。二是感谢首都师范大学初等教育学院会议筹备团队的全体老师,他们不辞辛苦、高效服务,为会议的圆满成功保驾护航,无此亦难有本书。三是感谢由首都师范大学初等教育学院研究生组成的论文编辑团队,疫情期间就开始投入联络和编辑工作。四是感谢天津人民出版社的编辑林雨、武建臣以及其他老师,感谢各位老师细致、严谨的付出!

　　在未来道路上,我们将一如既往、不忘初心,用理论、用实践、用对话铸就中国小学教师教育人的中国梦,不负时代的召唤与人民的期待!

唐斌、魏戈、杨天

2021 年 8 月 16 日